Immigrant Enterprise in Europe and the USA

Immigrant-owned enterprises are a highly visible phenomenon but, frequently and increasingly so after 9/11, immigration has been cast in pessimistic and apocalyptic terms which became associated with rising xenophobia and restrictive legislation, such as the Patriot Act in the United States.

This book examines the issue of immigration and the contribution immigrant enterprise plays in the economic development of gateway cities such as London, New York, Los Angeles, Paris, Amsterdam and Miami, cities which appear as the living embodiment of globalisation.

Immigrant Enterprise in Europe and the USA questions the extent to which cities are transformed by immigrants themselves, 'from below', and points to relationships with wider processes, such as the legal and political framework and the restructuring by capital of particular industries and localities. What happens to immigrants is shaped by membership of particular groups and the historical circumstances in which they find themselves. It is also shaped by the reproduction of social stratification rooted in class, gender, race and age. The book points to the development of social and economic differentiation amongst immigrant groups, which challenge popular stereotypes about immigrants in business i.e. that they invariably operate on the fringes of the law and are dependent on family labour. The findings, on the contrary, point to a highly differentiated enterprise structure. The recognition of diversity is a necessary first step to understanding winners and losers in immigrant enterprise.

Prodromos Panayiotopoulos is a lecturer in Development Studies and Sociology, currently at the School of Environment and Society at Swansea University, UK.

Routledge studies in the modern world economy

Immigrant Enterprise in Europe and the USA

Prodromos Panayiotopoulos

Routledge
Taylor & Francis Group

LONDON AND NEW YORK

First published 2006
by Routledge
2 Park Square, Milton Park, Abingdon, Oxon OX14 4RN

Simultaneously published in the USA and Canada
by Routledge
270 Madison Ave, New York, NY 10016

Routledge is an imprint of the Taylor & Francis Group, an informa business

Transferred to Digital Printing 2009

© 2006 Prodromos Panayiotopoulos

Typeset in Times by Wearset Ltd, Boldon, Tyne and Wear

British Library Cataloguing in Publication Data
A catalogue record for this book is available from the British Library

Library of Congress Cataloging in Publication Data
A catalog record for this book has been requested

ISBN10: 0-415-35371-8 (hbk)
ISBN10: 0-415-49418-4 (pbk)
ISBN10: 0-203-34685-8 (ebk)

ISBN13: 978-0-415-35371-8 (hbk)
ISBN13: 978-0-415-49418-2 (pbk)
ISBN13: 978-0-203-34685-3 (ebk)

This volume is dedicated to my mother, Kyriakou Panayiotopoulou, and the other machinists of her generation who would never be allowed in Britain under New Labour's 'points' system.

Contents

Illustrations

Figure

Tables

Preface

This book says nothing particularly original. It does, however, draw from 25 years of research, primarily about Cypriot entrepreneurs in the North London clothing industry. Immigrant businesses are evidently present in most high streets, shopping malls and neighbourhoods in the cities of Europe and the United States. Nothing grates against the xenophobe more than an immigrant doing well in business. This book attempts to explain this phenomenon and investigates in a comparative way the role of immigrant enterprise in Europe and the United States and assesses its contribution to the shaping of gateway cities such as London, New York, Los Angeles, Amsterdam and Paris. These cities act as points of entry into the metropolitan heartlands of Europe and the United States and appear as the living embodiment of globalisation. The book contains empirical and case study material which is used to investigate the globalisation 'from below' thesis, i.e. that contemporary patterns of migration have resulted in the undermining of the nation state leading to the formation of transnational communities which feel equally at home in receiving and sending countries. Immigrant enterprise is a social and highly visible phenomenon in the make up of gateway cities. Many of these cities have been transformed by immigrants, with limited assistance from government or the commercial banking sector. Indeed much of this is taking place in the face of governments and their restrictive immigration policies. This appears as confirmation of the globalisation 'from below' thesis.

Theoretically, questions asked include, whether cities are being transformed by immigrants themselves, or whether this involves relationships with wider processes, such as with the institutional framework and the restructuring by capital of particular sectors, industries and localities. What happens to immigrants is influenced by their membership of particular groups and the historical circumstances they find themselves in. It is also influenced by the reproduction of market relations and social stratification rooted in class, gender, race and age. Again, the book says nothing original in this. It merely makes the observation and demonstrates how immigrant communities are themselves socially differentiated in these and other ways. Another question asked is who benefits from immigrant enterprise? The book includes, for example, specific reference on the incorporation of women in immigrant enterprise. The reproduction of market relations are reflected in what the book calls a process of social and economic differentiation within immigrant communities. At one level we can see significant differences between immigrant workers and immigrant bosses. At another level we see differences between enterprises in terms of their size, purpose, and in how they relate to markets. Many enterprises are small, family firms or firms dependent on family labour whilst others are large employers who recruit labour from a wide range of ethnic groups. Some act as transnational entities. In the case of the garment and information technology industries, some immigrant enterprises operate as micro-multinational companies involved in outward processing.

The material challenges popular stereotypes about immigrants in business i.e. that they invariably operate on the margins of the law and are dependent on family or co-ethnic labour, and points to a highly differentiated enterprise structure. The book is a debate with those who see immigrant enterprise as invariably on the 'fringes' of economic and political systems. Another debate is with the advocates of the globalisation 'from below' thesis, about the social and economic differentiation of transnational communities and the role of the institutional framework in shaping significant variation in institutional behaviour towards immigrants.

The book is aimed at an academic, practitioner and popular audience. It will be of interest to a wide variety of undergraduate students of ethnicity, immigration, enterprise, globalisation and gender, and of relevance to courses in Geography, Cultural Studies, Sociology, Anthropology, Economics, Management Studies, Gender Studies, Development Studies, Urban Studies and Social Policy. The book is also aimed at local authority and voluntary sector staff involved in community and economic development with inner-city ethnic minority dimensions, as well as members of the general public who are themselves confronted by the issues raised in the book and are trying to make sense of the changes taking place around them.

There is a general interest about immigrant enterprises. There is also a considerable academic and wider literature which points to the influence of the political-institutional framework, the role of ethnic solidarity in negotiating adversity and the significance of small enterprises and particular sectors, such as retail, garments and restaurants, in shaping immigrant labour market incorporation. The book brings together these foci and makes the material available to a wider readership. The book adds to this body of work by critically challenging assumptions made by academic and popular audiences about homogeneous and compliant immigrant communities and histories, by assessing the impact of social and economic differentiation and the formation of new classes within immigrant communities. This allows readers to identify for themselves 'winners' and 'losers' in the processes of change they see around them.

Acknowledgements

There are too many acknowledgements to list individually. Clearly the entrepreneurs, who assisted research efforts by giving their time and knowledge, underpin credit where credit is due. Equally, this book would not have been possible without the work of other researchers who have made their work available. One general acknowledgement is to the pioneering and current work of Edna Bonacich and Ivan Light who, probably more than most, inspired the development of research on immigrant and ethnic minority enterprise as a significant field of study. The work of Saskia Sassen, Nigel Harris, Swasti Mitter, Sheila Rowbotham, Naila Kabeer and Annie Phizacklea, on immigration, informalisation and gender has influenced the direction of this work. The book has also been informed by the considerable research and published work produced by Roger Waldinger and Alejandro Portes and their associates, as well as Jan Rath and other staff at the Institute of Migration and Ethnic Studies at the University of Amsterdam. Whilst none of the above are responsible for the contents, the book attempts to present their views accurately.

Introduction

Immigration and globalisation

Introduction

The movement of people is the most visible face of globalisation. The International Organisation for Migration (IOM) Annual World Migration Report for 2003, estimates that over the past 35 years the number of international migrants has more than doubled to 175 million people, representing one in every 35 people, or nearly 3 per cent of the world's population. Nearly 95 million are in Europe and North America. In the United States, nearly one in ten of the population are first-generation immigrants. In France it is 6.3 per cent and in the UK 3.6 per cent. Germany at 9.0 per cent, has the highest rate in Europe. One estimate from Portes and Rumbaut is that one out of five Americans (more than 55 million people) are first- or second-generation immigrants (IOM, 2003; Harris, 2002:152; Portes and Rumbaut, 2001). One significant dimension of immigration is the role of remittances: the Inter-American Development Bank, for example, estimates that $38bn was sent back home by immigrants ($13.7bn of which went to Mexico) and that this was central to the economic stability of many countries in the region (Lapper, 2004:7).

Contemporary patterns of immigration have been made more complex by the large numbers of people seeking asylum and refugee status in Europe during the 1990s and in the United States since the 1970s. Asylum seekers, refugees and economic migrants are in many cases labour market substitutes for each other, and also with native workers. Frequently, however, refugees and asylum seekers (such as in UK legislation) are denied the right to work. Fleeing persecution is an indication that the world has become a more dangerous place and most refugees originate from areas of war and conflict: the break-up of Yugoslavia, the wars in Afghanistan, Iraq and the Great Lake Region of Africa, provided the bulk of refugees. Most seek refuge in adjoining countries, in the hope of a quick return to their homelands. Pakistan, Iran and Asia generally were home to nearly six million refugees out of an estimated global total of 12 million. Paradoxically, it is in the developed high-income economies, that those seeking refuge have been the most vilified by demagogues and scapegoated by anti-immigration parties. More than six million asylum applications were lodged in the high-income economies in the 1990s compared to 2.2 million in the 1980s. Most of these applications were rejected. According to the Organisation for Economic Co-operation and Development (OECD), in 2000, refugees made up fewer than a fifth of permanent migrants to the UK, the US, France, Canada and Portugal. In the Northern European countries of Denmark, Sweden and Norway, refugees made up between one fifth and two fifths of the total inflow. The rejection of refugee status and the tightening of immigration controls, particularly in the US since 9/11, has compounded undocumented immigration. The human traffic industry in the US is estimated to be worth $10bn a year. Undocumented migration may account for between a third and a half of entrants into high-income countries: in Europe an estimated 500,000 entrants were in this category in 1999 and the US hosts an estimated 12 million undocumented immigrants (OECD, 2003).

The desperation of economic immigrants and 'failed' asylum seekers has driven many of them into the arms of human traffickers who facilitate transit and in some cases employment. This was cruelly revealed in the UK, when 21 workers collecting cockles in Morecambe Bay, Lancashire were drowned by the oncoming tide: of these, 18 were Chinese, 13 of whom were seeking refugee status. The tragedy in Morecambe Bay followed 58 fatalities amongst Chinese illegal immigrants four years previously, at the port of Dover where they suffocated in the back of an airtight container truck during the five-hour ferry crossing from Zeebrugge, Belgium. In both cases 'Triad' (mainland China) gangsters were mentioned and attention focused on recent trends in a labour diaspora linking the province of Fujian in China with Europe. An extensive undercover Special Report by a Fujian-speaking journalist working for the British *Guardian*, and subsequent Parliamentary Inquiries on the Morecambe deaths, revealed a world of intimidation, misery, shared and overcrowded apartments and fear of the authorities (Pai, 2004). Other sources point to a wider relationship between gang masters and European agriculture. In the UK, reports from the UK Parliamentary Environment, Food and Rural Affairs Committee and the UK Agricultural and Allied Workers Union, estimated that there were 3,000 agents providing the agricultural sector with casual labour needed by the fruit and vegetable sector at peak picking times. In the last ten or 15 years this has become big business and some gang masters employ up to 2,000 people, looking primarily to Eastern and Southern Europe for sources of labour (Bell, 2002; Lawrence, 2005).

The role of gang masters and the provision of agricultural seasonal labour in unregulated and casualised labour markets, has focused on Eastern Europe as a source for labour, particularly from the newly-acceded states to the European Union such as Poland. It is also a reflection on transnational enterprise formation. In the Dover tragedy, the destination of the group was restaurants in Newport Street in London's

Chinatown. There they hoped to get £167 per week and pay off in two years or so the debts incurred for the journey. One factor driving this, is that 'there is a great shortage of workers there since many second generation Chinese go to universities and work in the professions' (Harris, 2002:xvi).

The contribution made by immigrants to the economies of the receiving countries is illustrated by US immigration trends which show that most immigrants are as skilled and educated as native-born workers and that the proportion with a college education is similar. This makes immigrants theoretically highly substitutable for native labour. The proportion of immigrants classified by the Immigration and Naturalisation Service (INS) as 'professionals' is in fact significantly higher than for the US population as a whole (Portes and Rumbaut, 2001). One factor driving the US economy during the 1990s was the convergence between high rates of growth and the highest ever rate of immigration recorded in the history of the US. More than 13.5 million people immigrated to the US during the 1990s, arriving in even greater numbers and more diversity than the three decades of the 'First Great Wave' of immigration during the end of the nineteenth century, when the Jewish ghettos of Eastern Europe and the villages of southern Italy provided the bulk of immigrants. Immigration during the 1990s accounted for 40 per cent of US population growth (Goldenberg, 2002). The 'Second Great Wave' is expected to restructure race and ethnicity in the US: with those categorised as 'white' declining from 73 per cent of the population in 1997, to 53 per cent in 2050. According to US Census Bureau projections, the proportion of Hispanic Americans is expected to rise from 11 per cent to 25 per cent of US population, Asian Americans are expected to increase from 4 to 8 per cent of population and 'Black' Americans to register a smaller increase, from 12 to 14 per cent (Booth, 1998b).

Another indicator of the impact of immigration is that the City of London has emerged as the principal western centre for Islamic finance. There are 250 Islamic banks worldwide managing funds of up to $500bn in Sharia-compliant (interest-free but profit-maximising) accounts and they are increasingly targeting the overseas Muslim communities. An estimated 20 million Muslims live in Europe and the US. In the UK, Sharia-compliant mortgages are expected to generate $4.5bn by 2006. During August 2004 the UK Financial Services Authority authorised the first fully Sharia-compliant Islamic bank to take deposits from the UK's estimated two million Muslim population and mainstream banks such as Lloyds of London and HSBC are also considering launching Sharia-compliant financial services (Burgess, 2004).

One continuity in immigration policy appears in processes of selectivity. Race, gender, nationality, religion and the status of migrants, as between refugees or economic migrants, documented and undocumented migrants, are significant factors in determining entry and the terms of integration. In the UK, for example, immigrants from the white Commonwealth countries (Australia, Canada, New Zealand) are many more times likely to be admitted than immigrants from the black, New Commonwealth countries (Caribbean, Indian subcontinent, Africa). Similarly, UK immigration legislation denied Asian women the right to independent migration for nearly a quarter of a century. The British Government introduced in 1905, for the first time, anti-immigrant legislation (the Aliens Act) which targeted poor Yiddish Eastern European immigrants, who had transformed the East End of London into a centre for Jewish economic, political and intellectual life, rivalling that of New York's Lower East Side. In 1962 the UK Commonwealth Immigrants Act targeted West Indian and Asian immigrants.

In the United States, a country built by immigrants, and which more than most actively encouraged immigration, similar processes are discernable. The first ever anti-immigrant legislation (Immigrant Act 1875) targeted women who worked in bars or were 'prostitutes'. In fact, young Irish women who worked as housemaids and in many cases travelled as independent female immigrants, were the first to feel this restriction. The Chinese Exclusion Act (1882) made Chinese labourers inadmissible, and this was extended in 1888 for 20 years (with a clause for a further 20 years to 1928). It was not repealed until 1943, in favour of meagre quotas (literally hundreds) which continued until 1965. Following the assassination of President William Mackinley by a freelance anarchist in 1901, the Immigration Act (1903) prohibited entry to 'polygamists' and 'anarchists'. Legislation in 1907 (The Gentlemen's Agreement) severely limited Japanese immigration. The Immigration Act (1917) imposed literacy tests for admission which virtually barred all Asian immigrants from entry. The National Quota Law (1921) limited immigration of each nationality to 3 per cent of the number of foreign-born of that nationality living in the US in 1910. This was extended in the National Origins Act (1924) which set annual quotas for each nationality at 2 per cent of that nationality living in the US in 1920 (Tichenor, 2002:3–5).

The quota system in the United States which discriminated against immigrants from Eastern and Southern European countries, followed on the heels of the Russian Revolution in 1917, and a real or imagined threat which gripped the law enforcement agencies about foreign 'anarchist' and Bolshevik revolutionaries. The Palmer Raids were launched to round up many 'undesirables' for deportation (in one instance 800 at a time), and in the process eroded civil liberties. Nicola Sacco and Bartolomeo Vanzetti, two Italian working-class immigrants, became victims of this climate and were executed on trumped-up charges, becoming international symbols of the last time the United States fought a 'war against terror'. Most cruelly, the Quota Acts were used to limit the number of Jewish refugees fleeing Nazi Germany admitted into the United States. Many German Jews faced 'double barriers' with, on the one hand, US consuls (responsible for processing applications) demanding evidence of economic self-sufficiency and, on the other, Nazi officials preventing immigrants from removing money and other assets from Germany. Tichenor (2002:151) writes that 'the State Department's Visa Bureau and consular officials were especially resistant to Jewish refugees and often did use their discretion to target European Jews for harsh treatment'.

The national origins quota system was dismantled in 1965. It became, during the 1960s, an anachronism in the face of increased economic inter-dependency and 'globalisation'. The labour demands of the US economy during the post-war boom, exhausted available supplies of labour. The return by the US towards policies actively encouraging immigration, was reflected in the dominance of free-market ideas in the Democratic and Republican parties: the conservatives in the Republican Party demanding a halt to immigration, while its polar opposite, the trade union and manu-facturing lobby in the Democratic Party (demanding import controls) became less significant in the shaping of policy (Watts, 2002). The advo-cates of less restrictive immigration policies, point to the contribution made by immigrants towards aggregate demand and in human capital formation. One third of immigrants to the US since 1990, for example, had a bachelor's degree, or higher. At the same time the social neo-conservatives are xenophobic and the keenest advocates for immigration controls in the Republican Party, which is an amalgam of these two positions. The con-sequences of 9/11, shifted the balance towards the direction of the social conservatives and the US has experienced the return of an aggressive American nativism, demanding tough controls against immigrants. One aspect of this climate has been the proposition that the 'sweatshop' is making a comeback in the US economy, with large 'waves' of undocu-mented workers providing the labour force.

The Patriot Act (2001) reflected the changing balance in the Republi-can Party. The Act targeted Muslim and Arab immigrants and visitors for special attention. The extension of surveillance has included bi-optic iden-tification, fingerprinting and photographing of all visa holders arriving to the US, as well as personal interviews of applicants by US embassy staff. This saw an estimated 23 million visitors to the US each year affected, with US universities complaining of falling enrolments and loss of competition with European institutions due to the burdensome new regulations. The decision by the Bush administration to create the Department of Home-land Security, a new federal agency dedicated to preventing terrorism, saw the entire immigration function of the government contained within the new department. This reorganisation is a powerful signal that all immi-grants will now be viewed as terrorist threats. Thousands of immigrants lost their jobs when 750,000 letters were sent out by the social security administration to employers, telling them that a social security number they have supplied did not match one on its database. Congress passed a law requiring all airport baggage screeners to be US citizens. Thousands of immigrants who had not yet become citizens, were fired from jobs which, in some cases, they had held for many years. The Justice Department started enforcing a little-used 50 year old law making it a crime for an immigrant not to report a change of address to the INS within ten days of moving (National Migration Forum, 2002).

The 'war against terror' in the US, was most keenly felt by the established Arab American and Middle Eastern communities in Detroit, Florida and South California. In a manner reminiscent of the Palmer Raids, between Monday 16 and Friday 20 December 2002, 700 men and boys were detained mostly in the Los Angeles area so that they could 'assist' the Immigration and Naturalisation Service with their inquiries (Parkes, 2002a:8). The climate which produced the Act contributed towards the erosion of civil liberties in the US and Europe. The US Department of Justice released a report from its own inspector detailing the treatment of hundreds of illegal immigrants detained in the wake of 9/11. Many were held for months without access to counsel, some were physically and verbally abused and none of them were charged with 'terrorist' offences. Many of the 600 'special interest' immigration cases were held in courtrooms closed to visitors and family. Many were held without being told why, without access to a lawyer, without anyone from the outside (including their families) knowing where they were being held (see, *Financial Times*, Editorial, 'America the scary. Not the country we thought we knew', 9 June 2003).

Frequently, in the absence of the ability by the law enforcement agencies to clearly identify Muslims, Asians are targeted. UK Home Office figures show that 'stop and search' of Asians under the new Terrorism Act increased by 302 per cent from 2002–2003 to 2003–2004. According to the Islamic Human Rights Group, 32,100 people were searched, with Muslims accounting for the vast majority of suspects. About 500 Muslims had been arrested on suspicion of terrorism offences by April 2004. In the biggest ever operation by the UK Government, 700 police officers raided 28 homes during March 2003. Of those arrested, a handful have been charged (with minor immigration violations) and most have been released (Cowan, 2004:7). Young Muslim women frequently bore the brunt of much of the day-to-day hostility. Some had the *hijab* (headscarf) torn off their faces by patriotic thugs. The French Government banned the wearing of the *hijab* in schools and a number of Muslim girls were expelled for continuing to wear it. This has major implications for France's estimated six million Muslims. The Government also banned Sikh turbans, Jewish *yarmulkes* (skull caps) and large crosses, all falling under the heading of 'conspicuous' religious symbols. In Germany, five states made legislation to ban the *hijab* from schools but not *yarmulkes*, crucifixes and habits (Graham, 2003; Benoit, 2003).

The history of immigration in both the United States and Europe offers insight into future development. Daniel Tichenor's *Dividing Lines: The Politics of Immigration Control in America*, raises an interesting question.

Why (asks Tichenor) did American Nativism during the late nineteenth century, despite repeated attempts, fail to restrict new European immigration and was defeated? The most formidable Nativist movement during the 1890s was the American Protective Association, which claimed a membership of over two million members. One explanatory factor is offered in the integration of European settlers as important voting blocks. The Democratic Party courted the immigrant vote and opposed Nativist policy. The role played by Irish Catholic community leaders as political brokers in the New York Democratic Party, is the grand example. The politics of Chinese exclusion offers a very different picture. Most Chinese immigrants were newcomers, and their lack of access to the political system rendered them relatively powerless to resist the racist alliance assembled against them.

Tichenor, however, is less convincing in offering theoretical explanation for immigration policy. The author makes use of a historical-institutionalist approach which dismisses lightly the relevance of economic factors and the conflict between interest groups in the shaping of policy. The book identifies the policy regime as the product of global pressures on governing institutions, group alliances and expert narratives. Primacy is attached to the quality of the legislative and expert narrative. The key argument is that, 'liberal democracies such as the United States, deeply rooted in Enlightenment traditions of thought, are systems in which ideas thrive and in which government actors need rational and knowledge-based justification for new policy initiatives' (Tichenor, 2002:42).

Two criticisms can be made of Tichenor. One is that the thesis appears less convincing after 9/11. Guantanamo Bay is a legislative tribute to the return of American nativism. Another is the need to reflect on the connectivity between history and politics as well as many other factors which shape the policy regime during different historical circumstances. Political pressure on the legislative, the impact of global events reflected in political crisis and exile, the quality of ethnic mobilisations, processes of racialisation and selectivity in immigration, and economic circumstances in the sending countries and receiving countries. The relationship between immigration policy and the economy needs to be revisited and disentangled. This relationship is often revealed in the study of particular sectors, cities and neighbourhoods. One example, as Tichenor notes, was the two-tiered regulatory regime operating during the 1930s and 1940s which denied admission to Jewish refugees fleeing for their lives, whilst simultaneously, agricultural employers, chairs of congressional immigration committees and the federal immigration bureaucracy, supported the legal and illicit importation of Mexican labour for California's rural economy. Similar histories can be found in other industries and amongst other immigrant groups.

The effects of immigration in Europe and the United States has been the source of heated debate. Frequently this is thought of in economic terms: about jobs filled, or 'taken' by immigrant workers. Yet, in many places we see evidence of immigrants creating their own jobs and making jobs for others. Immigrant-owned enterprises, have become an important part of that debate. Nowhere is this debate more intense than in the major cities of Europe and the United States. Immigration has underpinned the development of gateway cities. Today, the cities of Los Angeles, San Francisco, New York, Miami and Chicago account for approximately 14 million immigrants, or nearly 50 per cent of all immigrants in the United States (Clark, 2003:39). These and other gateway cities in Europe (London, Paris, Amsterdam), are the subject of this book and are elaborated in subsequent chapters.

1 Globalisation 'from below'

Enterprise and ethnicity

Introduction

This introductory chapter presents immigration as an example of globalisation 'from below' (and from above), and considers its influence in shaping the gateway cities of Europe and the United States. One mechanism of globalisation appears in the incorporation of diverse immigrant groups into informal labour markets and precarious forms of income generation. The relationship between immigration and the restructuring of cities and industries is complex, and the view that immigration causes informalisation needs to be treated with caution. The introduction points to key issues in the interaction between localities and the global economy and immigration and enterprise. It identifies and explains key analytical terms and concepts applied in subsequent sections of the book. One way of understanding the substantive issues is in the summary presented by Portes (1995a) on the convergence between economic sociology and the sociology of immigration. Economic sociology is research 'on the ways in which social influences modify the assumed maximising behaviour of individuals and lead to predictions differing from those of conventional economic models' (Portes, 1995a:3). The study of socially orientated economic action points towards action constrained by 'bounded solidarity', reciprocity and group expectations, the non-observance of which carries the threat of retribution. Terms such as 'embeddedness' point to the way transactions are inserted in given social networks and structures, which shape their specific form and content. Typically this appears in the form of 'social capital' which comes from membership of those networks. The sociology of immigration points to different models in the incorporation of immigrants, in the role of ethnic economies and the persistence of particular occupational 'niches'. Another significant contribution is by studies of the 'informal economy' i.e. the sum total of income-earning activities unregulated by legal codes.

Concepts such as the immigrant and ethnic enclave economy, social embeddedness, social capital, 'diaspora', transnational communities and social differentiation, point towards the role of agency i.e. outcomes determined in part, by the activities of immigrants themselves. Concepts and issues which point to the role of structure, include the political forces which shape the institutional framework, the nature of local economies, the impact of globalisation in particular sectors and sub-sectors. The relationship between structure and agency is critical in explaining processes of racialisation, structuration and variation in policy towards immigrants. It also provides the framework for examining social and economic differentiation between and within immigrant enterprise. Variation is frequently linked to complex relationships involving the role of particular industries and patterns of subcontracting, the traditions of particular urban centres and local economies, the impact of the regulatory framework and the quality of ethnic mobilisations and the degree to which immigrant groups achieve political representation.

Globalisation 'from below'

One way of explaining globalisation 'from below' is by comparing it with globalisation 'from above'. This is illustrated in the actions of states to facilitate labour migration. An example of this was the transfer of labour to Europe during the post-war boom. Current examples include the recruitment of foreign doctors, nurses and other skilled workers. A major sectoral illustration is the globalisation of care and the import of foreign domestic workers. An estimated 400,000 women from the Asian continent migrate annually with the vast bulk doing so as independent migrants. In the case of the Philippines, two thirds of all female migrant workers are in fact domestic workers. The Philippines is a concentrated example of a labour-sending country which actively encouraged the expansion of foreign migrant labour markets. The Government adopted low-wage female migration as a source for foreign exchange in response to structural adjustment and stabilisation policies and to the economic slowdown faced by the Gulf States, which had employed many men migrants during the 1970s and early 1980s on large-scale construction projects. It is in part due to the work of the Philippines Overseas Employment Administration (POEA) that an estimated 4.2 million people from the Philippines are migrant workers, working in more than 130 countries and accounting for 6–7 per cent of the national population. Remittances account for the single largest source of foreign exchange (Government of the Philippines, 1995).

The regulatory regime in the receiving countries is designed to ensure that foreign domestic workers are a transient workforce. Legislation regulates the number of workers allowed to work in a country and the length of their contracts. Typically this appears in the form of short-term contracts. Immigration rules ensure that a visa is designed to be valid only for the period of the contract. If the employer dismisses a foreign domestic worker, this also deprives them of residency status. The objective of policy is explicitly to prohibit carers from changing employers. Short-term contracts and temporary visas tied to particular employers, points to powerful constraints to job mobility and results in the artificial depression of wages through the creation of a captive labour pool which primarily benefits employers (Panayiotopoulos, 2005).

Whilst the above is an example of immigration as globalisation from above in the service sector, Sassen (1991) and Harris (1995a), also point to globalisation as substantially driven by the dispersion of industrialisation, due to multinational investment and export-orientated state-directed industrialisation, characterised by the economic development of the East Asian newly industrialising countries (NICs) and China. This may take the form of foreign direct investment and 'capital to men', or labour migration and 'men/women to capital'. The greater locational mobility explicit in dispersion requires new technological capability to maintain control over globalised production operations. An important practical dimension in the relationship between centralisation and decentralisation appears in the fragmentation of production typically in the form of extensive systems of international subcontracting. Under these conditions, the lessening of concentration, paradoxically, may demand increased levels of centralisation (Das and Panayiotopoulos, 1996; Panayiotopoulos, 1996b). Saskia Sassen (1988, 1991, 1996), directs our attention to the spatial impact of globalisation and restructuring in the heartland of the high-income economies (London, New York, Tokyo) and suggests that one critical mechanism of globalisation appears in the incorporation of diverse immigrant groups into informal labour markets, characterised by low pay, casual work, undocumented work, survival-orientated and precarious forms of income generation. Sassen (1996) suggests that it is not immigration which is causing informalisation, but rather a more complex interaction between localities and the global economy, involving the restructuring of gateway cities and particular sectors of the economy.

Globalisation from below is a process which denotes that the restructuring of gateway cities in Europe and the United States, has been shaped by immigrants themselves, in spite of official hostility and restrictions. It is a process which has to negotiate immense structural constraints and opportunities. Ivan Light (2000a) in a reworking of migration network theory ('chain migration'), challenges Sassen's view that informalisation and the expansion of low-wage jobs acts independently of immigration. Sassen's argument that globalisation involves structural relationships between immigration, localities and particular sectors, has been (mis)understood by Light as assigning no independent role for immigration in the formation of informal labour markets. Leaving aside whether this actually represents Sassen's argument – note for example the suggestion that 'immigrants, in so far as they form communities, may be in a favourable position to seize the opportunities presented by informalisation' (Sassen, 1996:588). Migration network theory purports to show that migration creates self-sustaining labour flows, which in gathering momentum begin to act independently of factors which initiated migration in the first place. Light argues that solidarity intrinsic in membership of an immigrant network sharing common experiences, also has strong cost-cutting capabilities linked to informal systems of production and in this sense, immigration 'co-causes' informalisation. Light writes,

> To a substantial extent, immigration has caused itself and also the economic informalisation that is a condition of its self-reproduction. This view explains immigration and informalisation by reference to the mature migrations network's capacity to lower the economic, social and emotional costs and hardships of immigration. This cost-cutting capacity increases the degrees of informalisation in and migration to developed countries by permitting the economic exploitation of unorganised and covert demand that would otherwise have remained inaccessible.
>
> (Light, 2000a:176)

Light proposes a reformulation of existing migration network analysis and introduces the concept of 'spill over immigration' to explain conditions in which mass migration becomes unresponsive to declining opportunities, resulting in an 'expanding supply of migrants and lowering their reservation cost' (Light, 2000a:177). This explanation points to the activities of immigrants themselves as key agency in the structuring of immigration, settlement and labour market incorporation. Light *et al.* (1999), however, also offer criticism of migration network theory and the way it has been used to substantiate the view that 'waves' of immigrants are 'taking over' American jobs. They argue that existing network theory as a theory about labour transfer is limited. Crucially, it cannot sufficiently take into account the labour demand created by the development of immigrant enterprise. In this respect, immigrants far from taking jobs away from native workers, create employment, typically linked to the employment of other immigrants. Light *et al.* use the term 'immigrant economy' to explain this expansive labour market formation. They suggest that existing network theory exaggerates both the capacities of immigrant networks and differences between native-born and immigrant workers.

Globalisation from below has informed research on 'diaspora' and 'transnational communities'. Diaspora is a term used to describe overseas communities, formed by immigrants who are frequently, but not exclusively, victims of displacement. A more general understanding of the term, 'denotes the spreading around the globe of people who share a number of common cultural traits' (Mohann, 2002:83). Congolese traders in Paris, Mexican immigrants in the New York construction industry, Cypriot entrepreneurs in the North London garment industry, Korean wig manufacturers in Los Angeles, the many 'Chinatowns' catering for diners and tourists, have been analysed as diasporic communities. One further observation by Giles Mohann (in an inversion of the invisible hand) is that social and economic action in the diaspora is reflected in people who by making 'use of their localised diasporic connections to secure economic and social well-being and, as by-product, contribute to the development of their locality' (Mohann, 2002:107).

Discussion on diaspora, arguably, provides supporting material for cultural endowment theories in explaining the development of immigrant enterprise. More substantively, perhaps, it also provides insight on the role of trade diaspora and the consequences of labour migration. Robin Cohen (1997:26) points to a number of defining characteristics of diaspora (see below). The concept of a return movement is intrinsic to community memory and myth, and this characteristic appears at odds with most conventional patterns of immigration to Europe and the United States. However, contemporary patterns have also been shaped by displacement and a growing role for asylum seekers and refugees and this has provided a material basis for victim-focus diaspora analysis. Another material basis has been the targeting of immigrant and expatriate communities by governments of their country of origin, or perceived origin, which makes use of the diaspora discourse in order to reinforce claims to national origins, identity and territory in the homeland.

Defining characteristics of diaspora

1   Dispersal from an original homeland, often under traumatic conditions, to two or more foreign countries.
2   The expansion from a homeland in search of work, trade or in furtherance of colonial goals.
3   A collective memory and myth about the homeland, including its location, history and achievement.
4   An idealisation of the claimed ancestral home and a collective commitment to its maintenance, restoration, safety, prosperity, even to its creation.
5   The development of a return movement that gains collective support.
6   A strong ethnic group consciousness sustained over a long period of time and based on a sense of distinctiveness, a common history and the belief in a common fate.
7   A possibly troubled relationship with host societies, suggesting a lack of acceptance and/or the possibility that another calamity might befall the group.
8   A sense of empathy and solidarity with co-ethnic members in other countries of settlement.
9   The possibility of a distinctive creative, enriching life in host countries with a tolerance of pluralism.

(Cohen, 1997:26)

Robin Cohen presents different types of diaspora. Some show the influence of the victim focus of the original research. Others focus on labour and trade diaspora (see, below). Labour diaspora involve groups either travelling voluntarily in search of employment opportunities, or under semi-forced conditions in the case of indentured labour, frequently employed in menial manual jobs and occupations such as agricultural labourers and housemaids. Mexican migration to the United States could be seen as an example of a contemporary labour diaspora. In many experiences, labour migrants provided the ranks of the first-generation entrepreneurs. More explicit to discussion on enterprise, is the role of trade diasporas.

Types of diaspora

- *Victim diasporas* involve concerted persecution of one group by another and the forcible eviction of the persecuted from their homeland. The Jewish, Palestinian, African, Armenian and Irish experiences are frequently analysed as victim diasporas.
- *Trade diasporas* involve a group proactively dispersing to serve one or more markets in places other than the homeland. They circulate between home and these distant places and tend to congregate with fellow traders in their host societies. They are identifiably different from their local communities, are reluctant to settle permanently and sojourning i.e. the desire to return home, is a strong characteristic. Examples cited include, the Phoenicians, Venetians, Lebanese and Chinese.
- *Labour diasporas* involve groups either travelling voluntarily in search of employment opportunities or under semi-forced conditions, in the case of indentured labour, to work in menial manual jobs. Examples include Indians, Chinese, Sikhs, Turks and Italians.
- *Imperial diasporas* involve the proactive colonisation of foreign lands to be used as resource bases to service the imperial homeland. Examples include, the Ancient Greeks, British, French, Dutch and Russians.
- *Cultural diasporas* have created shared cultural codes and styles which unite communities in their exiled status and lead to new de-territorialised identities. Examples include Caribbean and Indian diasporas.

(Cohen, 1997)

Analyses of labour diaspora have become a more significant area of research in attempts to move the concept of diaspora beyond its original focus on the study of victims. In many cases, these studies have revealed new vulnerabilities in globalisation. Contemporary labour diaspora include: independent female migration of large numbers of foreign domestic workers (or 'maids') from South-East Asia (see Panayiotopoulos, 2005); the often involuntary diaspora associated with the sex industry and the 'Natasha trade' (Hughes, 2000; Ehrenreich and Hochschild, 2003; Human Rights Watch, 2001); and the *Futzhounese* network linking southern rural China with urban Chinatowns worldwide (see Chapters 3 and 6).

Research on 'transnational communities' and reflected in the work of the Transnational Communities Programme (see, Gokturk, 1999; Pecoud, 2001; Henry *et al.*, 2001), purports to show that contemporary patterns of migration have resulted in the undermining of the nation state, leading to the formation of diaspora, transnational networks and communities which feel equally at home in receiving and sending countries. The term 'deterritorialized nation-states' has been used to describe such networks. Basch *et al.* (1994:6) define transnationalism 'as the process by which immigrants form and sustain multi-stranded social relations that link together their societies of origin and settlement', and which cut across geographic, cultural and political borders. Portes writes that transnational communities are,

> characterized by dense networks across space and by an increasing number of people who lead dual lives. Members are at least bilingual, move easily between different cultures, frequently maintain houses in two countries, and pursue economic, political and cultural interests that require a simultaneous presence in both.
>
> (Portes, 1997:15)

The emergence of transnational communities with immigrant enterprise as the epicentre, would indicate a distinct phenomenon at variance with traditional patterns of immigrant adaptation. Portes argues that whilst the process is set in motion by the interests and needs of capital in the advanced countries, it can nevertheless 'offer a broader field for autonomous popular initiatives'(Portes, 1997:3). These can act (as the argument runs) as alternative ways to deal with world-roaming capital, to those associated with international trade union solidarity or attempts to impose labour standards in developing countries. In this discourse, the emergence of immigrant enterprise and transnational communities, is presented as a response by working-class immigrants to the globalisation of capitalist production characterised by persistent global income inequality,

> what common people have done in response to the processes of globalization is to create communities that sit astride political borders and that, in a very real sense, are 'neither here nor there' but in both places simultaneously. The economic activities that sustain these communities are grounded precisely on the differentials of advantage created by state boundaries. In this respect, they are no different from the large corporations, except that these enterprises emerge at the grassroots level and its activities are often informal.
>
> (Portes, 1997:2)

The globalisation from below thesis converged with the 'rediscovery' of the 'informal sector' in the urban centres of Europe and North America during the 1980s recession (see Gerry, 1987). Sassen (1988), in a study of unregistered activities in New York's economy in sectors such as construction, garments, footwear, furniture, retail activity and electronics, argued that important sources for the informalisation of various activities are to be found in characteristics of the city's larger economy: among these being the demand for products and services that lend themselves to small-scale production, or are associated with rapid transformations brought about by commercial and residential gentrification, or are not satisfactorily provided by the formal sector. Sassen suggests 'that a good share of the informal sector is not the result of immigrant survival strategies, but rather an outcome of structural patterns or transformations in the larger economy of a city such as New York' (Sassen, 1988:3).

The analyses presented by Sassen, Light and Portes emphasise to varying degrees, the role of structure and agency and the relationship between the two, in shaping contemporary patterns of immigration and labour market incorporation. Global restructuring, spillover migration and the formation of diasporic or transnational communities, however, say little about the role of the institutional framework. Immigration controls and state regulation are (by most accounts) a critical factor in shaping the pattern of immigration and its selectivity. Asylum-seeking refugees, for example, who formed an increased component of European and North American migrants in the 1980s and 1990s, would be unresponsive to declining economic opportunities, yet are the most impacted by state regulation. Jenny Robinson, argues that the idea of de-territoralisation, explicit in various theories of globalisation and transnationalism, appears at its weakest in relation to the international refugee regime,

> *the phenomenon of displacement does not diminish the significance of territories or places.* For both refugees and resettlers, it is usually the nation-state which not only causes displacement, but which also assumes responsibility for attempting to deal with the undesirable effects of its consequences.
>
> (Robinson 2002:3, italics in original)

From labour migrants to immigrant entrepreneurs

Whilst it would be unwise to generalise about the composition of immigrant entrepreneurs, one important generalisation is that many were labour migrants who may or may not have seen the original purpose of migration as a temporary recourse. Many first-generation entrepreneurs came from the ranks of shop floor workers. Many more were employed by them as waiters, taxi drivers, shop assistants, pressers and cutters. A not unusual trajectory is that entrepreneurs began their working lives as 'apprentices' working for other immigrants before they became owners of their own shops, restaurants and factories. It is for this reason that entrepreneurs can come under moral pressure to assist their workers if they want to establish independent enterprise activities, such as in advancing them loans (see, Ram *et al.*, 2001; Panayiotopoulos, 1994; Wilpert, 2003). The repositioning of immigrants from the ranks of workers to the ranks of entrepreneurs is a complex process. It needs to be understood in the light of particular historical circumstances faced by different social strata of immigrants, the opportunity structure of the small-scale sector and the social characteristics of the entrepreneurs themselves.

In an introductory discussion we need to establish what is meant by the terms 'enterprise' and 'entrepreneur'. It is the case, for example, that most immigrant enterprises are small and this has important implications for how enterprises function and are managed. An enterprise can be understood as containing physical and social features, characteristics and functions (see, below). Frequently, however, an enterprise is thought of as the concrete result of just one of the factors of production namely 'entrepreneurship'. The fact that we often refer to the skills performed by entrepreneurs as 'enterprise' merely increases the potential confusion surrounding this term, or rather, its reduction to the activities and the personality of the owner. Clearly, in small enterprises involving face-to-face relations, the personality of the entrepreneur is a critical factor. Nowhere is this more apparent than amongst the self-employed. However, all enterprises involve relations with internal and external economic agents and institutional actors. Micro and small enterprises which employ other workers, necessarily acquire new functions, least of all those of the 'management' of labour.

Enterprise characteristics

- *Physical characteristics:* a building, for example, in which various factors of production (e.g. raw materials, capital equipment, labour and entrepreneurship) are assembled and combined to produce goods or services.
- *Social features:* comprising of (a) the *internal* relations between those owning its productive assets and those supplying labour (including a specific division of labour and internal organisation) and (b) its *external* relations with the market and with other (government and non-governmental) institutions, which make up the environment in which goods and services are produced and traded.

Whilst immigrant enterprises, as we shall see, are differentiated and it would be a reductionism to generalise about an essential enterprise with its requisite essential characteristics, there are a number of features which appear as common to immigrant-owned enterprise (see, below). Many of these characteristics, however, (for example, the combination of ownership and management, informal production systems) should not be seen as the property of immigrant enterprises. Many small-scale, family-owned and 'informal sector' enterprises have similar characteristics to those associated with immigrant enterprises. Barret *et al.* (1996:804) caution against the danger of identifying certain characteristics as 'immigrant' or 'ethnic' 'when in truth they are often variants on a universal small-business culture'. One selectivity in the structuring of immigrant enterprise appears in size. Most are small, measured in terms of assets, turnover, level of employment and other indicators of economic activity and this has implications for a range of internal and external enterprise functions.

Immigrant enterprise: characteristics

1   The entrepreneur combines ownership and management functions.
2   No clear division of labour exists between management and direct production.
3   Levels of productivity are low.
4   Both production and administration are conducted along traditional, personalised and paternalistic lines.
5   Close personal relations exist both among those active in the enterprise and between the entrepreneur and other enterprises.
6   There is a strong dependence on family labour.
7   The enterprise finds it difficult to access formal financial and credit markets.
8   There is a strong dependence on informal systems of labour recruitment, management and production. They frequently act as contractors and subcontractors in extensive and difficult to monitor production networks.

Analyses of immigrant enterprise which draw from international comparison, point to significant structural variables which influence the development of immigrant enterprise. These include: prominence in small enterprises; self-employment and the agglomeration of immigrant-owned enterprises in sectors and localities, typically as contractors and subcontractors in difficult to monitor systems of production and exchange; the political-institutional framework and the legal framework applied in the regulation of enterprises and immigration itself; the nature of the political system and the extent of political representation and mobilisation by immigrant communities; the role of local economies and the traditions of particular urban centres and industries (see, Rath, 2000a, 2002a; Sassen, 1995; Kabeer, 2000; Panayiotopoulos, 1992; London Skills Forecasting Unit, 2001; Rekers and van Kempen, 2000). The above provides the context for the immigrant or ethnic economy theses (see, Light and Roach, 1996; Watson *et al.*, 2000; Waldinger, 1986). We need to explain selectivity in the concentration of immigrant enterprise in particular industries, sub-sectors and localities. Why is it that so many entrepreneurs crowd around the small-scale spectrum in sectors such as restaurants, groceries, newsagents, or as contractors and subcontractors in the garment industry? How do we explain that so many are found in US ghettos and enclaves, British inner-city areas, or cast-out on the margins of Parisian suburbs or wherever land values are the cheapest? Land values and rent prices have important implications for the location of enterprises within particular cities and neighbourhoods.

The social characteristics of entrepreneurs are significant in defining the opportunity structure. Race, ethnicity, gender and age, are factors which influence selectivity in the formation and extension of immigrant enterprise. One widely observed tension appears in generational differences and second-generation resistance to entering the 'niche' immigrant sectors and activities. Selectivity appears in widely observed racial and gender disparities in enterprise formation and the accessing of bank loans, both in the UK and the US. Many African Caribbean entrepreneurs in the UK and African American entrepreneurs in the US, despite their different histories, have common tales of rejection by bank managers.

One report, commissioned by the British Bankers Association, noted that in the UK 9 per cent of all business start-ups were owned by non-white entrepreneurs, and that 20 per cent of enterprises in London were ethnic-minority owned. One major finding was that whilst ethnic minorities appear to suffer no disadvantage compared to white business people when accessing loans, significant variation was found in the treatment of black entrepreneurs: only 21 per cent of African Caribbean entrepreneurs secured start-up capital, compared to 34 per cent of those of white or Pakistani extraction and 49 per cent of those owned by people of Chinese extraction. This was despite the finding that 46 per cent of black entrepreneurs had formal management qualifications, more than whites or Asians. The report concludes that, 'whilst we are unable to prove that discrimination exists, there is clear evidence of disadvantage which cannot be satisfactorily explained in terms of other characteristics of the business or their ownership' (Ram *et al.*, 2002b:4). Representatives of Barclays Bank counter-argued that there was no data to suggest actual discrimination against African Caribbean applicants, and that the report's authors had been 'swayed' by anecdotal evidence from case study interviewees. The survey data from the report which show that African Caribbean entrepreneurs are much less likely to access loans, was (in a familiar incantation) partly explained as 'self-exclusion by black entrepreneurs who assume that banks will automatically turn them down' (Roberts, 2002:5). Whilst the above may be an accurate description of justifiable conclusions drawn by black entrepreneurs, blaming the victim is not an unusual defence by the commercial banking sector. Neither will it take us very far in understanding institutional behaviour. Lower priority in the processing and granting of loan applications to non-white groups can be seen as an example of racialisation i.e. a process which reproduces institutional behaviour attaching lower value to particular racial, immigrant or ethnic groups.

Whilst it is the case, as Portes noted previously, that immigrant enterprise can engage in transnational activities and in this (the argument continues) 'they are no different from the large corporations' (Portes, 1997:2), they are very different in many other respects. An appreciation of immigrant enterprise needs to understand the accumulated impact of selectivity and the manner in which this process structures the incorporation of immigrant groups in the enterprise sector. What is the impact of concentration in the small-scale sector of particular industries, sub-sectors and localities, typically in the weakest contractual positions? One conclusion is that enterprise formation is in part a function of the economic power of the entrepreneur and in this there are contradictory forces at work. One factor is that immigrant communities are characterised by a relative abundance of labour but limited supplies of capital. For this reason, many enter sectors which have lower entry costs and are labour intensive i.e. require less capital and more labour relative to other sectors, and this is a key factor in structuring the sectoral and spatial location of many immigrant enterprises. Immigrant entrepreneurs attempt to compensate for capital scarcity, frequently as the result of exclusion from the formal commercial lending sector, by making use of immigrant ethnic ties and networks. Light and Gold (2000) point in the United States to a historical transition from first-generation dependence on ethnic resources and 'peer-group based lending' (friends, relatives, Rotating Savings and Credit Associations (ROSCAs)) to subsequent generation use of class resources, reflected in 'collateral based lending' used to access the commercial lending sector.

Key concepts

The emergence of immigrant enterprise points to a quandary. Most immigrants face immense structural constraints and processes of selectivity, both as immigrants and as entrepreneurs. Yet, their enterprise has contributed towards reshaping cities and neighbourhoods which felt long-abandoned by capitalism, into centres of multiculturalism and 'good' globalisation. What gives immigrant entrepreneurs the ability to function and reproduce themselves in some of the most competitive market sectors and some of the meanest or warmest neighbourhoods in the gateway cities of Europe and the United States? In answering this question there are immense difficulties in identifying causality and effect. One generalisation is that immigrants, as with other people, exist and learn how to be people in clearly defined social spaces and institutions. Family, kinship, workplace relations, religious, social, sporting and political organisations, and homeland associations, become functional ways in which a broader solidarity is structured in immigrant communities. Often, 'ethnic solidarity' is presented as causation. It is the case, that in many circumstances the institutions and associations which underpin immigrant communities, act as 'the heart of a heartless world' and inform economic arrangements, labour market incorporation and enterprise formation.

One interpretation offered by Light in the preceding discussion, is the proposition that immigrant networks have cost-cutting functions and are effective economic and social support mechanisms which make immigration and settlement possible. Many analyses point to how the repositioning of immigrants, from workers to entrepreneurs, is also in part shaped by their own action and agency. This appears as a key assumption in analyses of transnational communities and diaspora. Views which emphasise the role of agency apply concepts such as, ethnicity, the ethnic enclave economy, the ethnic niche, the immigrant economy, social embeddedness, mixed embeddedness and social capital, in order to explain this transition. These concepts lean towards residual explanations i.e. the ethno-cultural or social endowment of particular groups as critical to enterprise formation (see, below, summary of key concepts).

At the same time, we know that there are important structural and relational continuities in the positioning of immigrant enterprise. These frequently appear in processes of structuration, racialisation, and social and economic differentiation (see, below) which surface in diverse experiences; the historical circumstances immigrants find themselves in, the nature of the institutional framework, immigration policy and what is happening to particular sectors, cities, local economies and the small enterprise sector. For example, the arrest of the historical decline in self-employment in both Europe and the United States during the early 1970s onwards, and international trends towards subcontracting, became important dimensions of economic restructuring during the onset of the recession years. These, arguably, facilitated the expansion of immigrant-owned enterprises (see, Light and Rosenstein, 1995:12; Boissevain, 1984; Gerry, 1985).

Summary of key concepts

Agency

- *Ethnicity* and ethnic solidarity can be understood as an emergent and submergent phenomenon, based in claims to common origins shared by members of the same group, and manifested in cultural, economic and political arrangements which underpin the economic incorporation of immigrant communities (see Barth, 1969; Portes, 1984; Waldinger, 2000).
- *The ethnic economy* is a semi-autonomous economic system characterised by entrepreneurs hiring co-ethnic workers. The 'ethnic niche' and 'ethnic enclave' are concentrated forms of the ethnic economy: the 'ethnic niche' refers to the tendency to concentrate in particular sectors of the economy. The 'ethnic enclave' refers to concentration in particular cities and neighbourhoods (see, Light et al., 1994; Light and Gold, 2000).

- *The ethnic enclave* is characterised by ethnic entrepreneurs employing co-ethnic workers. The thesis argues that workers and entrepreneurs in the enclave, receive earnings-returns to human capital commensurate with the earnings-returns of immigrants in the open labour market and that immigrant enterprise represents 'an effective vehicle for upward mobility among immigrant minorities' (Portes and Jensen, 1989:930; also see, Zhou Min, 1992).
- *The immigrant enclave economy* points to labour force interspersion. Unlike ethnic economies in which entrepreneurs employ co-ethnics, immigrant economies arise when entrepreneurs employ immigrant workers from a variety of ethnic backgrounds (see, Light *et al.*, 1999; Panayiotopoulos, 1996a).
- *Social capital* is described by Portes as 'the capacity of individuals to command scarce resources by virtue of their membership in networks or broader social structures'. Fernandez-Kelly refers to a 'process' which determines access to benefits from social networks, and points to complimentary cultural capital i.e. a repertoire of symbols held by all members of an immigrant or ethnic group which structure social and economic relations (Portes, 1994:14; Fernandez-Kelly, 1995:220; see also, Putnam, 1993; Coleman, 1988).
- *Social embeddedness* refers to the level of integration by immigrant entrepreneurs in the market *and* extra-market activities of immigrant workers and communities; much of the literature identifies this as a necessary precondition for enterprise formation and critical in the management of enterprise functions (see, Portes and Sensenbrenner, 1993; Granovetter, 1985, 1995; Uzzi, 1996).
- *Mixed embeddedness* refers to the level of integration by immigrant and ethnic minority entrepreneurs to immigrant and ethnic communities *and* to the host society and its institutional framework. The concept relates immigrant social relations and transactions to wider political and economic processes and structures (see, Rath, 2002b; Kloosterman and Rath, 2001, 2003).

Structure

- *The institutional framework* creates the legal framework for the regulation of enterprises, immigration itself and the structuring of formal political rights. It can facilitate or constrain, depending on the extent to which immigrant groups have political representation, capacities for political mobilisation and 'mixed' embeddedness (see, Rath, 2000a).
- *The local economy* refers to the structure and traditions of particular urban centres, neighbourhoods, localities and the role of particular sectors and sub-sectors of the economy within those localities (see, Rath, 2002c; Sassen, 1995; Panayiotopoulos, 1992; London Skills Forecasting Unit, 2001).

- *Small enterprises, the self-employment sector*, and the agglomeration of small immigrant-owned enterprises in particular sectors and localities, typically as contractors and subcontractors in difficult to monitor production systems, provides the basis for the immigrant/ethnic economy thesis (see, Light and Roach, 1996; Watson *et al.*, 2000; Waldinger, 1986).
- *The 'informal sector'*, refers to the sum total of economic activities which are not registered and within which labour is not protected by any social legislation and is, therefore, cheaper. The concept associated initially with analyses of Third World urban labour markets, was 'rediscovered' (Gerry, 1987) in Europe and the United States during the recession years of the 1970s. There is considerable debate over the extent to which the informal sector is capable of autonomous action, or is dependent and subordinate on larger organisations and suppliers (Gerry, 1985; Portes *et al.*, 1989; Portes, 1994; Sassen, 1994).
- *Social differentiation* points to the reproduction of social stratification inside immigrant and ethnic communities. For example, in the emergence of entrepreneurs from the ranks of wage workers and in the role of ascriptive disadvantage embedded in given social categories: class, gender, race, age, religious affiliation and intersections between them (Kabeer, 2000; Bonacich and Appelbaum, 2000).
- *'Racialisation'*, refers to processes initiated by the state, which constructs immigration in 'race' terms and shapes conditions under which certain categories of immigrant workers and entrepreneurs participate in labour markets. It points to immigration and citizenship policy as defining issues in the 'race making' process and in the construction of national identities (see Carter *et al.*, 1996; Trimikliniotis, 1999; Schonwalder, 2004).
- *Economic differentiation* refers to processes which explain the differences in immigrant enterprises in terms of purpose, size and labour input: many are small, survival-orientated, family enterprises dependent on family labour, whilst others are large employers, who recruit labour from a range of ethnic groups, and in cases operate as micro-multinational companies engaging in international outward processing (Panayiotopoulos, 2000b; Panayiotopoulos and Dreef, 2002; Rutherford and Blackburn, 2000).

Structure *and* agency

Definitions of structure and agency are complex and some of the concepts above, such as 'mixed embeddedness', can be thought of either in terms of structure or agency. Similarly, the 'informal sector' is frequently presented as the result of agency and as the property of particular ethnic groups or immigrant groups operating on the 'fringes'. More significantly, it is the relationship between structure and agency which offers insight into the categorisations presented above. It is the case that structure (the banking sector, for example), can act as a barrier which constrains the development and extension of immigrant enterprise. It is also evident that immigrants as agency can influence structures, such as for example, of local economies and local government, towards taking a more sympathetic policy position. This often reflects on the significance of entrepreneurs to local labour markets and on the quality of immigrant and ethnic political mobilisation (see, Rath, 2002b; Sassen, 1995; Panayiotopoulos, 1992). The extent to which immigrant communities can influence localities, becomes an important explanation for institutional variation. This is illustrated in the United States where Tammany Hall, as a path to Americanisation (i.e. mainline assimilation), has informed Roger Waldinger's analyses of 'ethnic succession' and/or a game of 'musical chairs', to describe the positioning of immigrant groups in New York and Miami (Chapters 3 and 4).

An important continuity, Carter *et al.* (1996) argue, is in the role played by the state in the racialisation of populations through immigration and nationality regulations. They point to the racialised nature of immigration controls and institutional perceptions which both structure the way in which immigrants are situated within the labour market and valorises notions of 'race' difference. Despite the different circumstances in which these processes developed in the US and Europe, comparative analyses also point to significant continuities. In both, the reconstitution of national identities was frequently articulated through concepts of 'race', in which colour remains a key signifier of difference. Through immigration and nationality laws, governments ranked human populations into hierarchies of assimilation, in which some groups were regarded as more likely to 'fit in' than others. Once racialised in this way, migrant workers and entrepreneurs find themselves allocated to particular areas of the labour market and confined to particular positions within production systems and the labour process. Waldinger's analysis of 'revealed' labour market preference, in many respects is describing the effects of what Carter *et al.* would analyse as processes of racialisation.

Ethnicity

Ethnicity is frequently presented as coming to life in an interaction between relatively cohesive and distinct culture groups. At the same time, ethnicity is an emergent and submergent phenomenon, which has to be contextually understood. Ethnic groups are defined as much by 'boundaries' based on shared values, customs and 'patterns of normative behaviour', as the historical circumstance they find themselves in. Abner Cohen pointed to the 'degree of conformity' to patterns of behaviour as a key indicator of what defined ethnicity (Cohen 1974:ix, xi). Barth described ethnic categories as 'organisational vessels' that may be given varying levels of intensity and contextual forms in different socio-cultural systems.

They can be of great relevance to behaviour, but they need not necessarily be so; they may embrace all social life, or they may be relevant only in limited areas of social activity (Barth, 1969:14).

Abner Cohen suggested that,

> This [Barth's] approach raises a number of logical and sociological difficulties. Its central theme is descriptive and is essentially circular. What it says is that people act as the members of ethnic categories because they identify themselves and are sometimes also identified by others with these ethnic categories. How do we know this? The actors say so, or so they act.
>
> (Cohen, 1974:xii–xiii)

The dangers of a one-sided i.e. 'culturalist' interpretation of ethnicity, are recognised by Cohen who notes that,

> Ethnicity is a complex phenomenon [. . .] which involves psychological, historical, economic and political factors. A full study of its nature – if this is at all possible, will require giving due weight to these and probably many other factors and will call for the co-operation of many disciplines. But if we seriously attempt to do this at one and the same time, we shall not be able to go far in our analysis.
>
> (Cohen, 1974:xi)

Cohen (1974:xv), in trying to understand the 'rise of ethnicity' in the newly-independent developing countries and the cities of the United States during the 1960s, suggested that a 'political analysis of ethnicity' may provide for a better overarching framework. Many analyses of immigrant enterprise point to ethnic mobilisation and solidarity as providing causal explanation for how immigrants cope in the face of adversity and to explain the development and management of enterprises. Portes and Sensenbrenner (1993:1343–1344) suggest that situations where immigrant and ethnic groups have faced prolonged periods of exclusion and blocked upward mobility, have led to 'the emergence of collective solidarity based on opposition to these conditions and an accompanying explanation of the group's social and economic position'. One implication for enterprise, Portes (1995a:29) argues, is that 'bounded solidarity and trust enables employers in ethnic enclaves to demand greater discipline and effort from their workers'. Waldinger (1995:555) suggests that embeddedness in ethnic networks 'leads to cooperation, if not conformist, behaviour among ethnic economic actors'. The application of culturally derived explanations for economic organisation and action, point to market transactions as systematically governed by reciprocity which, for practical purposes, links immigrant enterprise formation to ethnic niches, ethnic enclaves and ethnic economies. Whilst there are distinct analyses associated with these

approaches (see, Light *et al.*, 1994; Barret *et al.*, 1996) many share necessary assumptions about the centrality of ethnicity. This appears in theories
which point to ethnicity as the revealed interface between immigrant
enterprise and market transactions. It is frequently ethnicity which underpins the concerns of diaspora research and studies in the formation of
transnational communities.

Ethnicity has been a key research focus in the re-emergence of economic sociology in its attempts to show ways in which social influences
modify economic behaviour (Portes, 1995a). The new economic sociology
points to the social institutions of immigrant groups as determinant extra-
market cultural weapons, which underpin the competitive advantage of
ethnically specific forms of market organisation and informal economic
behaviour which parallel, compliment and, on occasions, disguise formal
systems of production. Analyses with a basis in neoclassical economics
point to the 'ethnic niche' as the typical and rational response by immigrants to (limited) market opportunity. Waldinger (1996a, 1996b) has
applied the concept of the ethnic 'labour queue' to explain how minorities
face, negotiate and generally overcome structural constraints in US cities.
This model makes use of ecological succession and niche theories to
explain employment changes amongst immigrant groups. One suggestion
is that some groups may be 'predisposed towards certain types of work'
(Waldinger 1996a:21). The concept of the 'queue' draws from a long tradition of succession theories applied in the US to explain the relationship
between ethnicity and enterprise, which share common assumptions in the
familiar theme about the assimilationist prowess of American society.

Portes and Jensen (1989:929–949) have pointed to the agglomeration of
immigrant enterprise in an 'ethnic enclave' as the most concentrated form
of social embeddedness. In drawing initially from studies of Cuban immigrants in Miami (see, Wilson and Portes, 1980), they present an attempt at
explaining the repositioning of an immigrant group which remains critical
of conventional theories of structural incorporation and assimilation. The
ethnic enclave economy thesis – with entrepreneurs at its epicentre – proposes that immigrants in the enclave-labour market, far from being disadvantaged in separation and segregation, receive earnings-returns to human
capital commensurate with the earnings-returns of immigrants in the
primary labour market. Portes and Jensen pointed in an optimistic way
towards enterprise as 'an effective vehicle for upward mobility among
immigrant minorities' (1989:930) and, more specifically still, as 'a vehicle
for first-generation upward mobility' (1987:769; also see, Portes and
Stepick, 1985). The assertion in the ethnic enclave thesis is that a social
mechanism based on reciprocity operates in which ethnic bosses assist co-
ethnic workers in their attempts at upward social and economic mobility.
This approach has influenced research amongst other ethnic groups (see,
Portes and Zhou, 1996). Zhou (1992) suggests that most members of the
Chinese community in New York's Chinatown are employed in the ethnic

enclave economy and enjoy greater returns on human capital than they would command in the wider labour market. In a previous work, however, Zhou and Logan (1989:810) argued that in practice 'only a modest proportion of persons identified as within the enclave actually are employed in minority-owned firms'.

Social embeddedness and social capital

Social embeddedness in the immigrant or ethnic economy assigns centrality to extensive and qualitative integration by immigrant entrepreneurs in the market *and* extra-market activities of immigrant workers and communities. In reverse, Portes and Sensenbrenner (1993) argue that a necessary price for embeddedness is that immigrant enterprises come under pressure to acquire redistributory functions. Uzzi (1996:695) pointed to the cultivation of long-term contractual relations in the New York garment industry as 'precapitalist' in nature, and as having the potential to stifle competition and to reduce innovation amongst contractor enterprises. 'Mixed embeddedness' relates social relations and transactions to wider political and economic structures.

'Social capital' refers to the relationships and norms which shape the quality and quantity of an ethnic group's social and economic interactions. It is made up of networks of varying density which connect immigrants and members of ethnic groups to each other and the wider economy, and which are presented as the collective memory of an immigrant or ethnic group. Fernandez-Kelly (1995:218–219, 241) argues that research on impoverished people show that their survival depends largely on 'relations of mutuality' based in trust and cooperation on the basis of which social capital is generated. It is important to note that in this discourse, social capital is a process which determines access to benefits from social networks and not the 'amount' of social capital accumulated, or assumptions that more affluent members of the network can mobilise even 'more' social capital (Fernandez-Kelly 1995:220).

The contemporary development of social capital analysis points to quite diverse traditions. One of the most significant influences was in the work of Pierre Bourdieu who pointed to the role of cultural capital in the reproduction of class rule. This was defined as competence in society's 'high-class culture' and contained in knowledge about art, music, literature, theatre and dance, or architecture, furniture, fashion and cuisine. Bourdieu argued that knowledge of these arts represented a form of capital, because this knowledge could be used to the owner's economic advantage at future points of development in a person's biography. He pointed to the parallel curriculum of formal education and the development of 'human capital', and the acquisition of cultural capital in the family. Whilst the former results in formal qualifications for all, the parallel curriculum of the home teaches class knowledge formal schooling ignores, and gives the children of the bourgeoisie a superior endowment in cultural capital (see, Bourdieu and Passeron, 1977). Light and Gold (2000:91) note that this cultural capital 'conveys prestige recognition on the strength of which people get desirable jobs, marriages and business contracts'. In the UK it is referred to as the 'Old Boys Network' (a gender specificity Bourdieu's work tended to ignore), denoting schooling in expensive private schools, such as Eton and Harrow, where the future elites bond with each other and form relationships which act as future networking for the advancement of political and business careers. In this sense, social capital creates human capital, or the ability to predict, to minimise risk and more generally to 'trust'.

An example was presented by James Coleman (1988) who pointed to Jewish diamond merchants in New York who saved a significant amount in lawyers' fees by conducting transactions informally. Jewels worth thousands of dollars are lent for examination overnight without any papers signed. By social capital, Coleman meant in this instance, 'trust' as a resource of individuals and their relations within a given social network. Subsequently, social capital became identified as the property (or not) of groups, such as immigrant and ethnic minority groups, communities, nations and even political ideologies (Fukayama, 1995; Putnam, 1993). The World Bank sees the promotion of social capital as critical for the development of 'civil society' in the Third World, and has funded many projects frequently involving collaboration with non-governmental organisations (NGOs), which emphasise the promotion of group savings and credit schemes and small enterprises, targeted at the urban poor, youth and women and which have community 'empowerment' and 'participation', as stated objectives (Fine, 1999; Panayiotopoulos, 1997). One optimistic expectation is that the social capital of the poor will make up for their deficiency in human capital. The World Bank and others see 'social capital as the ability to create and sustain voluntary associations, or the idea that a healthy community is essential to prosperity' (Portes and Landolt, 1996:1).

The ethnic enclave

The ethnic enclave thesis raises important questions for conventional sociology in the US and its key assumption that separation is not to the interest of most members of the excluded group. Portes and Sensenbrenner (1993:1340) note 'constraints that community norms put on individual action and receptivity to outside culture'. One pessimistic view of immigrant enterprise is that it simply allows a small minority inside various communities to exchange the role of marginal worker for that of marginal proprietor. As such, this view would suggest that immigrant enterprises represent, at best, a truce with inequality rather than any substantial victory over it. Light and Rosenstein, in noting the scale of human need in urban America, conclude that whilst poverty and disadvantage may create a powerful motive for entrepreneurship, 'markets will not make entrepreneurs out of disadvantaged Americans who lack resources entrepreneurship requires' (1995:203).

Kwong (1997) also argues that ethnicity can act as an agency for the reproduction of compliance inside immigrant and enclave communities, which serves the economic interests of the dominant ethnic elites. In a study of New York's Chinatown, he argues that immigrants often depend on ethnic mutual assistance to make a start, but, that the concept of ethnic solidarity can also be manipulated by employers to gain better control over their co-ethnic employees. Chinese employers often invoke ethnic and cultural symbols, to project an image that only co-ethnics can be trusted, thus blocking the new immigrants' attempts to seek better opportunities outside of their ethnic environment. Kwong questions the validity of the ethnic enclave thesis as an agency of social mobility for all members of an ethnic group. Similarly, Model (1992) found no significant variation in returns to labour in the ethnic enclave economy when compared to the general labour market.

Whilst ethnicity is a useful term in explaining processes of intermediation between immigrant capital and labour it is, at the same time, a highly problematic concept. One problem, as Rath (2002b:9) notes, is the *'apriori* categorisation of immigrants as ethnic groups' and the implication that immigrants arrive with fully-fledged ethnic identities in place, ready to do battle with others, when much of the evidence suggests that ethnicity is something learned in the process of immigration, the formation of support systems and communities. Another problem is how to understand expansive labour market formation. Light *et al.* (1994) use the term 'immigrant economy' (as distinct to the ethnic enclave) in order to explain labour markets characterised by high labour force interspersion, in which, unlike the ethnic enclave where co-ethnics hire co-ethnics, immigrants hire non-co-ethnic immigrants. One example is the relationship between Asian employers and Latina workers, which structures labour market relations in the Los Angeles garment industry (see Chapter 5).

Social and economic differentiation

Residual theories point to cultural endowment and the collective institutions of immigrants, such as their social capital, as causal explanation for the emergence of immigrant enterprise. These theories appear at their weakest in trying to explain processes of social and economic differentiation inside immigrant communities. 'Marginalisation' may be an accurate description of the precarious condition of many, possibly most, immigrant entrepreneurs on the fringes of European and American urban economies. At the same time, we know that there is considerable variation inside immigrant communities and between enterprises. Social differentiation points to the reproduction of social classes and social categories inside immigrant communities, such as in the emergence of entrepreneurs from the ranks of wage workers. Stratification also points to the role of ascriptive disadvantage in the construction of particular social categories such as, class, gender, race, age and religious affiliation, and intersections between them.

Economic differentiation refers to diversity in immigrant enterprises in terms of size and labour input. Some are small firms in the 'niche' sectors which depend on family labour (newsagents, Chinese takeaways), whilst others, as in the garment industry, are large employers and recruit labour from the range of ethnic groups available in local labour markets. Some operate as micro-multinational companies and engage in international outward processing (Panayiotopoulos, 2000b). At the other end of the enterprise spectrum, the precarious status of entrepreneur is itself frequently an emergent and submergent phenomenon characterised by high levels of entry and exit. The above points to significant variation within immigrant enterprise and suggests that it would be unwise to make generalisations about an 'essential' ethnic enterprise (typically in the form of the 'family firm').

Conclusions

The literature provides contradictory evidence on the meaning and substance of globalisation from below. One concluding and general observation is that an investigation on the relation between structure and agency in immigration, the formation of transnational communities and the emergence of immigrant enterprise, will not take us very far without an appreciation of the role of the state and the wider forces which shape the political-institutional environment. Nigel Harris (1995b) points to immigration controls as one contradiction within the neo-liberal model of globalisation, whether from 'above' or 'below'. The effects, he argues, partly explain persistent global income inequalities. The neo-liberal model assumes free trade as a prerequisite to rising incomes. This has seen very high levels of mobility by capital as exemplified by the role of foreign direct investment and the activities of multinational corporations. At the same time, there are expansive and increasing immigration controls. These restrictions on the free movement of labour, undermine the basic premise of free trade neo-liberal assumptions made by the World Bank and the Stolper-Samuelson theorum i.e. the belief that free trade will result in factor price equalisation, including the cost of labour, reflected in greater rewards to exporters in the form of rising incomes (Samuelson, 1948; World Bank, 1995). More significantly, Harris argues that the primary functions of immigration controls are not economic, and are least of all born from concern about what happens to workers, but rather serve to underpin the exercise of selection and regimentation in the construct of nation state and national identity. The current climate of xenophobia and moral panic in Europe over asylum seekers and in the US over aliens has reinforced selectivity in immigration. This is frequently ignored in the transnational thesis and the conventional literature on immigrant enterprise.

Immigration controls point to contradictions and selectivity within the current terms of globalisation, which challenge some of the assumptions about self-generating migration and transnational communities. Harris (2002:6) suggests that global networks are tending to supersede the old order of separate national economies and that workers too are becoming increasingly mobile but, at the same time, immigration controls 'severely limit this movement for the masses and results in a kind of global *apartheid*, with the majority of people legally disempowered from moving about the world'. The reality is much more complex and is influenced by many variables, least of all in the supply and demand for workers of requisite skills and the fact that most people would not put their hands up for living under apartheid. Working-class immigrants in coping, learn to negotiate new spaces and places. In doing so, many form durable and contradictory communities which make a significant contribution to the transformation of industries and cities in Europe and the United States. The relationship between globalisation from below (agency) and above (structure) needs to be more clearly understood and located in particular historical circumstances faced by different immigrant groups and social strata of immigrants.

The literature indicates contradictory evidence on the meaning and substance of social capital, ethnicity and embeddedness. A considerable body of evidence points to initial privileges enjoyed by ethnic entrepreneurs in the internalised mobilisation of co-ethnic resources. These privileges have been conceptualised as substantially deriving from their greater social integration into the ethnic economy. Advantages have been identified in the mobilisation of capital. The emergence of immigrant enterprise in the garment industry has been frequently linked to monopoly access to co-ethnic female labour (see, Phizacklea, 1988; Green, 2002; Anthias, 1992). Much of the literature on labour suggests that for the ethnic employer to benefit from access to co-ethnic labour, he/she actually had to be involved and exercise considerable control over the extra-productive activity of that labour. Typically this appears through the power entrepreneurs have inside community associations and in their frequent role as the public face of the community in discussions with local government and policy makers. As such, they provide a significant interface between the community and the world and some of them are significant political brokers (Panayiotopoulos, 1992; Rex and Josephides, 1987).

Theories grounded in ethnic solidarity have been less satisfactory at explaining expansive immigrant labour markets and processes of social and economic differentiation inside immigrant communities. One key thesis underlining this book is that processes of social and economic differentiation within and between immigrant communities and enterprises, have important implications for who benefits from immigrant or ethnic economies and in shaping institutional behaviour. The concept of mixed embeddedness has been applied to analyse the extent of integration by entrepreneurs in the ethnic economy and their qualitative relationships with the market and the institutional framework. It is here that the impact of economic differentiation is at its most significant. Emergent immigrant enterprises which have 'broken out' of the ranks of the many ethnic contractors and subcontractors, relate to the market at different levels of the production cycle, are subject to different outcomes and adopt different strategies to cope with market fluctuation, and in their relationships with the banking sector, branches of the state and in particular with local government (see Panayiotopoulos and Dreef, 2002; also Chapter 7).

The beneficiaries of institutional support are more likely to be entrepreneurs who are the most embedded in communities but also the most economically powerful and who are also the most politically embedded in host society. In reverse, the small contractors and subcontractors are the least likely to receive institutional support and the most likely to feel the wrath of the state, typically for not conforming to relevant legislation on taxation and labour standards. The above suggests that culturally derived organisational theory may not sufficiently take into account processes of competition, accumulation and differentiation between immigrant enterprises. Neither can they explain variation in the role of the institutional framework in the shaping of selectivity in immigration and enterprise.

As we shall see in the following chapters, the institutional and market framework facing immigrant entrepreneurs in Europe and the United States is subject to variation, and this has important implication for the development of differentiation itself. Variation in part derives from the nature of local markets and the extent to which an agglomeration of small enterprises exists in which immigrants can enter, both as workers and as entrepreneurs. In equal measure, variation derives from the nature of the institutional framework, the legal status of immigrants themselves and in policy towards immigration. One tentative conclusion is that European and United States cities characterised by vibrant local economies and protracted presence by immigrant groups who have civil rights somewhere nearer the average, are more likely to see the development of sustainable immigrant-owned enterprises. It is under these circumstances that enterprises begin not only to emerge but also, in cases, to differentiate themselves from the ranks of the many self-employed, small contractors and subcontractors.

Two poles of interpretation can be presented in the current climate. One represents the return of Wirthian pessimism about the future trajectory of immigrants in the urban centres of the high-income economies. *Anomie* was a concept used by Wirth (1938) to describe a prevalent process of social decomposition faced by immigrants in urban America, characterised by the erosion and non-replacement of ascriptive solidarities, isolation and uncertainty about values. The literature surveyed, and much of the case study material which follows, by pointing to the collective institutions of immigrant and ethnic groups in urban America and Europe, challenges such pessimism (see, Transnational Communities Programme, Light, Bonacich, Portes, passim). At the same time, one discontent with these analyses which are critical of conventional, assimilationist models of immigrant incorporation, appears in an uncertain, perverse adaptation of *anomie*. Thus for practical purposes *anomie* signifies the absence of durable networks of embeddedness and reciprocity based in shared cultural norms, 'social capital', and so on. Indeed, 'success' or 'failure' by immigrant enterprises is sometimes perceived as conditioned far more by the presence or absence of the above social institutions, than variables to do with the wider political economy or the opportunity structure itself. Waldinger (1995:566, 573) offers residual explanations for black under-representation in New York City's enterprise spectrum and points to deficiency in 'social capital' and limited ethnic resources available to black entrepreneurs as causal explanation (see also, Flap *et al.*, 2000). In a similar manner, Samuel Smiles pointed in his Victorian classic *Self Help,* to 'energetic' self-help as a prominent feature of English national character.

In conclusion, Portes and Landolt in criticising David Putnam's analysis of a benign (and normative) relationship between social capital and civil society (in the Third Italy), caution against sermons and the identification of particular communities, 'a posteriori with the presence or absence of social trust or capital', as explanation for 'failure' or 'success'. They further add that

> the call for higher social capital as a solution to the problems of the inner city misdiagnoses the problem and can lead to both a waste of resources and new frustrations. It is not the lack of social capital, but the lack of objective economic resources – beginning with descent jobs – that underlies the plight of impoverished urban groups.
>
> (Portes and Landolt 1996:4–5)

The above, perhaps, helps to place in context some of the more optimistic assertions made (frequently by the same authors) about the capacities of markets and immigrant enterprise to address the scale of need which exists amongst immigrant communities in the gateway cities of Europe and the United States.

2 Rise of ethnicity
Crisis of modernisation

Introduction

Modernisation theory and its application to analyses of immigration and ethnic relations in the form of assimilation theory faced a severe political and intellectual crisis in the United States during the 1960s. The emergence of ethnicity as both a cultural and political basis of mobilisation challenged 'melting-pot' theories, dominant at the time in US sociology. An associated crisis was experienced by European anthropology and its dominant discourse – structural functionalism – under the impact of the rising independence movements in the colonies and the migration, initially, of expatriates. The crisis of melting-pot theories was most strongly felt in the US given its own historical development as a country of diverse immigrants transformed into 'modern' Americans. This chapter offers explanation for the rise of ethnicity and the crisis of modernisation theory and points to the role of communal affiliation, self-help institutions and solidarity in the development of immigrant community, diaspora and enterprise. The chapter cautions against seeing ethnicity as the natural property of immigrants and argues that immigrants do not arrive with fully-fledged ethnic identities but on the contrary, learn how to be 'ethnic' and are racialised in and by the host society, frequently in response and as by-product to hostility and discrimination. This was a strong feature of the crisis of assimilation theory in Europe, which became more apparent under the impact of mass labour migration during the 1950s and 1960s and amongst second-generation immigrant youth faced with more hostile labour markets during the 1970s. Ethnicity under these circumstances became a defensive social posture adopted by immigrants and their children. One consequence was that many immigrants began to look to the ethnic or immigrant economy, self-employment and small enterprises, as alternatives to unemployment or low-pay employment.

Crisis of modernisation in the United States

A key influence on analyses of immigration, ethnicity and enterprise, was the impact and consequences of the black uprisings which took place in urban America during the 1960s. The end of the post-war boom and rising unemployment, the failure of programmes to end urban poverty in part due to the mounting costs of the Vietnam War, oppressive policing of black neighbourhoods and the persistence of racial exclusion in American society typified by the ghetto, were features of urban life for most black Americans, despite the achievements of the Civil Rights Movement in the southern states. One illustration is that the first inter-racial kiss broadcast on US television took place in 1964, when Uhura kissed Captain Kirk in one of the early *Star Trek* episodes. The failure of the 'American Dream' i.e. generation-on-generation material improvement, in the face of economic slowdown, underpinned the uprisings which initially broke out in Watts, Los Angeles during 1965, and subsequently spread across most American northern cities, reaching a peak with the assassination of Martin Luther King in April 1968. These mobilisations, riots and uprisings, became an important expression of self-definition, least of all, in terms of participation and in what people call themselves.

The Kerner Commission's Report established to investigate the 'disorders', revealed that in Watts, 15 per cent of the black population (22,000 people) described themselves as 'actively involved' in the riot and another 35–40 per cent (approximately 51,000) as 'active spectators'. In the 1967 Detroit riot, 11 per cent of the black population described themselves as 'active participants' and in Newark during the same year, 45 per cent of black men between the ages of 15 and 35, described themselves as 'rioters' (Kerner Commission, 1968). Douglas Glasgow in describing the impact of the uprising on a group of young people, observed,

> I sensed a new tone amongst the street youth of Watts. They had lost some of the quiet sullenness so typical of their Parking Lot attitudes and became vocal, animated, excited, involved. Like some strange alchemy, they adopted seemingly overnight something called *Blackness*. They disclaimed what had been fought for by the older generation; they were no longer to be *Negroes*, they were now *Black*.
>
> (Glasgow, 1980:2, italics in original)

The above, although less graphically put, was an experience felt by many American Indians, Mexican Americans and the multitude of immigrant groups which make up the US population. For many, counter-migration back to their countries of origin, or perceived origin, became a new phenomenon as Jews, Germans, Czechs, Poles, Italians emphasised their ethnic origins in a growing transnational relationship. This contrasted sharply with the prolonged period from the early years of the recession until the early 1960s, when as Glazer (1983:18) noted 'ethnicity withdrew as a theme in American life'. The rise of ethnicity was expressed in the mushrooming of organisations lobbying the political establishment with demands ranging from mother tongue language use in the education system, to the redress of historic injustices. These mobilisations and the wider construction of racial and ethnic identities, presented major analytical problems for the Parsonian ideas of modernity and assimilation which dominated the discourse on race, immigration and ethnic relations in the United States during the 1960s. The assumptions guiding conventional sociological thought both in the developed and developing countries, that we were involved in a trajectory, gradual or violent, which would see the subsumption of 'traditional' societies based on particular identities – such as kinship, religion, caste, race, ethnicity – into 'modern' societies in which rational individuals, sharing a universalist outlook, would interact (and transact) freely, liberated from the dark, irrational prejudices and loyalties of the past (Parsons, 1952; Parsons and Smelser, 1957). The mobilisations during the 1960s suggested that race and ethnicity as particularist identities, far from retreating, were on the ascendancy. The black American urban ghetto appeared as the most concentrated expression of the contradiction between modernisation theory (assimilation) and practice (segregation).

The (re)construction of cultural differences and boundaries between groups in ways which symbolised and actualised separate and possibly conflicting interests on the basis of a solidarity which did not conform with modernisation theory, created a major problem for conventional sociological thinking. This as Glazer and Moynihan (1970, 1975) and Glazer (1997) suggested, was most deeply felt in the US given its particular historical development and the role of immigration and 'melting pot' ideas in nation building. King (2000) refers to the 'New Ethnic Politics', to describe the emergence of ethnicity in the United States and demands for a fuller political role, and Rhea (1997) to a 'Race Pride Movement', manifested amongst Asian Americans, Indian Americans and African Americans, which fuelled multiculturalism and demands for 'equal respect for all cultural and ethnic identities in a political system' (King, 2000:266). The abandonment of the National Origins Act in 1965, which operated since the 1920s as a racially selective mechanism in structuring immigration policy, and the enactment of the Civil Rights Act in 1964 and of the Voting Rights Act of 1965, provided significant contextual explanation. To social conservatives, American Nativists and, paradoxically, modernisation advocates of mainline assimilation, the re-emergence of ethnicity, challenged basic premises. For example, it challenged widely-held views that 'a third-generation return to ethnicity is incompatible with the progressive decline across the generations in the salience of ethnic identities' (Alba, 1999:306). Schlesinger (1992:43) predictably, perhaps, wrote of the effects of ethnicity as a threat 'against the original theory of America as "one people," a common culture, a single nation'. Nathan Glazer (1997) pointed to multiculturalism as a fundamental rejection of the melting-pot ethos.

With considerable justification, Glazer argued that the rise of ethnicity, multiculturalism and, in cases, the growth of separatism, was above all a manifestation of the United State's failure towards its African American population. Above all, in the slow pace of 'integration' in the south and the meaninglessness of this Civil Rights agenda for black Americans living in the ostensibly Jim Crow-free and 'liberal' north and western American cities. It was this experience in the northern urban ghettos, more than any other, which laid the basis for the politics of Malcom X, Black Power and black separation, as the polar opposite to the integrationist politics of Martin Luther King in the rural south. Glazer (1997:95) identifies the rejection of assimilation as based 'in black experience in America, and the fundamental refusal of other Americans to accept blacks, despite their eagerness, as suitable candidates for assimilation'.

Ethnic identity politics (as one of the legacies of the ethnic mobilisations in the US during the 1960s) represent the retreat of conventional assimilation thinking on integration. Stratification, however, poses problems for racially and culturally driven analyses and claims to common identity. Huey P. Newton of the Black Panther Party for example, spoke dismissively of ethno-cultural nationalism as 'pork-chop' nationalism (see, Allen, 1969:167). Manning Marable wrote of an 'upwardly mobile black petty bourgeoisie', who found in 'vulgar Afrocentrism' a useful theory in their social advancement' (see also, Callinicos, 1993; Smith, 1994),

> vulgar Afrocentrists deliberately ignored or obscured the historical reality of social stratification inside the African diaspora. They essentially argued that the interests of all black people, from Joint Chiefs of Staff Chairman General Colin Powell to conservative Supreme Court Justice Clarence Thomas [or Gondoleeza Rice], to the unemployed, homeless and hungry of America's decaying urban ghettoes – were philosophically, culturally, and racially the same.
>
> (Marable, 1993:121)

The emergence of ethnicity was also felt in the epistemology of the social sciences i.e. how knowledge itself is produced. One illustration is in how academic writings of the time were unsure about whether to use the word 'negro' or 'black'. Nathan Glazer (1983:20) for example, inserts a footnote for 'negro' and writes, 'I retain the usage of the time, and thus it is "Negro" in the essays of the middle 1960s, "black" in later essays'.

Crisis of modernisation in Europe

The impact of ethnic mobilisations in the United States forced the social sciences to adopt new terminology e.g. as in whether 'negro' or 'black' was the appropriate unit of reference, and what constitutes an 'ethnic minority'. Whilst in the United States this was particularly felt in racial terms, ethnicity as a social phenomenon reframed the epistemology of ethnic relations in Europe and in its relations with the wider world in more complex ways. The crisis originated, not in issues to do with assimilation, but the 'colonial encounter' and how to understand the emergent independence movements in the colonies, and in the impact of decolonisation on the metropolitan areas. Changing perceptions and acceptance or rejection of immigrants and ethnic minorities in Europe was originally framed by the post-colonial experience, which itself was subject to considerable national variation (see Chapter 6).

The crisis of modernisation sociology in the US was paralleled in Europe with a crisis faced by anthropology and its dominant paradigm, structural functionalism i.e. the view that all parts of a given social structure have the necessary function of maintaining the integrity of the system as a whole. The crisis of anthropology was most deeply felt in the UK and France, given their extensive legacies as colonial powers. In the UK, the Chair in Applied Anthropology at the LSE (occupied by Lucy Mair, 1963–1968) was referred to as the 'Chair in Colonial Administration'. Radcliffe Brown had instituted a training scheme in Sydney for the expressed purpose of providing colonial administrative 'cadets'. In more general terms anthropologists tried to sell themselves to European colonial administration as a discipline which might be of some use in the management of increasingly diverse societies, over which knowledge was woefully inadequate (Asad, 1973; Kuper, 1973; Panayiotopoulos, 2002).

The loss of colonial confidence is illustrated by Sandra Wallman, in one of the small number of studies carried out on Europeans in Africa. As Wallman (1974) argued, the white 'experts' and 'technicians' appear to engage in an ambiguous relationship with Africans. On the one hand Africans appear to want and need European technology but, on the other, despise it and do not want European control. In the context of emergent independence movements, low trust and mistrust extended to hostility. As one European settler explained,

> In the old days the Basuto were polite and friendly. They greeted you first. They called you 'friend' and 'father' and your judgment was law. Now there are accusations of malice and exploitation, demands for independence and houses next door. Sometimes small boys throw stones at your car and shout *white man go home!!*
>
> (Wallman 1974:240)

Levi-Strauss (1967) articulated a European perspective in attempts to reposition the social sciences in the de- and post-colonial environment. He argued,

> Our science arrived at maturity the day that Western Man began to see that he [sic] would never understand himself as long as there was a single race or people on the surface of the earth that he treated as an object. Only then could anthropology declare itself in its true colours:

as an enterprise reviewing and atoning for the Renaissance, in order
to spread humanism to all humanity.

(Levi-Strauss, 1967:52)

The above view pointed towards a greater theoretical willingness to
accept diversity. One practical dimension born from de-colonisation, was,
in many cases, the hurried settlement of white expatriates from the erstwhile colonies. This was the first time that the issue of 'assimilation' and
integration surfaced in post-war Europe. An estimated five to seven
million people repatriated to Europe following de-colonisation: of these
3.3 million were 'Europeans' and another 4.0 million 'non-Europeans'
(Smith, 2003:32). The Netherlands is a case in point: of the estimated
300,000 exiles who arrived from the Dutch East Indies (Indonesia) in 1949,
virtually all were classified as 'Europeans'.

The Netherlands illustrates European attempts to negotiate issues to do
with race and ethnicity. The example is used because, surprisingly perhaps,
for a deeply religious and conservative society, Holland is seen (with Amsterdam in mind) as particularly 'liberal' and 'tolerant' towards different
cultures and lifestyles. Whilst many immigrants may well disagree with this
view, it is the case that, from the original expatriate immigrant wave in the
1940s to labour migration in the 1950s and 1960s, and subsequent entry
into the small enterprise sector by immigrant and second generation
groups in the 1970s and 1980s, Holland points to a diverse and institutionally complex composition in immigrant and ethnic minority groups
(Willems, 2003; Penninx *et al.*, 1993).

Yet, in the Netherlands, it was only during the 1980s that settlement
was seen as permanent and that immigrants 'should have the right to
develop their own cultural identity' accepted by policy makers (Penninx *et
al.*, 1993:102). Rights to family reunions and permanent residence permits
became more available after one year's settlement, as well as a significant
increase in naturalisation. One (necessary) definition of 'minority group'
in the Netherlands became that of a group whose 'social position is homo-
geneously low' (Penninx *et al.*, 1993:195). This followed from a widespread
view that low socio-economic status and the negative feedback effects of,
for example, discrimination, acted as the basis for defining ethnicity and
minority status itself (Portes, 1984:383–412). At the same time, however,
the view that 'immigrants' – and in particular illegal immigrants – were
taking Dutch jobs, or living off the Dutch social security system 'has
shown the ambivalence of Dutch society about the economic impact of
immigration' (Penninx *et al.*, 1993:209). In the current wave of xenophobia
in the Netherlands, this is an understatement (see Chapter 8).

The positioning of the Chinese community brought attention, in a practical manner, to many of the issues raised above. In 1949, when the Dutch
East Indies became independent many persons of Chinese origin were
amongst the 'non-Europeans' repatriated to Holland. Many more came to

join them following anti-Chinese pogroms in Indonesia between 1959 and in particular during 1964, when the Chinese community took the brunt of the massacre of an estimated one million members and supporters of the Indonesian Communist Party (largest in Asia after China) during the CIA-sponsored military coup led by Suharto. His fall in 1997 saw an engineered mini-pogrom by the regime, which proved ineffective in diverting the pro-democracy movement. Many of these displaced persons were profession-als. Another Chinese community emerged during the 1970s and 1980s consisting mainly of non-Dutch speaking immigrants from mainland China and Hong Kong. Many of them were part of trade and labour diaspora. By 1990 they made up 64 per cent of the Chinese community in Holland (Pieke, 1999:324). This increase reflected on the emergence of the Chinese–Indonesian restaurant trade as an early significant concentration of immigrant enterprise and labour demand in post-war Europe.

During the 1980s the Chinese community in Holland were subjected to the equivalent of an ecclesiastical court, the purpose of which was not to balance angels on the head of a needle, but rather to adjudicate on the question of whether the Chinese community was an ethnic minority or not. As we noted, the mid-1980s saw a (momentary) reappraisal by the Dutch government of its ethnic minority policies. The question was asked as to whether any additional ethnic groups should be officially recognised as minorities under government minority policies.

> The question of whether or not the Chinese community were a minor-ity like any other had never been posed before because the image of the Chinese community held by Dutch people and the Chinese them-selves. Chinese seemed to be well off; they rarely made any claim on the authorities.
>
> (Pieke, 1999:326)

The above anecdotal view reinforced the image of a community which was 'self-sufficient'. At the same time, it does show a community which was routinely, socially excluded from taking part in the wider society and in making use of its services. Leaders of Chinese community organisations pointed to the needs of the diverse Chinese immigrant and second-generation community, in terms of indicators of disadvantage such as unemployment, language difficulties and 'lack of integration'. These indic-ators would qualify the Chinese as an 'ethnic minority'. However, for this to apply, the government of the Netherlands had to accept 'special responsibility' for the many non-Dutch speaking Chinese immigrants. This it was not politically willing to do and appointed a commission to help it find a way out of this quandary. Partly as the result of the research report written by Frank Pieke (see Pieke, 1999; Pieke and Benton, 1998), the government declined to grant minority status to the Chinese community in the Netherlands. The report gave its reasons, that, the Chinese were not sufficiently underprivileged in terms of income, employment, education and housing ... [and] that minority status may have the unintended affect of stigmatizing an ethnic group, whose enjoyment of minority benefits could all too easily be seen as freeloading by the majority population.

(Pieke 1999:327)

The implications from the above are quite revealing: that a community whose cultural diversity is noted, whose economic arrangements are barely understood, whose invisibility and exclusion from society is seen as a positive asset, are 'not a minority' the moment they raise demands on a state to whose treasury they are significant contributors. Clearly, the image of the successful restaurateur allowed anecdotal evidence to obscure the social and economic differentiation of the Chinese community in terms of gender, class, immigration status, language proficiency and other intra-indicators of diverse needs and aspirations. For operational purposes, the many migrants from mainland China who provide the labour for Amsterdam's restaurants, are assumed to have the same needs and socio-economic positioning as the owners of the restaurants. The debate in Holland, perhaps, raised more questions than answers. One conclusion drawn by many in the Chinese community was, that to 'be visible' opens you up to attention, scrutiny and makes you a potential target in a perverse game of musical chairs. Pieke (1999:327) observes that, the 'discussions left permanent scars on the Chinese community'.

The economics of ethnicity

The ethnic mobilisations in the United States during the 1960s, also heralded a growing interest in the economic activities of ethnic minorities. The critique of conventional modernisation theory argued that assimilation theories were ill-equipped to understand the role of 'self-help institutions', 'communal affiliations' and collective rather than individual organisational forms of economic development amongst ethnic minorities. Cummings (1980:5–6) argued that the failure of the social sciences to recognise 'collectivism' was in part the legacy of Weberian sociology and its construction of the profit maximising, freely acting and transacting individual, as the pivotal agent in economic growth. Whether this is an accurate description of Weber is debatable. His work did point to the solidarity networks amongst Calvinist sects as providing the framework and precondition for individual enterprise (Weber, 1968:302–322).

A number of initial inter-exchangeable analyses and conceptual frameworks were applied to explain the development of immigrant and ethnic minority enterprise in the United States and subsequently Europe. In Europe the impact of mass unemployment from the 1970s onwards on 'second' and 'third' generation members of immigrant and minority groups, became an important push factor towards self-employment and small enterprise formation. One significant labour market trend during the 1970s and 1980s in Europe and North America, was the halting of a long period of historical decline in the contribution of self-employment (Boise-vain, 1981, 1984). Minority-owned enterprises acquired a new significance in the context of declining open labour market opportunities and a growing policy focus on small-scale enterprise promotion. The promotion of the 'enterprise culture' as a solution for inner-city poverty and regener-ation, remains an important continuity in diverse local economic and urban development policy (Panayiotopoulos, 1992).

Early explanations for immigrant enterprise formation

1   One early body of theory pointed towards *cultural endowment*, i.e. variables specific to the ethnic group itself, as causal explanation for a cultural disposition towards enterprise. Middleman Minorities and trade diasporas were frequently analysed as such (Fallers, 1967; Jiang, 1968; Hamilton, 1978).
2   A second body of thought pointed to minority enterprise as a *response to discrimination* in the (segmented) labour market and as a collective survival mechanism in the face of ethnic disadvantage and lack of opportunity (Bonacich, 1972, 1993b; Ladbury, 1984; Anthias, 1992). This (pessimistic) view of minority enterprise is summed-up as one which 'simply allows a small minority to exchange the role of marginal worker for that of marginal proprietor' and, as such, (they conclude) 'represents a truce with racial inequality rather than a victory over it' (Aldrich *et al.*, 1984:209). Mitter refers to a 'sideways shift from lumpen proletariat to lumpen bourgeoisie' (1986:59).
3   A third collection of theories with a basis in neo-liberal economics (i.e. analyses which look to markets for solutions to the problems facing immigrants, such as over employment and housing), pointed to the *ethnic niche* as the typical and rational response by minority entre-preneurs to (limited) market opportunity (Jenkins, 1984:231–232; Boissevain *et al.*, 1990:131–156; Waldinger, 1984; Waldinger *et al.*, 1990). One early attempt to explain the relationship between ethnicity and enterprise consisted of the optimising longitudinal theory of *ecological succession* (Aldrich and Reiss, 1981:846–866). This view suggested a gradual progression by an immigrant group into the lower rungs of enterprise from which they were displaced in an upward direction by the next immigrant group.

Middleman Minorities

One of the earliest and most widely used ethno-cultural explanation for the phenomenon of immigrant enterprise, pointed towards so-called

Middleman Minorities (MMs) in both the economies of the developed and developing countries (Bonacich, 1973; Bonacich and Modell, 1980; Cummings, 1980). MMs appear as a concentrated example of a 'trade diaspora'. They are presented as exceptions to most ethnic groups, in so far as most minorities are seen as peculiarly disadvantaged, 'within, or even beneath, the working class' (Bonacich, 1973:585). In MMs we find a group which is identified as wealthy. At the same time, the analyses proposed that,

> Despite the fact that they are found in capitalist societies, middle-men minorities are not themselves modern capitalists in orientation. Rather they are essentially petit bourgeois, failing to engage in the kind of activity that epitomises modern capitalism, namely the hiring of contracted wage labour from which profits are extracted. Instead they work as single units, in which the distinction between owner and employee is blurred. Their shops depend on the use of the ethnic and familiar ties, not on personal contacts.
>
> (Bonacich and Modell, 1980:31–32)

What equally distinguishes MMs, becomes their particular location in the stratification system and the occupational structure. As Edna Bonacich (1972:34–51) noted, they are likely to occupy middle rank positions and to act as economic middlemen, i.e. as brokers in the movement of goods and services. Their economic role is thus presented as a function of intermediation (i.e. traders or agents, labour contractors, money lenders and brokers) in relation to spaces between production and consumption, employer and employee, owner and rentier and ultimately act as a link between the 'elite' and the 'masses'. Other categorisations of this intermediary role have been 'middleman trading peoples' (Becker, 1956:225–237), 'marginal trading peoples' (Schermenhorn, 1970:74–76) and 'permanent minorities' (Stryker, 1959). One also notes the genesis of the term (perhaps) in 'pariah people', or 'pariah capitalism' as a term to describe the economics of the Jewish diaspora (Weber, 1958). Frequently, vulgar cultural theorists provide explanations for the activities of these peoples, in terms of particular cultural endowments, values and heritages – which paradoxically remain unmodified, despite (in cases) new found niches and diversification.

The location of MMs was presented by Edna Bonacich as the result of a combination of factors (see below), some alluding to cultural endowment and others to factors operating independently of this, such as the structure of host society labour markets, reaction to hostility or perceived hostility, and processes of marginalisation.

Factors facilitating Middleman Minority role

1 Distinctive cultural and social characteristics of a particular migrant group that might facilitate MM role;

2   the structure and nature of a host system which migrants find themselves in and which might facilitate the same role; and,
3   the position of some migrant groups as permanent strangers or *sojourners* with the desire for a portable or easily liquidated livelihood due to perceived transiency.

(Bonacich, 1973)

Thus, the argument runs, some immigrant groups, pushed out of desirable positions in labour markets, manage to escape the 'lower rungs' (assuming that they all begin in the lower rungs) and acquire considerable 'wealth'. Ethnicity, or the formation of solidary communities thus becomes partly a collective response to processes of hostility and marginalisation in the host society and exists independently of the origins and cultural propensities of any ethnic group. This is reinforced under conditions where host societies are characterised by what Rinder (1959:340–354) called a 'status gap', i.e. societies in which the middle class is numerically weak and which exhibit a marked division between elites and masses. Feudal society, colonial, post-colonial or modern industrial society can be characterised in the above (see, Bonacich, 1973:583). Under these circumstances, immigrants free of status preoccupations can transact and trade with anyone. Sometimes restrictions are placed on the kind of activities they can engage in. Asian immigrant labourers who built the railroads and settled in East Africa were prohibited from the ownership of land and hence agricultural employment by the colonial authorities. Many were pushed into employment as traders in the Native Reserves and acted as an extension of colonial administration, such as in the collection of sales taxes. In sharply polarised 'status gap' societies with little social mobility (as was the case with colonial regimes), MMs acted as a buffer for 'elites' and frequently bear the brunt of mass hostility which, thereby, as the argument runs, further reinforces MM group solidarity and sojourning orientation. Whilst Bonacich (1973:585) argues that sojourning is not a sufficient condition for MM status, it is nevertheless a necessary one for the development of MM roles.

Ethnicity and class

The reactive, collective institutions, associations and networks of immigrants and ethnic minorities, which critics argued were misunderstood or ignored by modernisation theory, were presented as key in offering explanations for how minorities participate in labour markets and in how they relate to wider processes. Cummings, Light, Bonacich and others, pointed to factors other than cultural endowment to explain the formation of solidarity networks applied to economic action. For example, they pointed to the relationship between ethnicity and class. One key argument was summed up by Bonacich and Modell, in this way,

It is our contention to show that economic factors play an important role in the retention or dissolution of ethnic ties [...] Our central thesis is that ethnic groups often act as economic-interest groups and when they cease to do so, they then tend to dissolve. Whatever else it may be, the primordial tie of ethnicity is a tool that can be used to invoke class actions.

(1980:3)

The analyses by Bonacich borrowed from the work of Abram Leon (1946:79–80) who pointed to the increased persecution of Jews from the twelfth century onwards, as a parallel with the economic development of cities and industries in Western Europe and argued that, '*Above all* [...] *Jews constitute historically a social group with a specific economic function. They are a class, or more precisely, a people-class*' (italics in original). Leon pointed to the identification of a class with people (or race) as not exceptional in pre-capitalist societies and went on to argue that the enforced economic role of European Jews as a 'people-class', driven by, in cases, legal bans and social prohibitions to entering many occupations, was such an example. In this we note analogies, and perhaps the origins of Middleman Minority notions. At the same time, however, Abram argued that the 'first' great wave of Jewish migration, not to the US, but the interior of Russia and Germany during the beginning of the nineteenth century, saw Jews, for the first time, penetrating the industrial and commercial centres and playing important roles as merchants and industrialists. This new and important development meant that 'a Jewish proletariat was born', and that for the first time, 'the people-class began to differentiate socially' (Leon, 1946:90–91).

Ivan Light introduced a historical perspective in pioneering analyses of ethnicity and second-generation immigrant enterprise, which made no necessary assumptions towards a fixed cultural disposition. In criticising attempts by culture theorists to explain over-representation in the small enterprise sector, Light pointed to a number of factors in entrepreneurial organisation which acted independently of cultural endowments but which relate to the 'alien status' of migrant groups. Light (1982:5–7) identified three important areas:

1 Relative satisfaction derived from the process of migration from low-wage countries.
2 Reactive solidarities which consist of extraordinarily well developed social networks, often formed in the experience of chain or forced migration which did not exist as such in their country of origin (see also, Wilson and Portes, 1980:295–319; Portes, 1984:383–412).
3 Sojourning and its implication for entrepreneurial motivation which gives MM groups a competitive advantage over non-sojourners.

Light, in a number of early studies (Light 1972, 1982; Light and Bhachu, 1993), pointed towards a tentative longitudinal transition in immigrant and minority enterprise in the US, from an initiation based on immigrant solidarity and the use of 'collective' ethnic resources, to one amongst the native-born generation showing a dependency on 'individual' class resources, the use of the commercial banking sector, and constraints associated with small enterprises in general. Light (1982:16) argued that in the US during the course of the 'last half century', a whole range of ethnic entrepreneurs (Chinese, Japanese, Polish, Finnish, Irish, Mormon, Jewish), 'appear to have undergone a shift in this historical period away from an immigrant generation dependence upon collective resources towards a native generation, dependent upon individual resources' (Light, 1982:16).

The above shift was presented in part as a 'response' to the higher price of admission due to the historical decrease in the size of the (small-scale) competitive sector and consequent capitalist concentration, as well as the fruits of 'social mobility' amongst second generation immigrants. Thus, from 'impoverished immigrants' needing to combine their small capital in rotating credit associations and, therefore, dependent on collective networks, to the present day native-born entrepreneurs who are more likely to borrow money from banks, or other individual creditors (Light 1982:16–18). In essence, Light postulates that ethnic resources depend on 'pre-modern values' and social solidarities and so long as these survive in the ethnic community, co-ethnic business owners are able to utilise them in business activities.

The relationship between ethnicity, class and class recomposition i.e. the emergence from labour migrants of a class of migrant entrepreneurs, raises important questions over how we understand enterprise. Light asks, is an ethnic bourgeoisie just a typical bourgeoisie, or one with unique access to ethnic resources and if so, what are the effects of a 'supplementation' to class resources by this variable, specific to the entrepreneurial group? (1982:9, 11). As we noted, others point to a 'privileged' access to co-ethnic labour and capital. Light writes in terms of an 'ethnic bourgeoisie' on the one hand and the tendency to 'cluster heavily' or to be over represented in 'small businesses' on the other (Light, 1982:21) and indeed sees the competitive 'edge' of ethnic resources to be partly accounted by its relationship to this milieu. One may draw an implicit conclusion that he is actually presenting a 'small' bourgeoisie – or more analytically – a 'petty bourgeoisie': a term which Bonacich and Modell use (1980:31, 32; Bonacich, 1973:589) implicitly or explicitly. Thus on MMs we find,

Despite the fact that they are found in capitalist societies, middle-men minorities are not themselves modern capitalists in orientation. Rather they are essentially petit bourgeois, failing to engage in the kind of activity that epitomises modern capitalism, namely the hiring of contracted wage labour from which profits are extracted. Instead they work as single units, in which the distinction between owner and employee is blurred. Their shops depend on the use of the ethnic and familiar ties, not on personal contacts.

(Bonacich and Modell, 1980:31–32)

One conclusion is that in MM analysis we are presented with the classical image of the petty-bourgeoisie as an international class of shopkeepers who, like merchants elsewhere, earn their keep within the sphere of circulation via the time-honoured tradition of the price 'mark-up'. Of course, this is a caricature of their activity – as Light showed in his description of the activities of Japanese trucking and market gardening enterprises in the US (1972) or the shift towards bank capital (1982). Nevertheless, the notion of the self-employed trader provided much of the focus of early analysis and this acted as a limitation to understanding the differentiated nature of immigrant enterprise, changes to the scale of employment and related questions. For example, periods of primary business formation are frequently associated with a high dependence on family and co-ethnic labour but subsequent extension may not be; or, that small scale enterprises appear as more relevant to particular sectors. Bonacich points to some degree of differentiation within MMs. On one hand the 'typical' business appears as the 'family store' using unpaid family labour whilst, on the other, the 'hallmark' becomes vertical organisation of a particular industry such as 'Jewish' control of the New York clothing trade (Bonacich, 1973:586) involving 'the hiring of contracted wage labour from which profits are extracted'. Family shops relying on unpaid family labour, however, imply different kind of relations from enterprises in capital intensive areas of production, which borrow capital from banks and employ wage labour.

Much of the MM literature pointed to 'traditional' middlemen merchants in authoritarian, pre-indusial societies and in many circumstances pre- and post-colonial systems. Clearly, the US differs from these experiences, in the existence of formal plurality and democratic norms, as well as economic development and a significant middle class. Despite these fundamental differences, Min Pyong (1996) has found the concept of MMs useful in offering explanations for the incorporation of Korean entrepreneurs in US cities. Min Pyong has applied the triangular relationship highlighted by Middleman Minority theory – ethnic solidarity, middleman trading activities and host society hostility – to explain the incorporation of Korean immigrant enterprise in cities such as New York, and in neighbourhoods such as South Central Los Angeles (see Chapter 5). The relationship between Korean liquor store owners and the black community in areas such as South Central Los Angeles, provides fertile ground for analyses of Korean entrepreneurs as a MM, bearing the brunt of popular hostility. In an attempt to 'refine and revise' MM theory, Min Pyong (1996:218–219) points to Korean intermediaries as 'non-traditional' MMs who, as with other MMs, bear the brunt of popular hostility, in this instance, from customers in black neighbourhoods but, unlike traditional MMs, also conflict with the elite, or, white and Jewish suppliers and landlords and government agencies. Thus, the argument continues, Edna Bonacich is wrong to see MMs generally, and Korean entrepreneurs in the LA garment industry specifically, as surrogates of elites. Min Pyong (1996:220) argues that, 'Korean merchants as middlemen have responded to White suppliers and government agencies, honing their political skills as they use collective strategies' and points to significant organisational skills of an entrepreneurial group recruited mainly from 'college-educated members of the middle class'.

Conclusions

The economics of ethnicity cannot be disengaged from the emergence of ethnicity as a political phenomenon. From the 1960s onwards assimilation theories in the US and Europe faced a crisis in trying to understand this phenomenon. Early attempts to explain the economic arrangements of ethnic minorities and immigrant groups pointed to the role of ethnocultural endowment i.e. variables specific to an ethnic group itself as causal explanation for a disposition towards enterprise, and this remains very much a contested term. One treats with scepticism the hypothesis that of immigrants who become Middlemen Minorities, 'almost all that do derive from Asia and the Near East' (Fallers, 1967), or that 'overseas Indians in general', 'overseas Greeks in general' (Jiang, 1968) or 'overseas Chinese, Indians, Lebanese *and* Armenians in general' (Hamilton, 1978 emphasis added), have a greater propensity for such economic roles. The discussion on MMs parallels the ethno-cultural assumptions which drive much of the diaspora literature. Examples of trade diaspora include the ancient Phoenicians, Venetians, Lebanese and Chinese. Criticisms made of the application of both trade diaspora and Middleman Minority notions are that they appear as ahistorical in content and cut across social and economic formations some of which pre-date the development of the nation state. One conclusion is that the expansive application of diaspora and MM analyses results in the majority of humanity described as showing a cultural disposition towards enterprise and, as such, may have limited analytical value. These approaches, by pointing towards cultural endowment, make necessary assumptions that all or most members of an immigrant or ethnic group will behave, roughly speaking, in similar ways. This presents stereotypes which, in the case of the Chinese community, they have paid for dearly at the hands of the Indonesian and Dutch states.

The early research also pointed, in a more substantial manner, to the development of immigrant enterprise as a tendency to cluster heavily and to be over represented in the small businesses sector (Light, 1982:21). Indeed, the competitive 'edge' of ethnic resources was frequently accounted for by its relationship to this milieu. Light and Bonacich's general critique of theories rooted in cultural endowment and conventional sociological thinking, by pointing to the role of other factors, such as the condition of sojourning, the fear of displacement, the experience of immigration itself, the relationship between ethnicity and class over time, laid the basis for further, and in many cases, more fruitful research. Much of the early analysis also focused on trading activities. In these initial approaches, the social and economic differentiation of immigrant or ethnic minority enterprise, was not a question, since most were seen as self-employed, or employers of family or co-ethnic labour at most. One criticism of both, ethno-cultural and approaches and theories grounded in political economy (such as Light and Bonacich), is that they are either methodologically indifferent, or underestimate processes of social and economic differentiation inside immigrant and ethnic communities.

3 Still they come
Immigrants of New York

Introduction

New York is a key gateway city. Ellis Island is a potent symbol of both American historical development and the life-stories of millions of immigrants. New York continues to act as a magnet for immigrants from all over the world. This is illustrated in the history of the garment industry. From Jewish dominance and Italian participation from the mid-nineteenth century until the post-Second World War period; to an industry dominated in the 1980s by the Chinese and Hispanic (Dominican) communities. Today some 500 garment factories employ 20,000 immigrant women workers in the extended Chinatown area in Lower East Manhattan alone. New York is also important ground for testing some of the assumptions of the new economic sociology, such as the extent to which ethnic paternalism modifies market relations, the practical manifestation of labour diaspora and the substance of transnational communities. This chapter points to the concept of the ethnic 'labour queue' and the way it has been used to explain mainline assimilation and how immigrants overcome structural constraints faced by them. Waldinger provides a model of 'ethnic ordering' in New York which makes use of ecological succession and 'niche' theory to explain employment changes amongst immigrants. One suggestion by Roger Waldinger (1996b:21) is that some groups may be 'predisposed towards certain types of work'. The chapter debates the application of the concept of the ethnic labour queue as a benign game of 'musical chairs' (Rath, 2001) in the positioning and repositioning of immigrants in New York and elsewhere.

Bring me your ...

During the First Great Wave of immigration to the United States, Ellis Island (New York's harbour) and the Statue of Liberty, became potent symbols of American historical development and the life-stories of millions of European immigrants. The Statue of Liberty is New York's most famous landmark which greeted immigrants as they approached Ellis

Island for disembarkation. The Statue of Liberty links America and Europe in another sense. It owes its origins to the French Revolution and was a gift by the French people to the people of the newly independent United States of America who had overthrown British colonial rule and the tyranny of King George III. The French revolutionary, Lafayette, was a direct link between the democratic ideals of the French Revolution and the struggle for independence in the North American British colonies. When 'French Fries' are renamed 'Liberty Fries', it is particularly important to remember where the Statue of Liberty came from.

Ellis Island was the first experience of the United States for many immigrants. It is an area of about 27 acres 1.6 km south-west of Manhattan Island and served as the country's major immigration station between 1892 and 1924. During this period an estimated 17 million people were processed by the immigration authorities. Of the 5,400,000 immigrants who arrived at the United States between 1820 and 1860 about 3,700,000 entered in New York. They disembarked, were numbered, processed, their names frequently were misspelled, in cases they were deloused and sometimes hosed down and then they were allowed to enter the United States of America (Howe, 1976:42–46). Many of them settled in New York. In 1890 an estimated 42 per cent of New York's population was born in Europe.

New York appears as the living embodiment of globalisation and has acted as the historic entry point into the United States for endless generations of immigrants and ethnic groups: Irish, Jewish, Italian, Greek, Dominican, Chinese and other nationalities. The 'Americanisation' of successive waves of European immigrants provided the basis for mainline assimilation theories (see Glazer and Moynihan, 1970). The example of New York's Irish community is a case in point. Irish immigration into New York shaped its politics for over a century. Of the 640,000 persons born in Europe and living in New York in 1890, 190,000 (29.6 per cent) were from Ireland. By 1910 the number of people living in the city who had been born in Europe stood at 1,944,000, with the number of Irish-born persons amongst them at 253,000 (13 per cent) (Lankevich, 1998:119).

Irish immigrants successfully fought the nativist backlash and indeed were a key force in defeating the considerable weight of the American Protectionist Movement and its Republican allies in attempts to restrict immigration during the 1890s. The development of political captains inside the Irish community which delivered the vote for Tammany Hall, made them into the dominant political force in New York. Tammany Hall began as one of a number of patriotic societies which sprang up to promote various political causes and economic interests after the American Revolution. The Tammany Society, or Columbian Order of New York, was such a society and formed in 1786. Its rites, ceremonies and titles of its officials were based on pseudo-native American forms. Its significance was that it became the executive committee of the Democratic Party in New

York City and held political power from 1821–1872 and 1905–1932. When it was first formed the Tammany Society was a middle-class organisation of native Americans who gravitated towards and dominated the local Democratic Party. Although always controlled by the wealthy it attracted the support of the working classes and immigrants. An important point in the transformations of Tammany was when Irish immigrants forced Tammany Hall to admit them as members in 1817 and became rapidly its major popular political force. Because in the 1820s Tammany successfully fought for the extension of the franchise to all propertyless white males, it attracted support from workers. Tammany Hall represented a system of political control by local bosses of Irish communities at ward level, typically through charity work, patronage and in opening doors for employment in the expanding public sector. In this long association with the political system through the local Democratic machinery, Tichenor (2002:73) observes that 'Irish Catholics remained one of the party's most dependable and important voting blocks' especially in New York, but also other northern urban cities, such as Chicago. Tichenor further notes that 'in growing cities like New York, the Democratic party enjoyed new strength largely to immigrant voting blocks and new Irish dominated party machines such as the Tweed Ring of Tammany Hall' (2002:67). William Tweed was Commissioner of Public Works from 1865 to 1871 which allowed him to carry out wholesale corruption, until convicted and imprisoned for 12 years. Incidents such as this made Tammany Hall into a symbol universally synonymous with urban political corruption.

Whilst Tammany Hall admitted the newly-arrived Irish, it was also long-controlled by Protestant leaders like Tweed. Lankevich (1998) points to 'an ethno-religious revolution' to describe the transformation of the Hall during the decade after the Civil War. By 1860, Catholics composed the largest religious group in the city, and Church records counted 350,000 Catholics in 32 parishes in 1865. In 1866 a crowd estimated at 100,000 demonstrated in support of Home Rule and the Fenian cause. By the 1870s the Irish, heirs of destitute immigrants of the 1840s, 'finally attained power in New York' (Lankevich, 1998:118). A major voice was the publication in 1871, of *Irish World*, today the oldest weekly in New York. The Orange Order, a significant ally of the Nativists, was the first to feel the wrath of Irish Catholics. In the same year, Tammany activists who supported the republican and nationalist cause, successfully stopped the annual Apprentice Boys parade held on 12 July – a celebration of Protestant supremacism in Northern Ireland and the Irish Protestant diaspora. 'During the 1870s, the almost traditional Protestant attacks on Catholic Irish functions simply came to an end because the Orangemen were simply overwhelmed by numbers' (Lankevich, 1998:118).

Tammany Hall, as a path to Americanisation and mainline assimilation, glosses over contradictions within immigrant communities and defines their outcome as synonymous with those of 'their' political patrons and brokers. Lankevich (1998:119) quotes (approvingly) the argument by Richard Croker (one of Tammany Hall's political bosses) that,

> Tammany Hall Americanized the immigrant: it took 'hold of the untrained, friendless man and converted him into a citizen'. All it asked was his vote. The system that Tammany Hall evolved worked well, and later history demonstrated its ability to fulfil the dreams of Italians, Jews, and blacks and Irish.

The history of New York is an Irish history, but it is also a Jewish history. Today, approximately 1.5 million persons of Jewish origins play an important role in the economy of New York. Many buildings in New York, particularly in Manhattan, are owned by Jewish landlords and this is a source of conflict with both private and commercial tenants, such as housing tenants from the black community or entrepreneurs from, for example, the Chinese and Korean communities. Many Chinese, Haitian, Dominican and Korean entrepreneurs, contractors and storekeepers, continue to depend on Jewish suppliers and garment manufacturers for ethnic produce and work (Min Pyong, 1996:179–183).

The history of Jewish immigration to New York offers insight into the settlement and social differentiation of an immigrant community. From 1880–1920 approximately 3.5 million Jewish immigrants passed through New York harbour. About 1.4 million of them came from Eastern Europe and Russia, many for economic reasons but also as the result of discrimination and religious persecution. Many were fleeing pogroms i.e. communal violence directed at Jewish ghettos and frequently organised by sections of the state apparatus. As noted, many Jewish immigrants were to face discriminatory immigration controls in the US (see Introduction). 'Uptown' New York, contained in the Upper West Side, was for the most part populated by Jewish immigrants from Germany. Some in this group adopted American culture relatively quickly. Many moved into white-collar jobs, became shopkeepers, or joined the self-employed. Typically the second generation adapted to the new world more than the first generation. This laid the basis for Reform Judaism (i.e. a less strict and more accepting form of Judaism). 'Downtown' (the Lower East Side) were the Jewish immigrants from Eastern Europe and Russia who lived and worked there. Many lived in crowded tenements and worked (indeed became the backbone) of the most significant centre of garment production in the US. The Lower East Side was similar to the Jewish ghettos in Eastern Europe. This experience was associated with loyalty to Orthodox Judaism (i.e. a 'fundamentalist' and less accepting form of Judaism) (see, Howe, 1976:67–118, 325–359).

New York continues to act as a magnet for immigrants from all over the world and remains a key interface of the Second Great Wave. This is reflected in the fact that New York's immigrants are more diverse, significantly younger and more recently arrived, even when compared to other gateway cities, such as London. In part this is the result of more restrictive immigration policies in the UK when compared to the US (Model and Lapido, 1996:493). Whilst Irish, Jewish and Southern European immigration underpinned the First Great Wave of immigration to New York, the Second Great Wave is associated with a more diverse and expansive immigration. One example is Bangladeshi taxi drivers. In 1990 they were only a handful and today they make up about 7,500 of New York's 50,000 taxi drivers. About two thirds are owner-drivers. Usually two or more persons buy the taxi in partnership at a cost of around $35,000. The main problem for them is acquiring a taxi medallion. The cost of each individual medallion is $250,000 and the number of Bangladeshi owners is estimated at only 400 people. In the past it was possible to rent the individual medallions within the community, but now this is illegal. The medallion owner now must drive the taxi himself and can only have one partner. This had a discouraging effect. However, since fewer people were buying medallions and given that one impact of the 9/11 attack on the New York service sector was that the price of medallions declined significantly, to $195,000, reports from the Bangladeshi community indicate that 'more people are buying medallions today, as the price has gone down' (Kashem, 2001:7)

Koreatown – it's official

Of Korean immigrants enumerated in the 1990 Census, 12.0 per cent lived in New York and 4.8 per cent in New Jersey. After California, the New York–New Jersey (NY–NJ) area with 134,000 people, is the second highest concentration of Koreans in the US. During 1980 the NY–NJ Korean community numbered 47,000 people, and by 1994 it was 150,000 (Min Pyong, 1996:32–33). By 1994 about 100,000 Koreans lived in New York City. This made Koreans the third largest Asian immigrant group after Chinese and Indian immigrants. Nearly half the Asian population lives in Queens and amongst them, Koreans show (at 70 per cent) the highest level of concentration (Min Pyong, 1996:37). This is questioning the previously held view of New York's Korean community as a 'nonterritorial' community. Indeed one prevalent view of the Korean community as a whole until the 1980s, was that they did not settle in clusters. This reflected, perhaps, more on immigration rules which made it difficult for Asians to enter the US until 1965, than Koreans themselves.

Min Pyong (1996) points to another 'overseas Seoul' which has emerged since the late 1980s in Flushing, a ward in the Borough of Queens, and writes that although 'this Koreatown is much smaller in scale than the one on Los Angeles, it possesses many characteristics of a typical ethnic ghetto' (Min Pyong, 1996:38–39). There are high levels of spatial concentration, with an estimated one quarter of New York's Koreans and more than one third of those in Queens, residing in Flushing. This makes Flushing the most significant social and cultural centre for the Korean community outside Los Angeles. It is also the centre of an ethnic economy, and many Korean restaurants, bakeries, beauty salons, barber shops, nightclubs, ethnic presses, book stores and real estate companies, Korean community associations and about 60 churches are located there. The city, however, had other ideas about the location of 'official' Koreatown. Manhattan, which was the centre of the earlier New York Korean community, sees a visible concentration in the so-called Broadway Korean Business District, a rectangular ten-block area from 24th to 34th Streets between Fifth and Sixth Avenues. The intersection of 32nd Street and Broadway is considered its centre. Here, are located approximately 400 Korean import and wholesale companies: most import wigs, hats, leather bags, clothing, jewellery, toys and other manufactured goods from South Korea and other Asian countries, which are then distributed to Korean retailers all over the country. Also, there are many accounting firms, law firms, real estate offices and travel agencies. 'In October 1995, the city named the district "Koreatown" and posted official signs at the intersection' (Min Pyong, 1996:39–40).

'Chinatown' or 'Little Fuzhou'?

The Chinese community has had a significant presence in the US since the Californian Gold Rush of 1848 and the construction of the western section of the transcontinental railroads during the 1860s to the 1880s. As we noted, they were also scapegoated by the 1882 Chinese Exclusion Act and denied entry by the Immigration Act of 1965 which abolished the national quota system. The growth is a more recent phenomenon. From the mid-1960s to the mid-1990s, the Chinese population in the US grew to an estimated two million people (0.7 per cent of the total population) with Los Angeles, New York and San Francisco (in which 10 per cent of the total population are Chinese), the most significant areas of settlement (Lai, 1998:273).

New York's 'Chinatown' has come to symbolise the public face of the Second Great Wave, in a more substantial way than the relatively smaller Koreatown. The 1987 *Survey of Minority-Owned Business Enterprises*, enumerated 89,717 Chinese-owned firms in the United States indicating a 286 per cent increase between 1982 and 1987, as compared with a 14 per cent increase for all firms nationwide. In the New York, NY–NJ Standard Metropolitan Statistical Area (SMSA), the number of Chinese firms increased from 2,667 in 1977 to 11,579 in 1987 (10,864 firms were based in New York) (Zhou, 1992:97). Some 500 garment factories employing 20,000 immigrant women workers in the extended area of Lower East Manhattan, forms the spatial clustering of Chinatown (Zhou, 2002).

Historically, Fujian and Guangdong Provinces on China's south-eastern shoreline have provided the majority of immigrants from China. Until recently, migrants from Fujian tended to migrate to South-East Asian countries. Within Fujian, Fuzhou City and its surrounding rural counties, provided fewer immigrants than the more outlying rural areas and accounted for just under 10 per cent of migrants. The Fuzhounese migrants developed a special relationship with the US.

> Never in the Chinese immigrant experience have so many from a single locale moved so far by clandestine means within such a short period of time. Between 1979 and 1995, 300,000 to 400,000 people found their way by some combination of air, land, and sea routes to the lower east side of Manhattan.
>
> (Hood, 1998:33)

Hood points to a Fuzhounese exodus. By 1994 many villages had half their population living in the US. In one case, Houyu in Changle county, as much as 80 per cent of the entire population had found its way to New York and its adjoining areas. The periodisation of this movement went through a number of stages in its development (see below) (Hood, 1998:33–34).

The Fuzhounese

First stage: before the Second World War, Fuzhounese seamen began to settle illegally in New York. By 1970, many graduated from labourers in Cantonese businesses to becoming entrepreneurs in their own right.
Second stage: the process of clandestine (in many cases) family reunifications which gathered momentum from 1979–1982, and eventually exhausted this supply of migrants.
Third stage: small numbers of migrants, with less than 5,000 entries into the US during the period 1982–1986.
Fourth stage: from 1986–1994, partly in response to US restrictive and liberal immigration policies (after the Tiananmen Massacre, 4 June 1989), human trafficking becomes a mass phenomenon and was transformed into a multi-billion dollar business: the result was a massive exodus of approximately 200,000 Fuzhounese to the US from 1991–1993.
Fifth stage: by 1994 migration declined dramatically, with the arrival of older women and young children, signalling that many villages in Fuzhou had reached a kind of equilibrium.

Immigrants and the restructuring of New York's economy

Today, the history of New York appears as the history of the world. Whilst Hispanic and Chinese communities have longer histories in the US, Korean, Bangladeshi, Indian and other communities are more recent arrivals. The Dominican community in the United States by 1990 had grown to over half a million people of whom three quarters resided in New York City with a high concentration (137,000) enumerated in the Borough of Manhattan. Between 1980 and 1990, Dominican immigrants made the single largest flow of immigrants to New York City (Hernandez, 2002:121).

Their experience of immigration during the Second Great Wave became linked to the social and economic restructuring of New York City. The restructuring of New York, as with other major cities (the familiar argument runs), saw during the recession years the decline of relatively highly paid jobs in manufacturing and their replacement with low-paid service sector employment. The term 'post-industrial' city has been widely advanced to define this perceived transformation (see, Waldinger, 1996b; Sassen, 1996; Drennan, 1991; Hernandez, 2002). Many of these analyses of labour market incorporation (such as Sassen's) are supply driven and point to the (global) restructuring of particular sectors as causal for the incorporation of immigrants as workers and entrepreneurs in informal labour markets. Saskia Sassen (1988) examined New York's 'informal sector' in terms of the number of unregistered commercial and manufacturing operations, and industrial sectors where informal practices were most common. Industries covered included construction, garments, footwear, furniture, retail activity and electronics. Many of the jobs in these industries rely on manual skills: homework in the apparel sector; general construction contractors and operative builders, heavy construction contractors, special trade contractors particularly in masonry, stonework and plastering; activities like packaging, the making of lampshades, artificial flowers, jewellery. There is also a strong tendency for such operations to be located in densely populated areas with very high shares of immigrants. Sassen observed that in branches of the construction industry work, particularly in foundations excavations and trenching, as well as in highly specialized crafts work (stone cutting, masonry and plastering), there was an 'extremely high incidence of informal work'. These branches have experienced severe labour shortages and employ largely skilled immigrants, mostly Hispanic immigrants. Sassen noted a growing presence of Hispanics among the subcontractors 'in an industry where Hispanics were excluded not long ago'. In other industries, Chinese immigrants were prominent with South Koreans and certain European nationalities increasingly so. One area (Brighton Beach), with an almost exclusively Russian émigré population, 'has an extremely developed informal economy' (Sassen, 1988:6). The significant contribution made by immigrant entrepreneurs to the revitalisation of New York's economy is widely recognised by policy makers. Another recognition is that a certain level of economic informality may be an acceptable and even necessary precondition for revitalisation strategies (see, Pavlova, 2001; Hum, 2001).

Sassen also pointed to a tendency for 'traditional' sweatshop activity (notably garments) to be forced out of areas undergoing residential and commercial gentrification and to be replaced by new forms of unregistered work catering to the new clientele, for example: high quality wood-cabinet making, has replaced garment manufacture in Jackson Heights, Queens; unregistered 'sweater mills' have replaced garment manufacture in Ridgewood, Queens; and there is strong evidence of a growing spatial dispersion of unlicensed and unregistered work to more outlying areas (certain counties in New Jersey have seen a massive development of such operations, most of it geared to demand by firms in New York City). Furthermore, in the case of the garment industry, Sassen pointed to 'a massive displacement to more peripheral areas' e.g. out of the Chinatown area in Manhattan and into Northern Manhattan, Brooklyn, Queens and New Jersey (Sassen, 1988:7). Harlem also has been impacted by 'gentrification', or rising commercial property prices and rents, which has particular implications for small enterprise in the area, of which an estimated 80 per cent do not have leases, rent business premises 'month to month' and face the threat of eviction (Grimes, 2003:9).

Rising rents are a major problem for immigrant entrepreneurs. In telephone interviews with 93 randomly selected Korean merchants in black neighbourhoods in New York, Min Pyong (1996:177–178) found that 81 per cent leased store buildings frequently, but not exclusively, from Jewish landlords. Many have experienced severe rent hikes, partly in response to perceived Korean 'success'. Most Korean merchants cannot change their landlord as easily as they can change suppliers. Many Korean produce owners in New York have had to open 24 hours a day to cover this escalating cost. Firms in the Broadway Korean Business District, were particularly badly hit, and this galvanised political lobbying, protests and the formation of the Coalition for Fair Rents during the mid-1980s. Rent regulation remains a burning issue.

Sassen concludes that the structural transformation of New York's economy and the growth of informal labour markets present opportunities for immigrant communities, conditioned by how,

> Workers and firms respond to the opportunities contained in these patterns and transformations. However, in order to respond, workers and firms need to be positioned in distinct ways. Immigrant communities represent what could be described as a 'favored' structural location to seize the opportunities for entrepreneurship as well as the more and less desirable jobs being generated by informalization.
>
> (Sassen, 1988:9)

Many immigrant-owned enterprises also had to negotiate the direct and indirect effects of the events of 11 September 2001. An estimated 500 undocumented immigrants who worked in low paid jobs as messengers and janitors, or delivering doughnuts and coffee to the offices in the World Trade Centre (WTC), were among the dead. Limousine and taxi drivers who account for the employment of 50,000 drivers, let alone valeting, butlers, housekeepers, waiters, nannies, bellhops, were occupations badly affected by the 9/11 attack. The estimated 75,000 workers in these occupations experienced sharply declining incomes as they worked fewer hours, carried fewer passengers and received lower tips. This was in addition to the 80,000 persons estimated to have been thrown out of work as a result of the attack (Greenhouse, 2001:8). Not only were service-related immigrant enterprises badly hit, but the consequence of the long clean-up, forced many production-related enterprises to relocate. Chinatown – the poorest neighbourhood in Lower Manhattan – is less than a mile from the WTC. Many garment shops relocated to Brooklyn because trucks couldn't make deliveries due to traffic restrictions which operated during the clean-up.

Immigrants in the New York garment industry

The history of immigrant workers and entrepreneurs in New York can be illustrated in the history of the garment industry. From the mid-nineteenth century until the post-Second World War period, the industry was dominated by the Jewish and Italian communities. During the late nineteenth century the garment industry dominated the city's employment structure. Eastern and Southern European immigrants – men, women, children – worked in the many shops and as homeworkers. By 1890, 91.5 per cent of male tailors were foreign born. Most families 'could not and did not get by on the wages of the adult garment worker'. During the busy season tailors or machinists worked up to 16 hours a day 'and then took large bundles of unfinished garments for their wives and children to make up at piece rates for additional waged income' (Friedman-Kasaba, 1996:123–124).

Whilst the garment industry was dominated by the Jewish community, in 1880 only 2 per cent of Jewish wives took jobs outside their homes and by 1905 it was only 1 per cent. Indeed according to the Bureau of Labour, at the time, 'the Hebrew men seldom allow the women of their family to do the [clothing] work at home, even though they had been shop workers before marriage' (quoted from Friedman-Kasaba, 1996:123, 125). Most Jewish-owned and other shops (i.e. small factories) depended for labour mainly on young unmarried girls and women from other immigrant groups. This was reflected in the wider New York labour market. Russian Jewish women ranked fourth and Italian women seventh, amongst the most numerous groups of female wage earners in New York City in 1900. Of all women employed in manufacturing industries in New York City in 1900, 53 per cent were between the ages of 16 and 25. Many Italian women were employed as home finishers (i.e. homeworkers). The pattern was different from that found amongst Jewish wives and many Italian women in

New York continued to work in 'outside' shops, or in formal employment, after marriage, and only moved into home finishing after having children (Friedman-Kasaba, 1996:126, 171). 'In contrast to Russian-Jewish women, young Italian immigrants women were not steered to limited areas of the labor market by an affluent group of co ethnic entrepreneurs or middle-class coethnic social reformers' (Friedman-Kasaba, 1996:167).

The uptown/downtown division in the Jewish community was also reflected in the socialisation of 'young girls'. The German Jewish immigrant community uptown predominated amongst the owners of the large garment enterprises and wholesaling activities. Russian Jewish immigrants primarily made up the ranks of the contractors and workers in the industry. One view is that uptown Jewish New York, 'made it a policy to steer young Russian Jewish women into training courses and then into semi-skilled and unskilled sectors of the garment trades' (Glanz, 1976:27–30). By 1900, 77 per cent of Russian Jewish women were employed in the garment industry. By 1914, the German Jewish entrepreneurs had been replaced by Russian and other Eastern European Jewish men who had, in many cases, been their previous employees (Friedman-Kasaba, 1996:160).

Many young Russian Jewish and Italian immigrant women, in trying to make sense of the world and the enclave around them, adopted the status of household 'earner' in the ethnic economy as part of 'becoming a person'. This as Friedman-Kasaba (1996:173) argues, 'was a source of self-esteem, pride, and accomplishment for many women, although never a free choice'. In doing so, however, many young women 'developed reputations as unruly and demanding workers' (Glanz, 1976:212). In November 1909, 30,000 garment workers began a 13-week long strike to organise the International Ladies Garment Union. This was known as the 'girls' strike, because young women led it. About 21,000 Jewish women, 2,000 Italian women, 1,000 American women and 6,000 Jewish men took part (Seller, 1986:255, 267).

During the last decade of the nineteenth century, and substantially due to the impact of mass Jewish immigration, New York was the most important centre of garment production in the US. In 1890, 44 per cent of all ready-made clothes manufactured in the US were made in New York (NY). Womenswear production in NY accounted for the employment of 54 per cent of all workers, most of them recently arrived young immigrant women. During the Second World War 65 per cent of all workers in womens wear were concentrated in NY (Zhou, 2002:114).

By the 1980s the New York garment industry became dominated on the production side by Chinese and Hispanic (Dominican) immigrant communities. By the end of the 1990s the NY garment industry was the major manufacturing employer. In 1998, it employed 133,000 workers. Today, more than one in four dresses made in the US are manufactured in NY City (Zhou, 2002:115–117). Significant relocation by garment enterprises to the southern states of the US took place during the 1950s to 1970s. The Border Industrial Programme (BIP) linking El Paso and

Cuidad Jerez on the USA/Mexico border acted as the basis for the relocation of much of the jeans wear industry. One of the beneficiaries of more recent relocation has been the State of California and in particular the Greater Los Angeles area.

Roger Waldinger's *Through the Eye of the Needle: Immigrants and Enterprise in New York's Garment Trades* (1986), is an important study of immigrant participation in the New York garment industry. It examined contractors and workers in the New York garment industry. It began as a doctoral thesis. Waldinger worked as a union official for the International Ladies and Garment Workers Union (ILGWU, later renamed UNITE) and subsequently for the employers association. Waldinger's sample found many Italians and Jews still active as contractors. The average age of these entrepreneurs, however, was 56 and most were ending their working lives. By 1980, Chinese and Dominican workers made up 20 per cent of official employment (Waldinger 1986:126). Today, these two groups monopolise employment.

The structure of garment production in NY and elsewhere involves vertical subcontracting relationships which link buyers, manufacturers and contractors. The most significant factor is the location of the vast bulk of immigrant entrepreneurs as 'cut, make, trim' (CMT) contractors and subcontractors. This consists of the three basic fragments of production which depend on different skills and are paid in different ways. Cutters and sample machinists, who make the first copy to 'show' other machinists, are on set wages and tend to be the best paid workers. On the making side most labour is made up of women machinists who are on piece rate. Trimming requires pressers and 'passers', cotton cleaners, and workers who do the bagging, labelling and ticketing. These workers (often younger women) are on agreed wages and are the lowest paid group of workers. A key group are drivers who link the homeworkers machining at home with the factory. Homeworkers are on piece rate. Drivers could be on a set wage or commission, or be operating independently by recruiting their 'own' machinists (see Figure 3.1).

The assembling and reassembling of workers, in the right numbers and the requisite skills in time for the fashion season, dominates the lives of most CMT contractors. In the above we find powerful structural constraints shaped by the organisation of production. The location of most immigrant entrepreneurs in the production chain as CMT contractors, the small size of most enterprises, the market sector immigrant firms operate in and local labour market variation in the supply and demand for workers of differing skills, provide significant contextual explanation for the structuring of garment production and workplace relations. The women's fashion-wear sector, for example, indicates specific production relations, including workplace relations, driven by demand for quick-turnaround delivery systems and which have specific implications for immigrant entrepreneurs and workers.

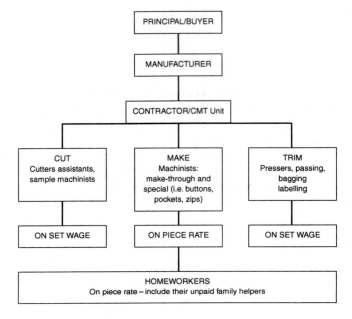

Figure 3.1 Organisation of production and system of payment in the garment
industry.

Waldinger (1986:97) offers two explanations for the continuity of the
garment industry in New York and the incorporation of diverse immigrant
groups. First, that 'thanks to a massive infusion of immigrant blood', we
have the effect that 'immigrants lower wages', and second, that the industry in New York has adapted to a 'spot-market' in the women's fashion-
wear sector, which requires quick-turnround delivery systems and an
agglomeration of buyers, manufacturers, designers, suppliers of textiles,
trimmings, specialised services to the trade, as well as CMT units in a
robust local economy.

In offering explanations for the expansion of New York's Chinatown,
Zhou Min (1992) and Zhou Yu (2002) point to the 500 garment factories
employing 20,000 immigrant women workers in the extended Lower East
Manhattan, as the heart of the community. The number of Chinese
garment firms increased massively from eight in 1960, to 480 by 1992
(Zhou, 2002:120). This provides the material basis for Zhou Min's description of Chinatown as an 'ethnic enclave'. Zhou Yu (2002:115) follows
Waldinger's explanation for the resilience of the garment industry, i.e. that
immigrants' lower wages and the development of a fashion-wear spot-
market, provide combined contextual explanation. The spatial agglomeration of Chinatown includes the Manhattan Fashion District which extends

between Sixth and Ninth Avenues, from 35th Street to 41st Street. Rents in Manhattan (and Chinatown), however, are rising so relocation is taking place to outer boroughs such as Queens and Brooklyn, or to other neighbouring states such as New Jersey. By the early 1990s immigrants made up 75 per cent of all labour; of garment workers, 33 per cent are Hispanics, 27 per cent Asian and 67 per cent are women (Zhou 2002:119–120).

Whilst agreeing with Waldinger (1986:102), that 'New York provides a concentration of small, highly flexible factories that are set up for small-batch production', there is a debate between the two explanations offered. What is determinant in the development of a fashion-wear spot-market? Is it that the garment industry grew up in New York *because* of the creativity of the city's huge pool of immigrants who provided the ample and flexible supply of labour the industry needed, lowered labour costs and provided many of its contractors? Or/and does this involve wider relationships which reflect on the nature of local economies and the restructuring of the women's fashion-wear sector by leading retailers?

Panayiotopoulos (2000a, 2001a) points to changes in multinational sourcing policy as critical in the relocation of production activities. Similarly, Elizabeth Petras (1992:92) in a study of the adjoining Philadelphia fashion industry argued that the industry was coming back to the urban sites of the US (and further, that 'garment sweatshops are proliferating in the U.S. at a rate unparalleled since the 19th century'), for two main reasons: sensitivity to labour costs and trends in fashion-wear market for quick delivery of smaller batches. In the case of international processing 'overseas orders must be placed 6 to 18 months in advance' (1992:78) and are incapable of mid-stream change, such as for example in changing the design or colour of the fabric. Petras argued that,

> the *central factor* stimulating the proliferation of sweatshops and homework in New York, New Jersey, and Philadelphia, as in California and Florida, has been the *decision of American manufacturers to shift their production orders back to the U.S. as a cost-cutting measure.*
>
> (Petras, 1992:93, italics in original)

The ethnic composition of the labour force in Philadelphia, consisted mostly of Chinese, Vietnamese and Cambodian women, a number of whom were refugees. Chinese co-ethnic relations were significant in structuring day to day relations. Hong Kong provided many entrepreneurs, after the transition of power to mainland China, in Philadelphia and elsewhere. 'During the 1980s as many as 1,000 garment shops' were reported to be owned by them (Petras, 1992:90). Labour conditions and employment were underpinned by informal labour practices – 'illegal, off-the-books, pay no minimum wages, unemployment insurance, or health benefits and ignore child labour laws'. Women 'often bring their children to the shops because they have no one to care for them'. Entrepreneurs 'may pay passage abroad for others, generally young women' and 'documented cases where the shop owner also requires women to take room and board on the shop premises' (Petras, 1992:77, 91, 92).

> Inside the shops, where the structure is organised like a family, with the owner in the paternal role, women are not likely to refuse to cooperate or make demands on their protectors. This is particularly true for women who do not speak English and don't venture outside their immediate neighbourhoods.
>
> (Petras, 1992:101)

Organised crime has a presence in many economic activities in the US and also in the experience of many US labour unions (such as the Teamsters) where rank and file members had to fight a very difficult battle to reclaim the union for its members. The garment industry is no exception. The New Jersey State Commission investigated connections between organised crime, illegal money transactions and garment sweatshops, and came to the conclusion that 'a number of "crime families" have controlling interests in a small number of factories in Northeastern Pennsylvania' (Pennsylvania Crime Commission, 1991) – Joseph Gambino, a leading and much surveiled Mafia figure, and two of his employees, were filmed visiting Philadelphia garment factories. Organised crime parallels the structures of subcontracting in the garment industry. To obtain work from the jobbers (manufacturers), a shop owner needs to establish contact with one of the established trucking lines. Many of them are controlled by crime families and the contractor is then 'married for life' to that trucker. Because of threat of violence, the only way to switch trucking companies may be that the firm has to shut down altogether and later to reopen with a new name. This reinforces the tendency in many firms to frequently relocate and change name.

Roger Waldinger and Michael Lapp, challenge the idea (such as from Petras) that 'the garment industry has gone back to the sweatshop' (1993:6). The view that waves of illegal immigrants employed in sweatshops were overwhelming the combined powers of corporate America and the US Immigration Department, underpinned the rise of xenophobia and restrictive immigration policies in States such as California (see Chapter 5). Primarily, they rely on official figures which tell us that in the New York garment industry 'only a small proportion' of the labour force is engaged in homeworking and there is in fact 'little evidence of a substantial underground garment industry' (1993:20). In this Waldinger has been criticised for ignoring evidence on 'sweatshops' in NY and elsewhere. According to academic and union sources, the number of sweatshops increased from 300 in the 1970s to about 3,000 by the early 1980s, 'employing approximately 50,000 unregistered workers and 10,000 home workers' (see, Bonacich, 1993a; Portes 1994:435; also see, Sassen, 1988).

Ethnic paternalism and transnational communities

Waldinger (1995:555) argues that embeddedness in ethnic networks 'leads to cooperation, if not conformist, behaviour among ethnic economic actors'. In an earlier study of immigrant participation in the New York garment industry, Waldinger (1985:325) found that workplace relations were structured by 'rules designed to constrain both managerial and worker behaviour' (and which) 'fosters a broader group identity that tends to eclipse relationships of authority'. Waldinger points to difficult terrain for ethnic paternalism in the New York garment industry. Jobs are unstable due to seasonality, but turnover was limited to a small number of hired workers, with family workers seen as part of a 'core' labour force. Immigrant firms relied heavily for labour recruitment on kinship and ethnic networks and this created the material basis for paternalistic relationships between employers and employees, who share a 'repertoire of symbols and customs' and values which 'can be cultivated on a more routine basis to broker patron–client relationships' (Waldinger, 1986:160). At the same time, a number of tensions were identified. First, between efficiency and paternalistic obligations in enterprise functions and constraints 'in the exercise of authority' amongst family workers and friends. Second, in factors associated with the structure of subcontracting in the New York garment industry and the 'severity of the competitive environment' which make patron–client–relationships inherently difficult to sustain (Waldinger, 1986:163, 166). Despite these constraints, Waldinger argues that 'immigrant firms enjoy a competitive advantage in small business industries because the social structures of the ethnic community provide a mechanism of connecting organisations to individuals and stabilise these relations'. In this discourse, ethnicity is identified as the key variable in the determination of 'the social structures that attach members of an ethnic group to one another and the ways those social structures are used' (Waldinger, 1986:15, 32). A further argument is that some ethnic groups may be 'predisposed towards certain types of work' (Waldinger, 1996b:21).

Gender-sensitive (and other) research in New York's Chinatown garment district, however, points to a more complex situation. One view, which would be supportive of Waldinger's argument, is that gender subordination is the result of 'frozen' traditional values, which define women in the ethnic enclave primarily as daughters, wives and mothers. In this discourse, 'to get rich for their family' and 'to help their family members to immigrate' (Zhou, 1992:156) is seen as a key part of the dominant enclave ideology. This can be particularly damaging to professional women trying to break out of low paid manufacturing and service sector jobs (see, Zhou and Logan, 1989). Analyses pointing towards resistance, identify the activities of trade unions and organisations which make a class appeal to immigrant women workers and which often arise in response to the structural characteristics of the garment industry, and in particular, job insecurity.

An estimated 20,000 Chinese women were members of UNITE, the garment workers union (Zhou, 2002:120). Chinatown garment workers were involved in mass demonstrations during 1982. On two occasions 15–20,000 mainly women workers marched in defence of the union contract. Chinese employers appealed (in vain) to their workers in the name of ethnic solidarity to abandon the union and resorted to denouncements of (sometimes co-ethnic) union activists, as 'communists' (see, Proper, 1997; Kwong, 1997; see also, Bonacich, 1998).

Peter Kwong (1997, 1998) has been studying the Chinese American community for 25 years, many of them as a social movement activist, and has conducted hundreds of personal interviews with Chinese undocumented workers, from south Manhattan's traditional Chinatown to the growing Chinese neighbourhoods in Queens and Brooklyn. His work provides insight into the role of ethnic paternalism in transnational communities linking ethnic enclaves to regions of the homeland. The focus of the research has been on illegal immigration from mainland China, primarily identified in a relationship linking New York's Chinatown with the rural areas of the southern province of Fujian. The Fuzhounese were relatively new and marginal within the Chinese community and for them, more than others, the use of existing ethnic social networks and resources was even more imperative in immigration and settlement given their lack of economic power (class resources).

The basic unit of Fujian rural social structure, as with other areas, were the clans and localised, unofficial civic organisations which sprung up during the Q'ing dynasty. Early Chinese immigrants who were mainly bachelors and tended to live communally, sharing apartments to save money. Until 1965, most US Chinatowns were largely bachelor societies. This arrangement evolved into a formal collective called a *fong*, which literally means a 'room'. Members of a *fong* developed close relationships and great loyalty to one another. Group savings and lending associations often sprung from these circumstances. *Fongs* made up of people from the same village, formed a *village association*; those made up of people with the same surname formed family or surname associations. They would raise money for good causes, such as building schools and hospitals in their home village. These associations were originally established to defend their members against a hostile world and to provide order within the community, but developed internal hierarchies: shopkeepers and restaurant owners became the patrons and big shots (*kiu ling*) who also controlled the associations. These associations became conduits of support for immigrant workers and underpinned the Chinese labour diaspora. Finding work through friends, co-villagers and patrons, forces newcomers into a system of social obligations. The patron performs a *ren-qing* (personal favour) by means of *quanxi* (connections) and then the newcomer owes *re-qing* to the patron/employer for giving him/her a job (Kwong, 1997:372).

Kwong pointed to the number of Chinese illegal workers as relatively small: 200,000 people out of an estimated five million illegal immigrants in the US at the time. Unlike other immigrant workers in other cities, such as Mexicans who work for Korean greengroceries in Los Angeles, the Ecuadorians who work for Cuban garment factories in Miami, and Polish and Eastern European illegals who work for Irish construction companies in New York, 'few Chinese are employed in the open and competitive labour market' (Kwong, 1997:368). One significant change to the make up of US Chinese communities in the US has been the consequence of liber-alisation in immigration policies during the late 1960s onwards, which saw the mushrooming of family reunions and the arrival of many women immi-grants, who provided the backbone for Chinese entry into the New York garment industry during the 1970s and 1980s, typically as contractor and subcontractors. In the case of the Fuzhounese he argued that,

> They are unique. They are victims of a large-scale and sophisticated international human smuggling network. After arrival in the US, they are forced to work for years under what amounts to indentured servi-tude to pay off large transportation debts, with constant threats of torture, rape and kidnapping.
>
> (Kwong, 1997:366)

Many live with the constant double fear 'of detection by immigration officials' and the 'threat of torture from fellow Chinese debt enforcers' (Kwong, 1997:367–368). The economic relationships in this labour dias-pora involve migrants from Fujian, southern China, traffickers ('Snake-heads'), labour contractors ('gang masters') and employers in the cities of the United States. Kwong (1998) estimated that Chinese traffickers charge migrants about US$1,000 as down payment, and if delivered successfully to the destination, have to pay the full fee, which ranges from US$10,000–50,000 and is deducted from future wages. The debt to finance the venture typically comes from family, friends or neighbours and come under legitimate moral pressure to repay. When a person cannot borrow sufficient sums they turn to loan sharks affiliated with the Snakeheads. In its traditional form, bonded labour involves a person who is tied, depend-ent and rendering services to another person, usually the person who has advanced the loan, in relationships which are direct and clear.

Restrictive immigration policies have contributed towards making the Fuzhounese into a phenomenon found in many Chinatowns in the United States and Europe, since Kwong's early description of the impact of a unique debt–bondage relationship in the structuring of New York's Chinese community. Whilst the literature has focused largely on North America (see Kwong, 1997, 1998; Chin, 1999), there is a growing literature in Europe on illegal Chinese migration and the 'invisible' phenomena within these communities (Skeldon, 2000; Salt, 2000). The International

Labour Office (ILO) in a report on Chinese migrants and forced labour in Europe, writes that 'global concern with human trafficking has risen quite dramatically in recent years'. Under the ILO's Convention No. 29, 'forced' or 'compulsory' labour is defined as 'all work or service which is extracted from any person under the menace of any penalty, and for which the said person has not offered himself [sic] voluntarily' (Yun, 2004:3). One manifestation of this condition appears, as Kwong observed, in the contemporary adaptation of traditional debtor–creditor bondage. The ILO notes that,

> In contemporary forms, the debtor–creditor relationship is more complicated and less direct due to the involvement of trafficker's. The labourer does not necessarily render services directly to the trafficker but rather works in the trafficker's interest. This is a form of covered or hidden debt bondage.
>
> (Yun, 2004:14)

Europe is a new destination and in the past most immigrants from Fujian had migrated to South-East Asia and lately North America (Pieke, 2002). Illegal Chinese immigrant labour is employed in the 'ethnic' economy but also in wider agricultural and industrial processing, where labour contractors ('gang masters') add another layer to the debtor–creditor bondage. The less an ethnic economy exists, as with more recent migrant labour from Eastern European, the more likely that they will be employed by native employers. Amongst the Chinese community in European cities, there appears to be a strong co-ethnic relation, in part to do with labour and trade diaspora linking various parts of China to Chinatowns and communities abroad (see Chapter 6). Workers describe their experiences as, 'we work like oxen, eat like pigs, and sleep in hens cages' (Beja and Chunguang, 1999:79). According to Pieke (2002:34), however, the possibility of entering the small enterprise sector at some future time, 'compensates for the period of working as a "slave"'.

It is worth reflecting on the Dover tragedy in the UK, during which nearly 60 Chinese illegal immigrants died for another purpose. According to Chinese community activist, Jabez Lam (2000:16) the local police were 'refusing to let relatives identify their loved ones until they first volunteered information about those who trade in refugees'. Relatives, even though they had legal status in Britain were too scared to claim the bodies. Ethnic stereotypes perpetuated about the Chinese community in Europe (and elsewhere) frequently focus on the Chinese community as an 'impenetrable' community, with illegal workers 'living in clandestinity and without legal rights of residence' (Yun, 2004:iii, 8). It is hardly surprising that illegal workers want to remain invisible and very likely that this kind of institutional behaviour drives people even further into the margins. Unlike other tragedies, there were no public announcements of sympathy or condolences from politicians or religious figures. One week after the deaths a demonstration to defend refugees made its way through London's Chinatown led by a group of Chinese restaurant workers (who in a rare show of militancy were trying to unionise their workplace) carrying a banner saying '58 Dead – Nothing Said'.

Whilst in diminishing proportions, uncle Tom, auntie Jemima and the underground railroad which smuggled slaves from the South to the abolitionist North elicit a positive response from liberal audiences, no such concessions are made for 'Snakeheads'. Let alone that they represent a form of transnational enterprise (see, Salt and Stein, 1997). The demonisation of human traffickers, detracts attention from the regulatory framework, processes of selectivity in immigration policy and the extent to which traffickers are a response to policies which make it impossible for many economic migrants to enter a country legally.

The ethnic 'labour queue'

Waldinger (1996a, 1996b) in analysing the structural incorporation of immigrant workers and entrepreneurs in New York and elsewhere, makes use of the terms 'ethnic niche', 'ethnic succession' and 'ethnic labour queue', to explain how minorities face, negotiate and generally overcome structural constraints they face in cities such as New York and Los Angeles.

The concept of the 'queue' draws from a long tradition of succession theories which share common assumptions in the familiar theme about the assimilationist prowess of American society. Waldinger provides a model of 'ethnic ordering' in New York which makes use of ecological succession and 'niche' theory to explain employment changes amongst minorities. Ethnic succession purports to show a 'straight-line' assimilation of the native-born or 'second-generation' immigrants, who benefit from acculturation and an enhanced social status which results in an economic improvement usually denied to 'first-generation' immigrants. The term 'niche' is borrowed from ecology where it is used to describe the interdependence of organisms in a community of plants and animals. Waldinger (1996a) points out that in every market economy, jobs are distributed according to the principles of desirability and availability. This is also affected, however, by prevailing ideas and practices in society both in Europe and the United States in which immigrants are ranked in terms of ethnic, racial, gender or religious characteristics, which form the basis for a pecking order, or queue. Typically, members of the dominant group are at the head and those with least economic power, such as first-generation immigrants, at the bottom. One necessary assumption made by Waldinger, is in the effect of upward social mobility amongst more established immigrant groups who, in vacating the lower levels of the queue, create vacancies which are filled by those in lower positions or by more recently arrived immigrants. It is this that Waldinger refers to as a 'game of ethnic musical chairs'. Another suggestion is that immigrants are primarily funnelled towards specialised economic activities by their own networks. In a familiar recap of migration network theory, as soon as the first wave have established themselves, others follow and thus, in time, chain migration results in ethnic concentrations and spatial and/or sectoral niches are formed. Waldinger and Lap extend the argument further and point to ethnic succession as a social mechanism in which 'the distribution of opportunities for informal income generation closely parallels the distribution of opportunities for income generation of any type' (Waldinger and Lapp, 1993:21).

There are many examples where immigrant workers and entrepreneurs or members of various ethnic groups, are concentrated in certain branches of trade and industry. We noted previously the term 'people-class' used by Abram Leon and Edna Bonacich to describe the association between particular groups of people, trades and economic functions, in both the experience of Jewish communities in pre-holocaust Europe and, less convincingly, in more general analyses of Middleman Minorities (see Chapter 2). Rath (2001) notes that niches can also appear in the form of labour diaspora. The experience of the Futzhounese is such an example. Frequently niches reflect on the opportunity structure, particularly for second-generation members of immigrant groups. They are also influenced by variation in the institutional framework regarding immigration policy and cyclical trends in global economic growth to which immigration has been linked during various historical periods.

Rath (2001) argues that Waldinger makes assumptions about durable migration networks and long historic periods in which there is continuous immigration, which itself is a necessary condition for the game of ethnic 'musical chairs'. This as he points out is subject to variation, with Europe, and more recently the United States, introducing more restrictive or selective immigration policies. Rath criticises Waldinger for exaggerating the role of durable ethnic social structures and migration networks and not giving sufficient attention to the role of the market, technological innovations and the institutional framework in the development of immigrant enterprise. Two pointed criticisms made by Rath are, first, that Waldinger supposes the long-term existence of more or less cohesive ethnic groups, with a large measure of solidarity and trust, 'when in reality, the social relationships are not often that harmonious' (Rath, 2001:25), as competitors, for example. More significantly, Rath points to the limited vision of ethnic political mobilisation, inherited in part from Tammany Hall, presented by Waldinger, as one where,

[he] seems to limit the role of the institutional framework to political arrangements steered by ethnic or racially based interest groups with the aim of influencing the allocation of jobs in the public sector. The

political system in New York is certainly not a blueprint for 'the' institutional framework.

(Rath, 2001:24)

Whilst Waldinger correctly points to the existence of a hierarchy of preferred population categories, this is not a factor sufficiently taken into account in his own work. For example, in an edited work entitled *Still the Promised City? African-Americans and New Immigrants in Postindustrial New York* (1996) – ostensibly a book about black New York – there is little explanation on the role of race in the game of 'musical chairs'. Indeed one a priori is the view, more widely articulated by William Wilson (1987), that racial 'discrimination has lost its force' in American society (Waldinger, 1996b:11). The grounds for (perverse) optimism are that since more African Americans work in New York's public sector rather than manufacturing, therefore, they have been little affected by declining employment in the manufacturing sector. According to Waldinger (1996b:81–82) African Americans have 'successfully adapted' to the postindustrial environment in New York and this is partly reflected in a 'growing internal stratification' within the community.

Whilst the rise in the significance of class in the black American community is an important phenomenon, it is debatable whether this has led to a diminishing significance for race in the social stratification of American society and barriers to entry in the enterprise spectrum. The relationship between race and imprisonment remains poignant. America has the highest rate of incarceration in the industrial world and for the first time the prison population exceeded two million people in 2003. Figures from the Federal Bureau of Justice Statistics indicate that 12 per cent of black men between the ages of 20 to 34 are in prison, compared with 1.6 per cent for white young males (Cornwell, 2003:10). In another report the Bureau of Justice indicates that black men born in 2001 will have a one in three chance of going to prison during their lifetime if current trends continue. These are rates of incarceration found only amongst the Palestinian population in West Bank and the Gaza Strip under Israeli occupation. With some justification, anti-custodial sentencing campaigners have argued that under these circumstances, 'prison had become the social policy of choice for low income people of colour' (Marc Mauer, assistant director of the Sentencing Project, quoted from Young, 2003:8; also see, Neale, 2004:87–111).

One critical factor in the incorporation of Dominican and other recently-arrived Hispanic immigrants from the Caribbean to the US, are processes of racialisation which intersect the relationship between ethnicity and race. Nancy Denton and Douglas Massey point to the particular racial traditions in the US, in which the black–white dichotomy typically shapes racial taxonomy, and subsumes the diverse racial codification (mulatto, Creole) common to the Hispanic and French Caribbean: *in extremis*, C. L. R. James (1980) pointed, in *The Black Jacobins*, to circumstances where the legal system of the French colony of Haiti recognised 147 different shades of colour between black and white. Denton and Massey (1989:790) in a breakdown of the 1970 and 1980 US Census data relevant to Hispanic and race, show that in residential terms 'people of mixed racial ancestry are accepted by white Hispanics on the basis of shared ethnicity but are rejected by Anglos on the basis of race'. Further, that 'Anglos will view people of mixed race as black no matter how they see themselves' (1989:802).

Similarly, Emily Rosenbaum's (1996:217) research on the influence of race in Hispanic housing choices in New York City, indicates that racial status determined where Hispanics moved and that 'white Hispanics are more successful than black Hispanics and other-race Hispanics in gaining access to predominantly Anglo sub areas, apparently by virtue of their non-black status'. One implication of this line of inquiry is that it reveals the persistence of race in the structuring of American society. More significantly, perhaps, it reflects on the incorporation of immigrant groups i.e. the most recently-arrived entrants into 'Americanization'. In their case, people who have never thought of themselves as 'black' in their own countries, have been forced to do so in the United States. Practically, this means that Hispanics of different colour are defined as 'Black' and live in similar (racially segregated) neighbourhoods as those of other black Americans, whilst many white Hispanics have the option, and many exercise that option, of moving out of the neighbourhood. The relationship between race and ethnicity is an important and recurring theme in Hispanic immigration and settlement (see Chapter 5). The above is one of many examples (others include gender) which suggests that ethnicity and ethnic succession is more complex and anything but a benign game of 'musical chairs'.

Conclusions

New York is a laboratory of human endeavour. Nowhere is this more applicable than as a description of the ingenuity of the immigrant masses and entrepreneurs who shaped and continue to shape its development. Irish political patrons in Tammany Hall gave us an early example of 'mixed embeddedness'. With one foot in the ward and the other in the Town Hall these brokers could identify each name on the electoral register and offer appropriate inducement. The experience of Jewish immigration is an early example of occupational clustering and social differentiation. How we analyse immigrant enterprise depends on the framework we adopt. Analyses rooted in structural functionalism look to the social structures of an ethnic community to provide explanation for competitive advantage in small business industries. Waldinger and others argue, in a familiar refrain about hyper-efficient migration networks, that networks of successive waves of immigrants, in lowering wages in the New York's garment industry and other sectors relying on the manual trades, have been a critical factor in the revitalisation of the local economy and run-down areas of New York City. Sassen places more emphasis on the complimentary effects of economic restructuring, the role of the 'informal sector' and 'trust' in shaping immigrant economic transactions.

Analyses rooted in theories of social stratification and social conflict question some of these basic assumptions. Frequently no distinction is made between 'immigrant' and 'ethnic'. Rather, as Jan Rath (2000:5) argues, Waldinger *et al.* 'assume that immigrants constitute ethnic groups and that their economic activities are mainly ethnic by nature'. Little attention is given to the role of immigration controls and selectivity in immigration policy and institutional behaviour as an important continuity which is a significant formative experience in itself. Analyses, such as by Kwong, provide insight into New York's Chinatown and other ethnic enclaves, and raise uncomfortable questions about the substance of ethnic paternalism, the nature of transnational communities and sectoral dynamics which surface in studies of trade and labour diaspora. These point to the external relationships with markets and the institutional framework and how these structure the internal relationships of the community (see also, Mahler, 1995). These constitute attempts to assess the specific impact of social and economic differentiation inside immigrant communities. Processes of racialisation and social differentiation are rarely revealed in the rooted assumptions of theories about homogeneous ethnic communities (such as Waldinger's), and their tendency to ignore conflict within immigrant communities and present, therefore, compliant histories and communities. Neither are processes of differentiation revealed in theories rooted in globalisation and economic restructuring (such as Sassen's) which point, in many cases correctly, to the role of local variation, sectoral detail, historical circumstance and restructuring, in the positioning and repositioning of immigrant workers to immigrant entrepreneurs. One general criticism of theories rooted in labour transfer and labour market incorporation is that these ideas do not fully take into account the accumulated impact of employment generated by immigrant-owned enterprises or the impact of economic differentiation between immigrant enterprises themselves.

4 Miami

The end of the Cuban ethnic enclave?

Introduction

Demographic projections indicate that by 2050 the Hispanic population will become the largest minority in US. Cubans are a small proportion of Hispanic immigrants but are highly concentrated in Dade County, Florida (which includes Miami). The historical development of the Cuban community becomes a microcosm of wider processes. It reflects on the role of ethnic mobilisations in the USA. In Miami attempts to end mother-tongue education during the mid-1980s galvanised the Cuban community into creating its first self-defence organisations. The Cuban community also reflects on specific characteristics. It is a spatially concentrated community of political exiles which captured City Hall and then remade the city in its own political image. The conventional analyses for Cuban immigrant enterprise, points to the 'bounded solidarity' and social capital of political exiles as essential mechanisms in transformation from political exiles to ethnic entrepreneurs.

Alejandro Portes and Leif Jensen (1987) point to the high concentration of enterprise as an 'enclave economy'. It is argued that immigrants in the enclave labour market, far from being disadvantaged in separation, receive earnings-returns to human capital commensurate with the earnings-returns of immigrants in the open labour market. The ethnic enclave is presented as an effective vehicle for upward mobility among immigrants. This chapter debates the enclave economy thesis by pointing to the classical assimilation view, based in substantial historical justification, that segregation tends to retard the economic achievement of minorities. The chapter argues that the enclave can be understood as both a process of social exclusion and as means for social mobility amongst Cuban immigrants. The proposition that different outcomes are possible between members of the same ethnic or immigrant group, is one criticism of the ethnic enclave thesis. This line of thinking suggests that the enclave economy thesis needs to be sensitive to differences between immigrant workers and immigrant bosses and between self-employment and the employment of others. On a wider level, we need to understand how

Cuban society in Miami is socially stratified in terms of race, gender and generational differences.

Given that the enclave economy thesis began out of Miami research, and subsequently applied to other areas, the chapter acquires increased significance.

Cuban Miami

Hispanic enterprise is a growing phenomenon in the US. One indication is the estimated 80,000 Hispanic Avon ladies, retailing a cosmetic and jewellery brochure specifically designed for Hispanic customers. The term 'Hispanic' refers to immigrants from Mexico, Cuba, Puerto Rico, the Dominican Republic and other Central and South American and Caribbean origins. The 2000 Census enumerated 35 million Hispanics, up from 22 million in 1990. They make up 12.5 per cent of the population and have overtaken blacks as the largest minority in the US. It is estimated that by 2010 Hispanics will make up one third of the US population and currently account for an estimated $580bn spending power. One indication is the growth in advertising spending on Spanish language television by leading companies. Another illustration on the role of Hispanics in American society is that an estimated 13.5 per cent of registered voters in 2005 were of Hispanic origins and, repeatedly, in the State of Florida played a pivotal role in Presidential elections. Mexican immigrants (at 65.2 per cent) make up the vast bulk of Hispanics in the US, followed by Central and Southern Americans (at 14.3 per cent) and Puerto Ricans (at 9.6 per cent). Cubans make a relatively small portion (4.3 per cent) of the overall US Hispanic population and (at 3.6 per cent) a small proportion of all US immigrants (Waldinger, 2001a:315; Yeager, 2000:10, 2002:11).

If Mexican immigration to the State of California defines the bulk of movement by Hispanics to the US (see Chapter 5), nowhere is the presence of Hispanic enterprise more apparent than Miami. Miami is a Hispanic Cuban city but also a black, white, Jewish and American city, where many retired persons from New York City and elsewhere try to find comfort in Florida's warm climate. The number of Hispanics in Miami increased from 50,000 in 1960 to 1,000,000 by 1990. This substantially drove Miami's quadrupling of population between 1950 to 1990 from 500,000 to two million persons, despite four decades of decline in the white (non-Hispanic) population in the Metropolitan Miami area, to less than one third of the total population by 1990 (Portes and Stepick, 1993:210). The evolution of the Hispanic Cuban community in Miami was defined by key moments – not least of all political exile – which gave the community particular characteristics (summary below) (see, Portes and Stepick, 1993; Portes, 1984; Portes and Bach, 1985; Wilson and Portes, 1980).

The evolution of Cuban Miami

- *Political exile* following the Cuban Revolution in 1959, first by officials of the deposed Batista regime and subsequently by large sections of the middle classes. Fiercely anti-communist, many of the exiles acted as proxies for the Central Intelligence Agency (CIA) in the abortive invasion of Cuba in the 1962 Bay of Pigs fiasco, and subsequent attempts to destabilise the Cuban economy.
- *High spatial concentration* with 65 per cent of all Cubans in the US living in the Miami Metropolitan Area, making them 'far more concentrated in one place than any other group' (Waldinger and Lee, 2001:48) and also in particular neighbourhoods within Miami itself, typified by 'Little Havana', which stands next to Liberty Hall, the largest black area in Miami.
- *Transformed by the impact of 'Mariel'* distress migration caused by the collapse of the Cuban economy during 1980, and changes this entailed in the class and racial composition of Cuban immigrants, as well as by the exceptional hostility shown towards these immigrants both by the US authorities and Cuban Government.
- *Political mobilisation*, initially in order to defend bilingual education under threat by proposed anti-bilingual legislation in Dade County, which includes Miami, and also in part, in support of the *Marielitos*. Ethnic mobilisation was subsequently applied by Cuban political patrons to the capture of political power in Miami.

The particular evolution of a community of anti-communist political exiles, forms the basis of much of the argument which points to the 'exceptional' nature of Cuban Miami. The Bay of Pigs fiasco, named after the Cuban shoreline where the CIA and Cuban exiles landed in 1962 and were routed, is an illustration. During the run up to the invasion the CIA was a major employer in Miami and its funds were an important source of income for many of the newly-arrived exiles. The role of political exile in shaping the Cuban ethnic enclave in Miami – lodged opposite Cuba – led Portes and Stepick (1993:204) to view the development of Miami as 'economically undetermined [...] a city more the product of chance and individual wills than of geographic or commercial imperative'. The origins of Cuban Miami lie in the first wave of political exiles who fled the Revolution in 1959, and which was initially made up of panic-stricken officials of the deposed Batista regime, other sections of the white Hispanic elite and the numerically more significant middle classes. Approximately 135,000 people arrived between 1959 and April 1961. The Hispanic population of Miami consisted of 50,000 people in 1960 and had grown by 1970 to 580,000 (Portes and Stepick, 1993:102, 211). Over half of all Cuban immigrants arrived in the US before 1980 (Clark, 2003:36).

After 1980, Cuban Miami was significantly reshaped by the *Mariel Exodus*. This began during April 1980 in the form of mass demonstrations by tens of thousands of Cubans who forced their way into the Peruvian Embassy demanding refugee status, the right to migrate and in many cases to reunite with families in Florida. This severely embarrassed the Cuban government which was forced by sheer force of numbers to open the Port of Mariel for all who wanted to leave. The circumstances in which Mariel took place were complex, but not substantially different from other circumstances which produce flows of economic and political refugees from other poor Third World countries, such as neighbouring Haiti. In this instance, refugees fled a collapsed economy characterised by a shortage of basic commodities – foodstuffs, petrol, insulin and other pharmaceuticals – an area in which Cuba is today acknowledged as a significant force. The collapse of the Soviet Union destroyed the sugar-for-petrol arrangement which drove economic policy for 30 years. The accumulated impact of the US embargo at this junction was particularly damaging to Cuba's attempts to restructure and reorientate its economy, increasingly towards tourism. The embargo was a major contributor towards the increase in poverty and malnourishment which appeared in Cuba for the first time since the Revolution. Fidel Castro's talk during 1980 of 'Year Zero', was an uncomfortable (and unintentioned) simile with phraseology used by Pol Pot in Cambodia. By 1980, even black Cubans – the bedrock of the Cuban Revolution – had enough and were leaving in droves.

Sieges of foreign embassies to obtain exit permits, and organised flotillas from Miami funded by relatives to ferry the *Marielitos*, initially characterised the 1980 events. Hundreds of boats picked up over 125,000 people, most of whom settled in Dade County. This gave way – given the large number of refugees – to mass and disorganised waves of 'boat people' heading towards Florida on anything that floated, with Miami and family reunion, in many cases, as a goal. At the same time, thousands of Haitian refugees, similarly escaping poverty and economic and political crisis, also headed for Miami and New York. During mid-May something like 50,000 people were camped in emergency accommodation in the Orange Bowl and in public land (Portes and Stepick, 1993:47). The arrival of many working class and black *Marielitos* was a shocking experience for the established white Cuban community in Miami. One white Cuban American official commented that 'the *Marielitos* are mostly Black and mulattoes of a color that I never saw or believed existed in Cuba' (quoted from Portes and Stepick, 1993:21). They were subjected to unusual hostility. Newspaper stories of 'undesirables' and 'Castro emptying his jails' fuelled hostility. Mariel refugees were stigmatised nationwide *and* within the Cuban community.

In *A Statement by the Revolutionary Government of Cuba*, published in *Granma*, the official organ of the Central Committee of the Communist Party of Cuba, Cuba's position on the *Marielitos* was made perfectly clear. They were referred to as 'common criminals and lumpen elements' or, alternatively, 'criminals, lumpen and anti-social elements and parasites'.

Granma further commented, that 'To judge from their dress, manners and language, seldom has such as "select" group gathered anywhere', and to further clarify, added,

> Even though in our country homosexuals are not persecuted or harassed, there are quite of few of them in the Peruvian embassy, aside from all those involved in gambling and drugs who find it diffi-cult to satisfy their vices here [...] Good riddance to the parasites! Good riddance to the antisocial elements! Good riddance to the lumpen! Good riddance to the scum!.
>
> ('Cuba's Position', *Granma*, 7 April 1980)

The White House also took a hard line on mass asylum, clarifying that Cuban and Haitian boat people, also fleeing poverty, if intercepted at sea would not be allowed to enter the United States. This, as Tichenor (2002:278–279) noted, 'marked a significant break from three decades of treating all Cuban escapees as refugees'. This contrasted sharply with the 300,000 admissions of Indo-Chinese refugees between 1975 and 1979 alone, all admitted under executive paroles (Tichenor, 2002:246; Portes and Rumbaut, 2001:275). The widely held belief that Cuba was emptying its jails and dumping undesirables on the shores of Florida, legitimised changes in US immigration policy. This view was confirmed in one study, which indicated that 42.25 per cent of all persons who left Cuba through the port of Mariel, had previous convictions. The single largest category came from Cuba's poor, as indicated in 40 per cent of all those with 'previ-ous' involving crimes against property (primarily theft). The second largest group of convictions (10.8 per cent) were for 'crimes against the normal development of sexual relations', charges used routinely to criminalise Cuba's gay community (Portes and Stepick, 1993:21). Far from being 'lumpen', the large numbers of *Marielitos* probably represented a far more accurate reflection of the breadth of Cuban society than the white, middle-class counter-revolutionaries who fled Cuba in 1959, and who had domin-ated the community in Miami since then. The new wave of refugees were met, in some cases, by Ku Klux Klan members burning crosses on beaches and shouting 'Spics Go Home'. This atmosphere was compounded by the return of American nativism in the form of the Anglo-dominated Citizens of Dade County, who placed on the ballot box for referendum, a proposi-tion that would have prohibited expenditure of any county funds for the purpose of using 'any language other than English or any culture other than that of the United States' (Portes and Stepick, 1993:161). The 'English Only' campaign directed primarily against Cuban but also other Hispanics, 'galvanised the refugee community into creating its first self defence organisations' (Portes, 1984:395).

During the decade following Mariel (1980–1990) the Hispanic popu-lation of Miami increased from 580,000 to 953,000 people (Portes and

Stepick, 1993:210). Not only did this represent a significant increase, but also a qualitative change in the make-up of the Cuban community in Miami. The defeat of the anti-bilingual proposal also gave the Cuban community more confidence. In a manner similar to the experience of Irish immigrants in nineteenth century New York, the 1980s saw the consolidation of Cuban control of local political institutions. The words 'take over', were frequently cited by both Anglos and black Americans. In part this reflected a high spatial concentration within which immigrants have political rights. The enclave economy is also a spatial phenomenon. This resulted in the political capture of City Hall by Cuban immigrants, who as Stepick and Portes argue, 'started to remake the city in its political own image' and 'as the Cuban community gained political power it imposed a monolithic outlook on the city, often with little regard for the concerns and interests of other sections of the population' (1993:138). One (of many) examples, which sums up the intolerance of the anti-communist, right-wing political leadership which dominates the Cuban community, involved Nelson Mandela. During summer 1990 the recently released Mandela was to arrive in Miami. The black community were exuberant about a visit from a leading figure of black liberation. When Nelson Mandela said (what was public knowledge) that he considered Fidel Castro a friend, who helped in the struggle against apartheid,

> Over the strenuous objections of Black community leaders, the Cuban-American mayors 'uninvited' Mandela. Although [he] came for a brief speech at a union convention and never accepted any local invitation, the mayors' action profoundly hurt Miami's Black community.
>
> (Portes and Stepick, 1993:141)

Blacks responded by a boycott of their own city, asking tourists and visitors to stay away until the mayors apologised. None of them did. This incident can be seen as representative of Cuban–black relations, in what Stepick *et al.* (2003) refer to as 'Miami's Cuban takeover'. Another high-profile incident which polarised Miami, including the Cuban community itself, was the case of Ellian Gonzalez – a young boy rescued from the sea when his mother died – and who was held prisoner by relatives and non-relatives in Miami against the wishes of his own father in Cuba. Eventually he was allowed to return home.

The ethnic enclave economy

The ethnic enclave economy thesis reflects on the ethnic mobilisations in the USA from the 1960s and the continuing crisis of US modernisation sociology and its assimilationist assumptions (see Chapter 2). A concentrated microcosm appears in the experience of the Cuban community in

Florida (Dade County, includes Miami). Portes and Jensen point to the ethnic enclave economy hypothesis as an attempt at explaining the positioning (and repositioning) of Cuban immigrants, which is critical of conventional theories of structural incorporation and assimilation. The enclave economy thesis – with minority-owned enterprise as its centre – proposes that, 'Immigrants in the enclave-labour market, far from being disadvantaged in separation, receive earnings-returns to human capital commensurate with the earnings-returns of immigrants in the primary labour market' (Portes and Jensen 1989:929–949).

The key assumption of the ethnic enclave economy thesis is its role as 'an effective vehicle for upward mobility among immigrant minorities' (Portes and Jensen, 1989:930) and, more specifically still, as 'a vehicle for first-generation upward mobility' (Portes and Jensen, 1987:769). Employers in the enclave, it is argued, come under pressure to assist co-ethnic workers in their own entry into entrepreneurship, self-employment and as petty or larger-scale employers. A recap of the conventional argument points to the 'bounded solidarity' and social capital of political exiles, as essential mechanisms in transformation from political exiles to ethnic entrepreneurs. This was facilitated by shared language and culture combined with closely-knit social networks and practices such as the tendency to patronise other Cuban-owned businesses and to prefer co-nationals as business associates (Portes and Stepick, 1993:135).

Portes and Jensen (1987:769; also see Stepick *et al.*, 2003) argue that they are not advancing a 'separate but equal' proposition. As they write, 'enclave workers and businessmen are neither "separate" (because their activities are closely intertwined with the broader economy), nor necessarily "equal" (because new arrivals are often much worse off in terms of occupational status and income)'.

The thesis originated in Wilson and Portes' (1980) analyses the Cuban enclave labour market. Within this discourse, concepts such as the split labour market and labour market segmentation are typically used to explain the positioning of immigrant workers. These ideas developed in the 1960s, partly in order to offer explanation for persistent labour market inequalities in American society (a continuing theme) but also as a response to the more general crisis of assimilation and modernisation theory. Light and Gold (2000:12–13) note that the earliest formulation of the ethnic enclave economy thesis by Wilson and Portes made use of dual labour market theory. It is for this reason that the enclave was originally defined as composed of co-ethnic bosses and workers. Subsequently, in Portes (1981) it was refined to include the self-employed, 'the first time dual labor market theorists had done so'. In other work (Portes and Bach, 1985) there is a reversion to its original formulation. Light refined the ethnic economy further to include 'the self-employed, employers, their co-ethnic employees and their unpaid family workers' (Light and Karageorgis, 1994:663).

The original concerns of Wilson and Portes' research, was the enclave made up of the large bulk of men employed in Cuban-owned firms. They began with concerns about the labour market because they were trying to understand the experience of the majority of the Cuban community who, as with other communities, are wage workers. One influence on Portes' early work was radical dependency theory, a variant of world system theory, applied amongst others, to analyses of international migration and Third World urban labour markets (see Portes, 1981:71–92). The 'informal sector' debate was a significant landmark in the literature of this period (see Gerry, 1987:101–119) and one which finds similarities with discussion on immigrant enterprise today. Wilson and Portes began from labour market theory because they saw the immigrant refugees and political exiles as a peculiar example of labour transfer. Whilst the model was extended to include the self-employed, wage workers and employers, one weakness remains in the non-disaggregation of these quite distinct employment categories and income groups.

Wilson and Portes (1980) argued that in Miami, protracted Cuban economic relations and retentive value adding activities differed in intensity from those typically associated with other ethnic economies. Substantial clustering and 'dense' co-ethnic links gave the Cuban ethnic economy an 'enclave' character. Horizontal and vertical linkages build on ethnic networks, trust and a common language underpinned the economic activities of the enclave. The locational cluster of Miami's Little Havana gave the Cuban economy a vibrant and concentrated nature which went beyond ethnic economies associated with other Hispanic immigrant groups. In comparing Cuban and Mexican immigrants they concluded, in rather general terms, that due to the absence of spatial clustering and many immigrant-owned firms which generated large numbers of jobs, Mexican immigrants were incorporated into 'low wage labor in the open economy' whist Cubans benefited from a 'setting dominated by business networks' (Portes and Bach, 1985:268).

Waldinger (2001a:318) points to the distinctive economic structure of Miami as not particularly fertile ground for social mobility amongst immigrant groups. It is part of a low wage region, 'a peripheral region of the world economy', with a limited manufacturing sector, a small representation for professional and advanced services and lack of opportunities when compared to other US cities. All the more remarkable then, as Waldinger writes, that it is 'still possible to conclude that the Cuban story is one of success'. One way of presenting the argument in labour market terms, is to note that in 1960, 46 per cent of Miami's citizens were foreign born and today it stands at 43 per cent (Harris, 2002:17; Clark 2003:39). Nearly one million people fled Cuba during the 1980s. Yet, as Harris observes, 'there were no effects seen in local unemployment levels' (2002:60).

Few Cuban businesses existed in Miami before 1962 and in this period the CIA was 'one of Miami's largest employers' (Portes and Stepick,

1993:126). Portes and Stepick summarise the early experience of the Cuban enclave as a response to constraint and opportunity. Opportunity appeared in the substantial ethnic Cuban market which generated the basis for many small firms and the self-employed and in 'privileged access to a pool of cheap labour' enjoyed by co-ethnic entrepreneurs. Constraint appeared mainly in barriers to accessing the commercial banking sector. By 1987, nearly 35,000 Cuban-owned enterprises existed in Dade County and Miami Metropolitan Area. The vast bulk consisted of the self-employed, but a significant proportion (one in six) employed other workers (Portes and Stepick, 1993:182).

Entry into enterprise followed a predictable sectoral trajectory. First came the gas stations, then came grocery shops and restaurants. Many used their skills as carpenters, plumbers and bricklayers to enter construction. They 'created their own home repair businesses by buying a truck and going door-to-door seeking work' and by 1979, approximately 50 per cent of major construction companies in Dade County were Cuban-owned (Portes and Stepick, 1993:133). From this followed entry into real estate. The concentration of Hispanic labour in the garment, construction, hotel and restaurant sectors, is an indicator of sectors in which Cuban entrepreneurs are located. In garment employment, by 1980, 82.6 per cent of all workers were Hispanic. In the other sectors it was between 30 and 40 per cent of all workers employed (Portes and Stepick, 1993:41).

Many entered low capital sectors, restaurants, construction, either as self-employed, or as owners of small enterprises which generated employment for others. The sectors are amongst the easiest to enter and as such generate immense competition. At the same time, many have come out of the fringes and have differentiated themselves from the ranks of the self-employed and subcontractors. Cuban enterprises in Miami are critical to the local labour market and monopolise particular sectors. Ethnic solidarity and networks in the Cuban enclave were used to generate 'character loans', as a means of circumventing restricted access to the commercial banking sector. Effectively, many mainstream banks realised the economic potential of the Cuban enclave and responded through the employment of Cuban staff and venture lending in which character acted *as* collateral. This implies more than the standard commercial knowledge, complicated by ever-changing credit managers. Portes and Stepick summarise the experience of one Cuban entrepreneur's experience of differing banking styles in this way,

> The American banker looks only at the balance sheet of the company. If he doesn't like it, he doesn't give you the loan. The Cuban banker has a different technique: he [sic] looks for signs of your character. If he knows you, knows that you will meet your obligations, he lends you without looking at the balance sheet [...] they often even knew their families in Cuba.
>
> (Portes and Stepick, 1993:133)

The garment industry was one early example of employment concentration by Cuban immigrants and one which played a strategic role, both in the maintenance of the community's integrity and in the development of enterprise. It began when New York Jewish garment manufacturers relocating production to low-union Southern States identified the Cuban community in Miami and in particular Cuban refugee women, as a low-wage recourse. Many of them were skilled sewing machinists. One estimation made by New York manufacturers was that 'bounded solidarity and trust enable employers in ethnic enclaves to demand greater discipline and effort from their workers' (Portes, 1995a:29). This created the conditions for garment production in Miami. By the middle 1980s, 'between 30 to 50 per cent of local garment production was traceable to homework' (Portes, 1994:435–436). One factor in the growth of homeworking was that many Cuban women progressively moved from factory work to homework under pressure from husbands and fathers, driven by 'cultural norms stemming from traditional Latin family norms' (Portes, 1995a:31). Under circumstances in which many factories in the Miami garment industry faced labour shortages due to a 'massive' shift in women's employment from garment factories to homeworking, and as the only initially available labour force, (at the time) Cuban first generation women remain in high demand. Stepick (1989: 116–118) points to the pay of homeworkers keeping pace with the minimum wage. Today, 15,000 workers – most Cuban women – sew the latest fashions in Miami. As Grennier and Stepick note,

> The large scale employment of Cuban women in the needle trade had two important consequences. First it allowed families to stay in Miami and bought time for husbands to learn English and find some local business niche. And second, in itself created some of these niches through independent subcontracting.
>
> (2002:137)

Perhaps, the most favourable conclusions which can be drawn about the Cuban ethnic enclave, are presented by Light and Gold (2000:97–98) in analyses of the post-Mariel environment, where they ask (rhetorically), 'why the penniless Haitian refugees in Miami have not been so successful in business as the penniless Cuban refugees in creating a prosperous ethnic enclave economy'. The answer is that 'Cubans in Miami retained their social capital, their human capital, and their cultural capital', and at the same time, developed class resources. Haitians in reverse lacked all the above and were poorer than Cubans, even though 'their level of material deprivation was initially the same'. In comparing Cuban and Haitian refugees, they point to the existence of a vibrant Cuban economy in Miami, which was responsible for absorbing nearly half (46.1 per cent) of the *Marielitos*, whilst amongst Haitian refugees it stood at less than 1

Table 4.1 Cuban and Haitian refugees: employment in Miami (1980) (per cent)

Type of economy	Cuban Mariel refugees	Haitian refugees
Immigrant economy		
Self-employed	15.2	0.5
Working in co-ethnic firm	30.9	0.2
General labour market		
Unemployed	26.8	58.5
Employees	27.1	40.8
Total	100.0	100.0

Source: Stepick 1989, cited from Light and Gold, 2000:44.

per cent (0.7 per cent). Those in self-employment made up 15.2 per cent of the total, whilst a larger proportion (30.9 per cent), were working in co-ethnically owned enterprises. An even larger proportion (53.1 per cent), however, were either employed in the general labour market (37.1 per cent) or were unemployed (26.8 per cent). Amongst Haitian refugees the unemployed made up over half (58.8 per cent) of the total (see Table 4.1).

Criticism of the ethnic enclave thesis

The ethnic enclave thesis as an analyses of labour market incorporation and explanation for social mobility amongst an immigrant group, raises important issues for debate. The argument by Portes and others that immigrants can earn similar returns to human capital in the enclave economy, as those associated with the wider economy, remains a point of intense debate. Another view grounded in theories of social stratification would point to ethnic enclave, both as product of social inequality and as means of social mobility amongst different sections of Cuban immigrants. This calls for the disaggregation of the Cuban community into social and economic categories and the need to analyse the distribution of the benefits of immigrant enterprise. Sanders and Nee (1987a:745) suggest the need to reformulate the enclave economy hypothesis so that it is 'sensitive to important differences between immigrant-workers and immigrant bosses'. They question the methodology applied by Portes and Bach, for failing to make a distinction between self-employment and the employment of others and for ignoring previous findings (Portes and Bach, 1985: 205–216), which 'report significant [income] differences between workers and bosses in the Cuban enclave', when estimating returns to human capital (Sanders and Nee, 1987a:747–748).

Frequently it depends what we are measuring (see Sanders and Nee, 1992, 1996). If we are measuring average returns to labour in the immigrant or ethnic economy when compared to the general labour market, as was the case with the ethnic enclave thesis, then this would disguise the possibility that entrepreneurship might produce a small but significant number of high income earners and a large mass of low paid hired workers. If we were to measure the redistributory impact of immigrant enterprise in income terms by class, gender, age and race, we might see differing trends and outcomes for different sections of the Cuban enclave. We note for example, that character loans are effectively class loans. Professionals and white-collar workers and 'those who brought money and contacts from Cuba [...] were more likely to access character loans' (Portes and Stepick, 1993:128), than workers or the *Marielitos* when compared to other classes and the elite exiles from 1959.

On a wider level we need to understand how the Cuban community in Miami is socially stratified. We note for example the impact on women of gender relations in the garment industry which manifests itself in global comparisons, in pressure on women towards homeworking. Labour market incorporation in the form of homeworking is found in the garment industry worldwide and, as such, may be impervious to particular ethnic categories, such as 'Latin'. The sexual division of labour in the garment industry (and the domiciliation of women) is a common enough phenomenon in diverse immigrant communities, from Chinatown in New York, to the Bangladeshi and Greek Cypriot communities in London and elsewhere (see Chapters 3, 9, 10). Whilst Cuban women machinists might be at a premium in the enclave economy, homeworking frequently involves the loss of rights by invisible and in many cases unregistered workers. It is largely due to this, that minimum pay legislation cannot reach those who are most likely to benefit from it.

The growing complexity of the Cuban enclave is reflected in generational differences. At one level there are differences between 'first'- and 'second'-generation immigrants of Cuban origins. At another level, there are qualitative differences between different waves of refugees. The elite exiles who fled the Cuban Revolution in 1959 and the *Marielitos* who fled during the mass exodus in 1980, represented different sections of Cuban society. The working-class and black *Marielitos* faced far more difficult circumstances than the exiles from 1959, who found an early niche as political entrepreneurs in the anti-communism industry. The differences between first and subsequent generations have also become more pronounced. The 'mummies' who have run the Cuban community in Miami since 1959 and their intolerance and arrogance towards the *Marielitos* and other refugee groups, such as Haitian and Nicaraguan refugees fleeing poverty and the US sponsored Contra War, have alienated many of the younger Cuban generation and have provoked a growing (class) polarisation inside the Cuban community. In one survey of perceptions and experiences of discrimination by Mariel refugees carried out in 1983 (three years after Mariel), 75 per cent of a random sample of 520 believed that 'Mariel Cubans are discriminated against by older-established Cubans' and that 52 per cent had 'personally experienced [such] discrimination' (Portes and Stepick, 1993:33).

The complex relationship between ethnicity and race in Hispanic immigrant communities, whilst it became more acutely posed in the Cuban enclave under the impact of Mariel, has not been fully noticed or recognised. Portes and Stepick (1993:41) in commentary on US Census Statistics write that 'in 1970 and 1980 Dade County had relatively few black Cubans or black Latin Americans, so the category "Black" and "Spanish" may be taken as mutually exclusive'. Elsewhere they note that for 1980, 11,000 persons and, for 1990, 28,300 persons were reported as 'blacks of Hispanic origin'. In 1990 those enumerated made up a small but significant section of the 'Hispanic' population (at 28,300 out of 953,000) (Portes and Stepick, 1993:211). Yet, little concern or special analyses is applied in explaining the relationship between race and ethnicity in the positioning of black Cubans in the enclave. It is a non-question, which hides behind not easily available data. At the same time, we do know that the reductionist racial bi-polarity in the US, dispenses with the categorisation of different colours and races and collapses them into 'White' or 'Black'. As with the experience of other non-white Hispanics (Dominican, Haitian) in cities such as New York and Los Angeles, many black Cubans also come under pressure by US racial taxonomy, towards racially specific modes of incorporation, such as pressures to reside in racially segregated neighbourhoods where other 'black' Americans live.

One telling criticism of the ethnic enclave thesis is the argument, presented by Sanders and Nee, which constitutes a theoretical defence of the key lesson learned from conventional sociology. Namely, that exclusion (such as in the form of the ethnic enclave or ghetto) and in particular the persistence of racial exclusion in the US, has generally not been in the interest of most members of the excluded group. Indeed, the demand for integration was the central plank of the Civil Rights Movement in the southern States. Sanders and Nee argue that the enclave economy hypothesis, 'contradicts the classical assimilation view that segregation retards the economic achievement of minorities' (1987a:745). In counter-defence, Portes and others argue that far from contradicting these views, the enclave economy thesis by pointing towards immigrant enterprise as a vehicle for upward social mobility by first-generation immigrants, can be seen as an *alternative* path to integration and assimilation. Portes *et al.* offer a model of integration which remains critical of conventional models of incorporation within which 'Americanization', rather than the acceptance of cultural diversity, was and remains in large part the end product. They invite studies on the social and economic development of second-generation immigrant workers and entrepreneurs, and the extent to which the ethnic enclave has acted in the long term (and by tortuous detours) as an agency for an economic and social integration. One conclusion on the ethnic enclave thesis is that the case is not proven. In order to show that the enclave has redistributory functions which result in social mobility for all or most members of an immigrant or ethnic group, we need to move beyond a trickle-down theory of income distribution and returns to human capital. We need to know more about the social political as well as economic structure of the enclave and how this, and the economy in general, impacts on the lives of different section of Cubans in Miami over time.

Conclusions

Immigrant entrepreneurs have played a major role in transforming what was a peripheral region of the US economy. Miami today is a global city and serves an important function as a continental intermediary between Latin and North America. In retrospect, the analyses by Portes and Stepick (1993) of the Cuban ethnic enclave in Miami, can also be in part understood as an early study of globalisation 'from below', albeit with large parts of it in cahoots with the US Defence Department. During the 1990s, accounts held by Latin American citizens in Miami, were equivalent to the total debt owed by Latin American countries to private creditors and the World Bank. There are widely-held views about the Cuban community in Miami as an 'achieving minority'. Frequently studies write of the 'remarkable success' of the Cuban exiles or the 'unique character' of the Cuban experience. Clark (2003:213–214) in a study of immigration and the 'remaking' of the American middle class, points to Cubans as an 'achieving' minority and writes that 'the children of Mexican immigrant meat packers in Omaha, Nebraska, do not have the same advantages as children of Cuban businessmen in suburban Dade County, Florida (Miami)'.

We noted that one conventional explanation offered (by Portes, Stepick, Bach) points towards a complex vision of 'success', substantially driven by the role of enterprise. Other explanations point towards grand political narratives of a community complicit and benefiting as an anti-communist 'show-case'. This account reflects on globalisation 'from above' and the treatment of the initial wave of political exiles as a favoured client group of US foreign policy. Waldinger (2001a:317) writes that 'macro political factors lie at the root of the Cuban ethnic enclave'. The transformation of mass waves of political exiles into entrepreneurs forms the basis of an 'exceptionalism' made in most analyses of Cuban incorporation in Miami. Waldinger (2001a:315) points to a picture 'unlikely to have been encountered elsewhere'. Yet, macro-politics – particularly those resulting in mass refugee status which create the basis for spatial concentration and an 'ethnic' economy – have been a significant factor in structuring immigrant communities in many countries, and this challenges some of the assumptions of 'exceptionalism'. There are many comparable experiences, most notably, the *Aussiedler* migration between 1945 and 1955 – comprised of 12 million people of German 'descent' who fled Eastern Europe to West Germany (Geddes, 2003:79) and the estimated five to seven million people repatriated to Europe following decolonisation. An estimated 300,000 exiles from the East Indies (Indonesia) to the Nether-lands, 800,000 *retornados* from Angola and Mozambique to Portugal and the over one million *pied-noir* from Algeria to France. As with Cuban refugees, one continuity appears in the massive and unexpected arrival of thousands of people during compressed periods of time. Most *retornados* arrived between 1974 and 1976 and made up 15 per cent of the total popu-lation. Most *pied-noir* arrived to France during 1960 and 1962. Between May and July 1962 Marseilles was overwhelmed by arrivals from Algeria. Many of these communities, such as the *pied-noir* in the southern regions of France, formed significant clustering and economic networks, which could be understood as ethnic enclaves, if we chose to see them as such (see, Smith, 2003:9–33; Jordi, 2003:61–74).

The view that the 'success' of the Cuban economic enclave was the result of either, the ingenuity of immigrant entrepreneurs, or, endeav-ours by the CIA to promote an anti-communist show case, are both unsatisfactory. Market relations and social stratification are rarely con-structs of ideology. One conclusion is that neither is an accurate descrip-tion. Neither can we assume that the benefits of the ethnic enclave, are such as to alter the disadvantages faced by all immigrants. Cuban Ameri-cans have fewer professionals than other immigrant groups. Cuban, as with Mexican immigrants, are 'more likely to be managers' (Clark, 2003:112); similarly, in levels of home ownership – a key indicator used by Clark as constituting 'middle class' status – 'a large number of Cuban households never managed to become owners, and those who did were not able to sustain the ownership rate' (Clark, 2003:134). Roger Waldinger, in examining the relationship between education and employment amongst Cuban (and other immigrant groups) with the native-born, comments on claims made by the ethnic enclave hypothesis, and suggests that,

> the presence of a Cuban business sector does nothing to depress employment opportunities among immigrant men. Low-skilled and relatively recent Cuban immigrants fare no differently than white high school graduates in the likelihood of holding a job [...] the employ-ment niche occupied by Miami's Cubans is not particularly impressive. Working Cubans are a good deal less likely than low-skilled whites to hold adequate jobs, which in turn generates a wide gap between Cuban men and comparable white natives.
>
> (Waldinger, 2001b:104)

Further, on Cubans who are recent arrivals, that they 'are about as likely as their Mexican, West Indian and Dominican counterparts elsewhere to be adequately employed, a finding hard to reconcile with the notion that Miami offers Cubans a distinct mode of entry into the U.S. economy' (2001b:105).

The above does not detract from the remarkable role played by Cuban refugee entrepreneurs in the transformation of Miami. It compares very favourably with most international comparison. It is quite unusual, for example, for an immigrant group to capture local political power within a generation. All the more remarkable given the particularly difficult circumstances faced by different waves of Cuban refugees. The *Marielitos* were demonised and discriminated against for their colour, their poverty and perceived or actual sexual orientation. Yet, they managed with little official assistance, indeed in the teeth of opposition by both Anglos and the established Cuban community, to make or earn a living. The Cuban ethnic economy in absorbing many of these refugees, acted as a market simile of classic Keynesian wage multiplier. The Cuban economy gave a push to the growth of the economy of Miami as a whole. This gave a push to the economy of Florida and the wider region. The demand for labour in tourism, construction, restaurants and other service-related enterprises – many of which are Cuban-owned – can be seen as a microcosm at city level of changes to aggregate demand brought about by immigration to the wider US economy.

One graphic illustration of labour market 'success' is that the Cuban ethnic enclave today has outstripped available supplies of co-ethnic labour for low paid sector employment. In part this is driven by the ageing of the Cuban population in the US, a decline in the size of households and second-generation resistance to entry in the niche sectors, if alternatives are available. In itself, this is not unusual, and can be found in the experiences of other immigrant groups. One consequence appears in a rising premium for co-ethnic workers. Another and more significant factor, in this instance, arises from the unusually high demand for labour created by the vibrant economy of Miami. This is sucking into the Miami immigrant workers and increasingly entrepreneurs from other Hispanic groups and from a wide geographical area, to compliment the previous flows of refugees from Haiti and Nicaragua from the 1980s. Currently a surge of immigration from other Hispanic groups over the past decade – from Central and South America, as well as north-east US states such as New York and New Jersey – has relegated Cuban Americans to a minority status in Florida's Hispanic community. Cubans are just 31 per cent of the state's 3.2 million Hispanics – less than the combined total of persons of Mexican and Puerto Rican origins. These trends are likely to continue as Cubans in the state tend to be older and have fewer children. This is even more pronounced in Miami. Puerto Ricans are the largest non-Cuban group accounting for 18 per cent of the state's Hispanics. One consequence – since Puerto Rico is a US territory – is that they are eligible to vote in Florida, and this is beginning to challenge the entrenched political machinery built by the political exiles which tied the Cuban community to the far-right in the Republican Party (Chaffin, 2004:12).

Miami is being reshaped, perhaps no longer in the image of the old politics of anti-communism which underpinned and legitimised the political dominance of the Cuban community in Miami by an embittered and socially conservative group of political exiles, many of them with a history on the CIA payroll. Paradoxically, the success of the Cuban ethnic economic enclave laid the conditions for its own destruction. The evolution of Cuban enterprise in Miami points to an economy which began as an ethnic economy. Due to its exceptional spatial concentration and density, typified by intense co-ethnic relations, such as in the hiring of co-ethnic workers and the consumption of goods and services produced in the ethnic economy, it became an economic and also political enclave constructed, in part, in the image of political exiles. The Cuban ethnic enclave is being transformed into an immigrant enclave, as second-generation Cuban entrepreneurs and workers become part of a wider and more ethnically diverse immigrant economy, typified by labour force interspersion and vertical as well as horizontal patterns of association. These reflect on the structures of particular industries and patterns of subcontracting. In the tourism industry, Cuban-owned enterprises cater for non-Cuban pensioners, are increasingly staffed by non-Cuban labour and depend on daily contractual negotiations with travel agencies and tour operators from all over the world in order to exist. Many of them would be surprised to read that, 'norms of solidarity within an ethnic community raise the reverse problem of social support expectations that are incompatible with the logic of capital accumulation' (Portes and Stepick, 1993:136). It is worth emphasising that unlike ethnic economies, in which entrepreneurs employ co-ethnics, in immigrant economies entrepreneurs employ workers from a variety of ethnic backgrounds, and this tendency thereby reduces the material basis for the 'logic' of ethnic solidarity.

Perhaps, one way of understanding likely future development in the enclave is by looking at the labour input of Cuban-owned enterprises in Miami. This would need to revisit the original research on the Cuban enclave, which began, paradoxically, in studies of the formation of enclave labour markets, and to compliment these with studies of development amongst second-generation members of an immigrant group in the light of the opportunity structure and alternatives available to different social and economic strata within the Cuban community in Miami. What is happening to workers, for example, could be better understood if it was possible to operationalise enclave participants in terms of place of work rather than place of residence. Census Bureau Statistics, however, do not provide this information, for example ethnic origins of entrepreneurs (Portes and Jensen, 1987:769).

An expanding literature on second-generation immigrant youth which overlaps with the literature on transnational communities, has provided important insight (see Portes and Zhou, 1993; Portes and Macleod, 1996; Perlmann and Waldinger, 1997; Waldinger and Feliciano, 2004). Much of this literature points to 'segmented assimilation' between and within different immigrant groups. Portes' model of the Cuban economic and political enclave as an alternative form of incorporation into American society, assigns a key role to outcomes amongst second-generation youth. Portes (1995c) in examining the incorporation of Haitian second-generation youth in Miami, points to pressures and processes of racialisation leading to 'downward' assimilation and mobility amongst the 'foreign' residents of 'Little Haiti', adjacent to Liberty City, where second-generation Haitian children are sometimes made fun of for their Haitian accents. This group find themselves torn between conflicting ideas and values: 'to remain "Haitian" they would have to face social ostracism and continuing attacks in school; to become "American" (black American in this case), they would forgo their parents' dreams of making it in America' (Portes, 1995c:249). Arguably, similar processes can be found amongst black Cubans. Amongst Cuban second-generation youth, he points to the benefits (and costs) of a strong and authoritarian community. It is argued that in the Cuban case, immigrant solidarity is grounded in a strong common cultural memory based on exile which attempted to replicate home country institutions. This allows for a greater density of social networks, which make even more social capital available, which is also applied as an agency of parental 'social control'. The above, lowers 'the probability of downward assimilation' (Portes, 1995c:258). At the same time Portes reminds us, in commenting on what are effectively hypotheses rooted in ethnic competition, that 'There is at present no data set for any immigrant group that allows a rigorous test of the hypotheses' (Portes, 1995c:262).

One cost which is apparent in all ethnic economies and which appears in an exaggerated form in the case of the Cuban economic and political enclave, is the loss of structural autonomy by individuals and social groups, or the loss of 'weak ties' as Portes refers to this condition in borrowing from Granovetter (1985). Arguably, this loss might be a necessary condition of dense relations and social capital processes which, in this instance, originated in over-defensive social posturing adopted by the exiles. Portes argues (1995c:259) that density in ethnic networks 'is not incompatible with weak ties'. Yet, the Cuban community in Miami has paid a heavy price for its lack of cultural heterogeneity and the dominance of the economic and political enclave by a revanchist ethnic solidarity, which reinforced homogeneity (or assumed homogeneity) and demands community compliance in the anti-communist project. This monolith broke down under the impact of Mariel and changes in the social composition of the Cuban community in Miami. To the political patrons in the community, power, ethnicity and ethnic organisations, are subordinated to the ideology of anti-communism and the grand ideal of overthrowing Castro and the Government of Cuba. This does not address the needs of Cubans actually living in Miami and in particular second-generation youth, many of whom were embarrassed by the Ellian incident. More fundamentally, the Cuban community in Miami has been transformed again, this time by the labour demands of Cuban enterprises and trends in the supply and demand for labour towards greater ethnic diversification in the enclave labour market. These changes in the economy of Miami are opening up the enclave to new ideas and influences.

5 Los Angeles

Between the old and the new

Introduction

The Californian rural economy has always depended on immigrant labour. Hispanic migrants – primarily from Mexico – have also provided the labour for domestic work, as cleaners, janitors, sewing machinists and construction workers, that keep the Los Angeles economy going. Hispanics in Los Angeles show social indicators which are even lower than those for black Americans. Whilst nearly four out of ten of black Americans are college graduates, amongst Hispanics it is nearer one in seven. More Hispanics are found amongst the low paid than black Americans. Many of them also have to live with the fear of deportation. It is for these reasons that some of the literature suggests a more 'savage capitalism' (when compared with a more unionised New York). The 'new' in Los Angeles appears in the form of a more expansive Asian migration and enterprise. Immigrants from Korea, Vietnam, China, India and Cambodia, have added to the diversity of Los Angeles and contributed to its economic development. Because Los Angeles is the largest concentration of garment production in the US, it is (after Chicago) the second largest concentration of manufacturing employment in the US. Many industries and services would not exist but for immigrant labour and entrepreneurs. Yet, immigrants in California have been subjected to a witch-hunt and accused (amongst others) of 'taking jobs away from African Americans'. This paved the way for an affirmative vote to Proposition 187 to target illegal Mexican migration. This chapter illustrates that far from 'stealing' American jobs, immigrants create new or maintain old areas of employment. Silicon Valley's Asian immigrants, for example, are a key part of the high technology industry which drives growth in California and the US generally. Almost 3,000 of the region's high-tech companies (a quarter of the total) are run by Chinese and Indian nationals. They employ 58,000 workers and generate annual sales of almost $20bn.

Los Angeles

Mike Davis (1992) in *City of Quartz* pointed to growing social polarisation in Los Angeles. It is the US city with the greatest gulf between rich and poor and has an estimated 30 per cent of its population living below the poverty line (Gumble, 2002:12). Davies also wrote in terms of 'futures past', i.e. Los Angeles and California as representing the future and the economic and cultural influence of this on the development of the United States as a nation state: but at the same time, 'past' in the sense that it represents the failure of various American utopias. California acted as a magnet for opportunity and distress migrants from pioneers, victims of the Dustbowl Depression and black Americans. Today it is a magnet for immigrants from the Asian continent and in this there are elements of continuity as well as change. Los Angeles has informed discussion on the formation of transnational communities and its image as 'the future' society is projected globally by Hollywood. Davis argues that this has come to an end, in a brutal, gated real-estate development, underpinned by heavy policing which has socially and economically excluded the majority of the city's black and Hispanic population. This suggests a contradiction in the development of contemporary Los Angeles: it is indeed a great metropolis, but for many it is also a great necropolis and a graveyard of hope and aspirations.

California is the world's eighth largest economy. It has also produced many influential ideas and social movements: Haight-Ashbury in San Francisco being a case in point. The diverse environmental lobby – which has acted as a check on corporate America – is another. This lobby has reproduced and reinforced a romanticisation of the countryside, and strong opposition in Los Angeles and elsewhere to further urban growth and sprawl (Fulton, 1997). This brought them into conflict with the 'urban growth bloc', often called the 'growth machine' i.e. local interest coalitions that make or earn a livelihood from population growth in their locality: construction, insurance, real estate and jobs in personal services, are examples. This version of local patriotism exists in direct relations to planning agencies and political machines of local government. Light (2000b) points to immigrants joining urban growth blocs or, more accurately, 'municipal growth blocs', and points to important practical and theoretical implications in this conflict for immigrants and their housing needs. On the supply side as a source for real-estate immigrant enterprise activities, and on the demand side, the needs of second-generation immigrants moving out of the original immigrant reception areas. Light points to the routine institutional ordering of housing location by estate agents, and writes that, 'regardless of race, estate agents steered customers to racially segregated neighbourhoods' and as such, segregation 'is not just a passive reflection of consumer preference. Brokers create it' (Light, 2000b:2). This is a globally recognised experience and indeed formed the conclusions of some of the earliest studies on the housing status of immigrants in local cities of the United Kingdom (Rex and Moore, 1967).

Los Angeles is the most diverse metropolis in the United States. It is a black, white, Asian and, above all, a Hispanic Mexican city. Roger Waldinger and Mehdi Bozorgmehr and their associates, in *Ethnic Los Angeles*, present a vision of an enduring pluralist society – 'ethnic Los Angeles is here to stay' (Waldinger, 1996a:470). But at the same time, it is an economy characterised by structural inequality within which race, ethnicity, class and immigration status, form key intersections in the incorporation of immigrant groups. Working-class Hispanics show education and income indicators which are even lower than those for black Americans (see Table 5.1). Portes and MacLeod (1996) point to ethnic 'self-identification' by second-generation children whose parents came from Latin America, in the adaptation the general label 'Hispanic' (rather than Cuban American, for example),

> Contrary to the commonly-held assumption that the label 'Hispanic' denotes greater assimilation into the mainstream of US society, our findings indicate that children who adopt the Hispanic label are the least well assimilated: they report poorer English skills, lower self-esteem and higher rates of poverty than their counterparts who identify themselves as Americans or as hyphenated Americans.
>
> (Portes and MacLeod, 1996:523)

Waldinger (1996c:1078–1086) points to the role of local urban economies in the structuring of immigrant receiving areas, most notably within New York and Los Angeles. Neighbourhoods and the economic and political structures of immigrant receiving areas are distinctive and have, therefore, particular implications for groups of newcomers. Those structures are not seen, in this instance, as 'all determining' but, rather, that immigrant outcomes are shaped by the interaction between distinctive

Table 5.1 Population of Los Angeles (CMSA) by ethnic group and key social indicators (per cent)

Ethnic group	1970	1990	Income less than $20,000	College graduates
White	71	47	8	46
Hispanic	14	32	26	15
Black	8	8	15	36
Asian	2.5	9	7	64

Source: Parkes, 2000b:11.

Notes
Consolidated Metropolitan Statistical Area (CMSA): Orange, Riverside, San Bernadino, Ventura and Los Angeles Counties. Indicators refer to State of California for 2000.

urban institutions and the specific characteristics of ethnic groups. In the last analysis, Waldinger argues, the urban context makes a critical difference. In the comparison, Waldinger points to more vigilance in New York about conformity to labour standards, when compared to the more 'savage capitalism' in Los Angeles (1996c:1081), and comments that 'the urban world of tomorrow, I suspect, looks a good deal like Los Angeles. And that possibility should give us some thought about immigrant's prospects in the years to come' (1996c:1086).

The case of black Americans is a case in point. Migration to the west coast and northern cities, characterised the restructured incorporation of black Americans in the US labour market during the drive to war in the 1930s and the post-war boom. Movement into manufacturing, transport and public services in Los Angeles and the northern cities involved significant and contradictory improvement, when compared to the south. Nowhere was this more pronounced than Detroit. 'Motown' was the fifth largest city in the US during the early 1970s, the major industrial centre of the nation's heartland and the headquarters of the automobile industry. Georgakas and Surkin (1998:95–96) point to black Americans as a key section of the American working class and nowhere more so than in the automobile industry. Many black Americans were amongst the 'estimated 65 on-the-job deaths per day amongst auto workers, or total of 16,000 annually'. This was contained in a report on the conditions of auto workers published during 1973. Approximately half of the deaths were from heart attacks. There were also some 63,000 cases of limiting illnesses and about 1.7 million cases of lost or impaired hearing.

The Watts Riot in 1965 which, more than any other event, symbolised the crisis of conventional assimilation theory and exposed historical 'unfinished business' in US society, was also, in part, the beginning of the end of the post-war boom and the closing of many employment opportunities previously available to black Americans.

South Central – which includes Watts – experienced another riot during April 1992 when four Los Angeles Police Department (LAPD) officers were acquitted by an all-white jury, of the (videotaped) beating of black motorist Rodney King. South Central erupted in spontaneous rioting. A State of Emergency was declared and nearly 10,000 National Guard, Federal troops and riot officers, retook America's second largest city at the cost of 55 lives. The 1992 riot was also an important proxy indicator of the extent to which Los Angeles has become a great multi-racial, multi-ethnic metropolis. Unlike the Watts Riot in 1965 – when the rioters were exclusively black Americans – the 1992 riot began in the same area, but very quickly became a rainbow expression of hostility to the police,

for the first in American history, Hispanics and white people joined a black riot. As African-American rioters moved north to the shopping malls in Hispanic neighbourhoods, local Hispanic working people joined in, because they had the same experience of prison, police, work and poverty. As the riot moved northwards, people became more confident. They moved into mixed neighbourhoods. By the time the riot reached Hollywood, young white men on skateboards were looting. Of the first 5000 people arrested, 52 per cent were Hispanic, 38 per cent were black and 10 per cent were white.

(Neale, 2004:110)

Ten years after the 1992 riot, Central Avenue – once South Central's main street – was described as 'devoid even of the most basic services [with a] fear-ridden loneliness to the district, the silence punctuated only by the regular sight of black men being pulled over and searched by police patrols' (Gumble, 2002:9). South Central has seen significant movement out by sections of the black middle classes to the suburbs, or even further to Atlanta City – a true black metropolis. Disproportionately, left behind are the poor, the old and high school dropouts. An estimated one in three black men in South Central is in prison, frequently for petty offences. Whilst many shopkeepers moved out after 1992, Koreatown is expanding to the north of South Central and working-class Hispanic immigrants are moving in from every direction. South Central is now as much a Hispanic (nearly 50 per cent of population) as it is an African American neighbourhood. One conclusion would point to black marginalisation. Another would point to the 'Americanization' of South Central or, at least, the integration of a greater diversity of humanity than was imagined possible even a decade ago (Parkes, 2002b:9).

Employment, ethnicity, race, gender and 'job channelling'

Mexican immigrants provide the labour force for the (seasonal) agricultural economy of California, the service sector (cleaners, janitors, porters), the construction industry, the garment industry and other, mainly manual work, which sustains the Los Angeles and Californian economy. Agriculture is a case in point. Martin (1994), points out that agriculture has been the major side door and back door through which unskilled immigrants have entered the United States for the past half century, and nowhere more so than the State of California. Immigration patterns during the 1980s–1990s indicate that up to one quarter of the working-aged immigrants who arrived during the period had their initial US employment in fruit and vegetable agriculture. Immigration reform was expected to reform agriculture's revolving-door labour market. Most farm employers did not make adjustments to retain newly legalized farm workers and, instead, sought the employment of newly arrived and often unauthorized immigrant workers (also see, Sorensen and Bean, 1994:1–17).

In the manufacturing industry, Hispanics made up 30.8 per cent and women 33.7 per cent of the labour force. Hispanic women provide most of the labour force in the garment industry and Asian and Hispanic women are close labour market substitutes, particularly in the garment industry and the personal service sector (Scott, 1996:222–223; also see Ehrenreich and Hochschild, 2003; Hondagneu-Sotelo, 2001). African-American workers are more concentrated in public sector employment, where employment has been more constant, but faced job losses in manufacturing (from 6 to 4.8 per cent between 1970 and 1990).

In a study of the Los Angeles labour market, Ellis and Wright (1999) examined the role of 'ethnic channelling' in sectoral employment concentration, amongst two groups. Recent immigrant and native-born migrant workers into the metropolitan Los Angeles area, i.e. the Los Angeles Consolidated Metropolitan Statistical Area (CMSA), which includes Orange, Riverside, San Bernadino, Ventura and Los Angeles Counties. During this period Los Angeles received about 400,000 foreign-born and 575,000 native-born workers. The main purpose of the study was to provide explanation for concentration, by comparing major immigrant groups (including Mexicans, Koreans and Chinese) with each other, and with native-born workers (white and African Americans). For longitudinal purposes, both groups were compared with resident foreign- and native-born workers.

The greatest concentration amongst Mexican recent immigrants was agriculture. This is a sector in which Mexican residents were also highly represented, but amongst immigrants it was twice the level of residents. High concentration also exists for Korean immigrants and residents (one third in each case) in the retail sector. At the same time, recent Korean immigrants also concentrated in agriculture and construction, unlike resident Koreans. Chinese immigrants and native-born were both equally concentrated in 'non-durable manufacturing' (includes the garment industry). One trend appears in the greater level of concentration and job channelling of recent immigrants, with sectoral concentration most pronounced amongst Korean and Mexican immigrants (Ellis and Wright, 1999:38, 49). In this, two explanations and an underlining trend were identified as causal. The first explanation points to the role of ethnic networks in the channelling of immigrants and internal migrants into sectors where co-ethnics and co-nationals were concentrated. The second, points to industrial distribution as a function of individual human capital and skills i.e. gravitation to sectors where their skills are in greatest demand, rather than ethnic 'job channelling'. For example, 'unskilled workers are more likely to find work in the ethnic niches than the skilled' (Ellis and Wright, 1999:31). Ellis and Wright (1999:29) further suggest that 'job placement of recent arrivals will depend on some combination of skills and network connection' but hypothesise 'that ethnicity will be more important determinant of sectoral employment than skill for recent immigrants'.

Another, and perhaps more significant factor in the job placement of recent immigrants into the LA economy, is the restructuring of the local economy and changes to sectoral demand for labour. An underpinning factor – which Ellis and Wright ignore – is the influence of gender and race in the channelling of both immigrant and native-born workers. The collapse of the aerospace industry and its many satellite contractors during the 1990s, saw the loss of 200,000 jobs. These job losses, mainly amongst men, had particular implications for black American men since (at 10.5 per cent) heavy manufacturing industry was the fourth highest area of employment concentration (Ellis and Wright, 1999:Table 3, 39). At the same time, the death of manufacturing in the Los Angeles area has been exaggerated. The metropolitan region's 606,000 jobs in manufacturing, almost put it level with national leader Chicago. It remains the case, however, that the jobs lost in manufacturing during the 1990s were significantly better paid, with rates above $15 an hour, whilst expanding areas such as textiles average less than $10 today. More than half of the manufacturing enterprises employ fewer than ten employees and only 38 firms in the entire region, have more than 1,000 people on the payroll (Parkes, 2002b:12).

Asian immigration and changing demographic composition of Los Angeles

The abolition of the national-origins system during 1965 – which militated against new immigrant groups – proved a path breaking decision for new Asian immigrants and contributed significantly to the population increase of Greater Los Angeles from 9.9 million in 1970, to 14.5 million in 1990. The increase was made up of 1.7 million additional native-born persons and 2.8 million who were foreign born. Asian first-generation immigrants made 911,130 (28.6 per cent) of the increase amongst all the foreign born (see Table 5.2). It is this population increase, which Light (2000b) argues, provided the basis for a reconstituted urban growth coalition, seen by Fulton (1997) as in terminal decline.

The growth of the Korean community is revealing: from less than 10,000 foreign born persons in 1970 to 155,500 by 1990. The Chinese community, although it has longer roots in California, similarly saw the number of foreign born rise from less than 30,000 to 231,361 by 1990. Another 414,427 Koreans and 75,769 Chinese were born in the US. Asians made up nearly 10 per cent of the population of Los Angeles by 1990 (Sabagh and Bozorgmehr, 1996:82–83). As we noted in the case of New York the terms 'Asian' and 'Chinese' contain immense diversity and many contradictory trends can be found between and within these groups (also see Chapter 6). Labour and trade diasporas linking the Chinese community to US cities and elsewhere, illustrate this complexity. Many Taiwanese, Malaysian, Laotian, Vietnamese and other immigrants from the globe are frequently members of the expatriate Chinese community. For example the estimated Chinese population in Cambodia declined from 64,500 in 1975 to under 5,300 in 1996 (Meng, 1998:171) and in Vietnam, from an

Table 5.2 Population of ethnic groups by nativity, Los Angeles region (CMSA) (1970–1990)

Ethnic group/nativity	1970	1980	1990
Hispanic	1,399,600	2,862,120	4,697,509[a]
Native-born	1,001,400	1,665,980	2,338,369
Foreign-born	398,200	1,196,140	2,359,140
Asian	256,200	596,080	1,326,559
Native-born	147,600	222,640	414,427
Foreign-born	108,600	373,440	912,132
African-American			
Native-born	778,700	1,026,800	1,114,269
Foreign-born	2,300	17,000	31,415
White			
Native-born	6,577,500	6,425,560	6,494,372
Foreign-born	506,000	450,980	398,884
All Other	88,600	243,640	432,419[b]
Native-born	55,200	144,360	214,596
Foreign-born	33,400	99,200	217,832
Total native-born	8,868,600	9,485,340	10,576,033
Total foreign-born	1,090,300	2,136,840	3,919,394

Source: Sabagh and Bozorgmehr 1996:Table 3, 95–96.

Notes
a Of these, 3,718,383 were Mexicans of whom two million are native born;
b Of these, 300,546 are 'Middle Easterners' (including Iranians) and 62,533 American Indians.

estimated one million people in 1975, to half of that by 1994. Between 1978 and 1989 about one million refugees left Vietnam, either to China (from North Vietnam) or as 'boat people' to other counties in the region and further on: an estimated '60–70 per cent of them were Chinese' (Tana, 1998:233). Policy on assimilation adopted by the Government of Vietnam after 1975, proposed a novel solution to the problem of 'integration'. A decree made children born to Chinese–Vietnamese couples, retrospectively, Vietnamese citizens 'whether they liked it or not' (Tana, 1998:232). All the more remarkable then, that commentators frequently point to high incomes amongst Asians, as proof of 'success'. The 2000 US Census indicated that the median family income in Asian households stood at $48,614, the highest of any group, and nearly $9,000 above the national average for all populations. Amongst Asian-Pacific Americans (APA), managers and professionals made up more than 41 per cent of the APA workforce. At the same time, 10 per cent of households lived below the poverty level (*AsianWeek*, 2001).

Min Pyong (1996) points to the Korean population in the United States before 1970 as an estimated 70,000 persons, most of whom were 'overlooked' by the 1970 Census. Despite the South Korean 'economic miracle', high rates of growth and progressively near-developed status (see Capps and Panayiotopoulos, 2001:133–147), more than 600,000 left the country between 1970 and 1993. The 1990 US Census enumerated the Korean population at 800,000. These immigrants drew disproportionately from the urban middle classes and the estimated 25 per cent of the population of Korea who are affiliated to (mainly) Protestant churches. In one survey of Korean immigrants in Chicago, 52.6 per cent indicated that they had been Christians in Korea. This affiliation – with a less tolerant and puritanical version of Christianity – is one factor according to Min Pyong (1996:30), which 'separates Korean immigrant from other Asian groups'.

One third of the Korean immigrants enumerated in the 1990 US Census, lived in California. Of these, 70 per cent lived in the Los Angeles and Orange Counties region. Many of them have relocated to Los Angeles from other areas of the United States and it is this growing spatial concentration which has laid the basis for an organic 'Koreatown'. Other Asian groups are even more concentrated in California than Koreans. Half of the Filipino population in the US lives in California. So does nearly half of the Vietnamese population (44.0 per cent) and 43.2 per cent of all persons enumerated as Chinese (Min Pyong, 1996:33–35).

Asian enterprise

Asian immigrant entrepreneurs make a significant contribution to the economy of Los Angeles and the State of California in its wider relationships with the Pacific Rim economy. Wigs are a case in point. The wig boom began in the early 1960s and continued until the early 1970s. During 1974, an estimated 38 per cent of American women over the age of 17 possessed at least one wig. Devine lampooned this in *Shampoo*. Ku-Sup Chin *et al.* (1996) point to the import–export of wigs as an early ethnic niche by Korean entrepreneurs in Los Angeles. Entrepreneurs formed transnational links in a vertical integration developed between Korean wig manufacturers in South Korea and Korea importers, wholesalers, and retailers in the US. This relationship reflected on South Korea's early industrialisation in light and labour-intensive industries, demand for this product in the US (world's largest market for wigs) and the existence of an immigrant community in the US who saw this as an initial business opportunity. This 'commodity chain' can be found in other products and markets. During the period 1968–1977, wig retailing 'became the most prevalent business among Korean immigrants during that time' (Ku-Sup Chin *et al.*, 1996:493). In an earlier study, Bonacich *et al.* (1976) found that during 1975 over 90 per cent of all wig stores in the Los Angeles area were Korean-owned. By the mid-1970s changes in fashion saw the bubble burst in wig retailing but, nevertheless, this was a formative experience for Korean enterprise.

Real estate and retail outlets illustrate the Janus-face of Asian enterprise. In the case of real estate, the increase in Korean and Chinese immigration and the size and spatial concentration of these communities, has impacted on the built environment of Los Angeles in ways which raise particularly challenging questions. The new Chinese and Korean immigration has also led to the recomposition of those communities. Light (2000b:5) notes in the case of Chinese settlement, a change from the working-class immigrants who lived in the dense and cramped conditions of Los Angeles' historic Chinatown, to the new immigrant entrepreneurs who draw disproportionately from the 'middle and upper middle class', and who pushed out of the traditional enclave into new residential and suburban areas. Monterey Park was created as a new residential neighbourhood, substantially as the result of Chinese real-estate developers and agents, who promoted Monterey Park in Hong Kong and Taiwan as 'the Chinese Beverly Hills'. Businesses not related to the housing sector, also benefited from this expansion. By 1994, the multiplier effect of Monterey Park, saw 66 Chinese restaurants, 14 Chinese mini-malls, two Chinese newspapers, 20 Chinese banks and six Chinese supermarkets *in situ* (Horton, 1995:30). The Monterey model was used to extend into the adjacent suburban cities of Alhabra and Rosemead, and subsequently San Gabriel Valley, Arcadia and San Marino.

> In 1983 about one-half of all the Chinese businesses listed in the Chinese telephone books covering Los Angeles were located in Chinatown and one-third in the San Gabriel Valley. By 1992, the San Gabriel had 55 per cent of all Chinese businesses in Los Angeles, and Chinatown only six per cent.
>
> (Horton, 1995:31)

Min Pyong (1996:35–36) argues that, 'a unique aspect of the Los Angeles Korean community is the development of a physically segregated community known as Koreatown'. Located about three miles west of downtown Los Angeles, it covers approximately 20 square miles and acts as a reception centre for many newly-arrived Korean immigrants. In 1965 whites made up 90 per cent of the population. Today most of the residents are Hispanic and one third Korean. Koreatown is a residential, commercial, social and cultural centre. Over 3,000 Korean-owned enterprises cater to the needs of the ethnic economy: native cuisine, groceries, books, magazines, accountancy firms, law firms, nightclubs and gambling houses, make up the visible face of the emergent enclave.

In 1970, Light (2000b:7) writes, Koreatown was known as the mid-Wiltshire district, 'a dreary residential and retail neighbourhood for poor black, and Hispanic renters'. In 1980 it was renamed 'Koreatown' and contained 21 per cent of Los Angeles' total Korean population. However, Koreans made up, at the time, only 7 per cent of the residents of 'Koreatown' (Light and Bonacich 1988:309) and many black and Hispanic residents were alienated by this insensitivity. In a similar fashion to the Chinese community, Korean developers, also impervious to the death of the growth machine in the Los Angeles area, 'assumed a leadership for effecting this transformation'. They promoted Koreatown in Seoul and its existence was well-known to newly-arrived immigrants (Light and Bonacich, 1988:200).

Many stores in the area were destroyed during the 1992 riots (Min Pyong, 1996:93) and this has reinforced the tendency for Koreatown to be the residence of necessity rather than choice. For the middle classes, co-ethnic developers provide the option of a suburban exit. For the poor, the old, recently-arrived immigrants and enterprises in the ethnic enclave, this choice is not a readily available option. In reverse, many Korean real-estate entrepreneurs benefited from lost property value in Koreatown and mid-Wiltshire as a result of the 1992 riot, and used it to acquire 'an additional 3.5 million square feet of commercial property' (Light, 2000b:9). Korean (and Chinese) real-estate agents, graphically challenge the view of immigrant enterprise as invariably operating on the margins of economic systems. These trends point to a polarisation inside the Korean and Chinese communities.

The polarisation inside the Korean community can be further illustrated in a sectoral comparison, between real estate and the retail sector. The retail sector is the highest area of employment concentration for Korean immigrants in Los Angeles. Most shops are located in black or Hispanic neighbourhoods. Spike Lee's cinematographic exposition in *Do the Right Thing*, illustrated the complex struggle for acceptance. The most frequently cited problems facing Korean storekeepers include, shoplifting, risk of armed robbery and 'the lower spending capacity of customers [. . .] Armed robbery is the major hazard confronting Korean merchants'. Twenty Korean shopkeepers in Los Angeles died in such incidents between 1987 to 1991 (Min Pyong, 1996:69–70).

The looting and partial or total destruction of an estimated 2,300 Korean stores during the 1992 riot was partly the result of a widely-held view in the black community, which associated Korean owners of liquor and grocery stores in South Central, with lack of respect to black consumers and the community in which they make a living. Many black consumers complain, for example, that they do not offer a broad range of services. Most are liquor stores. Perhaps a more significant factor in the looting of many Korean-owned stores – rather than the ethnicity of their owners – was that they were more accessible in terms of physical security and location; they were easier to rob and sometimes they were the only stores in the neighbourhood. One incident which illustrates the conflict between Korean shopkeepers and black consumers and which underpinned the events of 1992 – perhaps as much as Rodney King's televised beating – was the killing during the previous year of Latasha Harlins, a 15 year old black girl in a South Central Korean-owned store – over an unpaid bottle of orange juice. The extent of involvement in the liquor trade was illustrated in the post-riot reconstruction of South Central, when Los Angeles City Council refused to offer financial support for the reconstruction of destroyed liquor businesses. 'As a result only 28 per cent of the Korean stores destroyed during the riots were re-established, as of March 1993' (Min Pyong, 1996:90–91, 94)

Nutter (1997) points to Los Angeles as home to the largest concentration of garment production in North America. The sector has, as with New York and other gateway cities, been a key area of immigrant participation, both as workers and as entrepreneurs. It acts as the centre of the Californian industry. Between 120,000 and 140,000 workers are employed in over 5,000 factories and countless homes, cutting, making and trimming garments. Another significant cluster in the San Francisco/Oaklands area employs between 20,000 and 30,000 workers (Nutter, 1997:201; Light and Ojeda, 2002:152). These figures refer to official employment and exclude homeworkers, who are typically not registered. An estimated 30 to 50 per cent of value generated by Los Angeles garment contractors was produced by homeworkers and unregulated workshops. Over 90 per cent of homeworkers came from minority backgrounds (see, Portes, 1994:435; see also, Fernandez-Kelly and Garcia, 1989). Bonacich and Appelbaum (2000:150) estimate homeworking amongst Korean-owned firms at 40 per cent of the labour force.

The industry in Los Angeles has coped remarkably well with imports which 'devastated' the garment industry elsewhere. The crisis initially appeared in job relocation by US multinationals to the *maquiladoras*, when in the immediate post-NAFTA situation Mexico briefly displaced China as leading garment exporter to the US. The US garment industry faced the loss of one in ten jobs between 1982 and 1992, and was increasingly seen as a 'sunset' industry. In New York, over one in three jobs (35 per cent) were lost during the same period. By contrast, sectoral employment in Los Angeles had increased by one third (Nutter, 1997:200). The number of garment workshops in Los Angeles County increased from 2,332 to 6,364 between 1970 and 1996, as Light and Ojeda (2002:151) argue, 'mainly as a result of its superior access to immigrant labour'.

Nutter (1997:207) points to the ethnic composition of the labour force in the garment industry as primarily made up of Hispanic women. Mexican women make up three quarters of the labour force and other Central American Hispanic groups make up an additional 10 per cent of the workers. Asian workers, primarily from China and Vietnam, make up another 15 per cent of the labour force. The majority have arrived in the US during the last 15 years and 'most are undocumented'. The composition of the entrepreneurs is listed below (see Table 5.3).

The Los Angeles garment industry specialises in 'Women's Outerwear' (blouses, skirts, jackets and dresses) with a high 'fashion content'. As such, contractors need to meet the demands of the current season and production must, therefore, be delivered on time. The industry produces afford-

Table 5.3 Contribution by different immigrant groups to the Los Angeles garment industry (per cent)

Entrepreneurs		Workers/labour supply
Hispanic/Mexican	36%	Mostly Hispanic (mainly Mexican, also Central American)
Korean	19%	Mostly Hispanic and also Asian (Chinese, Vietnamese, Korean)
Vietnamese	13%	Mostly Southeast Asian (Cambodia, Laos) and also Hispanic
Chinese	9%	Only Chinese
Other Asian	10%	Mostly Hispanic and also Asian
Other, Anglo, Armenian, etc	13%	Mostly Hispanic

Source: Nutter, 1997:205.

able clothes, but also sells the 'California look', linked to Hollywood and global projection of the Los Angeles fashion industry. Effectively this has led to the development of a women's fashion-wear 'spot market' – characterised by rapidly changing styles which places even greater pressure on production and delivery systems (also see discussion on New York). Nutter (1997:199) argues that the spot market in Los Angeles exists because Los Angeles manufacturers created a casual sportswear niche market for low and moderately priced clothing for young women, and can meet retailer (principal) demands for reliable fashion delivered close to season and, thereby, reducing carrying costs. In order to do so, manufacturers use an extensive system of subcontracting to the many small immigrant-owned firms in order to produce a greater variety of styles, and to reduce labour costs. The average employment size of a garment workshop was 25 workers. Fashion seasons shape the pattern of employment in peaks and troughs, which indicate the volatility of the industry. Employment declines in July and August, picks up between September to December and declines in January to pick up again in February/March (1997:209).

Relations in the Los Angeles garment industry are not substantially different from the standard structure of subcontracting involving retailers, manufacturers and cut, make and trim (CMT) units which is applied in many situations (see Figure 3.1). Bonacich (1994:140) points to one variation which is indicative of the weak position of contractors in Los Angeles. Unlike, the standard C–M–T relation, many contractors were M–T units. They received already processed work from the manufacturer in the form of 'bundles' of cut fabric, which they simply sewed and trimmed. The workshop has less capacity for value-adding, or 'informal' appropriation of the manufacturer's fabric. At the same time, this further reduces the cost of entry by disposing some of the most expensive workers (cutters) and equipment, such as a cutting table. For this reason, Hispanic entrepreneurs are highly represented in this sector (38 per cent of all entrepreneurs), when in many others, they barely have a presence (see Table 5.2). In Bonacich's (1994) study of Asian entrepreneurs, the most common configuration was one of Korean employers and Hispanic workers – who made up 87 per cent of the employees of Korean-owned garment enterprises (Light and Ojeda, 2002:155). Bonacich argues that the (Korean) contractor is the 'immediate' but not 'main' exploiter of the women Hispanic workers, but also adds that, Korean contractors 'became the direct recipients of the (justified) wrath of the workers' (Bonacich, 1994:152). In this, Bonacich notes parallel discussion on the buffer role of 'middleman minorities'.

Conflict between immigrant entrepreneurs and the regulatory system provides insight on the institutional framework in which they operate and the labour conditions and relations associated with economic activity. Foo (1994) and Bonacich (1993b), point to the targeting of immigrant contractors in the Los Angeles garment industry for labour code violations which reveal systematic under-payment and non-receipt of benefits by employees, non-payment of taxes, non-conformity with health and safety regulations and the employment of child labour. The term 'sweatshop labour' is used by Foo (1994:2181) to describe 'multiple' or serial labour law violators.

Silicon Valley is not in Los Angeles, but it does reflect on the wider role of immigrant enterprise in the Californian economy. Participation by entrepreneurs in high-tech industries (as with real estate) challenges some of the assumptions made about sectoral confinement in areas of least resistance in terms of physical and 'human' capital, i.e. capital invested in the individual, such as in their education. A study by Analee Saxenian (1999) shows that Silicon Valley's Asian immigrants are a key part of the high technology industry which drives employment growth in California and the US generally. Almost 3,000 of the region's high-tech companies (a quarter of the total) were run by Chinese and Indian Chief Executive Officers who employed 58,000 workers and generated annual sales of almost $17bn. They have established long-distance business networks, specially with Taiwan, India and increasingly China. During 1980–1984, 12 per cent of the new start-ups in Silicon Valley were by Chinese and Indian nationals. During 1995–1998 it was significantly higher at 29 per cent (see Table 5.4). Many raise capital in Asia, subcontract manufacturing or software development to India and virtually sell all their products in Asian markets. Their activities illustrate processes of agglomeration and transnationalism. Silicon Valley acts as a key cluster of globalisation. Many successful Asian Silicon entrepreneurs, are effectively 'trans-Pacific commuters', or have relocated to home countries. In the case of Hsinchu Science Park in Taipei, some 40 per cent of enterprises were established by returnees, who in many cases went to the US in order to study (Parkes, 1999:12).

Table 5.4 Chinese and Indian-run high-tech companies in Silicon Valley

As share of total high-tech start ups	1980–1984 No.	%	1995–1998 No.	%
Indian	47	3	385	9
Chinese	121	9	809	20
Other	1,181	88	2869	71
Total	1,349	100	4063	100

Sales and employment of high-tech companies led by Chinese/Indian CEO	No. of companies	Sales ($m)	Employment
Indian	774	3,588	16,598
Chinese	2,001	13,236	41,684
Total	2,775	16,825	68,282
% share of Silicon Valley high-tech firms	24	17	14

Source: Saxenian, 1999; Parkes, 1999.

Notes
CEO: Chief Executive Officer.

The information technology (IT) sector with Silicon Valley as its epi-centre, saw temporary workers on H-1B visas starting a whole new wave of immigration, especially from India. This is an example of the interplay between the role of skills and job placement. In pre-9/11 America, with the high-tech boom at full swing, the initial limit of 115,000 H-1Bs was reached by March of 2000 and Congress increased the cap to 195,000 which was reached by September. Silicon Valley employers complained that, clearly, this was not sufficient and pointed to 340,000 vacancies in IT in California, alone (Harris, 2002:98). The dot.com fallout during 2000/2001, saw 75,000 jobs going, and this put pressure on H-1B workers laid off: the rules state that they must find a new job and the new employer must apply to the INS for a transfer within ten days. Many found alternative employment, some by using complimentary social networks and others in similar or related sectors. Some became self-employed (*AsianWeek*, 2001).

Xenophobia in California

The US has seen the return of an aggressive American nativism demand-ing tough controls against 'waves' of immigrants. Much of this has been driven by a moral panic over 'second-generation decline', which makes assumptions about all or most members of an ethnic or racial group. One aspect of this has been the idea that the 'sweatshop' is making a come back in the US economy, with large 'waves' of undocumented Mexican workers, in particular, providing the labour force. Roger Waldinger (1996a:445) writes that in Los Angeles, 'with good times gone, the regions hospitality to outsiders disappeared'. Light and Ojeda (2002:155) write that as the 'supply-driven' influx of Mexican workers increased, 'immigrant wages generally declined in Los Angeles, as did social conditions', particularly in the garment industry.

The above express the angst of the taxpayer in the State of California, who discovered that employers were passing health care costs through lack of medical insurance cover, to state hospital emergency and accident reception rooms. Light and Ojeda (2002:165) argue that 'the garment industry's employers had thus obtained a taxpayer subsidy. This taxpayer subsidy rendered their low-wage firms internationally competitive'. Why these particular 'subsidies' of some of the meanest hospital waiting corridors in the western hemisphere should irate academics so, is rather surprising. Subsidies to American and European farmers, for example, are far more significant in scale. Furthermore, it was not employers who became scapegoats. As the media and politicians publicised negative conditions in immigrant workshops, it was the workers themselves who were targeted. This has been reinforced by the post-9/11 environment which has seen stricter immigration and border-crossing policies, increased surveillance of the US–Mexico border, and the detention of Mexican illegal immigrants as part of 'Homeland Security'.

Scott (1996:236–237) writes that African American workers in Los Angeles, have 'been ousted from manufacturing labour markets by immigrants'. Scott's argument is not that low-wage immigrant workers have taken manufacturing jobs away from African Americans but, rather, that as Mexican and other Hispanics have moved into expanding industrial sectors in the region, *'their presence* [italics added] has come to constitute a set of barriers that have impeded African Americans'. Waldinger (1996c:1078) ponders pessimistically, 'how America's post-industrial cities can integrate the latest wave of newcomers just when the opportunities for native minorities seem to be at lowest ebb'.

Immigrants from Mexico and Central America, are presented as labour market substitutes for lower-level jobs such as domestics, janitor or sewing machine operator, 'which African Americans formerly held' (Waldinger, 1996a:452–453). In explaining labour market positioning and repositioning by Hispanics and black Americans, Waldinger confuses the concept of the 'underclass' with the working poor. They come from quite distinct traditions. The underclass concepts came out of social policy literature and attempts to offer residual explanations for poverty. An 'underclass', typically signified exposure to prolonged periods ('cycles') of poverty, deprivation, unemployment and dependency on welfare agencies. Waldinger points to the underclass as 'those groups whose jobs are at the very bottom of the totem pole' i.e. the working poor, and identifies Hispanic immigrants as filling that role: a group who have 'largely taken over the easy-entry positions once filled by less-educated black Angelinos'. Whilst low-paid jobs have grown enormously in Los Angeles, so has the supply of Mexican immigrant labour and effectively, from labour market substitution, Waldinger points to a process of labour market exclusion with African Americans presented as an 'outclass' rather than underclass.

'Spatial mismatch' theory is a more subtle application of the argument that Mexicans, are 'taking over' African American jobs. The argument here is that blacks 'refuse to work' – or to move to new areas of employment. It is summed up in the following proposition: the shift of industry and well-to-do residents from inner-city to suburban areas has resulted in a 'spatial mismatch' between,

1   the inner-city (ghetto/underclass) housing of African Americans and
2   new job opportunities available to them in manufacturing industry out of town.

With the new Asian migration in mind, the mismatch presents a quandary for Scott, 'if immigrants can shift hundreds even thousands of miles across frontiers, what keeps African-Americans from shifting twenty or thirty miles from one part of the metropolitan region to another?' (Scott, 1996:236).

In this analysis, mismatch theories reinforce underclass notions. Underclass theories see poverty as residual, i.e. rooted in 'deficiencies' of African American 'ghetto culture', and so on. Mismatch and possibly 'outcast' theories, also see poverty as residual, i.e. rooted in an unwillingness by African Americans to, (i) enter new areas of manufacturing employment (such as the garment industry) and/or (ii) move to areas where employment opportunities exist, rather than in factors to do with structural inequality.

Spatial mismatch theories, fail to recognise contextual manifestation of racial and gender segregation and exclusion. The experience of African American workers from the Deep South sucked into the shipbuilding, aircraft, auto and steel making industries of northern US cities and Los Angeles during the 1930s, showed vibrant population movement. It is this which laid the basis for an African American community in Los Angeles. The 1930s and subsequent post-war boom (1945–1973) were periods characterised by sustained economic growth and near full employment, fuelled by the needs of the arms-related and subsequently consumer durable industries – very different from the experiences faced by African American workers during the last three decades in recession-hit US cities. The recession years saw much greater selectivity in hiring and firing and this has reinforced the persistence of racial exclusion.

Racial inequality is not sufficiently recognised by spatial mismatch theories. Previous reference was made to the quandary presented by Scott (1996) i.e. that immigrants from Asia can move thousands of miles across frontiers but African Americans can't move 20 miles to where the jobs are. As the experience of Rodney King showed, travelling those 20 miles, may not be as easy as it appears. The video-taped beating of this black motorist by members of the LAPD and their initial acquittal sparked the 1992 riot. This incident also illustrated the wider institutional racism which underpins the work of the LAPD and the harassment faced by many black motorists. This can make it difficult for those most seeking work, i.e. young black males, to freely drive the freeways of Los Angeles. Many studies point to the role of race in patterns of residential segregation, the determining of access to housing and its relationship to employment (see Rosenbaum, 1996; Denton and Massey, 1989). At the same time, there is a substantial literature (see, Wilson, 1987; Holzer, 1991; Scott, 1996) on African Americans which points to a significant (but limited) flight by the black middle class. Often this consists of professionals who have retired after long careers in teaching, social services or other areas of public sector employment. The growing social polarisation and multi-ethnicisation of areas such as South Central, points to complex causation and outcomes.

Light *et al.* (1999) challenged the idea that immigrants are 'taking over' jobs from African American or other native-born workers. They suggest that existing migration network theory (applied by authors such as Scott, Ong, Valenzuela, Waldinger and others), 'exaggerates the extent to which hyper-efficient immigrant networks deprive native workers of jobs, thus exaggerating the conflict of economic interest between native and immigrant workers' (1999:8).

As we noted in Chapter 1, migration network theory purports to show how migration networks create self-sustaining labour flows which in gathering momentum begin to act independently of factors which initiated migration in the first place. Light *et al.* (1999) point to,

1   The limited use of migration network theory used to explain 'waves' of migration. They argue that as a theory about labour transfer, it cannot take into account the labour demand created by the development of immigrant enterprise itself.
2   The 'immigrant (enclave) economy' as a response to the labour supply problems faced by garment industry employers. This led to a situation where 'immigrant-owned [Korean] firms were pulling non-co ethnic [Latina] immigrant workers into Los Angeles' (1999:16).

The critique by Light *et al.* rests on the observation that labour demand outstripped available supplies of co-ethnic (Korean) labour, and entrepreneurs began to recruit from any available immigrant labour source (also see, Panayiotopoulos, 1996a). Light, *et al.* (1999) (also see, Nigel Harris, 2002) argue that far from immigrants 'taking jobs' away from native workers, they create employment typically linked to the employment of other immigrants, and which is a significant factor in the continuity of for example the garment sector in urban centres such as Los Angeles, New York, London, Amsterdam and elsewhere. Light *et al.* (1999) use the term 'immigrant (enclave) economy' to explain this expansive labour market formation, in contrast to the ethnic enclave or ethnic economies, resting on the employment of co-ethnics. One estimate of the immigrant and ethnic economies in the Los Angeles garment industry, is that only 6 per cent of the labour force are native-born Americans who are employed by native-born American entrepreneurs (see, Light and Ojeda, 2002:156).

One assumption, as we noted, is the view that Hispanic immigrants are labour substitutes for African Americans, and presumably vice versa. The logic of this argument would be that black men who lost their jobs in heavy industry, can substitute their lost jobs with those in growing sectors such as the garment industry. Clearly this is not the case for very good gender reasons: the sexual division of labour in the industry means that African American men cannot, at will, substitute for Hispanic women sewing machinists. The assumption is questionable in another way. African Americans are US citizens. Whilst the contribution made by African Americans to the development of the United States is outside the scope of this book, the refusal by many African American men to be treated 'in this way', like newly-arrived immigrants – or to work in low-paid sectors associated with them – blends into wider aspirations and demands over 'entitlement' (i.e. that 'we are American men and we are entitled to better than this'). These ideas can be used to legitimise resistance to employment in low-paying, low status, 'immigrant' jobs. *Skid Row* – a potent symbol of poverty in the US for many decades – adjoins the Los Angeles garment industry area and in this there are underlining reasons why this might not be endearing to Americans, be they white or African.

In the polarised debate over illegal workers in California, the view that illegal Mexican workers were taking jobs away from African Americans, provided support for anti-immigrant views and Proposition 187 (in US states, citizens can press for policy referendums). The purpose of referendum Proposition 187, was to drive a wedge between legal and illegal immigrants and to exclude illegal immigrants, as well as their dependents from basic services such as health and education (Tichenor, 2002:275–276). For example, it was envisaged that teachers would inform the immigration services about the children of illegal migrants, for eventual deportation. In what amounted to a one-sided pogrom directed mainly at the Mexican Hispanic community, Proposition 187 was approved by 59 per cent of the registered voters in the State of California. Most of the leaders of the black community, including some who came out of the Civil Rights Movement, campaigned in support of the Proposition. Despite this, a higher than average proportion of black Americans (50 per cent) voted against, as did 77 per cent of Hispanic voters. Mexican Americans 'rediscovered' their ethnicity during the referendum (see, Desnyder *et al.*, 1996;

Arbruster *et al.*, 1995). In a massive demonstration of solidarity in Los Angeles, up to 100,000 people marched carrying Mexican flags. This infuriated white America. On the demonstration a small but vocal group of white and black Americans took part, shouting '*We are All Mexicans*' (Panayiotopoulos, 2001a:105).

Proposition 187 was enjoined by a federal court ruling that denial of public education to the children of undocumented aliens, was 'unconstitutional' i.e. represented unusual and cruel treatment. Subsequently, federal judges nullified Proposition 187. California governor (at the time) Gray Davis (Democrat) received 78 per cent of the Hispanic vote in the 1998 campaign and 'had little incentive to appeal the ruling to higher courts' (Tichenor, 2002:287).

Proposition 227, however, was ratified in 1998. This ended bilingual education in California and reversed almost 30 years of policy. As we noted, attempts to end bilingual education in Miami galvanised the community into stopping the Nativists in their tracks (see Chapter 4). In California the opposite was the case. Proposition 227 replaced bilingual education with mandatory English tuition, except in limited cases where one-year immersion courses in mother-tongue education was allowed. In part this was the widely-held belief, including amongst a large sections of the Hispanic community, that its effects could not be any worse than the system in place (King, 2000:273). High school dropout rates amongst Hispanic youth range from two to four times the rate amongst whites. California is home to about half the children in the US deemed 'disadvantaged' by Limited English Proficiency (LEP). There are 1.4 million LEP children in the state – accounting for a quarter of California's school population – with half of them living in the Los Angeles metropolitan region (Parkes, 1998:12).

Conclusions

Between the old and the new points to change and continuity in the substantial contribution made by immigrants and immigrant enterprise to the making and remaking of Los Angeles. This is reflected in changes to sectoral employment and the changing composition of immigrants themselves. The new Asian immigration is an illustration of the Second Great Wave. Whilst Korean and Chinese immigrant entrepreneurs in Los Angeles represent elements of change, there are also important areas of continuity: in limited opportunities available for African Americans and Hispanic immigrants who provide the labour for California's agriculture and Los Angeles' sewing workshops. The term 'Hispanic' in Los Angeles denotes a different and subordinate meaning when compared to other ethnic groups, and indeed to the Cuban Hispanic community in Miami. The ending of bilingual education in California, but its successful defence in Dade County, says something about the two Hispanic communities, although its precise meaning is not clear.

Changes to the Los Angeles and wider Californian economy, driven in part by new Asian immigrant enterprise, are evident in commodities such as wigs and garments and sectors such as the IT sector and Silicon Valley, the retail sector in black and Hispanic neighbourhoods, in real estate with the evolution of 'Chinatown', 'Koreatown' and increased suburban development. New Asian enterprises are a significant force in the local economy and in the global IT sector.

Has the Los Angeles economy been transformed by immigrants, or is it the product of wider relations? The garment industry is the largest employer in Los Angeles county – the leading manufacturing county in the United States. This is substantially accounted for by employment immigrant-owned enterprises. It is perverse to see this, as is commonly the case, as an example of 'de-industrialisation' (Ong *et al.*, 1994:9). Rather, it points perhaps to a particular kind of industrialisation, which is in part the result of competition and economic restructuring. Nutter (1997) provides convincing explanation, that the spot market in Los Angeles (and elsewhere) developed because manufacturers created a niche market in young women's fashion wear which met retailer delivery demands by making use of immigrant contractors to produce the many styles required.

In real estate a more complex picture emerges. In pointing to the examples of immigrant participation in real-estate development, Light (2000b:9) draws the conclusion that 'in the period 1970–2000, Chinese and Korean immigrant entrepreneurs reorganised Los Angeles, building new communities to house fellow immigrants'. The 'Asian growth machine' broke the environmental impasse faced by the municipal growth bloc and became an important part of a new urban politics. This challenges the view, from Pyong Gap Min and Mehdi Bozorgmehr (2000:708) that Korean entrepreneurs are deficient in class resources and that the image remains, one of small 'mom-and-pop' businesses, which act as middleman minorities in low-income neighbourhoods. Clearly, the economic differentiation of the Korean community, has created conceptual problems for analyses which use ethnicity as the unit of investigation. Within the same ethnic group (Koreans) different trends are apparent which cannot be reduced to sectoral peculiarities. Rather, these trends reflect on the economic (and political) power, not of ethnic groups, but individuals and classes within ethnic groups and differential capacities of economic power and political influence.

In the face of widespread views over Asian Americans as an 'achieving' minority, Ong *et al.* (1994:4) point to indicators which show that whilst Asian immigration drew disproportionately from professionals, Asians also suffered twice the average rate of poverty. Cheng and Yang (1996:341), caution against using the overarching Asian American category to draw conclusions about social and economic status. They point to Asian Americans in Los Angeles as an increasingly diverse population, differing in ethnic composition, nativity, socio-economic status and patterns of incorporation. They argue, whether in demographic, cultural or class terms, 'treating Asian Americans as a group is likely to conceal more than it reveals'.

Ivan Light (2000b), in the study of Korean real-estate developers, perhaps, embellishes the significance of the Asian growth bloc in the shaping of the build environment in Los Angeles. The riot, for example, impacted on property values far more than Korean developers, and acted quite independently of them. Nevertheless, a challenging proposition is being raised here. To take the argument a step further: does it point towards the possible development of a 'rainbow' municipal growth bloc – with immigrant enterprise as its epicentre – which captures political power? In itself, this is not unusual development. The experience of the economic and political enclave in Miami, shows that Cuban exiles did not need an alliance at all. In historical terms, the experience of Tammany Hall can be seen as an important antecedent. Is this as good as it gets for immigrant communities in modern America? Representation in Tammany Hall made use of ethnic and religious categories as political units and reduced their outcomes to those of their political representatives, brokers and political captains.

Los Angeles is a contradictory metropolis in formation. Partly shaped by immigrants and other ethnic groups, and partly the restructuring by capital of particular industries and jobs. In between 'the growing gap between rich and poor [...] where many Angelinos span the entire social spectrum from metropolitan heaven to inner-city hell' (Waldinger, 1996a:451) lies the hope and the despair. One element of hope appeared in the actions of the mainly immigrant workers who clean the offices of Los Angeles (janitors and cleaners) who, after a three week strike, did manage to win an immediate bonus of $500 each and a 25 per cent pay rise over three years. This was seen widely as a significant landmark and likened to the victory achieved nearly 30 years ago by Hispanic farm workers (Campell, 2000:11). During May 2005 Los Angeles elected its first Hispanic Mayor.

6 From labour migrants to immigrant entrepreneurs

The European Union – an overview

Introduction

This chapter presents an overview of trends on immigration policy and immigrant enterprise formation in the major cities of the European Union (EU), and points to continuity as well as significant change in the development of immigrant enterprise. Emphasis is placed on cities in continental Europe not elaborated elsewhere in the book. It is in part, a debate with those who see immigrant enterprise as invariably on the 'fringes' of economic and political systems. One common Western European experience appeared in the labour demand created by the post-war boom in Europe during 1945 to 1973, and policies by governments to facilitate labour migration. This drew initially from the large number of refugees from Eastern Europe then labour migrants from the Southern European countries, the ex-European colonies and subsequently the former Yugoslavia and Turkey. Labour transfer was influenced by the nature of immigration policy which was managed in different ways by European countries. Britain, France and Holland, relied on their ex-colonies as labour reservoirs, whilst Germany, which lost its colonies during the First World War, relied on the 'guest worker' system. The chapter points to the (unintended) consequence of labour transfer and refers to the example of Turkish immigrants in Germany and the transition by a significant number of them from temporary guest workers to immigrant entrepreneurs. Variation in immigration policy had implications for political rights and the level of acceptance in the host society that settlement and enterprise was permanent, and that immigrants have the right to develop their own cultural identities. Another variation appears in participation in self-employment by immigrants groups. Some countries show higher rates than others, and there is considerable inter-ethnic variation. In the UK for example, indicators show that ethnic minorities have higher than white rates of self-employment (15.1 per cent, when compared to 12.8 per cent), but this disguises sharp differences between members of groups enumerated as 'South Asian' and 'black' (20.8 per cent when compared to 6.7 per cent), as well as between, 'South Asian' groups themselves (from India, Pakistan, Bangladesh) (Owen, 1997:29–66; Barett et al., 2003:109).

One introductory note is that policy in Europe towards immigration and enterprise is shaped in a relationship between convergent EU policies on the one hand, and significant variations in national policy and national histories on the other. Whilst labour transfer was handled in different ways by governments, the development of a 'European labour market' characterised and underpinned the economic development of post-war Europe (see, Kindleberger, 1967; Bohning, 1972; Castles and Kosack, 1973; Castles *et al.*, 1984). One response by European governments during the recession years was that aid and trade could be used in place of migration. Governments introduced financial incentives for returning immigrants targeting the countries of the Maghreb region and Turkey with little success. These policies misunderstood that migration today is more complex – economic migrants, refugees, asylum seekers, worker-students, ex-guest workers – and unlikely, therefore, to be responsive to this one set of policy measures. Further, as the accumulated experience indicates, the size of the immigrant settlement may owe more to natural population increase in the urban centres of Western Europe itself, rather than to any inward migration. These sorts of policies say little to the growing proportion of the 'immigrant' community who are second-generation persons born in the cities of Europe, and hence not immigrants. Rather, these policies diverted attention from the critical issues facing this group.

What is clear, is that post-war labour migration contributed to the unpredicted reshaping of European industries, services and cities over the next four decades, and its full social, economic and political consequences, are still barely understood (see, Borjas, 1999; Geddes, 2000, 2003; Cole and Dale, 1999). It is in part to this legacy of labour transfer that high levels of immigrant concentration in particular sectors and jobs, remains a characteristic feature of labour market incorporation: in the UK for example, one in six Pakistani men in employment are taxi drivers or chauffeurs, and two in five Bangladeshi men are cooks or waiters (compared with one in 100 white British men) (Turner, 2005:5).

Consequence of labour transfer: Turkish immigrants in Germany

Turkish immigration in Germany needs to be understood as the consequence of labour transfer and as part of a longer and continuing history of immigration to Germany. The first group of immigrants (between 1945 and 1955), were the *Aussiedler* and comprised of some 12 million people of German 'descent' who fled Eastern Europe. The guest-worker system was introduced during 1955 in response to the vibrant labour demand of the West German post-war 'economic miracle' and the exhaustion of available *Aussiedler* and female supplies of labour. The system envisaged immigrant workers as a temporary recourse tied to the needs of particular industries and the number of guest workers peaked at 1.3 million in 1966.

Whilst Turkish guest workers from Turkey were later arrivals, when compared to Greek and Italian workers, they more than made up in numbers, from 13 per cent of the foreign population in 1972, to one third by 1980 (Geddes, 2003:81).

The increase in immigration from Turkey was the result of family reunions between guest workers and their families, which proved the undoing of the guest-worker system envisaged as a temporary mechanism for fine-tuning Germany's labour market. The above provides support for Castles' thesis, that migration polices fail and that 'the self-sustaining nature of migratory processes once they are started' began to act independently of sending and receiving country policies, turning 'post-1945 labour migration into unplanned processes of settlement and community formation' (Castles, 2004:222–223). This view, grounded in migration network theory, parallels both Ivan Light's analyses of 'spill-over migration' and Alejandro Portes *et al.*'s thesis on the formation of transnational communities and globalisation from 'below' (see, Chapter 1). It is in part due to the legacy of labour transfer and the impact of contemporary displacement, that by 1999 an estimated 14 per cent of Germany's population had not been born in Germany (Geddes, 2003:79).

Immigration in Germany is revealed in the incorporation of the Turkish community – which typified the 1960s labour transfer. The Turkish population in Europe is diverse. Many are from the cities and others from villages in Anatolia. Many are Kurds. An increasing proportion is born in Europe. At an estimated three million people this represents a quarter of all immigrants in Europe and makes immigrants of Turkish origins the largest minority in Europe. In 1993, 2.1 million lived in Germany, which accounted for nearly two thirds of all Turkish immigration to the European Union (EU). The old industrial state of North Rhineland-Westphalia alone, accounts for nearly one quarter of Europe's Turkish population (Bayar, 1996:2; Manco, 2004:4).

It is difficult to find data on the number of Turkish workers and entrepreneurs in Europe, even in Germany. What we do know is that the Turkish community is made up of a young population, with an estimated one third of the total under 18 years of age. More than 80 per cent of these young people have been educated in Europe. Purely male migration was a feature between 1965 to 1973 and family reunions peaked between 1973 and 1985. For this reason, the Turkish population in Europe consists of families, with the male to female ratio moving nearer the average: in Germany 45.5 per cent (and in Belgium 49 per cent) of the Turkish population are women. Women form, typically though marriage, a significant and continuing source of new immigrants. Inter-ethnic marriages are relatively rare and many respect their parents' wishes for arranged marriages involving someone from their parents' village and region (Manco, 2004:2). The reproduction of hierarchy through marriage is by no means a particular feature of Turkish immigrants. Indeed amongst them, it appears at its weakest. In part due to popular Turkish music, satellite TV and proximity, many young Turkish men and women born and raised in Germany have a good knowledge of Turkey, and make frequent visits for holiday, social and family purposes, and in the process many form their own relationships and find their own partners.

Karen Schonwalder (2004) offers an explanation for why Germany's guest workers were largely European and, within that, largely Turkish. This stands in contrast to the UK and France which recruited labour from a wide range of ethnic and racial groups. The presence of vibrant black communities in London and Paris is testament to this. In Germany of 7.3 million immigrants admitted until 2000, 5.8 million were Europeans (including Turks). Schonwalder (2004:248) argues that this was 'the result of a deliberate policy pursued by West German governments of the 1950s to 1970s' to exclude persons referred to as 'Afro-Asians'. Where recruitment treaties existed, with North African countries such as Morocco and Tunisia, they excluded provisions on the immigration of family members. Effectively, policy ranked potential guest workers according to racial preference. In the case of Portugal and its significant African migrant population, it was decided to inform the Portuguese authorities that 'German employers were not interested in dark-skinned workers' (Schonwalder, 2004:250) and left it to the local authorities to ensure none were.

During 1960–1961, West Germany concluded recruitment treaties with Greece, Spain and Turkey, to add to Italy and Portugal. In response to inquiries from countries such as India, Iran, the West Indies, Togo and the Central African Federation, amongst others,

> it was decided not only to refrain from concluding recruitment treaties with non-European countries but actively to prevent employers from recruiting workers from Asian and African countries and to make sure that such individuals would not become settled in West Germany.
> (Schonwalder, 2004:249)

One legacy of German immigration policy is that only a fraction of the estimated 7.3 million persons of immigrant origins (those of Turkish origin account for 2.6 million) have the right to vote and to take part in the 'democratic process'. Of 2.6 million people of Turkish origin, only an estimated 370,000 are eligible to vote (Wassener, 2002:8), despite in many cases being born and educated in Germany, or having spent a lifetime on an Opal production line. This has implications both at central and local city levels in the capacity of so-called immigrants to politically integrate themselves and influence society as other people do.

One element of convergence in immigration policy is that the labour demands of national economies remain a key factor which drives immigration policy. One major contributing factor in the United States and Europe, is the ageing of the working population. For example, during 2002 and for the first time in the United Kingdom, those over the age of 60 overtook the number of young people under the age of 16 (see Harris, 1995a, 2002; Panayiotopoulos, 2005).

At the same time, variation in national policy towards immigrants is illustrated in a contrast between German, UK and French policy. In the latter, immigration from the ex-colonies allowed greater access (to the elites, at least), for citizenship and formal political rights. One significant consequence was the acceptance of family reconstitution and reunions. In Germany, by contrast, where immigrant labour was seen as a temporary measure, this was characterised by the absence of any political rights and representation. Lack of rights fostered insecurity and this delayed family reunions. Substantially, the intended non-incorporation of immigrants in Germany led to them being defined as 'foreigners', and this has continuing implications and raises wider questions not only about policy towards immigration and settlement, but also definitions of citizenship and 'rights'. Two poles can be presented in this respect, which in part reflect on the historical development of nation states. First, in whether an already exist- ing nation or people becomes the basis for claims to statehood (for example, Germany), or second, in whether the idea of nation is used to meld together a culturally and linguistically diverse population (for example, the United Kingdom and the United States). One area of con- vergence, as Turton (2002:25) reminds us, is that 'the nation-state exists, by definition, to protect the rights of only its own citizens', and this has important implications for immigrants.

The above was posed very sharply in the incorporation of guest workers in Germany given Germany's ethno-cultural definition of national community. An ethno-cultural definition does not see nationhood as a political construct, rather, the 1913 Nationality Law defined the German nation as comprised of a community based on 'descent'. This places immense obstacles in the path of non-Germans becoming citizens and has been referred to by Czarina Wilpert (1993) as a form of 'institutional racism'. Progressively, this position became untenable. In 1990, more than 70 per cent of the 'foreign' population had lived in Germany for more than ten years and Geddes (2003:95) notes, that around 1.5 million 'so-called foreigners had actually been born in Germany'. The 1990 Foreigners Law made some stringent amendments: it gave immigrants statutory residence and family rights for the first time and allowed for naturalisation after 15 years of residence, and eight in the case of second- and third-generation youth in the 16 to 25 age group. The uptake of German citizenship (and hence, right to vote) amongst Turkish nationals is low for various reasons. One factor is national pride. Many do not want to give up their nationality. Another and more significant factor is the result of defensive social pos- tures adopted by the Turkish community in response to racism. Turks in the EU have been subjected to exceptional hostility and physical attacks: Solingen is a case in point. A family of five Turkish people were killed in a

racially motivated attack and this saw one million Germans showing solidarity with the family in candlelit protests. For reasons of insecurity and
sense of impermanence, which the guest-worker system was designed to
produce, many see dual nationality as preferable and as an insurance and
are unwilling to give up their Turkish nationality and passports in order to
acquire German nationality. A dual nationality policy, which would have
addressed these concerns was rejected by both left and right in Germany.

'Fortress' versus 'social' Europe: a quandary

It is important to begin with a quandary. Only but the most blatant xenophobe, would not concede that restrictions on the free movement of
labour and the detention of asylum seekers and their children behind
barbed wire, makes Europe look like a 'Fortress'. However, despite
restrictions on immigration, it is equally undeniable that working-class
neighbourhoods in cities like Berlin, London, Amsterdam, Paris, have
been in part reshaped, some with more confidence than others, by immigrant enterprise. Is the Fortress being taken from 'within' and 'below'?

It is this quandary which gives Saskia Sassen (2004:23) the confidence to
argue that the European Union, far from representing a 'Fortress', is at
the cutting edge of 'innovatory' forms of immigrant incorporation and
social integration. Sassen points to the integration of fellow-Europeans
during the nineteenth century, for example, Irish immigrant construction
workers in the UK, Belgian bakers in Paris, Polish miners in Germany.
This could be extended to include the 12 million *Aussiedler* in Germany
and the millions of cross-border students currently within the EU member
countries. Leaving aside the broad brush the above implies – such as the
troubled incorporation of Irish immigrants in the UK – what this indicates
is that Europe has successfully 'integrated' diverse immigrant groups
during different periods in its historical development. Clearly in the light
of today's xenophobia this is an optimistic note. Sassen further argues that
the above would not have taken place but for the existence of 'highly
developed sense of civic and political community' in Europe, which forced
the creation of 'formal rules for including outsiders'. These innovations,
not least of all the acceptance of integration, were part of the fight against
natives who used existing institutions to argue against inclusion. The European Union's development represents 'the ultimate example of this effort'
at integration.

Sylvio Berlusconi (the Premier of Italy and EU Commissioner for
2004/2005), would probably have been surprised to see himself described
in this way. Spain and Italy account for two thirds of all immigration in the
European Union. Unlike Italy, whose tolerance of the 'informal sector'
does not extend to those who work in it and is deporting illegal immigrants
to detention camps in Libya, Spain has been (relatively) more willing to
accept the economic role immigrants play in seasonal agriculture and the

low paid jobs Spaniards no longer want to do. This takes the form of periodic amnesties for illegal workers. Something else is stirring in continental Europe and this is reflected in particular areas of the enterprise sector. In Madrid, domestic supermarket deliveries have been subcontracted to micro-enterprises – a man with a van – run mainly by Peruvian and Ecuadorean immigrants. In Barcelona, Pakistani immigrants dominate the distribution of butane gas and many corner shops are owned by Chinese immigrants, who are also moving into the retail of cheap fashion wear and accessories (Panayiotopoulos, 2003, personal observation, Madrid and Barcelona). In Venice and the southern European seaside resorts, a visible multitude of immigrant street-sellers of designer goods can be seen.

Clearly, there are major changes taking place in cities across Europe. How to interpret them is far more difficult, particularly in the context of rising xenophobia. We noted (see, Chapter 1) that one tendency in Sassen's analyses of globalisation is an unwillingness to show a (political) appreciation of the specific institutional arrangements which underpin processes of incorporation and selectivity in immigration and the formation of immigrant communities and enterprise. 'Racialisation' as a process which structured German immigration, is a case in point. If the Fortress is being taken from 'below' or 'within', it is under the difficult circumstances of increasing xenophobia in the European Union. Far-right parties made up of an amalgam of racists, populists, holocaust-deniers, Islamophobes and anti-Semites, campaigning under nationalist or regionalist banners, have made worrying advances. The Austrian Freedom Party led by Jorg Haider gained 27 per cent of the vote in 1999 and joined a coalition government with the Conservative Party. Internal disputes and opposition to Haider led to the loss of one third of its vote in 2002. In Italy, Umberto Bossi and the Northern League, rubs shoulders with Gianfranco Fini's 'post-fascist' National Alliance in Sylvio Berlusconi's *Forza Italia* government. In Holland, the Pim Fortuyn List, came second in the 2002 elections and entered government with the Conservatives, to subsequently implode as the result of its own internal contradictions. In Norway, the Progress Party won 15 per cent of the vote in 2001. The Vlaams Blok gained one third of the vote in the Flemish areas of Belgium. The National Front led by Le Pen, in France, came second in the first round of the Presidential elections in April 2001 and gained 20 per cent of the vote in the second round. The Danish Peoples Party, a hotchpotch collection, came third in the 2001 elections and joined the coalition government (Lloyd, 2002:21). In the 2005 elections it came third. The Swiss Peoples Party, led by businessman Christoph Blocher, nearly won a referendum to ban all but wealthy asylum-seekers from Switzerland – one of the richest nations on earth. It did win a referendum denying third-generation immigrants, rights to citizenship (Simonian, 2004:6). What unites them is opposition to immigration. All describe themselves as 'anti-immigration' parties. Most mainstream parties (cf. New Labour, in Britain) are engaged in a 'Dutch auction' (where you bid downwards), to see who can be harder on immigrants, Muslims, and in particular the most vulnerable amongst them, asylum seekers and refugees.

The above has created and legitimised a climate of hysteria including physical attacks against immigrants and refugees. It is important, however, to disentangle the alliance of the anti-immigration lobby and to show its weaknesses. Most racists, usually begin from economic arguments i.e. 'they' are taking our jobs, housing, school places and so on. Fascists begin from an ideological racial argument i.e. that all members of an ethnic or racial group not designated as part of the master race have to be physically dealt with. 'Repatriation' is an often stated codeword in this objective. The European-wide experience indicates that a significant proportion of the soft- to hard-core racists have joined and voted for fascist parties, when normally they would be opposed to them and what they stand for. For example, the swastika remains an offensive symbol for most people who vote for fascist parties. Due to the failure of the left in mainland Europe to challenge many of these movements as 'fascist' and the willingness of the right to go into government with them, this has legitimised the discourse of racism in official institutional politics. In the UK, anti-fascists partly contributed towards the failure of the neo-Nazi British National Party (BNP); it failed to make a widely-predicted breakthrough in the 2004 European elections. During the 2005 General Election, the vote of their leader in the Keighley constituency declined by one third.

In cases, sections of the revolutionary left (in the name of defending secular education) have gone along with ideas about 'forced' integration of minorities. The campaign to expel two young Muslim girls (Alma and Lila) from the French secondary school of Aubervilliers for wearing the *hijab*, was instigated by teachers who are members of *Lutte Ouvriere*. One of the leaders of the Revolutionary Communist League (LCR) who teaches Alma and Lila, 'voted for their exclusion at the disciplinary hearing' (Boulange, 2004:5). One poignant reminder of this climate is that Germany began to restrict Jewish immigration from the former Soviet Union during January 2005 (Benoit, 2005:9). Germany saw, after unification, the fastest growing Jewish community in Europe, mainly due to Russian immigrants who saw this as preferable to living in Israel. New conditions will include proficiency in German and academic qualifications.

Policy towards the 'informal economy'

Immigrant enterprises are part of wider European Union concerns (or panic) over unregistered and untaxed economic activity. This concern surfaced in the European drive towards common social and monetary policy. This has seen the adoption of the social chapter and enforcement of common social legislation (e.g. over minimum pay). In monetary policy, a precondition for reaching union was the reduction of public sector deficit, to 3 per cent of Gross Domestic Product (GDP) by all member states. These tight fiscal policies saw cuts in government spending, (e.g. pensions) and attempts to expand the tax-base. The most typical example of convergence in taxation was the introduction of Value Added Tax (VAT) as a precondition for EU membership and which currently stands at 17.5 per cent of the retail price. Also, more emphasis was placed to identify unregistered and untaxed economic activities, and to 'formalise' them. Estimates from the European Commission on the 'black economy' in a report adopted by the Commission, range from, a third to a quarter of GDP in Greece and Italy to less than 10 per cent in the Scandinavian countries. It is assumed that the EU's undeclared work amounts to 7 to 16 per cent of GDP, corresponding to 7 to 19 per cent of declared employment, or up to 28 million jobs (Smith, 1998:6).

Policy in the European Union is aimed at the reduction of the 'informal economy' through the greater enforcement of existing rules on taxation and labour legislation. The German (and Dutch) slogan 'illegal is unsozial' when coupled with the view that the 'black economy' goes hand in hand with illegal immigration, has specific implications for immigrants and sectors in which they are concentrated, such as services, restaurants and takeaways, the garment and construction industries and seasonal agricultural employment. Frequently, the relationship between immigrant entrepreneurs with the regulatory agencies involves conflict with various branches of central and local government over the avoidance of taxation, social insurance, health and safety at work and homeworking legislation. These relations are complex and can be influenced by factors such as the nature of the local economy and local political mobilisation. The European-wide offensive against the 'informal economy' was unusual in its scope and extent.

At the same time, policy in the EU is subjected to national variation through 'derogation' i.e. the right of member states to avoid the implementation of agreed policies and areas of legislation. The UK has done this on labour rights contained in the social chapter and Germany on immigration, where it retains national control over the number of immigrants it admits. Another variation derives from the nature of particular national economies and how these structure labour markets in the cities of Europe. Some countries are more tolerant of the 'informal sector' than others. There is a clear regional variation, with countries in Southern Europe characterised by the presence of large numbers of self-employed, micro-enterprises and subsistence economies. Italy, and the 'Third Italy' containing the dynamic sub-region of Emilia Romagna (in the centre and north-east of Italy), with Bologna as its cultural centre, is a case in point. The small-scale manufacturing sector goes hand in hand with the 'informal sector' and policy makers here and in other places, have drawn the conclusion that there is a trade-off between some acceptance of informality and economic growth (Quassoli, 1999; Magatti and Quassoli, 2003). In the

Northern European countries there is less tolerance towards unregistered economic activity. Germany has declared war on the *Schattenwirt-schaft* (shadow economy) and the Netherlands during the mid-1990s applied the full wrath of the 'social' state in an unprecedented crackdown on Turkish entrepreneurs in the Amsterdam garment industry (see Chapter 8).

The *Financial Times* in an Editorial commenting on the black economy in Europe, suggested that an alternative approach might be to 'see the black economy as the result of market forces outrunning the capacity of governments to adapt. It is for legislators to catch up' (*Financial Times*, Editorial, 8 April 1998, 'Black Economy'). Belatedly, the German government picked up on this advice. An attempt to 'formalise' the *Schattenwirt-schaft* appeared in the form of the 'mini-job' rule, making it easier to register low-paid employees. At the same time the government has created the FKS, an 120-strong customs cell overseeing a special customs and taxation force comprised of 7,000 officers, who are dressed 'in combat boots and green berets', unusual wear by most accounts of Her Majesty's Custom and Excise (Benoit, 2004:10).

The contrast between Germany and Italy is drawn in a comparison between two studies. Quassoli (1999) points to the tolerance of the informal sector by the institutional framework as explanation for a system of informal labour, estimated at 25 per cent of all labour in southern Italy. Hillmann (2000:7), argues that 'the opposite was true in Germany [...] here the polarisation of the new migration movements in the labour market has produced a highly stigmatised sector'.

The regulation of the informal economy has surfaced in concerns over the gang master system, which supplies intensive agriculture with illegal seasonal labour. This has reinforced closer scrutiny of immigrant enterprises in the provision of labour. In the Netherlands one third of all illegal workers (estimated at 100,000) are employed in market gardening. European governments created statuses for temporary, seasonal or fixed duration immigration. The intention was to formalise short-term stay for work (mini guest workers) but to preclude any possibility of obtaining the right to longer-term stay in the EU. In fact this system has operated in France since the 1960s, with seasonal workers from Morocco and Tunisia on OMI contracts (*l'Office des Migrations Internationales*) whereby workers 'are physically located in France, but as far as their rights are concerned they are in Morocco' (Bell, 2002:3). The accession into the European Union of Poland and other Eastern European states, has seen the entry of countries whose GDP per head is considerably lower. In the case of Poland and the Baltic states, it is 30–50 per cent below the EU-wide average, and in the case of future entrants, Rumania and Bulgaria, less than 30 per cent. This has created a new pool of cheap labour which has become increasingly important in seasonal agriculture and service sector employment. Over 15 per cent of all new national insurance numbers issued in the UK during 2001–2002, were to immigrant workers.

'Neo-American' versus 'Rhineland' model

The repositioning of a significant layer of immigrants from workers to entrepreneurs and their contribution to the transformation of sectors, cities and neighbourhoods, is an emergent area for research in continental Europe. One polarity is presented by Kloosterman (2000:98–103) between a 'neo-American' versus 'Rhineland' model of immigrant incorporation and enterprise development. At one level, the 'American' model can be understood in generalisation and necessary assumptions which surface in the work of Waldinger, Portes and Light, about the relationship between immigrants, labour markets and the institutional framework in the United States. They assume a framework which is consistent with 'unlimited supplies of labour'. Kloosterman presents these generalisations into a recognisable category, the 'neo-American' model, which is then contrasted (to its opposite) in the 'Rhineland' model as representative of the European continental experience (see below). In previous work Kloosterman (1996), in following Esping-Anderson (1990), pointed towards institutional variation in European states. First, in the form of the liberal welfare state offering limited protection. Second, in the social-democratic welfare state, typified by extensive protection and active labour market policies (such as, employment creation). And third, in the corporatist welfare state involving consensus i.e. 'paying people off' and underpinned as with (social-democracy) by tripartism between unions, employers and the state, usually in the name of the 'national interest'.

In the Rhineland model, the welfare state is identified as actively blocking the development of immigrant enterprise and employment opportunities due to its perceived over-regulated nature. This appears as a particularly strong feature of the personal services sector. Indeed in personal services, Kloosterman (2000:102) argued that immigrant enterprises are 'veering towards a permanent *Lumpen* bourgeoisie existence', whilst in production activities, subcontracting 'allows the circumvention of corporatist relations'. Personal services include child care, house-cleaning, care of the elderly, i.e. the commoditisation of large chunks of reproductive labour, much of which is provided by the public sector in which outsourcing is a growing phenomenon (see Panayiotopoulos, 2005). Kloosterman (2000:101–102) writes that labour in corporatist states is 'protected against market forces by high and easily obtainable social benefits, minimum wages and strict labour regulations'. This contributes towards higher unemployment, thereby, closing the door to low-paid job opportunities for low-skilled immigrants. Under these circumstances 'the less talented (the excluded) have a much greater incentive to become entrepreneurs'.

- *Neo-American model*, in which a continuous supply of immigrants expands aggregate demand typically in the form of low-paid jobs.

Under these circumstances, entrepreneurship in the little-regulated 'informal sector' may offer more opportunities for social mobility than the abundant but low-paid jobs in manufacturing and service employment.

- *Rhineland model*, in which continental European 'welfare states' retard the development of immigrant enterprise and employment opportunities due to their over-regulated nature. Labour is protected by social legislation, which contributes towards closing low-paid, 'informal sector' employment opportunities for low-skilled immigrants. Under these circumstances many unemployed immigrants are pushed into self-employment.

Two observations can be made of Kloosterman's argument First, there is a much greater diversity in the European institutional experience, for example in toleration towards the 'informal sector', than is suggested in the compression of the Rhineland model. Second, and more significantly for the theoretical premises of the argument, is the view that immigrant enterprise under these conditions, is therefore, invariably relegated to the 'fringes' of economic and political systems. Similarly, Haberfellner (2003) points to the example of Austria, as one where strict regulations, high barriers to start-ups and processes towards concentration of the retail sector, limit opportunities to less prosperous niches and create a 'disadvantaged' group of entrepreneurs. Hilmann (2000) defines immigrant enterprise in Germany as 'liminal' i.e. occupying a position like no others, typically at the intersection of formal or informal labour markets or, alternatively, at the 'fringes' of both the formal and informal economy.

The above (pessimistic) interpretation, may well be a more accurate description of some regions and cities within Europe when compared to the United States. At the same time, as much of the previous and coming material suggests, a general view of immigrant enterprise as essentially marginal, is highly prejudicial. Pang (2003) suggests that the failure to recognise the diversity and socio-economic differentiation of immigrant enterprises and immigrant communities themselves, is in part the result of the 'victim-driven' nature of most research in Belgium (and elsewhere) on immigrants and their economic activities. Neither is it clear to this reader, how an attack on the welfare state is to the benefit of most members of immigrant and ethnic minority groups who are more likely to be employed in it (one third of UK NHS staff, for example) and to use its services.

Turkish entrepreneurs: major cities as intersections

According to Manco (2004:6–7) an estimated 57,000 Turkish-owned enterprises during 1996, employed a total of 186,000 workers throughout Europe. The vast bulk of the firms (42,000) were in Germany, with the Netherlands, France and Austria making up the remainder. Findings from the Turkish Research Centre (TRC, 2000) at the University of Essen, Germany, estimate that in 1999 a total of 73,200 Turkish-owned enterprises employed a total of 366,000 workers throughout Europe (see, Table 6.1). Turkish immigrant entrepreneurs represent a significant and growing economic force in Europe. As the above indicates, during the five year period (1995 to 1999) nearly 20,000 more enterprises were added to the total representing a 34.5 per cent rate of increase. The estimated turnover of the firms (at 61.2 billion pre-Euro Deutch Marks) was equivalent to one fifth of Denmark's Gross Domestic Product (GDP). One conservative estimate of the total contribution made by Turks to the European economy is that it amounts to the equivalent of 51 per cent of Greece's GDP (TRC, 2000:3).

The distribution of enterprises reflects on the pattern of Turkish immigration and the formation of community ties. Working-class neighbourhoods in cities such as Berlin, Hamburg, Amsterdam, Vienna and London

Table 6.1 Turkish entrepreneurs in Europe (1995–1999)

	1995	*1997*	*1998*	*1999*
Number	54,300	62,100	67,000	73,000
Total investments (billion DM)	10.3	11.8	13.8	15.4
Average turnover for each company (DM)	777,000	812,000	832,00	836,000
Total annual turnover (billion DM)	42.2	50.4	56.1	61.2
Average number of workers in each company	3.9	4.1	4.8	5.0
Total number of workers	212,000	254,000	323,000	366,000

Source: Turkish Research Centre, Essen, April 2000:3.

Table 6.2 Turkish population in the main European countries and cities

Host country	Population (000s)	Per cent	City	Per cent of total
Germany	2,014	66.4	Berlin	7.0
France	261	8.6	Paris	25.0
Netherlands	260.1	8.6	Amsterdam	20.0
Austria	143.2	4.7	Vienna	32.0
Belgium	119.0	3.9	Brussels	33.0
Switzerland	79.4	2.6	Zurich	21.0
United Kingdom	58.2	1.9	London	64.0
Sweden	35.7	1.2	Stockholm	50.0
Denmark	35.7	1.2	Copenhagen	50.0

Source: Manco, 2004:4–5.

have seen the formation of communities which over the last two decades (some longer than others), have become centres for immigrant enterprise (see Table 6.2). In the cities of Brussels, Antwerp and Ghent, Turkish entrepreneurs form the largest group of immigrant entrepreneurs. Most started with little capital and tend to crowd around similar sectors, such as food processing, retail and catering. Turkish entrepreneurs come into conflict with the regulatory regime in 'old' Europe in more novel ways than those suggested by the (reductionist) Rhineland model. Pang writes that,

> Since the Middle Ages, each street in Ghent is organised in a 'dekenij', a merchant association with the status of a non-profit making organisation. It has been very difficult to convince these traditional merchant associations to include immigrant business people in their associations as equal members.
>
> (Pang, 2003:5)

One survey of 100 Turkish firms in Brussels, found that most of the entrepreneurs were young, below 35 years of age, and that one fifth were university graduates. Only one third of them had any training specific to their work. Nearly 45 per cent were in the retail sector (groceries) and had mainly Turkish customers. Over one third of them used start-up capital of $15,000 or less, and only one in five used the commercial banking sector to do so. In terms of labour input they are described as 'small-scale family enterprises', yet of the total of 412 persons employed, only 23 per cent were family workers and 65 per cent were of Turkish origin. A significant proportion of employment generated (35 per cent) consisted of the employment of other immigrant groups (Bayar, 1996:3, 6–7).

Berlin: the Turkish metropolis

Berlin is the major centre of settlement for immigrants from Turkey and accounts for 5 per cent of all Turkish immigrants in Europe (Manco, 2004:4). The development of immigrant enterprise has been influenced by the prolonged recession affecting the German economy and illustrated in rising levels of unemployment. During 1998, 4.8 million people were out of work. Nearly one in four (21.0 per cent) of the labour force in East Germany lost their jobs. The Turkish community (which makes up 2.5 per cent of the population), faced a 25 per cent rate of unemployment (Norman, 1998:8). During January 2005 Germany's unemployment levels rose to a post-war height of 5.04 million. Many Turkish immigrants lack vocational qualifications or 'transferable skills' and are over-represented in sectors which have seen most job losses – metal engineering, industrial and office cleaning, construction, local government manual work and the garment industry. Estimates of Turkish unemployment rates in Berlin are as high as 40 per cent (Hillmann, 2000:9). This has disproportionately affected young men. Only 6.4 per cent of 18 to 25 year olds in Germany go into higher education (Manco, 2004:5).

One powerful view is that the loss of employment was a significant 'push' factor for many ex-guest workers and their children to look to alternatives. Bayar (1996:1) argues that under these circumstances, many Turkish immigrants responded by 'creating their own businesses'. Hilmann suggests that 'it is likely that the very difficult situation of the Turkish population on the labour market might have contributed to the remarkable increase in Turkish entrepreneurship in the 1990' (Hilmann, 2000:12). One early 'niche' appeared in the grocery store and restaurant sectors. By 1992 one third of restaurants in West Germany were immigrant-owned. Immigrants appear to have levels of self-employment which are comparable to those of native workers. This, however, disguises sharp difference between rates of self-employment amongst Greek (16 per cent), Italian (12 per cent), and Turkish (5 per cent) ex-guest workers. Whilst amongst the Turkish community, self-employment was 'relatively modest' in 1998 (when the above comparisons were made) it represented a five-fold increase from 1980 when only 1 per cent of Turkish immigrants were self-employed (Wilpert, 2003:241–243). Given the large size of the Turkish community in Germany this amounts to tens of thousands of people. Most commentators (Wilpert, Kloosterman, Pang, and others) point to an acceleration of self-employment amongst Turkish immigrants in Germany and even more so in other countries in Europe.

Wilpert suggests that the later development of Turkish enterprise in Germany, when compared to other guest worker groups and to Turks in other European cities, may reflect on the 'differential treatment of former guest workers' and 'exclusionary processes towards certain groups' (Wilpert, 2003:233). Turkish immigrants were racialised and when compared to North Africans this worked to their advantage. Nevertheless, the historical Turkish experience in Germany has been one built on negative stereotypes, as 'foreigners', who only have an instrumental labour-market value. There are also significant institutional barriers and restrictions on self-employment by non-EU nationals as many Turks in Germany are classified. These include the requirement of eight years' legal residence and an assessment by the police and the Chamber of Industry and Commerce which determines 'whether or not the proposed venture is considered harmful or not to the overall economy', and which approves or not the permit to be self-employed (Wilpert, 2003:237).

There is an increasing body of knowledge about Turkish entrepreneurs in Berlin (see, Gokturk, 1999; Pecoud, 2001). Hilmann (2000:13–14) found some 3,600 firms listed in the Turkish Yellow Pages for 1998, and estimates that by the end of the 1990s, 6,000 enterprises were owned by immigrants from Turkey. Most of these were small enterprises relying on family labour (four fifths of employment) in the restaurant, services and retail sectors. The bulk of the enterprises were located in working-class neighbourhoods, such as Kreuzberg, Tiergarten, Wedding and Neukolm and impacted by economic recession translated to low spending power, leading to 'the collapse of many businesses'. The food sector in the form of ethnic restaurants, takeaways, groceries and vegetable stalls, initially in cases set up to cater to ethnic groups but which have become part of the neighbourhood shopping of many non-ethnic residents, are the most significant areas of sectoral concentration by immigrant entrepreneurs. About three quarters of Turkish owned enterprises in Germany are in retail and catering (Bayar, 1996:2). Wilpert (2003:246–247) also points to concentrations in manufacturing, construction and the ethnic service sector: travel agents, translation and community services, accountants.

The attitude of the Berlin City Council towards Turkish enterprise is a reflection of a wider continental European ambivalence. Policy makers recognise its instrumental economic value in creating jobs, revitalising decaying inner-city areas and so on. At the same time entrepreneurs are more likely to be associated with the 'informal economy' and are periodically subjected to repression, frequently by the same authorities.

The 'doner revolution'

The doner kebab, was 'invented in Berlin', according to Czarina Wilpert (2003:246). Leaving aside that a doner kebab could have been had in Hackney, East London in 1972, what the 'doner revolution' represented was the commodification of 'traditional' ethnic food (see, Hilmann and Rudolph, 1997). One common example is the 'Italian' pizza. The basis of the doner and much of Turkish food is the flat pitta bread, made up of two layers of bread knitted together. As with the Italian pizza it illustrates the influence of eastern cooking. The pizza and pitta derive from the influence of Arab and Turkish bread making. The Neapolitans added a layer of tomatoes on the flat pitta bread, baked it and called it a 'pizza'. The doner itself is an ovular lump of meat (usually lamb or chicken), which is skewered in the middle and grilled (upright) in a cooker with electric bars surrounding the meat. Slices of the meat and optional additions – onion, tomato, cucumber, salt, lemon juice, tahini (a sesame-based pulse) – are put into the sliced and warmed pitta bread. The commodification takes another dimension: for value-adding and western consumption purposes, cheaper material such as shredded cabbage and carrot are included in the pitta.

Whilst some Greek restaurants and takeaways have responded by including a version of the doner called 'Gyros' on their menu, the trade is monopolised by Turkish entrepreneurs and the expansion of doner takeaways has been the single most significant source of enterprise formation for Turkish immigrants in Germany and throughout Europe. In the UK, doner takeaways are an important part of the after-pub and after-club trade. Current moves in the UK to extend pub closing times, will in all probability, lead to the increased consumption of doner kebabs. The 'doner revolution' can be seen as the selective adaptation of traditional and now commoditised Turkish cuisine. It also displaced other forms of Middle-Eastern takeaway food. The shish kebab, which is widely consumed in the Middle East and the Balkans and is more popular in certain parts of Turkey, became a rarity. Its preparation and cooking is more labour intensive. Instead of one lump of meat (as with the doner), it involves cutting the meat into many smaller pieces which are individually skewered and placed on a flat cooker with the electric bars below the meat. Shish kebab requires more attention as the meat has to be manually turned over, whilst the doner turns and cooks automatically. Commoditisation represents an increase in the ratio of capital (equipment) to labour. Many of the takeaways can literally consist of one man in a kiosk. From the point of view of entry, when compared to other areas of takeaway consumption such as fish and chip shops and 'Chinese' takeaways, the doner takeaway sector has significantly reduced the cost of entry into entrepreneurship.

The above would not have been possible in Germany (or elsewhere) without the economic differentiation of Turkish entrepreneurs. Wilpert (2003:252–253) notes that some 'have moved from retail to wholesale'. The movement to a wholesaler position was an early feature of Turkish groceries in Berlin, where in 1972 a system (akin to a cooperative) saw bulk-buying in order to reduce the cost of goods imported from Turkey for consumption by the Turkish community. More significantly, we have seen the emergence of wholesalers of prepared meat used in the doner kebab trade. It is this, more than any other factor, which has made it possible for many entrepreneurs to start up. One Turkish Cypriot-owned company in London delivers to over 1,000 outlets. The industrial processing of meat has significantly lowered the labour costs of takeaways. For example, in the labour time that would otherwise be spent in kneading the meat manually into a cookable state. Factory processing has allowed the application of economies of scale which have significantly lowered the price of meat for the retailers of doner. The application of economies of scale has seen the resurgence of the shish kebab, as thousands of (mainly) immigrant workers cut and skewer individual pieces of meat onto sticks, which are delivered to retailers according to demand. These supply-side considerations need to be understood, as well as the popularity of the doner, due in part to millions of holidaymakers from Europe who visit Turkey every year.

One important example of food processing which surfaces in the wider continental European experience, is bread making. The flat Turkish bread has become widely consumed in Europe, particularly in the takeway trade as a necessary accompaniment to the doner kebab. In Belgium, the Netherlands and Germany, competition between Turkish bakers appears in the vicious under-cutting of the price ('bread wars'), sometimes leading to the deterioration of the quality of the product, such as for example, less flour is put in the bread than indicated. In Belgium, they fell foul of the Union of Bakeries and Confectionaries i.e. the relevant trade association. In Ghent and North Antwerp, local enterprise development initiatives by thinking practitioners, in collaboration with the Association of Turkish Merchants, successfully negotiated a standard price for Turkish bread. In North Antwerp, the project facilitated collaboration between eight Turkish and eight Arab-speaking bakers (Pang, 2000:7–8).

One consequence of the doner takeaway phenomenon, is that Turkish entrepreneurs have developed a specialisation in meat processing. Pork sausages, for example, are widely consumed in Europe and nowhere more so than Germany. Turkish entrepreneurs have become important suppliers to Turkish-owned groceries and also to some of the chain stores. They have also developed a speciality as bakers, particularly of pitta bread, but also other breads, sweets, dried nuts and confectionaries. The development of food processing, points to important differences between the mass of doner kebab takeaways on the one hand, and the fewer suppliers of these products, on the other. The suppliers are involved in value-adding manufacturing processing, whilst takeaways (and the retail sector generally) rely primarily on the price mark-up and consumer naivety. Groceries, and meat and bread processing, provide evidence of the development of Turkish wholesalers and the emergence of a significant layer of large enterprises which operate across borders. In doing so, they have significantly pushed out of the 'fringes'.

Chinese entrepreneurs and the fake designer goods industry

There is an expanding literature on Chinese immigration and the role of transnational links in the shaping of labour and trade diaspora in Europe. Much of the research reflects on the role of key gateway cities and harbour towns in Europe; Liverpool, Amsterdam, Rotterdam, Hamburg, London, Paris (see, Yun, 2004; Benton and Pieke, 1998; Pieke and Benton, 1998; Yu-Sion, 1998). One introductory note is the complexity contained within the term 'Chinese'. Frequently it refers to members of the expatriate community who are non-Chinese nationals and citizens of other countries, such as Vietnam, Hong Kong, Indonesia, Taiwan, Singapore and Malaysia. The above migrated at different times and faced different historical circumstances. One change in contemporary Chinese immigration, is that arrivals from mainland China have become more significant in the composition of the Chinese communities. This surfaced previously in discussion on New York's Chinatown (see, Chapter 3). During the 1980s, immigration from northern Fujian Province linked to human trafficking as a response to stringent immigration controls, became a significant factor in the restructuring of the many Chinatowns in the United States and Europe. Even more recently arrived labour migrants, such as immigrants from Dongbei, appear as the most marginalised. Yun notes that they do not yet have a chain of immigration ties,

> They are completely isolated. If there is a hierarchy within the Chinese communities, they are at the bottom. The Dongbei women are employed by Zhejiang families as nannies. The Chinese prostitutes who have appeared in the streets of Paris and Milan in the last years are mostly from Dongbei.
>
> (Yun, 2004:6)

Pieke (1998) points to the fact that Chinese immigrants established some of the oldest immigrant communities in Europe, initially in ports such as Cardiff, Rotterdam, Liverpool and Hamburg. Before the Second World War most migrants were temporary contract labourers. Many were recruited by shipping companies as a way of undermining the unions. Decolonisation brought several hundred thousand additional immigrants from South-East Asia to continental Europe (France, the Netherlands). Students have also become a growing source of new immigration (Pieke, 1998:3–5). The first independent immigration was by small merchants who originated from the hinterland of the port city of Wenzhou who built links with labour migrants and often supplied them with provisions.

Fake designer goods

The production and distribution of fake designer goods is by no means the property of any given ethnic group. Nevertheless, Chinese entre-preneurs offer an example of a significant specialisation or trade dias-pora in this sector. The sectoral focus, if there is one, involves leather goods (particularly, women's leather handbags), fashion-wear items and accessories.

The most visible dimension are hundreds of street-sellers, most of whom are not Chinese, trying to sell copies of Cartier watches, Dolce and Gabbana sunglasses, Prada scarves, Gucci bags and an assortment of other counterfeit designer fashion goods, which are widely distributed in Europe. These goods, which blend with legitimate products, are specifi-cally targeted at tourists, both in the holiday resorts of southern Spain, and also the major European city destinations, such as Venice, Paris, Florence, Barcelona and Rome. Frequently, they are sold in holiday shops owned by native workers. The army of mainly young male street-sellers, negotiate amongst themselves for the best spots i.e. those with more tourists, or wealthier tourists, or at bus and ferry stop-over points, or the best time of the day or night. Typically, it involves the display of hand-held goods, or goods laid on a blanket on the ground which can be gathered for a quick getaway from the police, depending on their attitude. Street-selling such as in the holiday sea resorts is a seasonal activity but in the perennial tourist cities there is more scope for all-year activity (Quassoli, 1999:221–222; Panayiotopoulos, 2000a, Venice, personal observation).

The attitude of the law to street-sellers is lenient in Italy and Spain, but less tolerant in Paris and even less so in other north-western European cities. Street-selling is more tolerated in Italy than most other countries. Many of the sellers are from Senegal, but also China, Sri Lanka and other countries. In one observation made of Barcelona's sea-front, which was developed to accommodate a previous Olympic Games, something like 100 sellers had their goods on the ground. The street-sellers were of different colours, gender and world distribution, but all were young. Amongst a group of nine Chinese street-sellers, eight were students, three were female, and for five of them this was their only source of income to cover daily expenses (Panayiotopoulos, 2003, Barcelona, personal observation).

A network of cities linking production and retail

The many street-sellers are the retail end-point of a production process which links tourists from all over the world, to the small workshops in the 'Third Italy' and the cities of Florence, Milan, Treviso, Prato, Naples and Paris. Chinese entrepreneurs have integrated themselves in this production and distribution cycle, partly by utilising the network of existing merchants and enterprises in the cities of Europe. Yun (2004) revealed a number of labour and trade diaspora: one diaspora built on the existing community from Zhejiang and the southern regions of Wenzhou and Qingtian, in the Arts-et-Métiers area in Paris where many specialise as dealers in leatherwear goods (Yu-Sion, 1998:213). Many of these Zhejiangnese immigrant entrepreneurs, bring with them (or so one argument runs) regional production systems from the Wenzhou area, in which each workshop specialises in the production of one part of the product, which is then assembled locally. Yun (2004:6) suggests that in the Chinese trade diaspora in France and Italy involved in the production of leather goods and clothing, 'we recognise an extension of the overseas "Wenzhou Economic Model"' (also see, Tomba, 1996).

The Chinese community in Italy, before 1986, was made up of an estimated 1,500 people. By 1992 it had increased to 23,000, primarily concentrated in the large cities of middle and northern Italy: Milan, Bologna, Florence, Rome and Turin. An equal number were estimated to be illegals (*clandestini*). Today the Chinese community is made up of approximately 100,000 people, forming in cases *i quartiery cinesi* (Chinese quarters) in working-class neighbourhoods. Rome has the largest concentration followed by the Tuscany metropolitan area which includes Florence, Prato and Campi Bisenzio. This area accounted for an estimated 25,000 Chinese *clandestini* during the mid-1990s and even more today. In some of the communes around Florence, 'the Chinese and Italian population are virtually equal in number' (Wong, 1999:320–321).

Table 6.3 Distribution of Chinese enterprises: Florence–Prato area (1995)

Sector	Florence	Prato	Campi Bisenzio
Leather	124	2	–
Clothing	14	261	81
Total manufacturing	*138*	*265*	*81*
Commercial	2	3	51
Restaurants	27	–	–
Other commercial activities	8	2	–
Total commercial activities	*37*	*5*	*51*
Grand total	175	270	132

Source: Tomba, 1996.

Unlike other immigrant groups in Italy, some formed enterprises initially employing family members and co-ethnics, and subsequently other immigrants groups, in handicrafts, restaurants, in street-selling activities and the import and distribution of goods from China. In Milan there are an estimated 200 Chinese restaurants and 600 leather firms which serve as an important centre for the industry. Similarly in Rome, these two sectors dominate the pattern of enterprise and employment. In the Tuscany metropolitan region, given that the region is the centre of the Italian clothing industry, many entrepreneurs have entered this sector also (see Table 6.3). Tomba (1996) pointed to the role of a Wenzhou network in Florence, specialising in the manufacture of leather handbags. In Prato, 'most of the Chinese businesses became sub-contractors [...] to the ready-to-wear manufacturers of that city' (Wong, 1999:321).

Treviso–Venice: an 'industrial district'

Magatti and Quassoli (2003:169) write that 'the "model" of Chinese business communities' has been 'exported' to 'traditional or new industrial districts' and cite Treviso, along with Prato and the hinterland of Naples, as one centre for the recent expansion in Chinese entrepreneurship. An 'industrial district' is a concept which derives from urban geography and is applied by economists to define an agglomeration of flexible producers, designers, contractors and subcontractors in a robust local economy, within which informal transactions and production relations (cf. New York's garment industry) take place. The 'district' is more expansive in this instance and is found across the cities of Europe. It is also highly specific to the production of fake designer goods. An ethnically informed 'Chinese' industrial district which links producers and consumers in the tourist cities of Europe.

Treviso is the north-east region of Venetto, historically the heart of right-wing politics in Italy and an area of strong support for the anti-immigrant Northern League. It is probably as near as one gets to an Italian 'Deep South'. In one incident, the Mayor of Treviso referred to all Africans as 'monkeys'. On the face of it, an unlikely place, institutionally, for the emergence of immigrant enterprise. It is, however, situated near Venice, which has more visitors than any other European tourist city (including Paris). During the early months of 2000, something akin to a 'moral panic' broke out in the Italian national media about the 'phenomenon' of Treviso. Researchers 'discovered' a total of 290 immigrant-owned enterprises, of which 230 had been established during a three year period (1997 to 1999). The largest grouping were 123 enterprises owned by men from the ex-Yugoslavian countries, with over 80 per cent of them in construction. The second largest group were Chinese women who accounted for 49 firms, with over 87 per cent of them in clothing (Magatti and Quassoli, 2000:16). In many cities, the emergence of a couple of hundred immigrant enterprises would not warrant this response. It became a national issue in Italy because the xenophobes, perversely, tried to use this example of immigrant innovation in the polarised debate in Italy about immigration.

The 'export' of the 'Wenzhou Economic Model' as explanation for the Treviso phenomenon and Chinese immigrant clustering, is insufficiently sensitive to the role of other factors. Magatti and Quassoli (2003:167) also argue that Chinese enterprises in the leather goods and clothing sector 'are located in regions and cities [such as in metropolitan Tuscany] characterized by a traditional diffusion of informal arrangements'. They point to the only particular characteristic of Chinese-owned workshops, as 'the employment of undocumented workers deeply indebted to their employers', and further add that,

> [Chinese] self-employment in small workshops and firms has not yet introduced any relevant innovation into the social organisation of these economic activities. On the contrary, there is exactly the same forms of organisation as in the small firms and workshops managed by Italian entrepreneurs.
>
> (Magatti and Quassoli, 2003:168)

In the above, Chinese entrepreneurs can be understood as an ethnic adaptation to the existing 'informal sector'. Other explanations point to the labour content of the diaspora and in the skills held by immigrants, which might be relevant to the garment and leather-craft industries. Many of the Wenzhou immigrant entrepreneurs were tailors and leather-workers in China. One study in Paris found that none of the Zhejian business owners had ever worked for local French companies, or claimed unemployment benefit before forming their own enterprises, and in this sense, 'they form something of an exception' (Yun, 2004:8). Another factor is in the effect of proximity. All enterprises in the fashion-wear and accessories sector in cities in Italy and France benefit from the reputation of 'Made in Italy' leather products and 'Made in France' clothing.

More significant, perhaps, is the impact of economic restructuring in Prato, Florence and the Tuscany metropolitan region, which saw the growth of subcontracting, and which created the space for Chinese entrepreneurs to enter the lower end of garment production (such as assembling). Indeed there are indications that this was a process actively promoted by manufacturers and other intermediaries in sectors such as leather goods, garments and construction (Magatti and Quassoli, 2003:170). Other 'niches' emerged for the production of low-quality and low-priced goods. A familiar enough immigrant story.

Conclusions

In Europe, far more than the United States, what happens to immigrant enterprise is 'in formation' and more finely balanced. Policy towards immigration and the 'informal economy' are examples. At the same time we see predictable trajectories, outcomes and debates. The immigrant story in Europe is, however, an increasingly more complex story as immigrant communities and enterprises become more socially and economically differentiated. It is worth reflecting on the typology of immigrant incorporation presented by Magatti and Quassoli (2000) and, in the light of the material reviewed, in order to revisit one major theme in the book. Does the experience indicate that immigrant enterprise is the result of the considerable ingenuity of the entrepreneurs operating under difficult circumstances? Or/and does it shed light on the wider restructuring of cities and sub-sectors and the role of the institutional framework in explaining convergence and variation in immigrant outcomes in the European Union?

A typology of enterprise formation can be presented in terms of whether immigrant or informal sector enterprises emerge from 'below' or 'above' and the degree of market autonomy i.e. relative capacity for independent decision making in economic actions. This is a complex issue which appears in different arrangements and is influenced by the extent of concentration and the nature of subcontracting in particular industries and services. However, 'independence' and market autonomy are ostensibly defining criteria for entrepreneurship itself. This issue raises substantive questions about the frontiers of control and older debate about the concept of the informal economy itself (see below) (Magatti and Quassoli, 2000:17; Gerry, 1985).

Enterprise formation: flow of control

- *From 'below'*, enterprises which emerge in relation to the community experience, such as in response to meeting demand for specific community goods and services, or through the mobilisation and concentration of internal resources in particular sectors and subsectors, in which many were previously employed as wage-workers.

• *From 'above'*, induced, artificial, supported and sponsored by local entrepreneurs, 'who in cases are actually active in the establishment of ethnic business' and who understand the benefits of having many competing contractors and subcontractors: reflected in significant institutional variation in tolerance towards the 'informal sector'.

This chapter drew from two immigrant groups involved in different subsectors in order to illustrate change and continuity in continental Europe. Turkish entrepreneurs have a presence of over four decades. Immigrant entrepreneurs from mainland China are a more recent phenomenon. The former show a concentration in the doner takeaway and clothing sectors, and the latter in the restaurant, leather, clothing and fake designer goods sectors (also see Chapter 8). Both appear to contain elements of enterprise development from 'above' and 'below'. In the case of Chinese enterprises in Florence and Prato involved in the production of leather goods, many were assisted in their entry by the sourcing preferences of native intermediaries. In the case of Turkish enterprises in the doner takeaway sector, many began from 'below', but some are now food processors and/or are wholesalers who promote other takeaways by lowering the cost of entry and guaranteeing weekly deliveries of a comprehensive package and product ('just like McDonald's', as one entrepreneur explained it).

Much of it hinges on how we analyse the phenomenon of immigrant enterprise. We noted previously, Felicitas Hilmann's (2000:8) thesis on the 'liminal' positioning of Turkish enterprise in Berlin i.e. as between and below both the formal and informal sectors. This view, of Turkish enterprise as essentially precarious, marginal and on the 'fringes' of economic systems, appears in diverse literature. Some of it draws, as we noted, from the Rhineland model, which points to the 'over-regulated' welfare state as (perverse) explanation for the 'underdevelopment' of Turkish and other immigrant enterprise in continental Europe (see, Kloosterman, 2000; Hilmann, 2000; Haberfellner, 2003). The view that the behaviour of immigrant entrepreneurs in Berlin (or elsewhere), is determined 'primarily due to relatively high level of social benefits in Germany' (Hilman, 2000:17) is a peculiar argument. Much of the evidence indicates that many Turkish immigrants saw self-employment as preferable to claiming benefits they had paid for, in cases, all their working lives.

The assumptions that immigrant enterprise and communities are on the 'fringes' of economic systems and need to be 'integrated', or are in the informal economy and need to be regulated, influence institutional behaviour towards immigrant communities. Both the Turkish and mainland immigrant Chinese communities (for all their historical differences) are commonly impacted by the immigration and naturalisation system in a negative way. The criminalisation and hindering of 'normal' economic transactions by men in combat boots and green berets, racist harassment, physical injury and high insurance premiums, lack of mother tongue provision and in the case of illegal entrepreneurs the fear of detention, deportation and family break-ups, contributed to the uneven (and in the Turkish case late) development and differentiation of immigrant enterprise.

The view that immigrant enterprise is on the 'fringes', however, is defied in one optimistic note about Turkish entrepreneurs. Despite the immense difficulties faced by them (least of all the long hours they work), they have not allowed the authorities to drive them into the margins. Their numerical expansion, the emergence of wholesalers and suppliers and diversification into other areas (most notably food processing), with greater control over value-adding parts of the commodity chain, indicates a vibrant economy, which as the doner kebab takeaway sector illustrates, has come into the mainstream. The economic restructuring of particular subsectors and neighbourhoods within cities and its relationship to the agency of immigrant enterprise is more complex than the level of benefits paid and assumptions made about how members of an ethnic group in all its diversity might behave.

Pieke (1998:13) in commenting on the many Chinatowns in the United States and South East Asia, reminds us that they 'were as much a product of racial segregation [...] as they were the natural outcome of Chinese cultural characteristics'. Pieke (1998:8,14) further argues that the 'vast differences between the Chinese communities in Europe are largely due to these differences in timing', and also, the impact of 'growing social stratification within the Chinese population'. The relationship between the historical circumstances immigrants find themselves in and the accumulated impact of immigrant enterprise on the social and economic stratification of the Chinese or Turkish communities in Europe, offers a far more useful avenue of investigation, than the perverse effects of the Rhineland model as causal explanation for the repositioning of Turkish and Chinese immigrants from workers to entrepreneurs. Another way of understanding the emergence of enterprise amongst immigrant groups in Europe, is to suggest that we are witnessing processes 'in formation', the future development of which might be difficult to predict. At the same time, accumulated evidence indicates that economic differentiation reveals far greater diversity than the 'fringe' literature suggests. Manco (2004:6) points to the emergence amongst the Turkish community,

> of a class of businessmen [sic] in Europe which increases the complexity of the Turkish immigrant population's social stratification while giving it a new dynamism. Henceforward, a Turkish population plagued by socio-economic marginalisation co-exists with a small class of businessmen that has the wind in its sails.

The potential entry of Turkey into the EU holds important implications for Turks in Germany. At a stroke, Turkey's entry into the EU would remove the ambiguity of their status and lack of political rights in Germany, by granting them rights as good as those that exist in any of the member countries. Europe is indeed testing ground for political innovation (as Sassen, 2004, reminds us). Turkish entrepreneurs in Europe are an example which should add weight to Sassen's benign view of the EU. After all, Turkish guest workers have been in Germany for over 40 years and were the bedrock of West Germany's post-war 'economic miracle'. The granting of automatic political rights implied in Turkish membership was an 'innovation' too much. When it came to Turkey negotiating entry into the EU, Frits Bolkestein, Single Market Commissioner, launched into a diatribe that Europe would be 'Islamisised' and went on to add that 'the liberation of Vienna [from the Turks] in 1683 would have been in vain' (quoted from Dombey, 2004:8). Turkey may have to accept emergency curbs on the free movement of its nationals, including most Turks in Germany, as a condition for joining the EU. In Berlin, the call to prayer remains banned, 'because it violates noise pollution rules' (Boyes, 2004:17).

The chapter concludes that the institutional and market environment provide the structure for the positioning and repositioning of the Turkish and Chinese immigrant communities and enterprises in Europe. This takes place through the immigration and naturalisation system, periodic drives against the informal economy and the economic restructuring of particular sectors and neighbourhoods within cities. The transition of some immigrants from guest worker to entrepreneurs is a potent symbol of this process. At the same time, we see immigrant communities applying forms of social organisation to take opportunities offered from 'above' and 'below'. One continuing tension arises from issues to do with embeddedness and representation in political systems and the implications this has for the sustainability of Turkish and other immigrant enterprise in Europe.

7 London

Enterprise in an immigrant metropolis

Introduction

London is the most cosmopolitan capital city in Europe and North America and this is reflected in the different languages spoken by school children, of whom nearly a quarter use a language other than English at home. It is estimated that more than one in three of London's population is either an immigrant or of immigrant origins, with nearly half of them born in the UK. London is also a centre of global wealth and an urban centre characterised by the persistence of poverty calculated in terms of material and social deprivation. For some of these reasons, London is a metropolis which amplifies issues to do with immigration, displacement, ethnicity, minority status, employment and enterprise. The East End of London is an illustration of this. In the sixteenth century French Huguenots established the lace industry. During the late nineteenth century, Jewish immigrants from Eastern Europe, transformed it into a major centre of garment production. Different flows of immigrants provided the labour and entrepreneurs: Greek and Turkish Cypriots; immigrants from the Indian subcontinent i.e. Pakistan, India and Bangladesh; and, more recently, mainland Turkish, Kurdish and Eastern European immigrants.

The Cypriot community is used as a case study. Cyprus was a British colony from 1871 to 1960 and for this reason, Cypriots migrated to Britain. The community has had a mass presence in London for over 50 years. Along with other immigrants from the British colonies, many of them arrived in large numbers during the 1950s as British passport holders. This facilitated family reunions. Many of the immigrants were artisans and this was a significant factor in their employment and subsequent enterprise activities. Cypriot entrepreneurs have become an important part of the local economy in a small number of north-east London boroughs (Haringey, Enfield, Hackney, Barnet, Islington) and many are concentrated in the catering, retail, garment, real-estate and financial services sectors. The Cypriot community have been presented by Roger Waldinger *et al.* (1985) as an 'achieving' minority, which other groups could emulate.

One question which surfaces in the book is over whether cities, such as London, are being transformed by immigrants themselves or whether this involves wider processes and relationships with the institutional framework and the restructuring by capital of particular sectors, industries and localities. This is investigated with reference to the garment industry and its long association with immigrant groups. In this, there are powerful elements of continuity. It is the case that many of them remain reliant on family labour and continue to crowd around the small-scale sector, typically as contractors and subcontractors in the women's fashion-wear sector. For many, life is precarious and they are constantly subjected to changes in the market place to which they appear as ill-equipped to respond. Being chased by the VAT Department of Her Majesty's Customs and Excise and other creditors is a regular experience. The informalisation of production remains an important continuity. This chapter, however, cautions against generalisations about immigrant enterprise and points to important changes. As has been previously argued, it is not the case that all firms are invariably small, operate on the fringes of the law and rely on the recruitment of family or co-ethnic workers. Much of the preceeding material challenges the view and points to a more complex process of economic differentiation. Some have become large firms. In some sectors, immigrant entrepreneurs dominate local employment. A significant proportion have broken out of the confines of the ethnic economy and entered the economic mainstream. The chapter considers the implications of informalisation, differentiation and economic restructuring for the positioning and repositioning of immigrant enterprise.

London: the capital city of immigrants

Whilst the overall impact of immigrant enterprise to the London economy is difficult to measure, London without immigrants would be demographically and economically a far less significant place. London is the most cosmopolitan capital city in Europe and North America, largely as the legacy of an expansive British colonialism reflected in immigration from the New Commonwealth countries. The largest groups of immigrants are from the New Commonwealth countries, with India first, followed by Jamaica, Kenya, Bangladesh and Cyprus (Storkey and Lewis, 1997:207). Currently, immigration is also driven by the opening-up of European cross-border migration to European Union nationals. London is also a reflection of how the world has become a more dangerous place reflected in an increased number of people seeking asylum and refuge. London's ethnic interspersion is reflected in the fact that it contains at least 50 different language groups with 10,000 or more speakers. At least a quarter of school children in London speak a language other than English at home, with the most common first language (other than English) being Bengali, which is spoken by 5 per cent of all pupils. Another 7 per cent speak either, Punjabi, Gujarati or Hindi (Storkey and Lewis, 1997).

The 1991 UK Census showed that London contained 12.2 per cent of the total population but nearly half (44.6 per cent) of Great Britain's ethnic minority population on the basis of country of birth data (Storkey and Lewis, 1997:201). The inclusion, for the first time, of the ethnic group question in the 1991 Census, allowed us to assess the relative size of the UK-born population of ethnic minority origin. This showed that 43 per cent of London's minority population were in fact born in the UK (Storkey, 1993:205). The 2001 Census registered a 40 per cent increase in people enumerated as 'black' and 'Asian' in England and Wales when compared to 1991. This stood in marked contrast to the 0.2 per cent growth in the population enumerated as 'white'. Half of the non-white population was born in the UK. The ethnic minority population in England and Wales increased from 6 per cent in 1991, to 9 per cent in 2001, and was made up of 4.21 million people. The biggest increase at 240 per cent and accounting for 514,000 people, was from the African continent. The Census also showed the arrival of significant numbers of immigrants from Eastern Europe. One contributing factor was the inclusion for the first time of 'mixed' ethnic groups in the Census (see, National Statistics Online, 2004a).

The 2001 Census showed that more than one in three of London's population were from minority origins. The decline in the white population was most pronounced in London, where it fell by 7 per cent to 71.3 per cent of the population. Data for Greater London shows the non-white population at more than two million people for the first time, when compared to 1.3 million in 1991. Another 795,000 people from 'other white' groups (Irish, Cypriot, Americans, continental Europeans) were also enumerated. Those defined as 'white British' made up 60 per cent of the total. Christians make up 70 per cent of England's population but in London account for 58 per cent of the population, with Muslims accounting for 8.5 per cent of all Londoners (National Statistics Online, 2004b). In two of London's 32 boroughs (excluding the City of London) ethnic minorities made up more than 50 per cent of the population, and in another three more than 40 per cent. These include the boroughs of Tower Hamlets, Newham and Hackney (see Table 7.1).

Significantly, the Census revealed that London accounted for 70 per cent of the UK's population growth between 1991 and 2001, even though it was home to only 12 per cent of the total population. It is in part due to immigration and higher birth rates amongst ethnic minority groups that London has seen the reversal of a long period of population decline. This lasted from the late 1930s when the population of London stood at 8.6 million, until the mid-1980s by which period it had fallen to 6.8 million, of whom only 2.5 million lived in inner London (made up of 13 out of the 32 London boroughs). During the 1990s, 400,000 people were added to London's population and another 700,000 people are projected to live in London by the year 2016. These trends were unpredicted by policy

Table 7.1 Ethnic minority population by London borough, 2001 (per cent)

London borough	Per cent	Per cent increase (1991–2001) (+)
Barking and Dagenham	14.8	118
Barnet	26.6	38
Bexley	8.6	46
Brent	54.7	21
Bromley	8.4	79
Camden	26.8	51
City of London	15.4	126
Croydon	29.8	67
Ealing	41.3	26
Enfield	22.9	60
Greenwich	22.9	77
Hackney	40.6	19
Havering	4.8	50
Hammersmith and Fulham	22.2	26
Haringey	34.4	17
Harrow	41.2	54
Hillington	20.9	69
Hounslow	35.1	42
Islington	24.6	30
Kensington and Chelsea	21.4	39
Kingston	15.5	78
Lambeth	37.6	23
Lewisham	34.1	52
Merton	25.0	51
Newham	60.6	41
Redbridge	36.5	60
Richmond	9.0	64
Southwark	37.0	49
Sutton	10.8	80
Tower Hamlets	48.6	34
Waltham Forest	35.5	37
Wandsworth	22.0	8
Westminster	26.8	28

Source: National Statistics Online, 2004b.

makers. In part, this was also the result of under-enumeration (subsequently adjusted) of young men, a disproportionate number of whom live in inner London and other major cities. The population of Manchester similarly saw Census figures adjusted upwards by 5 per cent (see, *Financial Times*, 26 June 2003, 'City's population baffles minister'; *Financial Times*, 28 August 2003, 'A rejuvenated London takes Government and policy planners by surprise').

Whilst information on the position of immigrants and their children is of variable quality, self-employment and employment in the small enterprise spectrum of the restaurant, retail and garment sectors are important areas of labour market participation by minorities, both as workers and as entrepreneurs. The Greater London Authority (GLA, 2003) estimates that 27 per cent of the inner London workforce comes from ethnic minority backgrounds. The London Skills Forecasting Unit (1999) estimated that 62,000 enterprises were owned by residents of ethnic minority origins, making up 19 per cent of all registered businesses in the London area. This is more pronounced in particular localities and sub-sectors of London's economy with the garment industry as a frequently cited example (see, London Skills Forecasting Unit, 2001). The average rate of participation in self-employment whilst (marginally) higher than amongst the white group, disguises sharp differences between members of minority groups enumerated as 'South Asian' and 'black', with self-employment rates of 20.8 per cent and 6.7 per cent respectively (see, Owen, 1997:53; Government Office for London, 2000, 2001). Explanations for the widely-observed disparity in UK enterprise formation between persons of Asian and Afro-Caribbean origin, point to much harsher processes of racial exclusion and the inability to access bank finance as critical factors in black under-representation (Ram and Jones, 1998). Another factor stems from important generational differences between first- and second-generation expectations and reluctance by second-generation young men and women to enter the 'niche' retail, restaurant or garment sectors in the face of other alternatives (Panayiotopoulos, 1990; Ram and Smallbone, 2001).

Data on income disparities and ethnic minorities in London is scarce, but unemployment is consistently higher amongst ethnic groups and this is also reflected in open registered unemployment. According to the International Labour Organisation (ILO) estimates, over one fifth of black men and Pakistani/Bangladeshi women were registered as unemployed in June 1998, when compared to an average white unemployment rate of 6 per cent (Panayiotopoulos, 2001a:100). At the same time, however, there are considerable inter-ethnic variations with estimates that three in four of Bangladeshi households are in the lower income group and Indian households nearer the income distribution associated with white households (Anderson and Flatley, 1997). What is certain, is that London is both a great centre of global wealth and an urban centre characterised by the persistence of poverty calculated in terms of material and social deprivation. In terms of material deprivation, using indicators such as the level of unemployment, number of lone parents, single pensioners, unemployed youth and those suffering from limiting illness, London is the most deprived city in England, with 13 inner and two outer London boroughs being amongst the 20 most deprived areas in the country. Whilst the relationship between wealth and poverty and the causation of social and spatial polarisation within the capital city are debatable (see, Sassen, 1991; Hamnett, 1996), indicators such as the rate of unemployment showed a rate which is eight times greater in poor wards when compared to richer wards in London. In the poorest inner-city wards of London 96 per cent of households do not own their own home and 74 per cent do not own a car when compared to only 3 and 5 per cent in the least deprived wards (Goodwin, 1996:1396–1397).

One recent study commissioned by the Mayor of London indicated that 53 per cent of children in inner London boroughs (including Hackney, Tower Hamlets, Newham, Lambeth and Southwark) were living in poverty. This is calculated as children living in households with disposable incomes below 60 per cent of the national average. Further, 40 per cent of children were living in households where at least one person was working. Child poverty was the highest amongst ethnic minority groups with, 73 per cent of Pakistani and Bangladeshi children, and 55 per cent of black children living in poverty (Gaffney, 2002). Whilst the position of immigrant groups in London shows considerable intra- and inter-variation one tendency is for members of minority groups to be over-represented in the inner London boroughs and wards which suffer most from deprivation (see, Storkey and Lewis, 1997:20–225). Another tendency is to work in sectors which are most systematically associated with low pay. The combined effect of being more likely to live in places where the representation of households with lower incomes is greater even by UK-wide standards, and the greater likelihood of working in low-pay sectors, offers substantial explanation for the positioning of immigrant and ethnic minorities in London.

Immigrants and the London garment industry

Immigrant entrepreneurs and workers have a long historical association with the London garment industry. Huguenot exiles in the sixteenth century, Eastern European Jewish refugees in the late nineteenth century and Cypriot and Bengali immigrants in the late twentieth century, all found a shelter in the trade. This is graphically illustrated by accounts of Victorian London, which show that it was not unusual for Jewish immigrant and local workers in the industry, who constituted a significant proportion of London's working poor, to hawk their own clothes in summer – when work was 'slack' – in order to buy them back in winter when work was more abundant (Steadman, 1976:19,152). The expansion of the piece-rate system and homeworking were new and growing features of the trade in the late nineteenth century. Much of the work was of a seasonal nature and casual employment characterised the industry. Many Jews fleeing pogroms in Eastern Europe during the 1880s and 1890s, found employment as pressers and machinists in the clothing workshops of the East End of London and for many this was an important stepping stone to Ellis Island or in opening their own workshops. Concerns about the social conditions of the London poor as well as a moral panic directed against the even poorer Jewish immigrant, informed the 'anti-sweating' campaign by Liberal reformers which led to the introduction in 1905 of the Aliens Act, the first ever anti-immigrant legislation in the UK (see, Steward and Hunter, 1964; Bermant, 1975; Fishman, 1976; Schmiechen, 1984).

The post-war boom and labour demand of the European economies and action by European governments to facilitate the migration of labour provided the conditions for the most significant expansion of immigration experienced by Western Europe. Whilst this was subject to considerable local variation, in the context of the post-war European experience the concept of a formalised 'European Labour Market' emerged as a description of systematised labour transfer (Kindleberger, 1967; Bohning, 1972; Castles and Kosack, 1973; Penninx *et al.*, 1993; Harris, 1995a). One consequence of this labour transfer was that African-Caribbean and Indian workers in the UK have higher rates of trade union membership than white workers (Jones, 1993:76). The migration of workers to the United Kingdom and Western Europe accelerated during the 1950s and 1960s and by 1970, 7 per cent of the UK labour force were immigrant workers with the single largest concentration in the textile and garment industry where immigrants made up more than one in ten of all workers. In the London garment industry during 1971 nearly one third of all registered workers were born outside the UK (UK Department of Employment, 1976:141). During 1962 the introduction of the Commonwealth Immigration Act severely curtailed New Commonwealth immigration to the UK. For an overview of immigrant participation in various branches of the London garment industry, see below (see, Basu and Altinay, 2003; Government Office for London, 2001; Panayiotopoulos, 1990; Panayiotopoulos and Dreef, 2002; Bermant, 1975; Schmiechen, 1984; Eade, 1989; Shaikh, 1995; Anthias, 1992; Luu, 1997; Kershen, 1990).

Immigrant groups in the London garment industry

- In the sixteenth century French Huguenots established the East London lace industry. After 1880, Jewish immigrants from Eastern Europe turned the East End into a major centre of garment production.
- In the post-war period immigrants from the New Commonwealth and, since 1950s and 1960s, Greek and Turkish Cypriots, both as workers and entrepreneurs.
- From the 1970s onwards, immigrants from the Indian subcontinent: Pakistani, Indian, and Bangladeshi.
- Since the mid-1980s, Turkish immigrants from mainland Turkey.
- Since the mid-1990s Kurdish exiles from Turkey and Iraq.
- From the late 1990s onwards, immigrants from Eastern Europe provide a new source of labour.

Spatial location

- Clothing production is concentrated in the East End London borough of Tower Hamlets, which is the major settlement area for the Bangladeshi community.

- It has also moved north to the borough of Hackney. Here predominantly people from Turkish Cypriot, Turkish and Kurdish background work as entrepreneurs and workers.
- Even further north, in the borough of Haringey, Islington and, to a lesser extent, Enfield; here Greek and Turkish Cypriots and people from the Turkish mainland, dominate the clothing sector. Recently Kurdish people have entered work in these (adjoining) areas.

Sub-sector of clothing industry and immigrant group

- Bangladeshi and Pakistani immigrants generate products for their own community, such as Asian women's outerwear, but also for the wider market, such as leather products (especially coats). Bangladeshi immigrants are concentrated in the leatherwear industry.
- Turkish and Kurdish immigrants specialise in the manufacturing of tailored wear, pleated skirts, menswear, suits and long and heavy coats.
- Greek and Turkish Cypriots (predominantly in Haringey, Islington and Enfield) produce cheap and fashionable women's outerwear, separates and dresses.

Despite large job losses in the UK clothing industry, garment production continues to have a significant presence in the London area. During the 1990s, an estimated 30,000 predominantly women workers were employed in 2,500 small firms. Most firms are small with production capacity at 1,000 garments or less per week (Graham and Spence, 1995; Anderson and Flatley, 1997). In part, the London garment industry owes its existence to the restructuring of the industry and the increased significance for the women's and girls' light outerwear (dresses, blouses, skirts) and casual wear sectors. In the early 1990s, London accounted for 12 per cent of all UK registered employment in the garment industry and in the womenswear considerably more at 20 per cent (Panayiotopoulos, 1996a).

There are specific factors in the continuity of the London womenswear sector, which derive from the (historic) relationship between buyers, manufacturers and fashion houses in the West End of London (Great Portland Street) and contractors in the East End and North London. The proximity of this relationship facilitates a fashion-wear spot-market, characterised by small-batch production of rapidly changing styles which places even greater pressure on meeting delivery times. A necessary precondition for such a market is the agglomeration of buyers, manufacturers, production units, designers, suppliers of textiles, trimmings and specialised services to the trade, in a robust local economy. Minority entrepreneurs have adapted to the London womenswear fashion spot-market, typically as contractors and subcontractors. An example of a spot-market, is in the role played by Fonthill Road in the Finsbury Park area of the London borough of Islington. It is a major centre of the UK women's fashion-wear sector and made up of approximately 150 Cypriot manufacturers and wholesalers. A growing proportion of their work is now sourced outside the UK and produced for non-UK markets. Two miles further in the neighbouring borough of Haringey, Florentia Clothing Village, a collection of units centring on the Vale Road Industrial Estate in Tottenham and other nearby Cypriot-owned units, employ an estimated 2,000 clothing workers.

The London garment industry (as with other cities) is dominated on the making side by immigrant entrepreneurs. It is characterised by a high representation for minority workers, women, small firms, low barriers to entry, hyper-competition, informality and seasonal troughs. The industry makes use of relatively simple technology and, importantly for immigrants, relies on demonstrable ways of learning skills. The organisation of production is structured in a series of subcontractual relationships. In a vertical direction these include the relations between the buyers (who place the orders), the manufacturers (who provide the cloth and design) and the contractors (who provide the labour) and are referred to in the trade as cut, make and trim (CMT) units. Labour consists to a large extent of homeworkers and their family helpers. Those moving in a horizontal direction include relations between contractors who frequently subcontract part of their production to other factories or to drivers who work on their own account. The womenswear 'fashion' sub-sector amplifies further the (above) structural characteristics. The tendency in womenswear for greater fashion change and even more frequent changes in style requiring even smaller 'dockets' (quantities of output) which are frequently delivered pre-cut, militates even more against large-scale assembly-line production and further reduces the cost of entry. This factor reinforces the role of small firms and hyper-competitive behaviour between ethnic contractors through the undercutting of the making price.

The basic fragments of production in CMT work require different skills and trades which are paid in different ways (see Figure 3.1, previously cited). Cutters, their assistants and sample machinists (who make first copies to show other machinists) are on pre-agreed wages. The making side which employs most of the labour, consists of sewing machinists who are paid through the piece-rate system. Trimming requires pressers and passers (cotton cleaners and workers who do the bagging, labelling, ticketing) who are also on pre-agreed set wages. Production also requires drivers who link homeworkers to the factory and who may be on a set wage or commission. Workplace relations are structured by the need to exercise control over women machinists who form the bulk of the labour force. Typically this appears in the form of the piece-rate system which links pay to effort. The rate paid for each garment is subject to individual negotiation and bargaining which involves variables such as experience, the time of the year, past rates and the availability of homeworkers (see Conclusion).

Most garment enterprises and employment within the London area is concentrated in the boroughs of Tower Hamlets, Hackney, Islington,

Haringey and Westminster, where many designers and wholesalers have their base. In the borough of Hackney, the sector is a major manufacturing employer and in particular sub-sectors such as tailored menswear and womenswear, and it remains a major centre for UK-wide production. The borough of Haringey is a major centre for women's fashion-wear production in the UK (Panayiotopoulos, 2001a; Panayiotopoulos and Dreef, 2002). The Government Office for London (2001) in a study of the sector, estimated that nearly 30,000 people were employed in 3,000 enterprises with most firms and employment being concentrated in the inner London area (see, Table 7.2). In the sample (of 40 companies) most (55 per cent) employed less than ten employees and the single largest turnover group (at 47.5 per cent) were those under £0.5 million a year. At the other pole 10 per cent had a turnover in excess of £10 million. Up to 40 per cent of companies were involved in manufacturing activities in other countries: Romania, Lithuania, Morocco, Turkey and China. Amongst North London firms many are also exporters, with 48 per cent indicating that their main market was overseas.

Ethnic solidarity provides an important but partial explanation for the pattern of employment. There is considerable variation in this, between different immigrant and ethnic groups, sub-sectors of the garment industry, firms of differing size and in skills held by different workers which may be in short supply. The ethnic interspersion of London's labour force may well be greater than the existing literature suggests. One study of Cypriot-owned garment factories in North London, revealed that whilst half of the workers were Cypriots, workers also come from a variety of ethnic backgrounds and this was a strong feature of medium and large enterprises

Table 7.2 Clothing and related establishments and employment: selected London boroughs (SITC 17+18), 2000 (000s)

Area	Enterprises	Employment
Greater London	3,000	29,455
Inner London	2,150	23,305
Of which		
Camden	140	875
Hackney	280	2,685
Haringey	355	2,475
Islington	225	1,890
Newham	160	785
Tower Hamlets	295	1,630
Westminister, City of	280	11,320
Enfield	110	715

Source: Government Office for London, 2001:Table 5.7, 53.

Note
SITC – Standard Industrial Trade Classification (17+18: women's fashion wear sub-sectors).

(Panayiotopoulos, 1994). Similarly, Bonacich (1993b, 1994) and Light *et al.* (1999) point to the most common configuration in the metropolitan Los Angeles garment industry as one of Asian contractors employing Latina workers. As we noted, Ivan Light refers to this labour market relationship as an 'immigrant economy'. By pointing to ethnically interspersed labour markets (see also, Green 2002), question marks are raised for ethno-cultural analyses which see co-ethnic employment and ethnic solidarity as necessary preconditions for enterprise activity.

Cypriot entrepreneurs in North London

The Cypriot community has had a physical presence in London since the 1930s, and in 1939 a total of 8,000 Cypriots were estimated to have settled in the UK. The 1951 Census enumerated 10,208 persons born in Cyprus. Most of the immigrants were men residing in lodging houses in the West End and central areas of London. The catering trade acted as the major employer for most Cypriot men. Indeed during 1939 it was reported that, '3,500, or one-third of the total membership of the Catering Trades Society, an approved society under the health Insurance Law(s) were Cypriot men and women' (Nearchou, 1960:16). Thirteen years later, the London Office of the Cypriot Colonial Government, itself set up under the impact of increased migration, wrote that,

> The catering trade still employs the main body of Cypriot labour and many of the first-class hotels and restaurants in London, such as the Savoy, the Ritz, the Berkeley and the Mayfair, are on the catering side entirely staffed by Cypriots.
>
> (Nearchou, 1960:18)

Cypriot emigrants were initially, therefore, employed as wage workers (mainly as waiters) in the catering industry of the West End of London. 'Fortune', however, was to smile on the army of young waiters. In coming from a colony which during wartime remained within British rule and provided the first voluntary recruits from the colonies (led by the mass-based Cypriot Communist Party) to the British Army, Cypriots escaped the pogrom directed against immigrants of German and in particular Italian derivation in wartime Britain. The internment of Italians (fascist and anti-fascist alike) provided Cypriots with the opportunity to oust their Italian supervisors from the catering trade. The number of Cypriot-owned catering establishments increased during the wartime period from 29 in 1939, to 200 by 1945. By 1950, this had increased to 510, with 230 of the establishments to be found outside the London area (Nearchou, 1960:19). The transition by this group from waitering to restaurant proprietorship, was the first significant expansion of Cypriot entrepreneurship.

Table 7.3 Cypriot emigrants, all destinations, by previous occupation, 1955–1962 (000s)

Year	Total	Not occupationally specifiable		Dressmakers and related industries	Other craft workers
		Total	Women, children and students		
1955	5,704	2,785	500 (est)	1,857	1,106	380
1956	6,461	3,949	500 (est)	2,689	838	499
1957	5,447	2,727	428	1,702	824	415
1958	5,273	2,231	765	1,223	868	483
1959	6,250	2,716	848	1,472	1,004	348
1960	14,589	6,937	2,410	1,768	2,264	1,130
1961	13,489	6,307	3,715	2,592	885	981
1962	6,277	3,291	1,829	1,289	857	639
Total	63,490	30,933	10,995	14,592	9,646	4,875

Source: Vital and Migration Statistics 1955–1962, Nicosia (from Panayiotopoulos, 1990:328).

During the late 1950s migration began to take on a mass form and between 1955 and 1962 a total of 63,490 persons emigrated from Cyprus of whom 55,633 (87.5 per cent) arrived in the UK. The two years of highest emigration were 1960 and 1961, which saw the arrival of 27,104 persons to the UK (or 48.7 per cent of all arrivees to the UK for the entire period) (see Table 7.3). The two years were also significant in the sense that in 1962 the expected Commonwealth Immigration Act came into force and many migrants were attempting to pre-empt restrictions, or perceived restrictions, on family reunions. This accounted for the large number of women and children amongst the migrants during 1960 and 1961 when they made up nearly half of the migrants. This period (1959–1962) was the formative experience for the Cypriot community in North London. It was a community reeling under the impact of mass immigration in the cramped reception areas of Tufnell Park, Kentish Town and Finsbury Park. Many were subjected to exceptional hostility, as the armed struggle for independence launched by Greek Cypriots which began in 1955 and ended in 1959, was fresh in the memory of the British public (Panayiotopoulos, 2001c). The word 'terrorist' was widely used by the British government and the *Daily Mail* (amongst others) at the time, to describe the five year emergency, and this impacted negatively in attitudes towards Cypriot immigrants in London.

The impact of accelerated migration saw, as the Ministry of Labour in Cyprus noted in its Annual Report for 1959, that 'out of 150,000 workers insured since 1956, 50,000 have either left the island, died, or left insurable employment' (Government of Cyprus, 1959:App. II). It is partly in this context that neoclassical economics applied to international migration theory were singularly unhelpful. Charles Kindleberger (1967:82) for example, wrote in his (classic) reworking of W. A. Lewis (1954:131–191) two sectoral model of labour transfer, that the 'less developed countries of Europe' act 'like the [subsistence] agricultural sector' in the developing countries. One notes that subsistence production is not usually characterised by insurable employment. Portes (1981:277–279) also pointed to evidence which showed that nearly half of Mexican migrants to the USA, were not only wage workers, but also skilled or semi-skilled.

According to UK Census statistics, Greater London was the major area of Cypriot settlement. During 1961 80.5 per cent of all Cyprus-born persons lived in the Greater London area. The subsequent censuses show a progressive reduction in the proportion residing in the London area. However, over half of the 78,031 Cyprus-born persons enumerated in the 1991 Census, continue to live in four boroughs situated in North London. During the 1980s and 1990s, second-generation Cypriots (i.e. persons of Cypriot origin born in the UK) began to make up a larger proportion of the settlement. During the 1980s they made up in the borough of Enfield (which has the highest concentration of Cypriots in the UK), 37.5 per cent of the Cypriot community. In the neighbouring borough of Hackney, the council estimated that 36.5 per cent of Cypriots were born in the UK. As a result of second-generation growth, estimates put the combined Greek and Turkish Cypriot community to over 200,000 people, with possibly more Cypriots living in London than the capital city of Cyprus, Nicosia (Panayiotopoulos, 2001c). The 1991 Census showed that over half of the Cypriots in London were born in the UK (Storkey, 1993:205).

In terms of previous occupation, out of the total of 63,490 emigrants from Cyprus to all destinations during the period 1955–1962, 30,933 did not specify an occupation on their embarkation cards. Of those specifying an occupation (32,557 or 51.3 per cent of the total) there is a high representation of artisans and occupations such as tailors, dressmakers, and other manual crafts such as shoemakers, barbers, builders, furniture and building carpenters, blacksmiths, car, bicycle and agricultural equipment mechanics. A few were well-diggers. These occupations made up over 40 per cent of all emigrants specifying a previous occupation and nearly a quarter of all the emigrants for the seven year period (see Table 7.3). Of the tailors, dressmakers and other craft workers, the vast bulk, as the business structure of Cyprus suggests, were employed in small workshops which showed a marked dependency on family and in particular, apprentice labour. A considerable proportion of them were classified as self-employed. In 1962 over half of the 17,400 industrial establishments (i.e. workshops) in Cyprus employed five or less workers (Government of Cyprus, 1970:7–8).

Other sources also point to emigration drawing from, and in a disproportionate way, the ranks of industrial, artisanal, clerical and service workers. Oakley (1972:303) in a study of the occupational composition of emigrants for the years 1960–1966, showed agriculture and related sectors contributed only 7.9 per cent of the immigrants. In part this is explained by the role of off-farm activities. The 1962 Industrial Census for Cyprus showed, for example, that of the 1,603 dressmaking establishments, 1,367 were to be found in rural areas (see, Government of Cyprus, 1962:25–26, Table 5).

Cypriot involvement in the London clothing industry and other sectors reliant on the skilled manual trades, rested in part on the artisanal (or 'archaic') manual crafts and skills brought by the migrants. This contrasted sharply, as we noted, with the decline of the manual skills amongst workers in the advanced capitalist economies of Western Europe and which was reflected in a historical decline for small enterprises and the reduction of the number of people working for their 'own account' i.e. the classical self-employed (Boissevain, 1981, 1984). Many of the migrants found employment opportunities in the garment industry in the small workshops of North and East London which were still dependent on the manual trades, not least, the sewing skills held by the women and, in smaller numbers, male tailors (Panayiotopoulos, 1990; Anthias, 1992). Another factor consisted of the changes taking place in sectors of the UK economy with a high labour and low capital ratio. These showed an increased use of subcontracting to smaller units of production. The women's and girls' outerwear sub-sector (Standard Industrial Trade Classification (SITC) 4536) in which many Cypriots entered as wage workers and subsequently as entrepreneurs, was emblematic of the 'arrest' of the historical decline for small enterprises in the UK economy. In SITC 4536, establishments employing 50 or less workers accounted for 76.2 per cent of all establishments in 1968, 85.7 per cent in 1973 and 91.6 per cent in 1985 (Panayiotopoulos, 1990:294).

The histories of Cypriot migrants were very closely bound up (and in gender sensitive ways) with the catering and clothing industries. A number of studies carried out during the period illustrate this. A study by Nearchou, on the types of employment amongst London Cypriots calling at the London Office for assistance during 1952 and 1958, found that during 1958, catering was the leading sectoral employer for men with nearly one third (30.5 per cent) followed by the clothing industry (11.5 per cent). The clothing industry employed, in 1952, 95.0 per cent and in 1958 85.2 per cent of the women (Nearchou, 1960:106, 110). During the 1960s the clothing industry accounted for 60.7 per cent of all females in employment (Oakley, 1972:307, 311–312). During the 1970s, Ladbury (1979, also see, 1984), pointed to the beginning of a significant reduction in open employment by Cypriot women in the garment industry. Employment diversification appeared in a trend away from the clothing industry and towards the service sector, with 37 per cent of males and 25 per cent of females employed in this sector. The clothing industry, however, continued to employ over half of Cypriot-born women and 18 per cent of men.

The availability of Cypriot female labour and the arrival of an increasing number of Cypriot women immigrants during the late 1950s and early 1960s, was a critical factor in the physical establishment of the community itself and the subsequent development of entrepreneurship. During the years of mass migration it was the availability of women's employment which kept the community together and influenced the pattern of settlement. Skilled machinists and seamstresses were in high demand and many households depended on the seasonal incomes earned by the women to survive on a day-to-day and week-to-week basis. As with the comparable example of Miami, this had the function of allowing men the time to adjust and to look for work. Many of the women skilled in the needle trades, whether previously employed as wage workers, apprentices or 'housewives' who in fact were highly competent in the trade through skills such as sewing and darning learned in the domestic economy, all found highly paid but seasonal employment. Some apprenticed women who worked in West End bespoke tailors workshops, such as in Soho, were amongst the highest earners in the community. The fact that it was easier for women to find work in North-east London, was one factor which influenced the residential location and neighbourhoods in which the Cypriot community settled.

The expansion of Cypriot-owned enterprises in the garment industry during the late 1950s and 1960s saw a process (as potent as in late nineteenth century New York) which, for near on half a century, saw Cypriot women ethnically channelled into the clothing industry (Oakley, 1972; Anthias, 1992; Josephides, 1988). The evolution of a class of Cypriot entrepreneurs was linked to the availability of this pool of labour, and this also exposed their weakness. This surfaced in the form of the 'labour question' as many of the entrepreneurs faced severe problems in recruiting machinists during the 1970s and 1980s, and for many this became a critical issue. This was driven by the ageing of first-generation women machinists, the unwillingness by many young second-generation women to enter the garment industry and compounded by tight immigration controls. Labour supply problems forced Cypriot entrepreneurs to make changes in the ethnic composition of the labour force and in how it was employed (also see Conclusion). The result was a greater degree of representation for non-Cypriot workers of whom more were homeworkers (Panayiotopoulos 1996a:442–445). One example is illustrated in the labour force composition of a Cypriot-owned garment factory in Tottenham, North London (see, Table 7.4).

The informalisation of production

The incorporation of diverse immigrant groups into informal labour markets characterised by casual work and precarious forms of income generation is a strong characteristic of the London garment industry. This

Table 7.4 A garment factory in Tottenham, North London: labour force characteristics

Factory		
1 entrepreneur	male	Greek Cypriot (brother)
1 master cutter	male	Greek Cypriot
1 assistant cutter	male	Greek Cypriot
1 sample machinist	female	Greek Cypriot (sister)
2 special machinists	female	Greek Cypriot (aunt)
7 machinists	female	4 Afro-Caribbean
		3 Greek Cypriot
1 driver	male	Greek Cypriot (brother)
3 passers	female	2 Greek Cypriot
		1 Irish
2 pressers	male	2 Afro-Caribbean
Sub-total 19		
Homeworkers		
4 machinists	female	4 Afro-Caribbean
6 machinists	female	6 Greek Cypriot
10 machinists	female	10 Indian
1 driver	male	1 Indian
Sub-total 21		
Total (40)	33 female	18 Greek Cypriot
(of whom 30	7 male	11 Indian
are machinists)		10 Afro-Caribbean

Source: Panayiotopoulos, 2001a:243.

could be understood with reference to the work of Sassen (1988, 1991, 1996) on the impact of globalisation and restructuring in the urban centres of the industrial economies (London, New York, Tokyo) which identifies one mechanism of globalisation in the incorporation of diverse immigrant groups in the informal labour market. Many studies of immigrant workers and entrepreneurs point in a pessimistic way to the re-emergence of 'sweatshops'. Mitter (1986:59), as we noted, refers to the emergence of Bangladeshi enterprise in the London garment industry as representing little more than 'a sideways shift from lumpen-proletariat to lumpen-bourgeoisie'. In this approach, immigrant participation in the garment industry is presented as a precarious response to discrimination in the (segmented) labour market, and as a collective survival-mechanism in the face of ethnic and racial disadvantage. Naila Kabeer (2000) similarly, in studies of women homeworkers in the Bangladeshi dominated East London garment industry, found that labour market preference for unregistered homeworking may owe more to 'defensive social relations' adopted in response to a more contemporary British racism, rather than cultural propensities of the Bangladeshi community. In this approach the 'split labour market' is a useful term in offering explanations for the positioning of immigrant workers at the lower rungs of labour markets (Bonacich, 1972, 1973).

In the London garment industry informalisation appears in a range of institutions, most notably, homeworking, 'clear-money', illegal selling activities ('cabbage sales'), 'design pinching' (of the latest fashion) as well as 'doing a liquidation', primarily in order to avoid value added tax (VAT) (see below). By institutions we mean a set of relationships which are structural characteristics of the garment industry and which should not be seen as the cultural property of any particular immigrant or ethnic group. At the same time, however, such institutions become an associated condition (and possibly a necessary one) of immigrant participation in the garment industry. The pattern of employment in the industry, the financial management of the enterprises and the organisation of production are sensitively linked to the institutions of informalisation. They shape management–worker relations and relations with the outside world. A not unusual relation between immigrant entrepreneurs and the regulatory agencies, involves conflict with various branches of central and local government over the avoidance of taxation, social insurance, health and safety at work, and homeworking legislation.

Institutions of informality

- *Cabbage sales*' are a critical institution in the day-to-day financial management and liquidity of the enterprise and represent unregistered sales. *Cabbage* is essentially an official or unofficial 'allowance' that the contractor squeezes out of the cloth (and design) provided by the manufacturer. That is, if the cloth makes 1,000 garments and the firm manages, through the skill of its cutter, to squeeze another 75–100 garments out of the same cloth, then this amount is referred to as 'your cabbage' which is then sold privately to shop and stall owners. Cabbage sales by contractors represent a response to weakness in production reflected in low making prices. Amongst some contractors selling activities also represents a conscious attempt to diversify the source of income, typically in the form of pseudo-wholesale activities.
- *Doing a liquidation*', or, more commonly, carrying out a voluntary liquidation as a means of avoiding paying creditors and in particular the payment of VAT which stands at 17.5 per cent of retail price. This tax which is added to the retail price is recoupable by the entrepreneur, but it has to be paid in the first place. However, as the question of liquidity (often posed in the shape of late payments) assumes a disproportionate weight in this sector, so the money is spent, frequently in order to retain machinists during 'slack' periods. It is of note that HM Customs and Excise do not routinely pursue the relatively small amounts owed by small contractor firms given that the cost of pursuit (of mobile enterprises) can be prohibitive. Studies of companies undergoing liquidations and insolvencies in the London garment industry indicated that the majority of companies undergoing liquidation in the womenswear sub-sector were identifiable as Cypriot-owned.

- *Design-pinching*' (of the latest fashion) has become a significant phenomenon amongst immigrant entrepreneurs in the London womenswear sector and this can be seen as a perverse reflection of the differentiation of the milieu. Many emergent ethnic contractor enterprises (now) as manufacturers use design input as a negotiating lever with buyers. In legal terms it affects all cabbage sales since, along with the cloth, it is the manufacturer's designs (samples) which are put to use. 'Design-pinching' represents a considerable and strategic saving for emergent entrepreneurs. This sort of activity is also a source of friction with undertones of potential (and sometimes actual) physical violence to persons and property in centres such as Fonthill Road, North London.

Many workers are employed illegally and paid off-the-books by firms which regularly carry out voluntary liquidations and are run by 'serial' failures. According to research carried out by the Greater Universal Stores (GUS) retail group, nearly 4,000 company directors of United Kingdom garment companies (four times more than previously thought) have been associated with ten or more failed companies. Many deliberately closed down their companies to avoid paying debts, and then set up new ones. Nearly half of them lived in London and the south-east region (see, *Financial Times*, 28 October 1998, '4,000 directors thought to be serial failures'). 'Unethical' insolvency practitioners in the garment industry have been a source of particular concern to the regulatory bodies for a long period. They have come under closer scrutiny as the number of disqualifications for previous misdemeanours have increased. The six months to the end of September 2002 saw a 24 per cent increase in disqualifications. Construction was the biggest sector followed by textiles and clothing. One third of the disqualifications were in the London area (*Financial Times*, 2 January 2002, 'New rules push up number of directors being disqualified' and 14 May 2001, ' "Cowboy" practitioners face crackdown').

'Management' for many entrepreneurs simply consists of following advice from the many ethnic accountants and 'liquidators'. Many rely on them, and their services are highly valued. Estimates of their earnings range between 10 and 20 per cent of VAT payment avoided. Many accountants have become very wealthy and are major proxy beneficiaries of immigrant participation in the London garment industry. Many workers in the industry use pejorative words to describe their activities with the word *karharia* (shark) prominent amongst them (Panayiotopoulos, 1994:175–187). These practices reinforce the casualisation of employment and loss of rights by workers. The implications of such trends – particularly regarding liquidations – have not been missed by the UK Customs and Excise department. This has led to increased regulation, some of it specific to the London garment industry. The London-based UK Fashion Design Protection Association (FDPA) was established by some of the largest Greek-Cypriot manufacturers and has successfully campaigned for the creation of special legislation to cover copyright infringement (i.e. 'design pinching'). There are now new statutory guidelines on company directors to bar 'repeat' liquidations. HM Customs and Excise has created special surveillance units targeting the North and East London garment industry, in addition to periodic joint raids by HM Customs and Excise and the Home Office searching for illegal workers (Panayiotopoulos and Dreef, 2002).

Transnational corporation strategy and immigrant enterprise

One factor in structuring enterprise functions is in the role of subcontracting relationships which link immigrant entrepreneurs to large corporations. The clothing industry is an example of this. The UK garment industry until recently, was characterised by onshore production in which labour costs were minimised by equipping factories with the best available technology, by making use of local contractors (including ethnic contractors) and by purchasing fabrics from the lowest cost source. This approach had the objectives of strengthening quality and minimising delivery times and was substantially driven by a highly concentrated UK clothing retail sector. This is illustrated by Marks and Spencer (M&S) and its commitment for many years to a 'made in the UK' policy. M&S placed textile and garment orders to the value of £5.7 billion in 1997, of which about 70 per cent was produced in the UK. In the 1980s this was significantly higher at 90 per cent of sales (see, Anson, 1997).

The ability of the retail sector to structure (and restructure) the UK garment industry is a reflection of its highly concentrated nature and considerable corporate power. In the womenswear sub-sector (which accounts for 40 per cent of the market) M&S was the market leader at 18 per cent, with Burtons its nearest rival at 8 per cent. Womenswear made up 60.5 per cent of M&S clothing sales. During the 1990s the power of M&S was challenged by the growth of specialised UK clothing retailers such as Arcadia (an offshoot of Burtons), Next and mail-order firms (such as GUS), which between them control over one fifth of market share. Many of them source production overseas and this has put pressure on M&S to do the same (Barnes, 1994). During May 1998, M&S asked openly for the first time, for its suppliers to source more of their production abroad. This put considerable pressure on M&S domestic suppliers such as SR Gent (its major ready-to-wear manufacturer), Courtalds Textiles and Coats Viyela (its major textile suppliers) and Dewhirst (major womenswear manufacturer). Many of these suppliers either closed down or have contracted capacity in their own larger factories in areas such as south Wales and Northern Ireland. Union sources estimate that 20,000 jobs were 'lost' in the UK as the result of this one change in M&S sourcing policy (Booth, 1998a:14).

Suppliers have put pressure on their manufacturers and they in turn on their contractors to remain price competitive in the face of global competition and this has impacted on immigrant entrepreneurs and workers.

The restructuring of the UK clothing industry led to an acute crisis faced by many immigrant workers and entrepreneurs in the London garment industry which began during the late 1990s, and was substantially driven by a reinvigorated outward processing, and recent developments in the market for clothing. Whilst the long-term implication of changes to the market for clothing are not certain, what is clear is that many contractors in the London womenswear sector – who as contractors are the least capable of adapting to the changes in the market for clothing – have come under intense pressure. Many factories have closed down and even more were working below capacity. All faced lower making prices from the manufacturers which in turn lead to lower piece-rate payments for machinists. Many of the contractors in the quantity market, where price competition and labour costs are more critical factors in production, pointed to a situation where, with comparable technology a machinist in London is paid £800 per month, when similar work in Bulgaria and Romania can be undertaken for only £60 per month. This was the subject of intensive discussion in the minority press (see, *Parikiaki*, 'Endymatoviomihania: apo to kako sto hirotero', 15 October 1998). Another indication was in the form of an empirical observation. Of 20 garment-related workplaces known to me in the London N15 post code area in research conducted during June 1994, only five were still visibly such during January 2001. Ethnic manufacturers have responded to changes in the market for clothing in quite different ways: many are pursuing an even more active policy of outward processing. Amongst Cypriots this was typically associated with subcontracting to Cyprus for most of the 1980s (see Panayiotopoulos, 2000b). Labour costs, however, have progressively risen in Cyprus and entrepreneurs began to look for alternative locations, such as North Africa and Eastern Europe. The Government Office for London (2001:19, 28) found that 'Former Eastern European block countries [are] buying up the contents of whole factories and are shipping the machinery out to those countries' and that the CMT sector was in particular decline. Most severely affected were the boroughs of Hackney and Tower Hamlets. Other manufacturers who have progressively added greater design and fashion input to production and established 'own' brand labels, responded to uncertainties in the mass market in clothes by pursuing with increased vigour a policy of moving away from quantity and towards quality production. For the contractors, these sorts of options are not readily available.

Economic differentiation and responses to crisis

Much of the material reviewed provides insights into our understanding of how immigrant workers and entrepreneurs are incorporated in the

London garment industry. At the same time they fail to reveal important differences between firms. For example, that immigrant manufacturers and CMT contractors relate to the market at different levels of the production cycle, are subject to different outcomes and adopt different strategies to cope with market fluctuation and crisis. Another dimension is the diversification of activities. One illustration of economic differentiation is the life history of Mr Chris Lazari, Greek Cypriot who began in the rag trade, and now has property assets of £701 million. This includes sizable chunks of the West End of London (Tottenham Court Road, Baker Street and Mayfair) (Molyva, 2005:15).

It is in marketing that one observes the differentiation of immigrant enterprise in its most concentrated form. For many of the contractors the issue of diversification is problematic, and marketing is formally not relevant. Producing to order on specifications set by the manufacturer for a given buyer allows little formal scope for choice in market segment or product style. By and large they produce what they are given and this tends to be in the quantity market. It is for this reason that contractors appear as the least capable of adapting to changes in the market environment. For many of them it is a struggle to maintain cut, make and trim activities and they resist, if they can, becoming mere make and trim assembly units of pre-cut work since in this way they cannot make any 'cabbage'. At the same time, however, there is considerable scope between being a CMT contractor and producing on 'own account'. Some large CMT units also produce independently of manufacturers (often with the cloth and design provided by the manufacturer) and this has been an important entry route into becoming an ethnic manufacturer.

It is illustrative to note (see, below) how emergent enterprises in the London garment industry have responded in different ways to market changes, and in particular the crisis which followed the decision by M&S to relocate more of its production offshore.

Economic differentiation and responses to market change

- *Outsourcing* is strongly associated with enterprises which are sensitive to price competition (quantity production) and have resorted to a more expansive system of international subcontracting to lower cost production centres. Amongst Cypriot entrepreneurs, relocation to Cyprus, Asian-owned enterprises in the West Midlands and increasingly to Eastern Europe and North Africa, provided production locations during different periods. One case reputedly involves the employment of 2,000 workers in Morocco by one Greek Cypriot manufacturer. This firm was a major beneficiary of financial support by the London borough of Haringey (Mavrou, 1994; Panayiotopoulos and Dreef, 2002).
- *Developing new products* is most common amongst enterprises in the women's fashion-wear sector in which product differentiation is a

more important factor in competition and branded style may command a considerable price mark-up. Attempts to engage in more value-adding production and marketing activities typically take the form of increased design and fashion input and this has been an important factor in the differentiation of minority enterprise. One such enterprise (Ariella Fashions Ltd) is a leading UK women's fashion-wear manufacturer, designer, exporter and producer on own account of brand name goods. It has an extensive collection of agents and collaborators in most European countries and has won both the British Apparel Export Award for 1996 and the Queen's Award for Export Achievement in 1998.

- *Direct sales.* Some CMT firms have circumvented the 'traditional' West End manufacturers who act as middlemen, and now enjoy direct relations with the buyers. This has been facilitated by buyers themselves who have designated such firms as 'top factory' (i.e. first to get offers of work). In reverse they seek cost advantages for the supply of regular work, increasingly in the cost of design and development of new products.

Conclusions

London is being continually reshaped by immigration. It is also being shaped by the growing number of second- and third-generation members of different ethnic groups, who do not see themselves as 'immigrants' and see London as their city, and the city which shaped their formative years. Visible but contradictory signs of this new confidence include the contribution made to the small enterprise sector and increasingly in public sector employment. The Cypriot community in North London, is a case in point. After 50 years, many neighbourhoods and arterial roads such as Green Lanes would not be the same. Everything changes, yet everything stays the same. Now Turkish and Kurdish enterprise flourish in the same streets, as Cypriots move further north into Enfield, Barnet, and many even further, returning home for retirement or burial in Southgate Cemetery.

The chapter concludes by returning to three main questions. The first is whether the London garment industry has been restructured by immigrant entrepreneurs themselves, or whether this was shaped by wider processes, not least, restructuring by capital of particular sectors, sub-sectors and in relationships with the institutional and regulatory framework. The chapter suggests that in women's fashion wear, be it in London or elsewhere, specific dynamics created the need for shorter and more flexible production systems. One major purpose of corporate restructuring in the women's fashion-wear industry (such as Marks and Spencer) was to find shorter and cheaper supply lines. Greek and Turkish Cypriots in London, Hispanic and Chinese immigrants in New York and Miami, Asian and Latino immigrants in Los Angeles, are as the literature indicates strongly associated with the sector. The suggestion in these sectoral studies of immigration, ethnicity and enterprise, is that the restructuring of the garment industry and the fashion-wear sector may be a more critical factor in the incorporation of immigrants than characteristics associated with any particular ethnic or immigrant group (Panayiotopoulos, 1996a; Blackburn and Rutherford, 1999).

Second, the chapter argues that participation by immigrant entrepreneurs in the London garment industry cannot be understood without reference to the informalisation of production. At one level this appeared initially as a response to a macro-economic environment characterised by falling or static making prices given by manufacturers to contractors and increases in value added tax. Many contractors tried to compensate for depressed prices by increasing volume output in extra-legal ways, such as by resorting to unregistered homeworking. The informalisation of production, such as in voluntary liquidations, can be understood as a response by the entrepreneurs to changes in the market and the institutional environment which developed into a general survival strategy adopted by many contractors. At another level, the informalisation of production can be understood as a conscious strategy adapted by buyers and manufacturers who deliberately make use of difficult to monitor and regulate production chains. In the case of liquidations, they involve the loss of rights by workers, co-ethnic or not.

The third question returns to the implications of economic differentiation for the proposition that immigrant enterprise invariably operates on the margins of economic and legal systems and is the victim of discrimination and disadvantage. As the material suggests, the increasing diversification of enterprises between a majority of CMT contractors, and a much smaller number of manufacturers, designers and wholesalers, points to significant variation between immigrant enterprises. One consequence of 'formalisation' is that enterprises which began in the margins are now part of the economic mainstream. The chapter concludes that in considering the role of social and economic differentiation amongst immigrant-owned enterprises in London and elsewhere, there are predictable winners and losers. In order to further analyse this contradictory phenomenon further, we need to apply social and economic analysis grounded in theories of social stratification.

8   The state versus immigrant enterprise in Amsterdam

Introduction

Amsterdam due in part to its historical development and its contemporary incorporation as an emergent European gateway city, can be understood as a 'small' global city. Whilst in population terms it is much smaller than others and its future is less certain than most, it appears as a lively, multi-racial, multi-ethnic city, which stands as a beacon for liberal causes. Or, so it appears. Amsterdam provides a significant vantage point for the study of immigration and the development of immigrant enterprise in two specific ways. First, as one of Europe's earliest global trading centres, it is perhaps not surprising that it became one of the earliest cities in Europe to experience the settlement of immigrant communities from the Third World (or expatriates, depending on the view taken) following the loss of the Dutch East Indies colonies in 1947. We saw previously that one legacy was the debate over the status of the Chinese community (see Chapter 2). In part due to this migration, the Netherlands and its largest cities (Amsterdam, Rotterdam, The Hague) saw the first major expansion of non-European immigrant enterprise in the form of Chinese–Indonesian restaurants. This example reveals important insight and reflections on the role of location and sector in shaping the pattern of immigrant settlement, how this influences where immigrants live, the extent of 'integration' in the host society and the nature of adapted social organisation. This is a case explored in the chapter.

Second, Amsterdam allows us to examine the incorporation of immigrant 'informal' enterprise into production systems which operate outside the legal structures, but are also subordinate to other larger and 'formal' companies, which dominate particular sectors and sub-sectors. This raises wider issues about the autonomy of entrepreneurs, the limits of formal/informal sector dual analyses and the selectivity of the institutional response. Immigrant entrepreneurs from Turkey operating as contractors in the women's fashion-wear sector are another case study. The number of registered contractors in Amsterdam peaked at 1,000 in 1992 and troughed at an estimated 50 firms by 1997. Employment dramatically declined from an estimated 20,000 workers to several hundred (IMES, 1998). One factor for the crisis was that sourcing policy began to look to Eastern Europe as a low-cost production centre of cheap ready-to-wear women's garments. Another, and perhaps more significant factor, was the comprehensive offensive launched against the informal economy by the Dutch 'social' state which led to numerous raids against workshops, the expulsion of undocumented workers, the fining of entrepreneurs and the bankruptcy by most of the firms. The extension of the Law on Chain Liability made retailers formally responsible for their contractor's illegal practices.

In this example, we see the significance of what Rath (2002), Klooster-man (2000) and Kloosterman and Rath (2001) mean by 'mixed' embed-dedness, and the implications of its absence. The embeddedness of entrepreneurs in immigrant communities, could not compensate in this instance for its absence in the wider political and institutional framework, when compared to other cities such as Miami, London and New York. This chapter is in part, a study of 'who gets hurt' when state repression is launched. This speaks loudly about the political weakness of immigrant communities in formation and raises question marks over the long-term sustainability of immigrant enterprises. The chapter, however, also sug-gests that we need to move beyond generalities about the 'corporatist' state and the influence of the political-institutional framework in structur-ing immigrant incorporation and the development of immigrant enter-prise, and to identify the social and political mechanisms of selectivity in institutional behaviour.

Immigration and 'forced' integration

The political-institutional framework towards immigrants in the Nether-lands began to change after Indonesia became independent in 1949, and over the next few years, when a quarter of a million 'East Indies Nether-landers' were repatriated, in what is a complex part of Dutch history (see, Locher-Scholten, 2003). Indonesia became the first source of post-war immigration and accounts for the largest number of persons (at 405,000) of immigrant origin in the Netherlands today. It was made up of colonial repatriates and also Dutch passport holders, some of them of Chinese origins. Given the early arrival of many of these 'immigrants', one con-sequence is that about 65 per cent were born in the Netherlands. The second largest group (at 302,000 persons) are from the ex-colony of Surinam which became independent in 1975 and of whom nearly half are black (Kloosterman and Rath, 2003:128; Geddes, 2003:104). Chinese immigration is a complex phenomenon because it involves significant cross-national dimensions. In 1939 an estimated 1,000 Chinese persons lived in the port towns of Rotterdam and Amsterdam, most of whom were unemployed seamen. In 1990 an estimated 59,000 people of Chinese origins lived in the Netherlands (Pieke, 1999:324). More Chinese immigrants arrived following various pogroms in Indonesia, most notably during the 1965 massacre of an estimated one million 'communists' which followed the Suharto-led military coup.

As with continental Europe, the Netherlands also made use of the guest worker system during the 1960s and abandoned it in 1973 with the onset of world recession. New work permits ceased and sanctions were imposed against employers hiring illegal workers (Geddes, 2003:105). It is largely due to the legacy of the guest worker system that more than half a million immigrants from Turkey and Morocco live in the Netherlands. Failed attempts at return migration, family reunions, the constitution of new families and the development of a second generation, have seen the establishment of permanent communities of increasing complexity. With the exception of immigrants from Surinam and Indonesia, it was only during the 1980s that the Dutch political system began to accept settlement as permanent (Penninx *et al.*, 1993; Pieke, 1998).

One significant departure in policy towards immigrants, followed the defeat of the Christian Democrats in 1994. The new coalition led by the Labour Party placed 'integration' and participation in society by 'individuals and groups' at the heart of policy towards ethnic minorities. The definition of 'minority' in the Netherlands is as we noted, a problematic concept (see Chapter 2). Institutionally, a member of a minority is defined in a combination of a person's birthplace and the birthplace of the person's parents. If one of the three birthplaces is outside the Netherlands, then the person is defined as belonging to an 'ethnic minority'. At the same time, the change in policy made no specific provision for ethnic minorities and their needs. Indeed, Geddes argues that, in effect, 'integration' became a substitute for policy on ethnic minorities. 'This new approach implied socio-economic and civil integration with individuals the focus, not groups. Culture, identity and post-national trends would be replaced by an emphasis on Dutch society and its values' (Geddes, 2003:116).

One practical manifestation of the move away from cultural explanations of minority status and an emphasis on barriers to civic integration, was education. The Law on Civic Integration of Newcomers (1998) proposed for lower levels of achievement to be tackled through compulsory civic integration courses, 500 hours of language training and 100 hours of civic education. The Netherlands, once on the frontiers of ethnic minority policy making, 'now seems to be at the forefront of moves towards civic nationalism' (Geddes, 2003:116, 124).

The drive towards 'forced' integration during the late 1990s, was underpinned by stereotypical representations of particular ethnic groups (such as the Chinese and Turkish communities) and xenophobic outbursts in the media about the 'ethnic underclass', unwilling and unable to integrate. The 'moral panic' and identification of immigrants as 'the' problem, prepared the ground for further institutional assaults on immigrants and legitimised the far right. Whilst this was a European-wide phenomenon (see Chapter 6) it appeared as more shocking to many outside the Netherlands, given its association with lifestyle tolerance. Partly this shock was the result of limited knowledge of the Netherlands by most visitors, which tends to be extracted from short stays in major cities such as Amsterdam. The political commoditisation of Amsterdam as a tourist attraction emphasised liberal values as a significant marketing strategy for nearly three decades. Today, coffee houses which retail cannabis and marihuana, red-light districts and 'magic mushrooms', still provide a significant but diminishing source of tourism income and related entrepreneurship (Panayiotopoulos, 2004, Amsterdam, personal observation).

The Netherlands is also a deeply conservative society where religion remains a potent force. In parts of the country, referred to as the 'bible belt', devout households in Calvinist villages ban television and any form of entertainment on Sundays. The origins of Holland as an independent Republic two centuries before the French Revolution, was effectively as a dictatorship of merchants who went on to colonise large parts of the Third World. The Boers, i.e. Dutch settlers in South Africa are a case in point. Current xenophobia is in part a continuity of these authoritarian traditions. More significantly it has been shaped by anti-immigrant political mobilisations, such as, *Leefbaar Nederland* (Livable Netherlands) which during the elections in March 2002 captured 35 per cent of the vote in Rotterdam. Its leader, Pim Fortuijn (he himself preferred the more 'aristocratic' spelling Fortuyn), was expelled for inciting hatred against Muslims and went on to form his own List Pim Fortuyn (LPM) for the national elections. The LPM won 26 seats (three more than the Labour Party) and more than it expected, largely due to public sympathy which followed the killing of Pim Fortuijn, by a radical environmentalist (Geddes, 2003:119). The 'phenomenon' of Pim Fortuijn and public outbursts of grief were compared by commentators to the death of Lady Diana which spoke loudly about the poverty of Dutch society.

The rising Islamophobia which followed 9/11, legitimised the use of language and practices which previously were unacceptable. The Muslim population in the Netherlands is comprised of Turkish, Moroccan and Indonesian immigrants who make up nearly one million people, or an estimated 5.8 per cent of the population of 16 million. In Amsterdam, there are more than 100,000 Muslims, 13 per cent of the population (Bickerton, 2004a:7).

One incident which summed up this environment was the consequences which followed the killing of Dutch film maker Theo van Gogh, during November 2004. He was killed by an individual, Mohammed Bouyeri, who is also a young Muslim, raised in the Netherlands of Moroccan descent and holding dual nationality. Two years previously, Mohammed had been cited in the west Amsterdam community press as a model example of 'integration': a photograph and article of a smiling young man urging others to use community services and to 'join' society (Bickerton, 2004a:7). He left a rambling five-page letter and was known that he was upset by his mother's death and by TV footage showing US troops in Iraq shooting prisoners. There was no indication that he did not act alone. The screening of the three-minute film, *Submission*, made jointly by van Gogh and Ayaan Hirshi Ali (reputedly of ex-Somalian aristocratic lineage) an MP for the anti-immigrant VVD, prompted the attack. The theme of the film depicted the 'oppression' of women by Islam and how the Koran sanctioned the beating of wives. The film included naked actresses playing Muslim women in soft-porn settings, which alienated the women who took part for trivialising the issue of domestic violence. Given that Amsterdam is a centre for the human trafficking of Eastern European women and that van Gogh was on record as saying that, 'gentlemen who give a tough hiding are quite attractive to some ladies really', there is an irony here. Van Gogh publicly referred to Muslims as 'goatfuckers'. In his book *Allah Knows Best* (2001) he routinely substitutes 'goatfucker' for 'immigrant from an Islamic country' (Tollenaere 2004:2). Previously he had been found guilty of anti-Semitism and received a petty fine. Theo van Gogh reaped the bitter fruit of his own hate politics and should be disengaged from secular cinematographic critiques of dominant religions, such as of Catholicism, by Buñuel and Scorsese.

What followed the killing of van Gogh (as with Pim Fortuijn's) were two reactions: first, the use by government of the discourse of 'the war on terror' and conspiracies, with raids on mosques, homes and organisations; and second, organised physical attacks by the far right. A bomb attack on an Islamic primary school in the small town of Helden, attacks on mosques and individuals, clashes with Moroccan youth in Amsterdam who mobilised in large numbers to drive fascist skinheads out of their neighbourhoods, were reported in the aftermath of van Gogh's death (Bickerton, 2004b:8). This environment and calls by the right (and the left, in the name of 'integration') that mosques should be closed down, that preachers should use the Dutch language and that the *hijab* should be banned, have grown. One conclusion from these brief notes, is that the Dutch political system and wider politico-institutional framework, which began to accept settlement as permanent during the 1980s and 1990s, has since moved in the opposite direction under the impact of xenophobia and anti-immigrant political mobilisations. The most concentrated expression of this was the mass expulsion of tens of thousands of the weakest of immigrants, refugees, including Somali women, no doubt driven into female circumcision and 'Islamic' oppression. This also provoked the largest demonstration in opposition seen in the Netherlands since the mid-1990s. Ayaan Hirshi Ali was an enthusiastic supporter of the expulsions, and further proposed that 'the African continent should not get a cent of aid' (Tollenaere, 2004:1).

Immigrant enterprise in Amsterdam

Nearly half of all immigrants in the Netherlands settled in Amsterdam and the major cities (Rotterdam, The Hague and Utrecht) (Kloosterman *et al.*, 1999:254). In part, this relatively wide distribution in settlement, was shaped by the location of particular industries, services and workplaces, recruiting guest workers, who also had to live somewhere. Immigrant neighbourhoods created the initial basis for an 'ethnic economy', and is one reason why nearly one fifth of all immigrant enterprises are located in Amsterdam, which accounts for 14 per cent of all Turkish and 24 per cent of all Moroccan-owned enterprises. That the location of these entrepreneurs reflects the pattern of dispersal associated the incorporation of ex-guest worker, becomes more noticeable when compared with entrepreneurs who are more recent immigrant entrants and of whom a far greater proportion are concentrated in Amsterdam. Over 65 per cent of all entrepreneurs from Ghana, 41 per cent from India and 40 per cent from Pakistan are located in Amsterdam (Kloosterman and Rath, 2003:131).

The development of services to local communities, such as Surinamese, Turkish and Moroccan butchers, food, vegetable and clothing stores and market stalls, confectionaries and bakers, provided one early entry route into entrepreneurship. Some of the earliest examples of immigrant enterprise were guest workers' hostels run by immigrants themselves, coffee houses and butchers. Another route was taken by most Chinese immigrant entrepreneurs in the form of restaurants and takeaways, which catered for the wider market. Turkish entrepreneurs became significant contractors in garment production and in confectionery. Many Italian artisans specialised in construction and renovation (Boissevain and Grotenbreg, 1988; Pieke, 1998; Hartog and Zorlu, 1999). Self-employment amongst some immigrant groups, such as Turkish immigrants at 12.2 per cent for 1997, were significantly higher than the national average of 10.2 per cent. Indeed the growth in self-employment amongst Turkish immigrants, provided the single most significant source of net additions to employment during the period 1986 to 1992 (Rath and Kloosterman, 2000:659).

One of the earliest examples of immigrant enterprise was butchers, who had established themselves during the 1960s and expanded in proportion to immigration from Turkey and Morocco. Many of these butchers responded to demand for Islam-compliant *halal* meat. This requires the meat to be drained of blood after slaughter and it is not specific to Islam. The Jewish faith, also observes similar religious rituals and had statutory rights to do so, lacking to Islamic butchers, which brought many of them into conflict with the Ministry of Public Health. It was not until 1975 that a licensing system was put in place. In 1985, 224 *halal* butchers existed of whom 138 were in Amsterdam and the largest cities. Several hundred others were assumed to be doing so illegally. By 1997 an estimated 360 butchers shops were run by immigrants in the Netherlands, of which most were Moroccan (51 per cent) and Turkish (38 per cent) owned (Klooster-man *et al.*, 1999:260–269).

A continuity which surfaces in many studies is about the influence of the local economy, sectoral and sub-sectoral patterns of subcontracting, the traditions in particular urban centres, and the way in which these shape the incorporation of immigrants and the emergence of enterprise. This is equally true of Amsterdam. For example, as Rekers and van Kempen (2000) note, whilst Rotterdam has a larger Turkish population than Amsterdam, there are five times more Turkish restaurants in Amsterdam. The concentration of amenities in Amsterdam is driven in part by urban traditions where 'going out' to eat or to be entertained is more pronounced, not least of all amongst the many tourists who visit the city, and reflected in the amount of money spent in restaurants and cafés, which in turn influences the number of establishments in this sector. It is, however, a highly segmented restaurant and leisure sector, with on one hand restaurants in the centre and on the other Turkish coffee houses in working class neighbourhoods, where most Turkish immigrants live.

The early experience of *halal* butchers is an illustration of a wider sectoral phenomenon. During the mid-1990s, nearly 60 per cent of immigrant enterprises were in the retail, wholesale and restaurant sectors. During 2000, it stood at 57 per cent (Kloosterman *et al.*, 1999:255; Kloosterman and Rath, 2003:133). If we considered the three most significant areas of sectoral participation for particular immigrant groups, the level of concentration rises even further. Amongst Moroccan entrepreneurs, nearly 60 per cent are concentrated in three sectors, and amongst Chinese and Hong Kong immigrants entrepreneurs this rises to 93 and 89 per cent respectively (see Table 8.1).

Table 8.1 Immigrant entrepreneurs in the Netherlands: three major areas of sectoral concentration, 2000 (per cent)

Immigrant group	No. of enterprises	Sectoral concentration		
		A	B	C
Turkey	7,478	Catering 22	Retail 17	Wholesale 15
Surinam	5,690	Personal services 17	Wholesale 14	Retail 14
China	2,297	Catering 79	Wholesale 10	Retail 4
Morocco	2,883	Retail 26	Catering 23	Personal services 10
Hong Kong	1,113	Catering 75	Wholesale 8	Retail 6

Source: Kloosterman and Rath, 2003:131, 133.

The above provides the material circumstances which point to affirmation of the conventional wisdom articulated in analyses of immigrant enterprise as existing in 'niches' or on the 'fringes' of mainstream economies. The argument by Kloosterman *et al.*, that entry in sectors with the lowest barriers to entry, leading to over-crowded and limited markets with high rates of firm turnover is, in itself, not an inaccurate description. The example of Islamic butchers seems to conform to this experience (Kloosterman *et al.*, 1999:260). Attempts by entrepreneurs to reduce costs through the informalisation and casualisation of employment, add to this argument. At the same time, it is a highly partial picture. Not all entrepreneurs responded to constraints and opportunities in the same way. This is illustrated in the material below, with one example being the differential way in which Chinese entrepreneurs in the catering industry responded to economic recession during the 1980s. Material on Turkish enterprise in the garment industry examines why entrepreneurs are institutionally impacted in different ways i.e. what 'mixed' embeddedness purports to reveal.

Turkish entrepreneurs in the Amsterdam garment industry

The idea that there should be 'order in the house' is a strange concept in these neo-liberal times. Self-regulation by markets is the conventional creed, but it appears as more selective in relation to particular immigrant groups and sectors and in policy towards the 'informal economy'. We noted in Chapter 6 that there is significant variation in tolerance towards the informal sector inside the European Union, with the 'Rhineland' belt of (German-speaking) erstwhile welfare corporatist states, appearing as the driving force in attempts to regulate the shadow or black economy. Often this is undertaken in the name of social, health and environmental standards, which themselves become the basis for future patterns of informality. Informality can be understood, in part, as a response by entrepreneurs to state regulation. As the level of regulation increases, so does the level of 'informality'. For example, every butcher in the Netherlands is legally obliged to register at the Chamber of Commerce and Trading Association of Butchers and is also required to have proper professional qualifications. Exemptions can be given if the applicant provides evidence of a need that otherwise would not be met,

> Such exemptions have often been granted. Initially, it was assumed that butchers were eligible to exemption if catering for less than 1000 Islamic inhabitants in a neighbourhood. In the meantime, this threshold had been raised to 2000 per inhabitants for the first butcher in an area, 3000 for the second one, 5000 for the third one and so forth.
> (Kloosterman *et al.*, 1999:261)

Many butchers worked illegally because they did not understand the language and rules and could not access exemptions. This example and the wider experience of Turkish entrepreneurs in the Amsterdam garment industry can be seen as a concentrated manifestation of a process which begins with attempts to impose social standards and result in the criminalisation of entrepreneurs, communities and the food they eat. Turkish garment enterprises in Amsterdam are an illustration of this process.

One of the earliest studies – during the mid-1980s – of immigrant enterprise in Amsterdam was carried out by Roeland van Geuns. The study focused on the women's fashion-wear industry and investigated the relationship between informal labour markets and Turkish 'sweatshops' in the Netherlands. It presented an analysis of the restructuring in the garment industry and the incorporation of an immigrant group into production channels which operate outside the legal structures, but which are also 'subordinate to other companies operating on a formal basis' (van Geuns, 1992:126). This and other studies (see previous discussion on Italy), raise wider questions, about the autonomy of immigrant or 'informal' enterprises.

Van Geuns (1992) pointed to (familiar) structural characteristics of informal labour markets amongst garment contractors. Infringement and avoidance of legislation and regulations regarding taxation, national insurance, minimum wages, holiday entitlements, and health and safety at work. Some of the workers were housed beneath or above the workshops in which they worked, with passports held by the employer. Work 'can consist of seven days a week and up to 18 hour a day, during the busy season' (van Geuns, 1992:133). The study also pointed to a low degree of autonomy in economic action – with most entrepreneurs constrained by their position as relatively weak contractors and subcontractors. Van Geuns also noted developments which surface in other studies of the women's fashion-wear industry. Restructuring – driven in substance by the sourcing preferences of the principal buyers in the women's fashion-wear sector – leading to a demand for rapidly changing styles requiring smaller 'batches' and shorter turnaround supply lines. This can require production on a week-to-week basis and lays the basis, in the case of Amsterdam, for a limited 'spot-market'. Limited in the sense that whilst it plays the role of a fashion centre, it lacks the designer and supporting infrastructure for the development of a robust local economy, as with world fashion centres such as Paris, London and New York.

For the large 'formal' companies, inward processing allows them the ability to respond to fashion changes to which international outward processing cannot address itself. Orders in the Far East have to be 'placed six months or more in advance' and are extremely difficult to change afterwards (a different colour for example), with the principal and associated manufacturers left having to carry large stocks in their warehouses, leading to interest losses and inability to respond to market trends (van Geuns, 1992:126–127). This is quite different in mass standardised garments (such as menswear and even more so work-wear and uniforms) in which the (relative) lack of choice in the variety of styles can result in more accurate predictions on market preference, and which continue to be driven by sourcing to low-wage economies. Other research confirms that the search for shorter supply lines also looked for sourcing in-country which was cheaper, with contracting and subcontracting often used for this purpose. In Amsterdam it was the Turkish community which provided the raw material by setting up clothing workshops during the 1970s making 'almost exclusively women's clothing' (van Geuns, 1992:128).

The Institute for Migration and Ethnic Studies (IMES) at the University of Amsterdam, is a major concentration of researchers on immigration and ethnicity in Europe. During the 1990s one major research project involved the study of Turkish contractors in the Amsterdam garment industry, as part of a wider comparative project. Much of these material has been published or has found its way in edited works (see, Rath, 2000, 2002; Kloosterman and Rath, 2003; Raes, 2000; Raes *et al.*, 2002; Rath, 2001; Hartog and Zorlu, 1999). This research pointed towards a dramatic growth in Turkish-owned garment enterprises in Amsterdam between 1987 and 1992. The vast bulk were small contractors who produced lower to medium quality women's fashion wear and in cases lacked the capacity to cut garments. At the same time an increasing number began to engage in wholesaling and import–export activities. The number of registered contractors increased from 275 in 1987 to 1,000 by 1992. After 1993 the sector went into sharp decline and was reduced to an estimated 300 firms by 1995 (IMES, 1998:21). Subsequent accounts point to the same broad picture. Dramatic growth followed by collapse. By 1997, there were only 40 to 50 firms left in existence (see Table 8.2). Different estimations on the number of contractors were provided by the Trade Register of the Amsterdam Chamber of Commerce and the IMES researchers. Whilst IMES staff identified over 1,000 firms for 1992, less than 500 were in fact registered. Most of these firms were located in the neighbourhoods of Pijp, the western part of Oost, the Jordaan and the southern part of Oud West.

According to the Chamber of Commerce, during the peak of 1992/1993, the overwhelming majority of entrepreneurs (some 60 per cent) were first-

Table 8.2 Number of contractor clothing firms in Amsterdam and level of employment by average number of workers per firm (1980–1996)

Period	Number/ contractors	Number/ workers	Number/workers per firm
early 1980s	100	1,304	12
mid-1980s	192	2,500	15
early 1990s	550	20,000	20
1996/1997	40–50	900	18

Source: Raes, 2000:78, 82.

generation immigrants from Turkey. Raes *et al.* (2002:98) estimated this to be significantly higher (at 76 per cent). During 1981, approximately 25 per cent of the workers were of Turkish origin and at the beginning of the 1990s, as much as 75 per cent (Raes, 2000a:77). Some of the Turkish entrepreneurs were naturalised i.e. had Dutch citizenship. The average length of stay in Netherlands by legal migrants was 14 to 17 years and many of them had previously worked in the clothing industry for Dutch contractors, most of whom abandoned the sector. During the 1980s most of the initial entrepreneurs were older men, many of whom were ex-guest workers in Holland and Germany, and 'their success encouraged an increasing number of youngsters to follow'. Many were without valid documents and their 'shaky legal status', relative short duration of stay, lack of familiarity with Dutch society or language, along with low level of formal education, 'impacted on their entrepreneurial opportunities' (Raes *et al.*, 2002:96, 98). The firms initially produced medium-quality women's fashion wear (blouses, skirts, dresses) but many of the large number of new entrants did so in the lower quality end of the market. At the same time, 'an increasing number of firms started to engage in other activities in wholesaling or import–export' (Raes *et al.*, 2002:92–93).

Volatility appeared as a strong feature. Many firms had been in existence for a short period of time, often less than a year. Raes *et al.* (2002:92) argue that high firm turnover and fluctuation, in part, reflected the fashion calendar: with the number of firms declining during the low season (December to February) and increasing during the high seasons (July to September). Volatility translated to employment levels with, in the early 1990s, up to 20,000 workers employed and by 1997 dramatically reduced to 900. Most the Turkish entrepreneurs recruited Turkish or Kurdish workers, 'many' of whom were undocumented. 'Some five or six Turkish coffee houses served as informal labour offices operating on a spot labour market [...] a contractor in need of workers would simply call the coffee shop owner and ask for machinists or ironers [pressers]' (Raes *et al.*, 2002:101).

The growth in Turkish-owned garment enterprises led to an ethnic and gender re-composition in the labour force. Whilst until 1980 most workers were women, unusual by international comparison, most of the workers by 1987 were men. Women made up 56 per cent of the labour force in 1987 and 20 per cent by 1997. As firms expanded rapidly in number, and restrictive immigration controls made it particularly difficult for women to migrate independently or for family reunion purposes, so, therefore, this exhausted available supplies of female labour i.e. 'the low percentage of Turkish women seemed to be linked to the relatively low percentage of Turkish women migrating to the Netherlands' (Raes *et al.*, 2002:99; IMES, 1998:51, 57). As Raes points out, the recovery of employment in the Dutch clothing industry was linked to 'the *presence* of migrant workers, but even more to the *arrival* of new migrant workers' (2000a:78, italics in original).

The rise and subsequent crisis faced by Turkish entrepreneurs in the Amsterdam garment industry was also impacted by significant changes in sourcing policy which began to look to Eastern Europe as a low-cost production centre of cheap ready-to-wear women's garments. This cannot, however, fully explain the crisis, since other centres of immigrant garment production (London, Birmingham, Paris) continue in the face of similar circumstances. What was specific about the Amsterdam experience was the severity of repression launched by the Dutch state which consisted of a comprehensive offensive against the informal practices in the industry leading to numerous raids against workshops.

As IMES (1998:62) noted, 'when undocumented workers were found, or when the payment of taxes and social benefits were evaded, entrepreneurs were heavily fined, leading to bankruptcy of a lot of firms, and undocumented workers were expelled'. Stricter law enforcement took the form of the extension of the Law on Chain Liability to 'make retailers formally responsible for their contractor's illegal practices'. Contractors had to open accounts where retailers or manufacturers, i.e. the suppliers, 'had to deposit 35 per cent of the price of each order as a guarantee that this sum would be paid to the tax and social security services'. The creation of the Clothing Intervention Team (CIT) brought together for the first time the courts, and other enforcement agencies (Labour Relations, Taxation, Aliens Police, Industrial Insurance) who launched numerous raids, targeting in particular violations of the Law on Work by Foreigners (Raes *et al.*, 2002:106–107).

The Compulsory Identification Act introduced in June 1994, made it necessary for all employers to provide documentation on their employees. The issuing of social insurance numbers was changed in 1991 and made conditional on having a residence permit. Previously, being a registered resident of the city was sufficient. These measures had the effect, as Staring (2000:187–188) argues, of effectively closing 'formal' sector employment and driving immigrant workers further into unregistered and casual employment.

Chinese–Indonesian restaurants: coping with crisis

A characteristic feature of the post-war boom, along with package holidays and the increased use of domestic appliances, was that more people in Western Europe were eating in restaurants and takeaways. Rising (and falling) living standards are sensitively linked to the catering industry. Often, 'eating out', is the first item to be retrenched in personal budgeting. The prolonged post-war boom created the material basis for the increase in the number of restaurants, but it was unlikely to have taken the course it did without the contribution of various Chinese immigrant flows which link Amsterdam and Rotterdam with villages in Fujian and elsewhere, in barely understood trade and labour diaspora. The emergence of the catering sector amongst the Chinese community in the form of an adaptation of 'Chinese–Indonesian' cuisine, was initially aimed at colonial repatriates from the East Indies and became an early 'ethnic niche'.

Pieke (1999:323) suggests that one factor was the lack of a culinary tradition of 'affordable restaurants for ordinary people' in the Netherlands at the time (when compared to Italy and France) and that this was a pioneering experience, initially monopolised by the small group of early immigrants in the cities of Amsterdam, Rotterdam and The Hague. Frank Pieke pointed to chain-migration as a labour market response linked to the rapid growth in restaurants and the exhaustion of available supplies of labour. By the 1980s, an estimated 60 per cent of the Chinese community were employed in catering, indicating the highest rates of protracted employment concentration by any ethnic group in the Netherlands (Pieke, 1999:324). Labour supply issues have been compounded by second-generation young people who are 'especially reluctant' to enter in the ethnic 'niche' of the catering trade. The boom in Chinese–Indonesian restaurants during the 1970s attracted other flows of immigrants. Indeed its expansion was dependent on these new arrivals. One early group were workers and entrepreneurs from Hong Kong, many of whom had previously lived and worked in Britain. By the late 1960s they became the dominant entrepreneurial group. Another group were immigrants from Singapore and Malaysia. During the 1980s immigrants from Fujian became the main source of labour and pool for new entrepreneurs. Immigrants from mainland China and Hong Kong make up the majority of the Netherlands Chinese population today.

The number of restaurants increased from 225 in 1960, to 618 by 1970. The massive expansion took place during the 1970s when by 1982 the number increased to 1,916. Despite the break-up of the post-war boom, Chinese–Indonesian restaurants coped remarkably well during the economic recession of the 1980s, in the face of high rates of unemployment and reduction in personal expenditure. Indeed by 1991, the number of Chinese restaurants registered a modest increase to 1,988 establishments (see, Table 8.3). This can be deceptive, however. Whilst the number of enterprises remained constant, they were in many cases owned by different entrepreneurs. Most analysis points to the scissors effect of very high firm turnover rates and constant flows of new entrants willing to enter the vacated space. Pieke pointed to one tension about the 'ethnic niche' which surfaces in the wider experience. In offering explanation for the observed saturation in the number of restaurants, he noted that, 'new entrepreneurs learned their skills by serving as apprentices in sponsor's restaurants; new ideas could hardly penetrate the community because of its essential isolation from Dutch society' (Pieke, 1998:145). As such, this pool of 'reserve' entrepreneurs, appear as 'prisoners' of the 'niche', in the sense that they lack not only information but also transferable skills, to allow them to enter other sectors. Whilst Pieke borrows from the work of Clifford

Table 8.3 Chinese–Indonesian restaurants in the Netherlands (1960–1991)

Year	Number	Change	Average yearly change (%)
1960	225	–	–
1970	618	+393	+17
1982	1,916	+1,298	+17
1987	1,842	−84	−1
1991	1,988	+146	+2

Source: Pieke, 1998:145.

Geertz to point to the 'involution' of immigrant enterprise in the sector, this can be understood as a variation on the theme of immigrant enterprise as essentially on the 'fringes' of economic systems.

One dimension of the crisis and concerns over saturated markets and new arrivals 'killing the trade', have been attempts at self-regulation. Some of the more economically powerful entrepreneurs who have time to attend meetings, have formed professional and employers associations. The largest is the Chinese section of the Dutch Catering Union with 600 members (Pieke, 1998:150).

The response to the 1980s economic recession by the entrepreneurs revealed an emergent and more complex pattern. One assumption is that enterprises such as restaurants (or shops) dependent on family labour, sometimes involving co-habitation, can be understood as Family Units of Production (FUPs). FUPs and, by implication, large chunks of immigrant enterprise, raise challenging theoretical questions about market functions. One function is over the extent they can act like capitalist firms, not least of all in the hiring and firing of labour (see, Conclusion). Nevertheless, the average employment size declined from 4.6 workers in 1982 to 2.7 by 1987 (Pieke, 1998:145). Other responses to the crisis were to convert restaurants to takeaways and remove the labour cost of employing waiters, or/and to move to cheaper premises in more outlying working class neighbourhoods. Some employed cheaper illegal labour. One general response was to work longer hours. At the same time, as Pieke also notes, the restructuring of the catering sector also saw the emergence of more clearly defined and market-functional enterprises relying more on hired labour, which adopted another strategy,

> The new type of Chinese restaurant that emerged in the Netherlands in the 1980s was no longer first and foremost a family enterprise but a calculated business venture aimed at profit maximisation. Location, decoration, size, menu and personnel were carefully chosen with the objective of catering for, or even creating, specific new markets, such as business lunches and dinners, exclusive parties and receptions.
>
> (Pieke, 1998:147)

The socio-economic differentiation between FUPs and more clearly delineated capitalist firms, accelerated under the impact of economic crisis and added to the existing patterns of differentiation articulated in more traditional relationships between the few wholesalers and the many restaurateurs and distributors of ethnic foodstuff. As the Dutch economy came out of the 1980s recession, talk of the collapse of Chinese–Indonesian restaurants subsided.

Conclusions: disadvantage and enterprise sustainability

One continuity in wider studies, appears in debates over the role of the immigrant 'informal economy' in urban restructuring, the sustainability of the 'ethnic niche' and the capacity of immigrant enterprise to act as a vehicle for 'integration'. The example of Chinese immigrant entrepreneurs in the catering industry revealed significant variation in responses to economic recession and restructuring. They also point to the limits of the 'ethnic niche', when its often positively described multiplier effect went into (temporary) reverse during the 1980s recession. Chinese entrepreneurs point to the limits of Dutch 'integration'. If 'forced' integration means anything, it sums up the experience of Chinese immigrant entrepreneurs in the restaurant trade. Substantially this flows from the nature of the 'niche' itself i.e. catering. The industry is characterised by dispersal and isolation. Only 6 per cent of Chinese-owned enterprises are actually located in Amsterdam. Indeed 81 per cent were found outside the major cities (Kloosterman and Rath, 2003:131). Unlike other employment concentrations, the nature of the restaurant trade does not in this instance lend itself to the physical formation of communities and neighbourhoods, such as in garment, leather and other production centres, which concentrate labour to a much greater extent in adjacent neighbouring urban districts and conurbations. Frequently, as was the case of Turkish-owned garment factories in Amsterdam, they were situated in residential areas where many Turkish and other immigrants live. The contrast with the Chinese community is striking. This is revealed in the fact that whilst Amsterdam has a district known as Chinatown (*Chinese buurt*), it is a commercial and leisure centre but, unlike most of its counterparts in the United States, it is not a residential area.

The idea that the Chinese community is more dispersed and, if this is an indicator of 'integration', more 'assimilated' than any other ethnic group, it is not the image projected by politicians or researchers whose emphasis on ethno-cultural variables, point to either an 'achieving' and discrete community, or a community impacted by human trafficking and the activities of criminal gangs. 'Specialisation in the restaurant sector, and regional dispersal, do not – contrary to some expectations and predictions – lead to integration, at least not for the first generation' (Pieke, 1998:143).

In short, many Chinese entrepreneurs are 'integrated', whilst at the same time excluded from most functioning parts of society. The nature of the work itself precludes much scope for social contact. Contact with Dutch society in work time is limited to superficial and subservient relationships. Long hours of work mean that few social spaces are available when the restaurants close. At that time in the morning, gambling places and casinos are some of the few places which are still open, and this is one major reason why many workers and entrepreneurs meet in these places to socialise.

The experience of Turkish entrepreneurs in the garment industry, reveals an important insight into the debate over the 'informal sector'. We noted that in this instance the entrepreneurs were mainly comprised of subordinate contractors producing on order for Dutch chain stores. In what sense are these immigrant enterprises 'informal' and 'ethnic' and how do they constitute a sector? To what extent are they capable of autonomous economic action? These issues previously surfaced in the urban informal sector debate over the role of artisans, cottage industries and the self-employed in Third World labour markets (see, Gerry, 1987; Atema and Panayiotopoulos, 1995); in analyses of the incorporation of immigrant enterprise in the Third Italy (see Chapter 6); and in debate over flexible specialisation in Southern Europe, London and elsewhere (see, Panayiotopoulos, 1992; 2000b). These debates, partly about the linkages between the informal and formal sectors, provide food for thought for the unproblematic and descriptive use of the contested term 'informal sector', by Kloosterman *et al.*, Saskia Sassen and most of the literature on immigrant enterprise. What the above do have in common is the identification of subcontracting as a significant route into entrepreneurship.

The most commonly accepted definition of the informal sector as we noted in a review of key concepts (see, Chapter 1), begins from a legal definition i.e. economic activity which is not registered for the purposes of GNP and in which labour is not protected by any social legislation. The ambiguity of the concept of the informal sector, particularly in contractor firms, rests on a legal superficiality: it is that suppliers and contractors are separate legal entities which are not liable for each other's action. This is a standard legal defence used in every market economy, by firms such as NIKE, Marks and Spencer and GAP, in the face of corporate critics (see, Panayiotopoulos, 2001b). All economies that is, except in the Netherlands when it came to Turkish entrepreneurs in the Amsterdam garment industry. In this instance – at a stroke – this legal defence was dissolved by the Law on Chain Liability which made suppliers responsible for the actions of their contractors. In one action, the Dutch state removed this synthetic construct which forms the basis for various 'dualist' theories, i.e. explanations of economic activity rooted in bi-polar presentation, such as between formal and informal, or between fringe and mainstream economies. Not only were theories rooted in superficial legality torn asunder, but the argument became reformulated. The 'informal sector' could not exist *but* for

the pivotal role played by established Dutch-owned retail chains in difficult to monitor systems of subcontracting. We noted that the evolution of
a 'spot-market' requiring weekly production allowed the buyers to
respond to fashion changes in ways they could not by sourcing to the Far
East. Subcontracting is more generally used as a strategy by larger firms in
order to avoid certain costs: transaction costs through transfer pricing,
costs in the recruitment and management of labour, the expulsion of marginal costs in the form of heating and electricity and, more problemati-
cally, the avoidance of institutional costs in the shape of value added tax
(VAT), income tax and other contributions. The incorporation of Turkish
contractors in structures of informality, can be understood as substantially
driven by the restructuring of the fashion-wear industry and that this may
have been a more significant factor than informal practices associated with
any particular immigrant or ethnic group. The argument, however, that
'immigrants play a pivotal role in these informal economic activities'
(Kloosterman *et al.*, 1999:252) did legitimise the drive against the entrepreneurs.

The example of Amsterdam shows a gateway city in crisis. Whilst there
are continuities found in this with other urban centres, there are also specific differences in institutional relationships with immigrant groups. The
political-institutional framework in the Netherlands, and less so in Amsterdam, has swung against immigrants. Rising Islamophobia, the absence
of ethnic minority policy and failed 'forced' integration, have impacted on
immigrant entrepreneurs and made life, hard as it is for most, a little bit
tougher. The experience of Turkish entrepreneurs in the garment industry
is a case in point. In Amsterdam we have a (painful example) of lack of
'mixed' embeddedness (with host political structures) when compared to
other gateway cities in the United States and Europe (see, Panayiotopoulos and Dreef, 2002) (e.g. only two Turkish contractors were members of
the established association of garment manufacturers, Raes *et al.*,
2002:107).

Kloosterman *et al.* (1999:257–258) in following Karl Polanyi, pointed to
mixed embeddedness as located in the 'intersection' between changes in
the social-cultural framework and the transformation of urban economies
and cities. The concept points to the relationship between immigrant
entrepreneurs and structural changes in the urban economy and the institutional framework within which entrepreneurs operate. It is a critique of
residual theories which 'reduce immigrant entrepreneurship to an ethno-
cultural phenomenon existing within an economic and institutional
vacuum' (Rath and Kloosterman, 2000:666). It is also a critique of the
'corporatist' welfare state. In a familiar restatement, it is argued that the
locational intersection of immigrant enterprise has been fundamentally
shaped by the consequences of the 'Rhineland model' (see, Chapter 6). In
this model the over-regulated state puts up barriers in the start-up of
immigrant enterprises and participation in low-wage employment. One

way it does this is by effectively pricing immigrants out of the labour market through measures such as minimum pay legislation. As Klooster-man (1996:650) writes, 'The corporatist institutional framework has effect-ively blocked [in Holland] a sufficient expansion of low-wage services to absorb the migrants as has happened, in for instance, New York in the 1980s'.

The influence of the institutional framework underpins, yet rarely sur-faces in most analyses of immigrant enterprise. In this sense, Rath, Kloost-erman, and the literature on 'mixed' embeddedness, are making an important and explicit contribution. At the same time, the critique pre-sented by Kloosterman *et al.*, needs to move beyond generalisations about the corporatist state, and to identify the political mechanisms which render a group of immigrant entrepreneurs particularly vulnerable to institutional repression, i.e. 'lacking' in mixed embeddedness. In order to understand lack of embeddedness in the political-institutional framework, we need to consider processes of exclusion and inclusion in political systems and the implications this has for how immigrant entrepreneurs operate in markets. Above all, we need to explain the selectivity in institutional behaviour. Why the Turkish community? Why the garment industry?

It is debatable whether much of the repression would have taken place, if it was directed at Dutch nationals. In part this derived from the continu-ing legacy of the guest worker system and the lack of citizenship amongst many ex-guest worker and new immigrant entrepreneurs. In important ways, rights to citizenship were actually taken away. The Nationality Law was changed in 1992 to permit dual nationality, but reversed in 1997. The 2001 Aliens Act included Turkey amongst the countries from which trav-ellers would require visas for the first time (Geddes, 2003:106, 117).

In part, institutional behaviour can be seen as the product of the politics of the irrational embedded in racist discourses. The moral panic which was directed at the Turkish community, became one of the most (if not most) significant examples of repression directed at immigrant enterprise in Europe. Its origins may well derive from the already coiled and ready to spring xenophobia stoked up in Dutch society. At the same time, it began (as panics often do) with an 'incident' and subsequent media amplification, involving a plane which crashed into a block of flats in a working class neighbourhood in south-east Amsterdam, overlooking Schipol Inter-national Airport. The Israeli plane (reputedly carrying nuclear waste – uranium ballast as it transpired) killed an unspecified number of people. The problem was that many of the victims were undocumented immi-grants and it was impossible to carry out a full inventory of the fatalities. Therefore, the government declared an amnesty by offering to legalise the status of such workers in the block. According to Husbands (1994), the sight of illegal workers (many of whom had suffered the loss of family and friends) queuing up to legalise their status, incensed the xenophobes and was exploited by the right-wing administration to legitimise the initial raids. In this experience, Husband also noted, the crystallisation of 'new' moral panics based in a 'crisis of national identity'. This was a foretaste of the more intensive repression which followed the killing of Fortuijn and Theo van Gogh in (2001 and 2004 respectively) and the mass expulsion of tens of thousands of refugees.

The chapter concludes that debate over the development of immigrant enterprise and the capacities of markets generally and immigrant enterprise specifically, to offer solutions to the complex social needs facing diverse immigrant communities, such as 'integration', cannot be understood without reference to the changing political-institutional framework. This raises question marks over the sustainability of immigrant enterprise in gateway cities in formation.

9 Paris

Immigrant enterprise in historical perspective

Introduction: key issues

Paris – like New York – has acted as a key gateway city for immigrants over two centuries. A review of the historical and contemporary incorporation of immigrants as workers and entrepreneurs in the Parisian economy, points to significant elements of continuity and change. One continuity appears in the relationship between spatial and sectoral variables, such as in the significance of particular neighbourhoods, places and industries for immigrant economic activity. Another appears in generalisation founded in labour market traditions, which indicate that North Africans tend to be shopkeepers and Southern Europeans are usually craftsmen or artisans (Mung and Lacroix, 2003:185). Other continuities can be found in a range of sectors of the Parisian economy. A long historical association exists between immigrants and the garment industry. At the turn of the twentieth century Paris was the fashion capital of the world, and one continuity remains in global demand for Parisian fashion. This has implications for immigrant contractors today.

Significant change is illustrated in the construction industry, where trends towards a growing role for contractors have been a significant factor in the entry route of many Portuguese immigrants from guest workers to entrepreneurs. In the retail sector, one trend has been towards grocery specialisation to fill the needs of particular neighbourhoods and communities and many immigrant entrepreneurs have responded to these market changes. Frequently, this involves regional trade networks of wholesalers and retailers, linking the Maghreb (Algeria, Morocco and Tunisia) to Paris and other urban conurbations. In the restaurant sector, diversification by the Chinese community into 'nouvelle cuisine' has been a recognisable trend. Similarly, diversification by Chinese entrepreneurs in the leather goods sector has seen the production and wholesaling of middle to lower end 'designer' goods, as well as the continuation of more traditional areas of activity such as furniture making and joinery (Yu-Sion, 1999:311–317).

Another continuity, as with the nineteenth and twentieth centuries, is that Paris continues to act as a magnet for refugees and asylum seekers who provided a rich source of new entrepreneurs. The example of immigrant enterprise in Paris reflects on two broader questions raised in the book. First, it provides fertile ground for examining Sassen's (2004) observation, that contrary to the current xenophobia, Europe has successfully 'integrated' many different groups of immigrants in its contemporary history. Paris is a concentrated example of this proposition which reveals significant historical continuities in the incorporation of immigrant entrepreneurs, which add to this argument. More problematic, however, are the political conclusions drawn by Sassen about the role of the European Union (EU) as an agency for integration. We noted that this fails to explain selectivity and variation in institutional behaviour and policy on immigration and naturalisation and the prejudicial construction of difference expressed in moral panic and xenophobia which has swept anti-immigrant parties into office in most EU member states.

Second, the chapter provides material critical of 'mixed' embeddedness theories, by pointing to alternative, ethno-cultural explanations for the development of immigrant enterprise. We noted that mixed embeddedness theories are critical of ethno-cultural analyses and their tendency to attach primacy to the origins and cultural endowment of entrepreneurs, as a priori for social embeddedness in the ethnic economy and as causal explanation for entrepreneurship. Rather, Rath (2000a) argued, this needs to be understood in a relationship with the wider political-institutional framework. It is in part due to lack of integration in the political systems of Europe (so the argument continues) that most, if not all, immigrant enterprises in the Rhineland countries are confined to the economic margins, with the Amsterdam garment industry as a case in point (see, Chapter 8).

One criticism of this approach is, as Mung and Lacroix (2003:188) infer, that mixed embeddedness theory may undervalue the role of 'how group strategies and individual desire for social mobility fit into the structure'. This is particularly relevant when the theory becomes associated with the 'fringe' literature on immigrant enterprise and its tendency to structurally over determine the positioning of immigrant enterprise. This may underestimate the extent to which ethnic and immigrant groups act as their own agency, or at least shape economic activity in specific ways that would not have existed otherwise. One inference is that ethno-cultural explanations are dismissed too easily and that, perhaps, in their haste to bring immigrant enterprise out of the 'fringe' and to propose practical ideas for policy makers to 'integrate' it, Kloosterman and Rath show insufficient appreciation of ethnicity or immigration status as a basis for economic and political mobilisation. Further criticism can be offered with reference to MacGaffey and Bazenguissa-Ganga's study of Congolese traders in Paris, many of whom were refugees, and the light this sheds on issues usually ignored in conventional analyses of immigrant enterprise (MacGaffey and Bazenguissa-Ganga, 2000).

Paris-France: a city and country built by immigrants

France has a long history of encouraging inward migration, dating to the nineteenth century partly in response to low levels of population growth. France was the major country of immigration in Europe for most of the late nineteenth and the first half of the twentieth centuries. Jews from Eastern Europe, Armenians from the ex-Ottoman Empire, but mainly migrants from neighbouring countries, such as Italy, Poland, Spain and Belgium, made up the vast bulk of migrants. During 1881, immigrants made up 2.2 per cent, in 1931 6.6 per cent and in 1990 6.4 per cent of the population. One consequence of this history is that by the 1980s, 25 per cent of people living in France were either immigrants or had at least one immigrant relative (Body-Gendrot, 1996:595–596).

Partly for the above reason, naturalisation plays a more significant role in France than most other European countries. In 1999, 3.2 million immigrants were classified as 'foreigners' and another 2.3 million had acquired French nationality. Collectively they made up 9.4 per cent of France's total population of 58.5 million people (Geddes, 2003:54). This is also reflected amongst entrepreneurs. Of the 73,972 immigrant shopkeepers enumerated in the French Census, 33,000 (45 per cent) were naturalised. Amongst the 86,734 immigrant craftsmen, 41 per cent were naturalised, as were 41 per cent of entrepreneurs employing ten workers or more (see Table 9.1).

'Artisanal', is also an important labour market concept in France, used to describe skilled workers e.g. carpenters, bricklayers, plasterers, tailors, bakers, watch-repairers. These were often the labour migrants who characterised much of French inward population movement during the nineteenth century. Belgians specialised in hotels and cafés and the Italians in construction, with the Swiss in hotels, watch and clock, and woodwork workshops. After the Russian Revolution, whilst the ex-White generals and aristocrats had no skills in this trade, many of them became taxi owners and chauffeurs. A large proportion of these artisans worked for themselves and this was reflected in high rates of self-employment which stood in 1911 at 20.4 per cent, when compared to 5.8 per cent (i.e. four times less) for 1988 (Simon, 1990:6). The rate of self-employment is widely used as a proxy indicator of entrepreneurship.

Table 9.1 France: naturalised and foreign immigrant shopkeepers, craftsmen and employers of ten or more workers (1990)

	Shopkeepers	*Craftsmen*	*Employ 10+ (all sectors)*
Naturalised	33,208 (45%)	35,692 (41%)	75,576 (43%)
Alien	40,764	51,042	98,394
Total	73,972	86,734	173,970

Source: Mung and Lacroix, 2003:183.

France has a complex history in negotiating difference, immigration and the status of minorities. One (optimistic) historical continuity appears in the many Roma villages in northern Rumania which have depended on remittances sent from Paris, where many are clandestinely employed in seasonal work in construction and in independent income generating activities, such as street-selling and entertainment. This annual labour migration has been recorded since 1992, 'as if this were still the nineteenth century and border controls did not exist' (Harris, 2002:34). One other reminder is that during the Nazi occupation of France, many Jewish entrepreneurs in the Parisian urban district were eliminated in the concentration camps, and this impacted on the overall (declining) number of persons registered as self-employed.

During the post-war period, France signed labour recruitment agreements with 16 European and non-European countries. Decolonisation in the 1950s and 1960s saw an increase in non-European migration, primarily from the countries of the Maghreb region. Geddes (2003:52) argues that immigration and debate about nationality and citizenship in France from the 1960s onwards has been shaped primarily by responses to movement from the ex-colonies of the Maghreb. As with other European countries, the 'crisis of integration' became a codeword for legitimising xenophobia directed at 'Muslim' immigrants and (given the absence of religious passports), brown and black people in general. Given that France has the largest Muslim population in Europe, this has added significance. Geddes (2003:56) writes that 'there's little to suggest that Muslim immigrants were any more or less assimilable' than other immigrant groups. One illustration of the post-9/11 environment was the banning of the *hijab* in French schools.

That the crisis was not shaped by the even larger numbers of Southern European immigrants is revealing. During 1982 nearly 1.5 million immigrants from Southern Europe, as well as 1.4 million from the Maghreb lived in France (Geddes, 2003:54). Paris is as much a Portuguese as a French city and during the 1960s they constituted the single largest source of immigrants, making Paris the second largest concentration of people of Portuguese origins after Lisbon. There are many stories of villagers from Villa Real, northern Portugal, walking to Paris (Panayiotopoulos, 1984). In 1990, Portuguese immigrants still made up 22 per cent of all immigrants in the greater Parisian region, compared to 23 per cent who were Algerians (Body-Gendrot, 1996:597). Castles and Cossack (1973) in their classic study of labour transfer and the guest worker system during the 1960s, pointed to the *bidonville* – not as a Third World phenomenon – but as the domicile of Portuguese construction workers on building sites in the Paris region.

The economic recession which lead to the abandonment of the French guest worker system in 1974, also saw immigrants impacted by rising unemployment in mining, iron and steel, and construction, in which many were concentrated. Some companies, like Renault, tried to link redundancy payments to Moroccan workers, with support in setting up enterprises. Simon, in a study of Moroccan entrepreneurs noted that in the repositioning of workers,

> it was less the loss than the fear of losing a salaried post that triggered the conversion of the salaried to independent work. Prior to setting up on their own behalf, nearly half the Moroccan businessmen in Paris had been on the payroll in the local mines of the North (7%) and industry (36%) for over ten years on average.
>
> (Simon, 1990:9)

During the recession years and despite restrictions on the recruitment of guest workers, the immigrant flow into France continued and changed in composition. In ways which are historically recognisable, between 1975 and 1987 some 145,000 refugees, not made up of Jewish refugees from Eastern Europe but from Indo-China, arrived in France, of whom an estimated 50 to 60 per cent were of Chinese origins. Other immigrant groups arrived from Hong Kong, mainland China and other European countries. Yu-Sion (1998:96,102) estimated a Chinese community of 120,000 people. Mung and Lacroix (2000:7,13) estimated people of Chinese origin significantly higher at 250,000 to 300,000 people, with immigrants from South-east Asia (Cambodia, Laos, Vietnam) making up the majority. Displacement, as well as economic migration, has led to the formation of new communities and the transformation of existing communities. This has made France into a more complex place. Turkish immigrants, refugees from ex-Yugoslavia, Congo and clandestine migrants from Eastern Europe, have made the composition of immigrants in France more diverse, and the causes of their immigration more difficult to generalise about or to predict.

Today, the 'failure' of integration and the 'crisis' of 'French' national identity, dominate debate and policy on immigration in France. Recent research, interestingly from the Interior Ministry, points to two million people in France living in urban ghettos, blighted by social exclusion, domestic violence, racial discrimination and 'religious extremism'. Nearly 300 out of 630 so-called *quartiers chauds* were dominated by immigrant groups. One conclusion was that integration into the economic and social mainstream has actually 'gone into reverse' (Johnson, 2004:8). The dominant view amongst policy makers in France is to point to residual explanations for exclusion, such as that the 'culture' of particular ethnic groups, or Islamic 'militants', are the main barrier to integration. This ignores existing discrimination against Maghrebian, Chinese and African immigrants of Orwellian proportions. Quite independently of any Rhineland model, France has a vast array of institutional restrictions on the employment of immigrants. Many sectors are closed to immigrants, whilst they are open for nationals from other EU states. For example, immigrants in France cannot practice as physicians, dentists, pharmacists, veterinarians, architects, surveyors, accountants, bailiffs or lawyers. Hardly surprising, perhaps, only about 1 per cent of the total number of licensed professionals in France, are foreigners. Neither can they own a periodical, a television or broadcasting agency, to sell tobacco or alcoholic beverages (Mung and Lacroix, 2003:175). It is partly due to restrictions such as the above that immigrants are forced to resort to naturalisation, which can close jobs and political rights in their own countries of origin.

Nearly 40 per cent of all immigrants in France live in the Ile de France region. This region is a vast sprawling urban development agglomeration, made up of the city of Paris, the inner and outer circles (the Parisian 'agglomeration') and smaller towns and 'suburbs'. The region accounts for a population of over 11 million people. One in three green cards between 1965 to 1971, were issued for this area and over the last 40 years the region gained an additional 3.5 million residents (Body-Gendrot, 1996:596). A defining characteristic of social polarisation in Paris is the significance of the suburb (*banlieue*) in the structuring of social exclusion. In most cities, the suburbs represent a form of social mobility and flight by the well-to-do. In Paris, the suburbs are where the poor and the immigrants live. The *banlieue* represents the area sprawling between the city and more distant urbanised zones. Frequently this appears in concentrations of high-rise apartment blocks attached to arterial roads. The origin of the term, contains a paradox in the current climate of xenophobia. It goes back to early medieval times and refers to the, then, perimeter of one league (*lieue*) around the city which acted, amongst other things, as an exclusion zone for victims of the plague.

In the city of Paris itself, Sophie Body-Gendrot (1996:595) points to the articulation of social polarisation in terms of a 'dual' system with, on the one hand, the few *arrondissements* (the XIIth and XIIIth) out of 20, which along with coastal retreats such as Nice and Biarritz act as the residence of 'more than half of French dominant social economic categories', and on the other, the 12 *arrondissements* which account for one fifth of all immigrants in Ile de France, such as the older inner-city areas such as Goutte d'Or and Bellevile ('Chinatown') in the XIIIth *arrondissement*, which constitute key areas of immigrant concentration (Body-Gendrot: 1996:601).

New Year's Eve – Champs-Elysees and Sevran Beaudottes

The centre of Paris is very white, unless you are up early in the morning to see the rubbish collected, the offices cleaned and the windows made pristine for the tourists. Very few people from the Maghreb stand in the queue to visit the Louvre or the Eiffel Tower, unless they are newly-wedded couples.

Sevran Beaudottes is far from the centre of Paris. It is part of the *banlieue* sprawl and was built between 1975 and 1990, with the intention of housing Paris' immigrant labour force. With approximately 50,000 residents, of whom an estimated 61 per cent are under the age of 14, it has experienced the fastest urban growth in France. Outside the RER station at 2 am on New Year's Eve 2003–2004, it was very different from the centre. No taxis in sight. Everybody at the bus stop was young, and most were either black or North African. Waiting for a bus for 40 minutes, with a 40-minute journey further on to look, left plenty of time for talking in broken French, Turkish, Greek, English and Spanish. 'Inshallah' was a common denominator. Sevran Beaudottes was the centre of rioting during 2001, which began on 2 July and lasted for six nights, 'because' as a number of the young people said 'there are not enough busses'. The riots involved young people and the police in pitched battles during which police cars were overturned and burned as were private cars, 'but they were old and people made money on the insurance'. The youths gained the upper hand during the first night by learning how to make and use petrol bombs, such that 'the lit bottle must be held upright ... like this ... otherwise the burning rag on the top can burn your hand'. They also had superior knowledge of the local streets and terrain. Frequently, young people have to walk for over one hour from the RER station to get to their homes. 'Home' is blocks of flats on main roads interspersed with Turkish-owned doner kebab takeaways and devoid of any other services. In order to buy cigarettes you have to go to the petrol station, where the Senegalese entrepreneur franchising the outlet will sell them to you under the counter, because he has no licence to sell tobacco.

The New Year celebration on the Champs-Elysees is one of the few occasions during which the central historical-ceremonial and tourist areas of Paris become visually interconnected with people who live in Paris, in places such as Sevran Beaudottes and other *banlieue*. The traditional party centring at the Arc de Triomphe is an annual event, which attracts people from outside Paris. It was a seething mass of multi-colour and multi-ethnic humanity. French, African, Algerian, Turkish, Chinese and Indian people were amongst the estimated one million-plus revellers. Groups of Moroccan youths ran about and played with the police, letting off fireworks and trying to wind them up. They established it was 'their' thing, too.

(Panayiotopoulos, 2003/2004, New Year, Champs-Elysees and
Sevran Beaudottes, Personal observation)

Sectoral and spatial analyses

Particular neighbourhoods and sectors in Paris, as with other places, become the physical location and entry point of immigrant enterprises and communities. Whilst Paris is characterised by high levels of ethnic

interspersion in sectors such as the garment industry, some neighbourhoods and sectors see high levels of ethnic concentration. Some neighbourhoods like the Sentier garment district, are commercial districts which
'close' after hours, on Sundays and during public holidays (Panayiotopoulos, 2004, Sentier, personal observation). Others combine both commercial
and residential functions. This is typified by the North African Goutte
d'Or district and Paris' 'Chinatown' in the Triangle de Choisy (Mung and
Lacroix, 2003:174).

The XIIIth *arrondissement* is the centre for Chinese immigrant entrepreneurship in Paris, with 20.5 per cent of firms concentrated in this area
and another 23 per cent in the four adjoining *arrondissements* of north-
east Paris (Yu-Sion, 1998:107). Unlike in Amsterdam, where 'Chinatown'
is effectively a tourist attraction, it is also a residential area which has
(paradoxically) grown as the result of urban development. The ranks of
the Chinese community were invigorated by Zhejiangese migrants from
the 1980s onwards and have withstood attempts to drive them out of Triangle de Choisy. From the early 1970s a number of 30-storey blocks were
built in the Porte de Choisy area, which were boycotted at the time by
French Parisians because of their expense and lack of taste. Refugees from
South-East Asia moved into the flats which became over-populated by the
1980s. Similarly, the dilapidated buildings of the Belleville area in the
XXth *arrondissement* were also restored. In both cases, many bought
apartments in the renovated neighbourhoods and settled there between
1980 and 1985 (Yu-Sion, 1998:106). In the XIIIth *arrondissement* there are
a variety of Chinese and other immigrant enterprises: garment manufacturing, estate agents, jewellers, bakers, butchers, grocers, driving schools,
as well as more traditional activities such as catering, the manufacture of
leatherwear and furniture making.

Trade, retail, wholesale: Maghreb-Paris

The retail sector has been the most significant area of expansion in enterprise by Maghrebian immigrants. It is a sector relevant to many immigrant
groups and one of the earliest to enter. Many have been forced to adapt to
changing and difficult circumstances. Indeed, the increase in immigrant-
owned retail enterprises and in particular groceries, is all the more
remarkable given that it has been achieved in the face of advances by
supermarkets and massive sectoral decline in France. The number of small
shopkeepers, i.e. those with a commercial surface of $400\,m^2$, declined by 43
per cent between 1982 and 1992 (Mung and Lacroix, 2000:2).

One form of adaptation has been towards grocery specialisation in
filling the needs of both rich and poor consumers. Entrepreneurs from the
Maghreb engage in 'neighbourhood' and 'community' trade (Simon,
1990:14). Neighbourhood trade consists of shops catering for the wealthy,
many of whom are elderly. The general advantages consist of shops which

are conveniently located, are available every day, even during weekends and the summer vacation and have long opening hours (12–15 hours). The main segmentation lies in the culinary crisis of the bourgeoisie. Whilst much of this specialisation has been driven by consumer concerns over periodic food–health crises, such as 'mad cow' disease and over the possible impact of genetically modified food, the appetite of wealthy consumers has transformed this into specialised markets for food labelled as healthy, organic, authentic, natural and local, or more typically, vintage, as in wine and olive oil (Mung and Lacroix, 2000). Clearly things have moved on since the 1950s when the only place one could buy olive oil in the UK, other than a handful of specialist traders, was in pharmacists' shops. The increased familiarity by native consumers for specialised products has created an important and growing new niche.

Community trade is mainly targeted at immigrant customers. As with neighbourhood trade, convenience appears in the form of easy access shopping for small purchases of hand-carried household items, often made on a daily basis. In both, the small scale of purchase is offset by higher prices, when compared to supermarkets. In community shops, however, higher prices are compensated further through the offering of other services, such as credit to customers and in acting as centres for the sharing of information about jobs, housing, schools and news from home. Many Maghrebian entrepreneurs have also established restaurants and eating places. Some are 'popular' restaurants with North African cooking in the old industrial suburbs of Paris (St. Denis, Gennevilliers), and others are more exotic restaurants for diners looking for somewhere different, often mixing Maghrebian with European cooking. Most entrepreneurs raised the start-up capital from close relatives and compatriots. Frequently this takes the form of buying back establishments within the same ethnic group and extended family chain ownership (Simon, 1990:14).

Construction: Portugal-Paris

Construction was the single largest area of employment concentration by Portuguese immigrant workers in Paris from the 1950s to the early 1970s. During the 1980s many became contractors in the industry, either in private sector construction or in public work involving municipalities and other bodies in civil engineering projects work. The number of 'self-employed' Portuguese contractors increased from 4,540 in 1982 to 15,800 in 1990 (Mung and Lacroix, 2000:4). One factor for entry into business reflected on family histories of involvement in the industry as workers, and considerations about the future employment needs of second-generation family members. This was one reason why Portuguese contractors were 'younger than their French colleagues' (Simon, 1990:16).

Another, and possibly more significant, factor was the recovery and restructuring of the construction industry during the 1980s, which accelerated trends towards subcontracting. The building boom of the late 1980s required the assembling of men with relevant skills at short notice. The Portuguese contractors had the skills and could make labour available, either from Portugal through seasonal contracts or prior to Portugal's entry into the EU, in the employment of undocumented workers, or amongst second-generation youth, following in their fathers' trade. The shortage of labour drove subcontracting, as much as the needs of ex-guest workers and their families to look to future employment needs. This was by no means an easy task. As with other second-generation young people faced with labour market alternatives, there is considerable resistance to entry in the niche sector. Simon (1990:17) noted that, 'the educational level of the youth has risen, and they don't wish to reproduce the situation – they henceforth can't bear its attendant constraints – of their tradesmen or artisanal parents'. Many have looked to alternatives in the service sector, mini-markets, transport and security.

Restaurants and world fusion cuisine: the world-Paris

Restaurants, doner kebab takeaways and sandwich bars are a highly visible area of immigrant enterprise. Amongst Chinese immigrant entrepreneurs, the most significant area of expansion has been in the catering industry. The numerical increase primarily of restaurants, and also fast-food places and other food-related activities, has seen over half (51.4 per cent) of all Chinese-owned enterprises in Paris in this sector (Yu-Sion, 1999:316). Expansion, however, has also taken a qualitative dimension in terms of diversification by Chinese and other entrepreneurs into fusion-food which, in part, has been made possible by the role of Paris as a global city in the culinary inter-exchange fusion-food implies. Many Chinese entrepreneurs own establishments classified as 'nouvelle cuisine', Japanese cuisine, tapas bars, Greek restaurants, kosher Chinese food. Frequently they involve innovation and adaptation. The sectoral composition of Chinese enterprise, despite the high representation for the catering industry, shows more diversity than in the Netherlands, where the Indonesian–Chinese restaurant 'niche' sector monopolised the lives of the Chinese community for four decades. In the Netherlands, we noted that the economic differentiation of enterprises was in part a response to economic crisis, which led some firms to reposition themselves as more clearly defined capitalist firms in their relationships with markets and labour (see, Chapter 8). Economic differentiation in Paris is illustrated in diversification and the existence of large enterprises such as the Tang Brothers Company, importers and wholesalers mainly of foodstuff, who employ 450 persons (Yu-Sion, 1998:108).

Furniture, leather: the 'Chinese economic arrangement'

Chinese entrepreneurs are involved in leather and garment production in many European cities. Whilst these sectors are in relative decline amongst the Chinese community in Paris, Paris remains an important centre of leatherwear production, with a long history of participation by the Chinese community. Wenzhounese itinerant merchants, abandoned their trade in fancy goods, moved from the XIIth to the IIIrd *arrondissement* (the old Jewish quarter) and established leather workshops after the Second World War. These involve the production and wholesaling of middle to lower end leather goods such as wallets and women's handbags. Emmanuel Mung estimated about 140 Chinese wholesalers distributed the merchandise produced in the small workshops. One development from the 1990s onwards was that 'they have began carrying more products imported from Italy (manufactured in Chinese workshops) and from Asia' (Mung and Lacroix, 2000:5). Some of the workshops simply attach 'designer' labels to goods produced in centres such as Florence, Prato and Treviso.

Furniture is an even more significant example. Many immigrant Chinese joiners, craftsmen and dealers concentrated in Faubourg Saint-Antoine, situated in the XIth and XIIth *arrondissements*, and turned it into 'the most important furniture centre of Europe' during the period 1960–1980 (Yu-Sion, 1998:105).

The garment industry: Sentier, the world-Paris

The Parisian garment industry illustrates a long historical association between immigrants and like its counterparts elsewhere, women immigrants. Nancy Green (a labour historian) points to the paradox, therefore, of the 'lack of historical memory on the part of many industry participants' (2002:29). The turn of the twentieth century saw Paris as fashion capital of the world and this was reflected in the segmentation of women's labour. The higher skilled *couturières* were employed in the production of custom-made fashion items, whilst the lower skilled *grisettes* made clothes for the popular market. Custom-made (*couturière*) rather than ready-to wear women's garments (*confection*) continued to be the norm in France longer than in the US (until after the Second World War). For these reasons employment in the Parisian garment industry dominated the labour market and accounted in 1906 for 290,340 jobs, twice those in metalworking, its nearest manufacturing comparison. By 1926 employment declined to 192,853 and collapsed to 85,461 in 1946, due to the deportation of Jewish workers and the subsequent impact of automation. Even in 1946, however, Jews made up 60 per cent of male workers. Many worked and hid in the small workshops during the Nazi occupation of Paris (Green, 2002:36). In 1962, 90,000 and in 1993, 40,000 workers (on 2,000 payrolls) were employed in the garment industry in Paris and its suburbs (Green,

2002:31). The Parisian garment industry provided a shelter for diverse immigrant groups in different historical periods (see, below) Green, 2002:35–38).

Parisian garment industry: immigrant waves (1840–2000)

1840s	Immigrants from Germany, Hungary, Poland
1880s	Eastern European Jews
1908	Jews, Poles, Czechs, Austrians, Romanians, Italians
1930s	Armenians, Poles, Italians
1950s–1960s	North African (Tunisian and Moroccan Jews)
1960s–1970s	Yugoslavian, Chinese, South-East Asian (Cambodia, Laos, Vietnam)
Mid-1980s	An estimated 800 out of 1,200 firms in Sentier owned by Jews (90 per cent from North Africa)
1990s–2000	Turkish, Pakistani, Sri Lankan.

Nancy Green asks, 'why have so many immigrants flocked into this industry?' and points to historical-structural explanations articulated in 'low' skill and capital requirements to set up a workshop in the sector, with start-up capital frequently raised internally; the limited labour market options available to immigrant groups; the role of immigrant networks in channelling women immigrants to the sector. Green points, empirically, to the growth of subcontracting and the 'high feminisation of sector'. In these and other respects the structure of the industry has not changed since the mid-nineteenth century, when the Courts of Europe used to come to Paris to purchase the latest fashion. At the top end we see the international buyers who come to Paris to purchase *haute couture* patterns and the right to reproduce them. At the bottom end are the contractors (*faconnier*, or entrepreneur) and subcontractors. Some 96 per cent of firms employ 20 workers or less. Most immigrant entrepreneurs are to be at the bottom of the commodity chain and are made up of small-scale production units which are under constant pressure for a quick turn around of merchandise in line with seasonal demand. The above is underpinned by high rates of firm turnover (failures). Many contractors' status changes between employer and employee. Some regularly shift from one status to another several times a year, and illustrate a high degree of mobility in both an upward and downward direction (Morokvasic *et al.*, 1990).

Collectively, the above point to a familiar enough picture of the women's fashion-wear sector. What is specific about Paris is the role of fashion and the compounded nature of relationships typified by *le system Sentier*, or *circuit court* (the short cycle), driven by rapid (and uncertain) fashion change, but also a worship of the 'new' and the 'modern'. Sentier is the district in Paris in which much of the garment industry is situated. *Le system Sentier*, concerns a very specific section of subcontracting of the sewing and pressing functions in the women's fashion-wear industry. It is an industry characterised by great uncertainty about style and what will sell. The way it works is that 'a few weeks before the start of each season' (spring, summer, autumn, winter) a manufacturer will put on the market a limited number of models (say, seven or eight) of dresses, trousers, skirts, blouses. These are produced in a limited quantity to 'test' the trends of the coming season. After a few days, the manufacturer has a clearer idea of which models will sell the most, based on information from the retailers who are selling the 'test' product. 'He [sic] must then produce, in a short period of time (one week), several thousand models in order to satisfy the demand [...] Therefore, this system requires a very flexible workforce, instantly available and ready to work intensely for a short period' (Mung and Lacroix, 2000:6).

Ethno-cultural explanations: immigrant and refugee entrepreneurs

As we have seen from the brief notes above, the development of Paris over the last two centuries has been shaped by the enterprise of diverse immigrant groups. Refugee entrepreneurs have been a significant part of this story. The role of Paris as sanctuary, followed traditions inherited in part from the ideas of the French Revolution. One group of early refugees consisted of English poets and authors, such as Percy Shelley, Byron, Keats, Wordsworth, Coleridge and Mary Shelley, who found republican France preferable to King George III's spies and the sickening hypocrisy of the English bourgeoisie. Percy Shelley was also fleeing religious persecution, or rather persecution by Christians, who expelled him from school at the age of 18 for defending atheism. Italian republican and Polish democrats and nationalists during the mid- and late-nineteenth century, Armenian survivors of genocide from the ex-Ottoman Empire during the early twentieth century, and waves of oppressed national and religious minorities fleeing the Tsarist Empire, provided constant streams of economic migrants, displaced persons, political exiles and refugees. Many of these refugees were also craftsmen and women in sectors such as the garment industry and most of the manual trades, who became over time an integral part of the French working class. Some were also anarcho-syndicalists and socialists, who added to the political culture of the left in France, much to the concern of the right, which as in other places was quick to point the finger at 'foreign agitators'.

Contemporary flows of refugees are mainly made up of persons displaced by conflict, such as in ex-Yugoslavia, the Central African lake region, centring on the Democratic Republic of Congo (DCR), Algeria and Iraq. As with refugees during the nineteenth century, amongst them are also some of most resolute advocates of freedom and liberty in their own countries and those of their displacement. Many of them have paid dearly for this. Manifestations of refugee economic activities are visibly evident in Congolese traders, Roma street-entertainers and diverse groups of street-sellers who frequently have in common lack of immigration status and an ambiguous relationship with the police on the street. Street-selling has few barriers to entry and there are no overheads. Old complexities in new forms, reinforce the view that Europe and in particular France and its major cities, have negotiated and in many cases successfully incorporated, diverse groups of immigrants, including refugees, for two centuries.

Ethno-cultural explanations for the phenomenon of immigrant and refugee enterprise, surface in analyses of trade and labour diaspora i.e. analyses which point to the significance of societies of origins. Simon (1990) described trades people originating mainly from the Berber communities: Jerbians and Jebalias from southern Tunisia, and the Mozabits from the Algerian Sahara. According to Simon (1990:12) in the Paris urban district, '90 per cent of the Moroccan businessmen [...] originate from Souss'. The activities of the entrepreneurs as grocers, patisserie proprietors and confectioners is articulated in a wider system of exchange involving the Maghreb and the Paris–Lyons–Marseilles conglomerations. These communities have long-standing trading traditions and monopolise retail and wholesale commerce in the Maghreb. Some, such as the Soussi entrepreneurs in France, 'have set up large-scale businesses in their regions of origins', such as hotels in Agadir and Casablanca (Simon, 1990:14).

Economic arrangements articulated in the idiom of ethnicity, are described by Mung and Lacroix (2000) in terms of a 'Chinese' economic arrangement, or 'an ensemble of interconnected enterprises [...] moving toward relative autonomy'. The number of Chinese-owned enterprises in Paris has increased from 1,044 in 1985 to 1,646 by 1992 (Yu-Sion, 1999:316). Most of them show very high levels of intra-community employment, with one estimate that 'somewhere between half and three fourths of the active Chinese population in France works for a Chinese business' (Mung and Lacroix, 2000:10). The Chinese economic circuit is presented at one level as a two-sectoral model (Mung and Lacroix, 2000:9) characterised by:

The Chinese economic arrangement

- *Intra-community market*: orientated towards (the limited) Chinese household market for consumption items such as food, clothing, beauty, cultural items; and also, business support and other services, accountants, real estate agents, GPs, machinery, suppliers.
- *Extra-community market*: orientated towards non-Chinese households, such as for example restaurants and takeaways; and also non-Chinese businesses in the sectors such as the garment industry).

Mung and Lacroix, make an important observation in pointing towards a progressive autonomy of the Chinese ethnic economic arrangement, characterised by a move from intra- to extra-orientation and illustrated in a growing diversification of Chinese-owned enterprises in Paris. At the same time, as some of the preceding material suggests, a two-sectoral model can over-simplify Chinese enterprise and undervalue its contribution in the shaping of particular sectors and urban spaces, and in the opening up of new centres of production and distribution in many European cities such as for leather and fake designer goods targeting tourists. Mung and Lacroix (2000), use the concept of the 'arrangement' in a more wide-ranging manner than the constraints the two-sectoral model implies. They write, 'the expression "arrangement" puts the fluid and circumstantial interactions and exchanges of the phenomenon under observation, rather than insisting on a structural constraint' (2000:8).

Immigration from West Central Africa to Paris, whether for economic reasons or as the result of displacement, has created increased demand for specific commodities and services. Typically this appears in demand for traditional foodstuffs. In 1990, some 2,000 shopkeepers from French-speaking Africa were enumerated in the French Census (Mung and Lacroix, 2003:183). Demand also exists for a range of products with a high cultural significance: wax-print cloth (*pangnes*) sold in six metre lengths and used to make women's outfits, as well as accessories, shoes, jewellery, beauty products, CDs, video cassettes of popular musicians, as well as a range of services such as hairdressers, seamstresses, financial transfer services, taxis, garages, people who take the initiative to break into 'squats' i.e. occupy an empty buildings and play a leading role in working with others for a common social or economic objective; photographers of important social occasions, manufacturers of false papers (MacGaffey and Bazenguissa-Ganga (2000:59). One key focus is in the role of *nganda* i.e. unlicensed bars, which act as social clubs and centres, some of which are 'squats'.

The above lays the basis for regional and continental trade based in informal networks of exchange. Much of this activity has the hallmark of an ethnic economy servicing the needs of particular communities. Mac-Gaffey and Bazenguissa-Ganga's study points to an extensive network of trade, whereby Congolese traders in Paris travel to different European countries to buy goods. In Italy they buy clothes, accessories, shoes; in Germany, clothes, leather goods; and in Holland sportswear. They either sell them amongst the African community in Paris, or travel to sell them in Congo Brazzaville or Congo Kinshasa. In paraphrasing James Scott (1985) and much of the globalisation 'from below' thesis, informality is presented as one of the 'weapons of the weak' and includes behaviour such as evading taxes, licensing requirements and other commercial regulations. Whilst tax evasion is not the exclusive property of the weak, informality does depend heavily on personal relations because activities that are often outside the law and its sanctions, reinforces (and enforces) therefore, the importance of trust which often relies on past experience. Relations with a basis in kinship, ethnicity, religion, neighbourhood, workplace and school-boy/girl friendships and rooted in reciprocity, underpin unlicensed, itiner-ant trade. These relations in turn, place 'pressures on the traders for redistribution of the wealth they accumulate' (MacGaffey and Bazen-guissa-Ganga, 2000:7). Despite the fact that respondents 'came of the ranks of those excluded from social and economic opportunities' (p. 3) they argue that,

> Our perspective differs from that of other analysts of informal trade in that we do not take the depressed view which sees commerce outside the law as a mere coping mechanism or survival strategy. It can indeed be such a strategy, but we view it in addition, as a means employed by individuals to evade and resist exclusion from opportunity to better their lives in circumstances of state decay, economic crisis and civil violence.
>
> (2000:28)

MacGaffey and Bazenguissa-Ganga's study, as an example of the con-tribution made by ethno-cultural approaches to explaining social and economic behaviour, points to a number of specific lacunae. One key issue is in the role of consumption, and the observation that all con-sumers buy goods within a specific cultural framework and use them to 'create cultural categories [...] construct notions of the self, and create (and survive) social change' (McCracken, 1988:xi). More contentious is the influence of Douglas and Isherwood's reduction of a commodity chain to the act of (reflexive) consumption itself, 'Forget that commodi-ties are good for eating, clothing and shelter; forget their usefulness and try instead the idea that commodities are good for thinking; treat them as nonverbal medium for human creative faculty' (Douglas and Isher-wood, 1979:62).

The most significant contribution made by the study is as an insight into the specific way in which 'the self' is shaped by consumption, in this instance amongst a subgroup of Congolese traders in Paris. Many were of indeterminate immigration status, but all were hard-core *sapeurs*. *La Sape* stands for the *Societe des Ambianceurs et Personnes Elegantes* (The Society of Ambience Creators and Elegant People). *Se saper* in French, means to dress elegantly. Half of the traders were *sapeurs*. They dealt in designer clothes and accessories, but also wore the clothes and were (so it seemed) defined in relation to the changing items of Parisian fashion. Images of Paris life through films and café life, influenced the development of a youth culture in Brazzaville during the 1950s, when groups of young people began to imitate the existentialist look (*existos*). During the 1960s another wave of *la Sape* emerged amongst unemployed and marginalised young people. They contrasted with the *existos* who had been older, married and employed.

These young people competed through the wearing of French designer brand-name clothing to achieve the position of a *Grand* or Great Man. This practice led them to migrate to France in order to acquire these clothes, which they paraded ostentatiously in Paris and Brazzaville.

(MacGaffey and Bazenguissa-Ganga, 2000:138)

All the traders began their lives in the respective capitals of Congo Kinshasa or Congo Brazzaville. The expansion of trade began in city-to-city trade and then towards trade between other cities in the two countries, then with other African countries, with Europe and even further (US, South-East Asia).

One argument is that this trade is being driven by 'the cult of appearance' and in attempts by people to take control over the image they present to the world in the form of the clothes they wear, and also in how their bodies look; frequently, in order to compensate for the lack of control in most other areas of life. Anorexia can be understood as an extreme example of body self-modification. Similarly, amongst *sapeurs,* some attempted via specialised diets to give themselves larger buttocks and stomachs, associated with Grand Men, or by having haircuts that simulated the early stages of baldness and ageing, to imitate 'the look of a well-to-do man' (Friedman, 1990:116–118).

MacGaffey and Bazenguissa-Ganga write (2000:139–140) that, in this context 'luxury clothes are transformed [...] the clothes themselves become secondary because it is the designer label that counts'. Further, that the parade of designer clothes indicates a more profound resistance. Despite living in Paris without residence permits, 'the *sapeurs* do not hide. Rather, they flaunt themselves through ostentatious practices, which are necessary to confirm the new status that will claim and make use of in their home country'. Competition between *sapeurs* over who is the best turned out, meaning who has what designer labels, is adjudicated by panels of friends. These ostentatious displays, the authors argue, 'recall both the kula trade of the Tobriand Islanders' and 'the potlatch of the peoples of the north-west coast of North America' (2000:154).

The primary concerns of the study were to investigate the construction of the 'self' in the *sapeur* phenomenon, in order to explain it. In doing so, one is reminded of Goffman's analysis of the social process by which people are labelled 'mentally ill' or 'deviant'. Goffman in *Asylum*, wrote of a 'belief that any group of persons develop a life of their own that becomes meaningful, reasonable, and normal once you get close to it' (1968:7). The study by MacGaffey and Bazenguissa-Ganga brings the subject closer and helps us to make sense of the phenomenon of Congolese traders in Paris and the material circumstances faced by them.

The focus of the study on ostentatious and ritualised consumption, however, fails to explain fully how the consumption of commodities is realised. Or, alternatively, how consumption is decommoditised. The elevation of consumption above all other spheres, represents what Karl Marx and Guy Debord referred to as the fetishisation of the commodity i.e. the reduction of commodity relations to the act of consumption itself. This raises a number of logical objections.

Any commodity involves an exchange value (price) and a use value, however defined and in whatever cultural form this may appear to the consumer. Price, under certain circumstances, is not the main consideration. In ritualised consumption, as in the *nganda* unlicensed bars, for example, prices for alcohol and food are inevitably higher than in French bars. Price, however, is important in the process of the realisation of consumption. This typically appears in the price 'mark-up' traders pass on to consumers. The price is also influenced by the production of commodities. Much of the research on immigrant enterprise in Europe points to a wider commodity chain, linking consumption to production in extensive manufacturing systems for fake and real designer goods, mainly of clothing, leather and accessories, which centres on northern Italian cities such as Florence, Prato, Treviso, as well as, Paris. One criticism is that the study presents only a partial picture of the commodity chain, and that we need to investigate the phenomenon in its totality (see Chapter 6).

The study of Congolese *sapeurs* in Paris provides important insights into consumption as an act and expression of human personality under conditions of duress. In France, today, this is a more complex affair than the authors could have imagined during their research in the 1990s. The banning of the *hijab* in French schools has turned the way people look into a matter of national 'debate'. The banning of the *hijab* also illustrates the limits of consumption-based analysis of the 'self'. Only the most naive would believe that it is 'consumption' which has led to the expulsion of young Muslim girls from French schools. Rather, attention has to focus on the rise of xenophobia and the actions of the French state, which turns consumption items such as garments, food, music, prayer, into living symbols of moral panic. What the literature on the 'self' and 'consumption' ignore, is that the self of the oppressed is also an oppressed self. There are many parallels with Compton, Harlem and other places, where youth cultures are associated with artefacts as necessary attachments to expression of human personality and in the gaining of status through conspicuous acts of disciplined consumption. This has provided the basis amongst Congolese youth for a transnational system of trade centring on Paris and made up of refugees, displaced persons, political exiles, ex-torturers from the previous regime and an assortment of adventurers. A large factor driving this process is contempt for the dominant culture. Much of this is articulated in Congolese dance music, and more widely in the music of Souad Massi, Renaud, Lo-Jo, Ismael Lo, Nass El Ghiwani and cinematographic interpretation such as by Mathieu Kassovitz in *La Haine*, who have brought the Maghreb and Senegal into the mainstream of

post-French popular culture. Like Tupac (RIP), the above represent manifestations of contradictory, commoditised and traumatised cultural expression. The *sapeur* are part of the process.

Conclusions

Paris is a city physically built by immigrants over two centuries. If Paris is
the City of Light, it is a light which was kept burning largely by the efforts
of immigrants and refugees and the ideas which made them welcome. Now
the xenophobes want to turn off that light. One difficulty is that many
'immigrants' for historical reasons are French citizens. Whilst this allows
for formal political rights and the ability to overcome aspects of discrimination, particularly in the professions, the incorporation of immigrants in
many respects reflects and reinforces the social polarisation of Paris.
Inequalities reflected in residential, occupational, and racial oppression
and disadvantage, exist independently of the passport held by Moroccan
youth in places like Sevran Beaudottes. The incorporation of immigrants
in reservations and dumping grounds on the edge of Paris, or its most
dilapidated inner-city areas, hardly speaks well of the substance of
Sassen's argument of the European Union as a paragon of 'integration'
(Sassen, 2004).

Body-Gendrot (1996) points to a dual system in the articulation of
social polarisation in Paris and in the structural incorporation of immigrant enterprise. Another argument is that we have not two, but one
system, where one part, say the fashion and construction industries, would
not exist without immigrant contractors and occupations such as carpenters, bricklayers, janitors, window and office cleaners, mail carriers, food
caterers, would find it difficult to fill these posts without the immigrant
residents of the *quartiers chauds*. In reverse, many of them could not exist,
certainly in Paris, without the specific needs of the Parisian labour market.
One example, as we noted, is the 'de-salarisation' and repositioning of
Portuguese immigrants from workers to entrepreneurs in the Parisian construction industry. This example raises wider questions about the role of
subcontracting in the relationship between structure and agency and the
degree of autonomy in economic decision making by entrepreneurs, which
are revealed in other studies. In this case, Mung and Lacroix (2000:4)
writing on French construction employers, noted that 'it is not unheard of
for employers to help workers to start their own business (often under
threat of being laid off) only to subcontract construction projects to them',
as a way of dealing with seasonal and project fluctuation. Similarly, many
of the entrepreneurs nominally registered as independent companies,
come under pressure from 'an informal obligation to work for their last
employers' (Mung and Lacroix, 2003:187).

Ethno-cultural explanations of immigrant enterprise rarely recognise
the specific institutional traditions of Paris, which flow from the

contradictory historical experiences of hospitality and hostility, shown to immigrants and their enterprise in France over a protracted historical period. Arguably, immigrant enterprise laid the basis for a multi-racialism and multi-ethnicity of the poor in Paris, which challenges the assumptions of ethnic heterogeneity and claims to common origins, which underpin ethno-cultural approaches. The Sentier is, above all, living testament to multi-culturalism and toleration between the poor and diverse ethnic and immigrant groups, from which the dominant culture could learn. One example is 'The King of the Sentier', Maxi Librati, son of Moroccan Jews, who 'began with Polish Jewish and Armenian homeworkers; today he works with Turkish, Serbian, and Chinese contractors' (Green, 2002:43).

Nancy Green, with reference to 'mixed' embeddedness points to the limitation of ethnically driven network theory and analyses of 'economic arrangements', be they Congolese, Maghrebian or Chinese, and argues that in the garment industry, 'networks are not the whole story. The economic, political and social environment must be taken into account' and further, writes that 'in a sector characterised by cut-throat pricing, those in charge of hiring will look beyond their own circle when the next wave of (cheaper) newcomers arrives' (2002:40). In the Sentier district, Green argues that the multi-ethnic nature of many firms' employment, 'reminds us that cultural complicity is not the only framework of labour relations' and that 'network theory may imply ipso facto ethnicisation of the history of the garment industry'. One consequence is that internal 'conflicts within ethnic networks have been minimised by optimists' (such as, Roger Waldinger, Giles Mohan, Alejandro Portes). The focus on the co-ethnic workplace (or diaspora) has too often overlooked the 'truly mixed character' of the garment districts (2002:41).

Issues raised by ethno-cultural approaches, in terms of extensive regional trade networks, whether amongst Congolese or Maghrebian immigrants, are a useful antidote to the generalisations made, particularly amongst policy makers who want to 'integrate' immigrant enterprise into the mainstream.

They remind us of the construction of the 'self' and the specific ideological and practical arrangements which all people, including immigrant entrepreneurs, use to make sense of the world around them. In terms of economic and institutional analyses, however, ethno-cultural explanations are the least sensitive to internal economic differentiation amongst ethnic or immigrant groups and its effects on the positioning of different social strata of immigrants. Nor do they consider the role of particular industries and patterns of subcontracting associated with them. Rather, they lead to generalisations, such as, 'the key debate concerns why the Chinese diaspora has been so successful' (Mohann, 2002:117) and explanations such as embeddedness, social capital and the ability of diasporic commerce 'to spot opportunities and exploit these through flexible networks' (p. 120) and/or, 'to take advantage of the opportunities that globalization offer' (p.

121). The view of an 'achieving' and precarious Chinese diasporic capitalism, is partly a reflection of not very satisfactory Middleman Minority
notions and their influence in the framing of diasporic literature (see,
Chapter 2). Much of the material in this book points towards a more
complex and contradictory phenomenon and one subject to significant sectoral and intra- and inter-ethnic variation.

Conclusion
Who benefits?

Introduction: résumé of the book

The conclusions return to the main issues raised by the phenomenon of immigrant enterprise in Europe and the United States and its contribution to the shaping of gateway cities such as London, New York, Los Angeles, Amsterdam and Paris. Many neighbourhoods in these cities seem to have been transformed by immigrants themselves acting as their own agency, with limited assistance from government or the banking sector. This transformation is taken as affirmation of the globalisation 'from below' thesis. The book questioned whether cities are transformed by the considerable ingenuity of immigrants themselves or whether this involves wider processes and relationships with the institutional framework and the restructuring by capital of particular sectors, industries and localities. Crucially, it is in the relationship between structure and agency, such as in the forces which shape the political-institutional framework, that variation in immigration enterprise becomes more evident. This variation is frequently also linked to complex patterns of subcontracting and more widely to the traditions of particular urban centres and local economies, the impact of the regulatory framework and the quality of ethnic mobilisations and the degree to which immigrant groups have formal political rights and representation.

The book has argued that whilst economic development amongst immigrants is influenced by membership of particular groups, it is also influenced by the historical circumstances they find themselves in and the reproduction of social stratification rooted in class, gender, race and age. That immigrant communities are themselves socially differentiated in these and other ways, raises the question about who benefits from immigrant enterprise. The incorporation of ethnic minority women in immigrant enterprise is an example. The reproduction of market relations are reflected in what the book calls a process of social and economic differentiation within and between immigrant enterprises and communities. The material challenged popular stereotypes about immigrants in business i.e. that they operate on the margins of the law and that they are dependent on family or co-ethnic labour. The book is a debate with those who see immigrant enterprise as invariably on the 'fringes' of economic and political systems. The book is also a debate with the advocates of the globalisation 'from below' thesis and their unwillingness to consider in a serious manner the social and economic differentiation of transnational communities, or the role of the institutional framework in shaping significant variation in institutional behaviour towards particular immigrant groups and sectors they work in and reflected in policy on immigration and the informal economy.

We noted that the 'rise' of ethnicity contributed to a political and intellectual crisis in the United States during the 1960s. The emergence of ethnicity as both a basis for cultural and political mobilisation challenged 'melting-pot' theories, dominant at the time in US sociology. This crisis and subsequent research on the economic arrangements of ethnicity, pointed to the role of communal affiliation, self-help institutions and solidarity in the development of immigrant enterprise. New York felt this crisis more than most places and is important testing ground for many of the assumptions of the new economic sociology, such as the extent to which ethnic paternalism modifies workplace relations, the practical manifestation of labour diasporas and the substance of transnational communities. The book argued that the positioning and repositioning of some immigrants from workers to entrepreneurs in New York (and elsewhere) is anything but an orderly ethnic labour queue or a benign game of 'musical chairs'. It is punctuated by selectivity in the ranking order of social groups with persistence in the reproduction of race, gender and class in the economic positioning of immigrants and members of ethnic minority groups.

One example of the (contradictory) ranking of ethnic groups is in the location of Hispanic immigrants in the United States. We noted that processes of racialisation mean that whilst 'Hispanics' are frequently presented as constituting an ethnic group, they also find themselves racially segregated in New York, Miami and other US cities. In terms of housing, black Hispanics become effectively a section of black America. Trends indicate that by 2050 the Hispanic population will become the largest minority in the US. This sends shivers down the spines of xenophobes. Yet, Dade County, Florida (which includes Miami) illustrates probably more than most places the contribution made by Hispanic immigrant enterprise. Cuban entrepreneurs turned vast areas of swampland into the 'hubs of the Americas' i.e. a gateway city with specific trans-continental purposes as well as an international tourist resort. As we noted, Alejandro Portes pointed to the high concentration of enterprises in Miami as an 'enclave economy', in which immigrants, far from being disadvantaged, received earnings-returns to human capital similar to the earnings-returns of immigrants in the open labour market. The view that the ethnic enclave presents an effective vehicle for upward mobility amongst immigrant groups challenges the key lesson of conventional sociology in the United

States i.e. that segregation tends to retard the economic achievement of minorities. One way of understanding the enclave economy is to see it as both a process of social exclusion and as means for social mobility for some immigrants. The proposition that different outcomes are possible between members of the same ethnic or immigrant group, is one criticism of the ethnic enclave thesis, and lies at the heart of this book.

In Los Angeles, unlike Miami, 'Hispanic' is a codeword for downward mobility, with social-economic indicators lower even than those for black Americans. Many also have to live with the fear of deportation. As we noted many industries and services would not exist but for Mexican immigrant labour and entrepreneurs. Without Mexican women workers, Los Angeles would not be the largest concentration of garment production in the US, making it (after Chicago) the second largest concentration of manufacturing employment in the US. Yet, immigrants in California have been subjected to a witch-hunt and accused (amongst others) of 'taking jobs away from African Americans'. Xenophobia is as American as cherry pie and in this there are elements of continuity. New developments appear in the 'new' Asian migration, from Korea, Vietnam, China, India and Cambodia, which has added to the diversity of Los Angeles and the State of California as a whole, and has contributed to its urban and economic development with Silicon Valley's Asian migrants as a case in point.

The theme of institutionalised xenophobia surfaces in Los Angeles and the wider European experience. Indeed much of the Northern European literature argues that exclusion is so effective that immigrant enterprise is driven into the fringes. What is clearer is that much of the European experience was shaped by the unintended consequence of labour transfer during the post-war boom. The example of Turkish immigrants to Germany and the transition by a significant number of them from temporary guest workers to immigrant entrepreneurs is another case in point. One salient lesson in the emergence of racial and ethnic identities in the United States and Europe is that immigrants do not arrive with fully-fledged ethnic identities ready to do battle with other ethnic groups but learn how to be 'ethnic' in the host society. Many 'Hispanic' immigrants discovered that they are 'black' in the United States. West Indian and Turkish youths in London and Berlin, respectively, faced mass unemployment and encountered very different circumstances from those of their labour migrant and guest worker parents. Under these conditions ethnic and racial identities became a defensive social position adopted by second-generation youth. *Rastafari* in London during the 1970s and the *Karnak* movement in Berlin during the 1990s (as much as young Muslim women defiantly wearing the *hijab* following 9/11) developed as significant cultural and political expressions, which either challenged or coexisted with the dominant culture, but equally revealed the crisis of modernisation and assimilation in Europe and the United States.

Nowhere in Europe has the struggle for acceptance been more apparent than in London. It is the most cosmopolitan capital city in Europe and

North America with more than one in three of its population either an immigrant or of immigrant origins and of whom nearly half were born in the UK. Immigrant enterprise in London points to elements of continuity and change. The informalisation of production remains an important continuity. Important changes, however, indicate that it is not the case that all firms are invariably small, operate on the fringes of the law and rely on the recruitment of family or co-ethnic workers. Much of the material challenges the view and points to more complex processes of economic differentiation. Some have become large firms. In some sub-sectors, immigrant entrepreneurs dominate local employment. Many of them have broken out of the confines of the ethnic economy and have entered the economic mainstream. The experience of immigrant enterprise in London reflects on wider issues and the implications of informalisation, differentiation and economic restructuring for the positioning and repositioning of immigrant enterprise.

Amsterdam provides a significant vantage point for the study of immigration and the development of immigrant enterprise in three ways. First, as one of Europe's oldest empires, the Netherlands and its largest cities also became the location for one of the earliest examples of enterprise by immigrants from the Third World in Europe. This saw the major expansion of the Chinese–Indonesian restaurant sector. This example reveals important insight and reflections on the role of particular sectors and location in shaping the pattern of immigrant settlement and the limited extent of 'integration' in Dutch society. Second, Amsterdam allows us to examine the incorporation of immigrant 'informal' enterprise into production systems which operate outside the legal structures, but are also subordinate to other larger and 'formal' companies, which dominate particular sectors and sub-sectors. This raises wider issues about the autonomy of entrepreneurs, the limits of formal/informal sector dual analyses and the selectivity of the institutional response. Third, immigrant entrepreneurs from Turkey operating as contractors in the women's fashion-wear sector are another case study, which allowed us to consider the significance of what Rath (2002b), Kloosterman (2000) and Kloosterman and Rath (2001) mean by 'mixed' embeddedness, and the implications of its absence. As we noted, the embeddedness of entrepreneurs in immigrant communities could not compensate in this instance for its absence in the wider political and institutional framework, when compared to other cities such as Miami, London, New York. The example of Amsterdam shows what happens when state repression is launched. This speaks loudly about the political weakness of immigrant communities in formation and raises question marks over the long-term sustainability of immigrant enterprises.

Paris offers opposing conclusions. Like the nineteenth and twentieth centuries, Paris continues to act as a magnet for economic migrants and refugees who provided a rich source of new entrepreneurs. The example of immigrant enterprise in Paris reflects on two broader questions raised in the book. It provides fertile ground for examining Saskia Sassen's observation that, contrary to the current wave of xenophobia, Europe has successfully 'integrated' many different groups of immigrants over the last two centuries (Sassen, 2004). Paris is a concentrated example of this proposition. At the same time, the political conclusions drawn by Sassen about the role of the European Union as an agency of integration, fail to explain selectivity in immigration and naturalisation policy and wider institutional behaviour; or the continuation of discriminatory restrictions on immigrant sectoral employment in many countries, including France. The chapter on Paris provided material critical of 'mixed' embeddedness theories, by pointing to alternative ethno-cultural explanations for the development of immigrant enterprise. One criticism of structural explanations for the development of immigrant enterprise is that they often ignore, misunderstand and in cases appear to have forgotten, that ethnicity and culture as the constructs of everyday life, frequently articulate self-defence positions adopted by immigrant groups who are ethnicised and racialised in an unequal relationship with the dominant culture and institutions of state and society.

Main theme of the book: social and economic differentiation

Much of the material reviewed in the book provides useful insight into how immigrant workers and entrepreneurs are incorporated in the labour markets of gateway cities in Europe and the United States. The book also argued that the analyses adopted by many approaches, have a more limited theoretical use in revealing tensions inside ethnic communities about the distribution of the benefits of immigrant enterprise. Both optimistic and pessimistic analyses of immigrant enterprise, in drawing from the sociology of immigration and ethnic relations, necessarily apply a methodology, which consists of counter-positioning of immigrants to host society, or of one ethnic or immigrant group to another. This methodology whilst useful in allowing us to analyse the economic and political position of a particular immigrant or ethnic group, does not allow us the ability to investigate fully (if at all) processes of social and economic differentiation within immigrant groups and ethnic minorities themselves and to consider its implications for the redistributory functions of enterprise. Frequently it depends what we are measuring. If we are measuring average returns to labour in the ethnic enclave economy when compared to the general labour market, for example, this would disguise the possibility that entrepreneurship might produce a small but significant number of high-income earners and a large mass of low-paid hired workers. If we were to measure income distribution within immigrant communities by class, gender, age, race, proximity to entrepreneur and other variables we might see differing trends and outcomes.

The main theme of the book has been to show that immigrant enterprise is more economically differentiated than most of the conventional literature implies. This has implications for whether immigrant enterprise represents a victory over discrimination and disadvantage, or at best a truce. The experiences of immigrant entrepreneurs in many cities and industries contain powerful elements of continuity as well as change. It is the case that most continue to crowd around the small-scale sector, typically as contractors and subcontractors in the garment, catering and retail industries. For many, life is precarious and they are constantly subjected to changes in the market place, which they find difficult to respond to. At the same time, however, there are important changes and variation in immigrant enterprise between and within diverse ethnic groups and in how they relate to particular sectors and sub-sectors.

The book made the observation that immigrant enterprise is far more diverse than it is generally assumed, both in terms of scale and purpose. It is not unusual in international comparison, for trends to reveal that most entrepreneurs from a variety of ethnic backgrounds have to struggle and work very long hours simply in order to survive. 'Marginalisation' is an accurate description of the precarious condition of many, possibly most, immigrant entrepreneurs in the gateway cities of Europe and the United States. Comparative research on immigrant contractors in the women's fashion-wear industry offers powerful illustrations of this condition. At the same time, however, a significant proportion have, or are trying to, break out of the confines of the ethnic economy and to enter the economic mainstream (Rutherford and Blackburn, 2000; Ram and Jones, 1998; Poutziouris, 1998, 1999). In the garment industry 'breaking out' represented a move away from the ranks of the many CMT contractors and towards the ranks of the fewer manufacturers (see, below). Some operate as micro-multinational companies. A small number have become owners of considerable real estate and industrial property.

Social differentiation can be understood at one level in the emergence of entrepreneurs themselves, typically from the ranks of manual workers and artisans. Economic differentiation is a feature of variation between enterprises. One key dimension, as we noted is in labour input. Some are small, family enterprises, dependent on family labour input, whilst others are large employers who recruit labour from a wide range of immigrant groups (Panayiotopoulos, 1996a). Differentiation represents a move away from weak positions in production and distribution systems in which many immigrant entrepreneurs operate as contractors, franchisees or are disadvantaged in some way or other by distortions to the price mechanism imposed by quasi-monopolistic suppliers. Since entrepreneurs operate in given sectors, they are differentiated in ways which reflect the structures of subcontracting in particular sectors. In the garment industry emergent immigrant enterprises have typically taken on the functions associated with the role of the manufacturer or 'jobber'. Buyers who have found it more convenient to deal directly with some of their larger ethnic CMT units have encouraged the repositioning of the entrepreneurs.

Differentiation influences relationships with the market and the institutional framework and it is here that the impact of differentiation is at its most significant. Immigrant manufacturers and contractors relate to the market at different levels of the production cycle, are subject to different outcomes and adopt different strategies to cope with market fluctuation. The same broad polarity can be applied in relationships with the banking sector, branches of the state, and in particular with local government. The beneficiaries of institutional support are more likely to be entrepreneurs who are the most economically powerful and who are also the most politically embedded whilst, in reverse, the contractors, subcontractors and multitude of self-employed, are the least likely to receive institutional support and the most likely to feel the wrath of the state, typically for not conforming to relevant legislation on taxation and labour standards (Panayiotopoulos, 1992). One important dimension of differentiation is the way it influences firm mobility, transnational positioning and relations with the political-institutional framework. In many respects the 'most' globalised entrepreneurs tend to be those with the greatest economic power and connectivity not simply with immigrant communities, but also the dominant institutions of the host society.

Differentiation is also influenced and in many respects structured by the political-institutional and market environment facing immigrant entrepreneurs and this, as the example of Amsterdam shows, is itself far from certain. One tentative conclusion on the European experience is that cities characterised by a protracted presence by immigrant groups who have civil rights somewhere nearer the average, are more likely (perhaps) to see the development of conditions necessary for sustainable immigrant-owned enterprises. The diverse experiences of immigrant entrepreneurs point to the need to consider the relationship between economic differentiation and how this influences the way entrepreneurs manage their enterprises and relate to the market and institutional environment in which they operate.

One caution is that the complexity of an increasingly differentiated milieu makes it difficult to draw overarching conclusions. Another suggestion from sectoral studies of immigrant enterprise is that the restructuring of sectors such as retailing, catering and sub-sectors of the garment industry, such as the fashion-wear sector in particular, may be a more critical factor in the incorporation of immigrant groups, the differentiation of enterprise and the modification of economic behaviour, than characteristics associated with any single immigrant or ethnic group. This introduces a note of caution on the assumption that an optimistic or pessimistic causal connection exists between enterprise, work norms, practices and the ethnic origin of entrepreneurs and workers employed by them. This observation challenges basic assumptions held by the new economic sociology.

Portes and Sensenbrenner (1993:1343) do point to differentiation and selectivity in the process of social mobility 'between successful members of the minority group and those left behind'. Fernandez-Kelly (1995:218) also points to the 'unevenness of social capital'. Neither, however, provides an analysis of the social mechanisms of selection in this contradictory process. We noted that the major criticism made by Sanders and Nee of the work of Portes and others concerns issues to do with the social stratification and workplace relations of ethnic groups. They suggest the need to reformulate the enclave economy hypothesis so that it is 'sensitive to important differences between immigrant-workers and immigrant bosses' (1987a:745). They question the methodology applied by Portes and others for failing to make a distinction between self-employment and the employment of others, and for ignoring previous findings (Portes and Bach, 1985:205–216) which 'report significant [income] differences between workers and bosses in the Cuban enclave' when estimating returns to human capital (Sanders and Nee, 1987a:747–748). Model (1992) found no significant variation in returns to labour in the ethnic enclave economy when compared to the general labour market.

This debate suggests that the particular location of immigrants as wage workers, contractors or manufacturers may have profound implications for how members of an ethnic group live, work and benefit from participation in minority enterprise. Differentiation points to considerable variation within immigrant enterprise and suggests that it would be unwise to make generalisations for research and policy purposes about an 'essential' ethnic enterprise (typically in the form of the 'family firm'). There is the need to consider the implications of differentiation for 'who benefits' and on how diverse entrepreneurs manage their enterprises and in how they relate to the market and institutional environment in which they have to operate.

Economic differentiation: a case study

The case study draws from research on the Cypriot community in the London garment industry (also see, Chapter 7). It was an attempt to understand the processes and effects of social and economic differentiation characterised by the emergence from the ranks of Cypriot immigrants of a class of employers in the garment industry, who confronted Cypriot women and members of other ethnic groups in that capacity. A further dimension was to explore the more contemporary rise from the ranks of ethnic employers of a layer of manufacturers who relate to other co-ethnic contractors in ways which parallel the structure of subcontracting in the London garment industry. The research was an attempt to consider the relationship between economic differentiation and ethnic solidarity.

An ethnographic approach proved relevant in a situation where the economic activity investigated is of the sort which can – and indeed frequently has to – escape the attention of HM Customs and Excise department and other official organisations. Use was made in initial approaches to the entrepreneurs of relatives and old school friends in North London who were themselves entrepreneurs or workers in the garment industry. An initial group of six entrepreneurs inducted me into words such as 'cabbage' and 'doing liquidation', as well as providing me with background information and rumour. Advice was offered such as, 'don't carry that black case – they'll think you are the tax-man'. Advice from this original internal network was critical in the framing of questions to ask and the structure of the interview sheet used. The advantages of using a questionnaire sheet were estimated to be, the use of a simple-to-recognise technique, but also (and mainly) as a means of legitimising physical entry into a work place. As a general rule the arrival was unannounced and without prior appointment. In this way access would be gained into the building and observations made, even if cooperation was ultimately refused.

An attempt was made to gather qualitative information from a total of 122 entrepreneurs and enterprises of varying complexity, which were approached for assistance in gathering information in North London. Attempts were made to select entrepreneurs in ways which reflected the known spatial distribution of the establishments, the concentration of Cypriot entrepreneurs in the womenswear sub-sector, and which recognised the diverse locations of the enterprises in the structure of subcontracting – whether a firm was a contractor, referred to as a cut, make and trim (CMT) unit, or whether the firm was a manufacturer acting for some buyer or other and which supplied the CMT units with work. These estimations pointed towards an extensive representation by Cypriots mainly as contractors in the dresses and separates sub-sector of womenswear (see Panayiotopoulos, 1996a:Table 1). Of the entrepreneurs approached, 78 formal interviews were conducted using a predetermined list of questions. In another 20 cases unstructured discussions took place whilst, in another 24 cases (a significant amount), I was shown the door. In the cases of the 78 respondents where formal/structured interviews were conducted, a statistical database was constructed. These 78 entrepreneurs employed a combined total of 2,504 workers, 58 per cent of them as homeworkers (Panayiotopoulos, 1994:232).

Most of the respondents were CMT contractors whose concerns were concentrated by a collection of problems. Low making prices given by manufacturers, finding work and irregular supplies of work, a fear of 'losing machinists' particularly during 'slack' periods and concerns over the quality of work produced by homeworkers. The accumulation of these problems is referred to in the trade as the 'CMT-syndrome' and this should be seen as key to an appreciation of the subordinate position of the contractors. The vast bulk of the respondents (66 out of 78) were in fact CMT contractors (see, Panayiotopoulos 1996a:Table 2). At the same time, however, the research revealed that considerable deviation was possible within the sharp structural constraints facing contractors. A more rigorous investigation of the contractors, revealed that a substantial number of them (16) also partly produced their 'own work', meaning by this that they had circumvented the manufacturers and were forming direct links with the buyers. In ten cases this consisted of 50.0 per cent or more of their output. The clearest expression of movement was found in seven respondents who were manufacturers, but who previously had been contractors. This issue was explored in five specific ways, which provided insights into economic differentiation between the entrepreneurs.

1 *A comparison was made between the total number of workers employed at the point of entry into proprietorship by 54 entrepreneurs and the number currently employed. Also there was a comparison made amongst the 54 entrepreneurs, of how many of the workers they employed were family workers and what proportion they represented of all workers in the first and current factory.*

In aggregate terms the 54 entrepreneurs increased employment from 517 workers at the point of entry to 1,642 in the current operations. In terms of labour force composition a key area for employment expansion was to be found in the proportion of workers employed as homeworkers. This had increased from 198 workers (38.5 per cent) to 806 or approximately half of all workers currently employed. The proportion of labour described as family workers made up 19.0 per cent of total employment in the first factory, rising to nearly one third (30.1 per cent) of indoor workers. In the current factory, however, this decreases to 4.7 per cent of all workers and a higher proportion (9.7 per cent) of all indoor workers (see Panayiotopoulos 1996a: Table 3). Indeed, since the number of family workers has also decreased absolutely over time, this suggests that a significant proportion of family labour has actually withdrawn from a working relationship with the establishment.

The above suggests that in a general sense, Cypriot entrepreneurs show a decreasing dependency on family workers and an increasing one for waged workers in production activities. This tendency is sensitive to employment size. In 18 of the 19 factories where family labour currently made up 40 per cent or more of indoor workers, none employed more than ten workers indoors and nearly all were small contractors (Panayiotopoulos 1996a: Table 4). The significance of family labour may be more suggestive on the formative experiences of the entrepreneurs themselves, rather than how most entrepreneurs actually produce garments. A considerable proportion of the entrepreneurs began their working lives as family workers. In terms of labour supply however, the idea that Cypriot clothing factories address labour supply through their family labour, as a general characteristic, is not representative of the actual situation. Neither should this be exaggerated in the historical sense: many entrepreneurs began as family workers, many depended heavily upon family workers in their initial entry, but few began and fewer continue as 'family units of production'.

2 *Amongst the larger sample of 78 firms, there was an attempt to estimate the ethnic interspersion (diversification) of the labour force.*

Another key dimension of employment growth to which the increase in use of homeworking was critical, consists of a considerable ethnic interspersion (diversification) in the composition of the labour force. In the 78 establishments, Greek and Turkish Cypriot workers made up (marginally) the majority of all labour (at 51.0 per cent) but considerably less of homeworkers at 43.0 per cent. Asian women made up a significant 25.0 per cent of all homeworkers: nearly half were employed by firms in the N4 post code area, which includes Fonthill Road, something of a centre for Cypriot participation in the garment industry. Afro-Caribbean women made up 16.0 per cent of all indoor workers with many concentrated in the N15 post code area (Tottenham), an important centre for the West Indian community. Greek Cypriot labour, whilst making up half of the total indoor labour, accounted for less than a third of homeworkers (see Panayiotopoulos, 1996a: Table 5).

The negotiation of labour supply problems – substantially resolved through the use of non-Cypriot homeworkers – is a concrete manifestation of the objective existence of a class of employers. The recourse to alternative supplies of labour was set in motion by the scissors effect of the need to expand employment and volume output in order to compensate for falling making prices in the face of the ageing of Cypriot machinists and the unwillingness by young 'second' generation women to enter the garment industry. This ('chasing of women') was identified by entrepreneurs as a key constraint to employment growth. The expansion of homeworking in order to address labour supply problems saw, however, the intensification of problems over quality control (see Panayiotopoulos, 1996a: Table 2). One dimension of labour supply problems, was a scheme established by local authorities in North London for the training of flat-bed machinists (Panayiotopoulos, 1992).

3 *An estimation was made of the extent that the entrepreneurs were working proprietors and carried out manual work, or not.*

The role of the working proprietor – at its most simple level distinguished by whether the entrepreneur carried out manual labour or not – was certainly a strong feature in the London sample. Amongst the entrepreneurs, 71 out of 78 carried out physical labour of some sort or other. The vast bulk (57 cases) described themselves as undertaking all types of manual labour, although they tended to emphasise one manual task as being more significant than others. Most of the (men) entrepreneurs cited cutting, pressing or driving as specific tasks in which they were mostly involved. Another group (eight cases) specified undertaking all tasks 'except' those requiring skills such as cutting or machining which is associated, by men and women in the production of light womenswear, as 'women's work'. Another group described themselves, more pragmatically, as undertaking all manner of tasks 'if the need arose'.

Seven entrepreneurs did not carry out any manual labour and they were characterised by the following features: they were large employers; five were manufacturers and two were CMT units, which also partly produced their 'own' work; none was simply a contractor. It was also of note that members of the immediate household did not undertake manual labour either and this was an important aspect of socially differentiated enterprise (Panayiotopoulos, 1996a:450). It is suggestive in the above, that whether the entrepreneur (or members of the household) carried out manual labour or not, was sensitive to the employment size and location of the enterprise in the structure of subcontracting (see Panayiotopoulos, 1996a: Table 6).

4   *An estimation was made of the significance of the rise from the ranks of CMT contractors of a layer of Cypriot Manufacturers.*

The clearest expression of differentiation from 'the mass' was found in the seven respondents who were manufacturers, but who previously had been contractors. This was also reflected in the growing role of Cypriot manufacturers in providing contractor respondents with work. In a sample of 52 entrepreneurs, 75.0 per cent cited 'Jewish' manufacturers as the providers of work in their first factory. In a sample of 68 entrepreneurs' current operations, whilst 54.5 per cent cited a 'Jewish' manufacturer, another 39.5 per cent cited a Cypriot manufacturer as the supplier of work (see Panayiotopoulos, 1996a: Table 7). A further elaboration of differentiation 'from the mass' was to be found in the London Cypriot manufacturers who were involved in outward processing activities to Cyprus. These activities were expressed in a number of networks which made use of the discourse of kinship and/or political affinity. The latter appeared in the shape of a 'communist' entrepreneurial network, which paralleled the organisational structures of outward processing. The context for the increasing profile of London Cypriot manufacturers in Cyprus was a crisis in Cyprus' exports to Libya (Cyprus' largest market at the time) due to the US economic embargo imposed on Libya, which resulted (amongst others) in the shortage of foreign exchange by Libya and delayed payments to Cyprus' exporters. This, reinforced the London market and London Cypriots as an alternative source of work for clothing producers in Cyprus (Panayiotopoulos, 1996b, 2000b).

5   *An evaluation was made of an aborted attempt by Cypriot employers to organise as employers in a North and East London-based organisation (the Dressmakers and Allied Contractors Association – DACA).*

Whilst points (1) to (5) above, suggest that in an objective sense many of the entrepreneurs are a class of employers willing to employ members of any ethnic group, another dimension of class formation was explored in the capacity of the entrepreneurs to act as a class 'for itself' however defined. The extent to which the entrepreneurs may be seen as a class in the double sense that the term is used, was investigated in the light of an attempt by respondents to organise (i.e. embed themselves) in a class-conscious way as employers, into a London Cypriot garment employers association, the Dressmakers and Allied Contractors Association (DACA). Ex-members of DACA made up a significant number of the respondents.

The establishment of an employers association suggests that the entrepreneurs perceived themselves as having interests separate from and indeed in opposition to labour irrespective of its ethnic identity. Many of the entrepreneurs saw the formation of an Association as a critical question: it is of note in this respect that it is actually quite unusual for entrepreneurs in the London garment industry to form collective organisations in the first place. Most small entrepreneurs tend not to be members of, for example, a local Chamber of Commerce. Working proprietors have little time to attend meetings and those who have more time tend to be the more powerful or politically committed of the entrepreneurs – such as cadres of the London Branch of the Cypriot Communist Party (AKEL). Indeed in the sample itself only two entrepreneurs were actually members, but another 20 were ex-members. At the same time, the vast bulk, (56) were not at any time members.

The purposes of the Association were initially to organise contractors in order to get a better making price from the manufacturers and to counter the vicious undercutting of prices which characterises the trade. For some it was also seen as an attempt to halt the growing role of homeworking (Panayiotopoulos 1992, interview with DACA Secretary). DACA was also, however, a response to labour supply problems and an attempt to undermine the freedom of labour by placing restrictions on the ability of workers to move from one factory to another in search of better paid employment. A number of women machinists and men pressers who remembered the initial attempts by the Contractors to organise, tended to emphasise the latter (Panayiotopoulos, 1994: Chapter 7.5).

As an organisation of relatively weak contractors, DACA proved extremely difficult to hold together as a representative body and it gradually decomposed, amidst allegations of financial irregularity. Ex-members spoke of the demise of DACA as the result of the 'breaking of ranks' by the contractors, many of whom effectively acted as clients for manufacturers who were eventually admitted to DACA membership and came to dominate the Association. A number of the small contractors, who were instrumental in initiating DACA, were themselves to become larger employers and indeed some became manufacturers in their own right. In substance, DACA did not simply fall apart because of a 'takeover' by manufacturers but, rather, that many of the ex-DACA members who broke ranks did so in order to expand. However, to expand in the much harsher economic climate of the slump years meant the extension of informalisation as a method for undercutting the making price through the extension of homeworking and the recourse to voluntary liquidations. In this context, any attempt to establish an organisation – even one which objectively articulated the interests of the entrepreneurs as a class – but which was about regulating the industry, was to prove for many an intolerable constraint. This experience also suggested that if the co-ethnic entrepreneurs were 'brothers', they were also brothers-at-war (Panayiotopoulos, 1994).

Social differentiation: ethnic minority women

One major illustration of social differentiation in immigrant enterprise is in the role of gender, the sexual division of labour and how this structures the work which immigrant men and women are frequently channelled into. Sassen (1995) notes that whilst there is little recognition of this factor in most analyses of immigrant enterprise, a number of studies on immigrant women in New York, Berlin and Southern European cities, or in sectors such as Chinese takeaways or the garment industry, show that labour market participation (and pay) 'vary according to gender' and in cases 'gender can override nationality or culture' (see, Gilbertson, 1995; Hilmann, 1999; Anthias and Lazaridis, 2000; Bhachu, 1988). The gendering of work and the incorporation of immigrant workers in sectors where the sexual division of labour is an already existing feature (such as garment production), points to an important continuity and adaptation by immigrant enterprise. Women in many sectors provide the labour power for immigrant enterprises. Frequently enterprises are extensions of household work carried out by women, such as cooking, sewing, cleaning. Sometimes it is women themselves who head such enterprises driven in part by the increased economic pressure to be providers and indicated in the growing number of households headed by women.

The way in which women learn skills, acquire training and employment in sectors such as garments, footwear, electronic component assembly, the personal service sector is neither 'natural' nor a simple matter of individual decision making. Women's skills and employment are structured by prevalent ideas in society about what constitutes 'women's work' and frequently there are conflicts between the economic needs of working-class women and dominant ideas in society about the role of women. Explanations for labour market incorporation frequently resort to crude biological reductionism, i.e. that women as a group have a range of 'natural' and 'feminine' aptitudes such as, 'nimble fingers', 'quick eyes', greater 'docility' and 'dexterity' than men as a group (see, Spielberg, 1997). This is often used to legitimise the prevalence of women in low-paid assembly-line work. It also finds a parallel expression in explanations for the concentration of women workers either in the middle and lower grades of 'caring' professions such as, nursing, teaching and voluntary work, or as 'housemaids' (Panayiotopoulos, 2005). More substantial explanations are offered by the social construction of gendered work. This directs our attention towards the way young girls and young boys are socialised, i.e. learn according to prevailing norms to become men and women and the way this is reflected in the learning of skills. This influences formal education, vocational training programmes and apprenticeships. It is also reflected in the learning of skills through the domestic economy (such as sewing and make-through machining) frequently from older women family members. Because these skills are often learned in the domestic economy, they are attached with low value and are frequently classed as 'unskilled'.

Women's work, whether as hired or waged workers, or as entrepreneurs, cannot be understood without reference to the relationship between productive and reproductive activities and the 'double burden' faced by women both as workers and as mothers, wives and daughters, with major responsibility for a range of 'reproductive' activities. These include childbearing, child caring and daily household maintenance (cooking, cleaning and so on). Homeworking is a prevalent way of organising work in the garment industry because it combines domestic work with paid labour and it addresses these two dimensions of women's lives. One major reason for homeworking is that women have children of pre-school age with no one to help in looking after them. The relationship between women's productive and reproductive activities influences the hours that women work, choice of sector and the kind of work carried out by them (Panayiotopoulos, 2001b). Frequently, shift patterns are adjusted or designed to accommodate women with school children

Patriarchy theory, i.e. the view that gender forms the basic social division in society, has applied the concept of 'relations of dependence' in offering explanations for the economic positioning of ethnic minority women. This view merely sees the extension of the (assumed) patriarchal relations of the family to those of work. Anthias (1983:74) writes that Cypriot homeworkers and their employment 'often involves the extension of the patriarchical relations of the family to those of work'. Mitter draws similar conclusions and argues that the ideology of the nuclear family in which a woman is expected to be the main carer for the children, 'makes it easy for large companies to have access to a captive pool of labour', or a 'captive and disposable workforce' in which 'husbands become the middlemen between the homeworkers and the sub-contractors' (Mitter, 1986:47,

60). Westwood and Bhachu write that minority women are 'more likely to be in the labour market than their white counterparts in full-time employment', but at the same time that 'many' (migrant women) are not part of the open labour market because they are working within the 'ethnic economy' (1988:7). Mitter, summarises the experience of minority entrepreneurs as one which is conditioned by the relation to co-ethnic women's labour and argues that,

> Ethnic minority entrepreneurs definitely have a competitive edge over their white counterparts. They can make use of the cheap labour of their women, who have very little opportunity to find jobs elsewhere. Intensive use of female labour is the cornerstone of the burgeoning ethnic economy [...] The ideology of the extended family amongst Asians or of village and ethnic loyalty among Cypriots, provides the ideal situation for recruiting such a docile and cheap – and overwhelmingly female – labour force.
>
> (Mitter 1986:53, 55)

Whilst the above approaches are useful in exploring processes of inclusion and exclusion in minority women's employment, one necessary assumption made (as in the wider 'enclave economy' thesis) is that ethnic employers would only employ family and co-ethnic labour, and that relations of dependence – over and above market relations – generally characterise minority women's participation in labour markets. There are a number of questions raised from this conventional application of patriarchy theory. One immediate question, for example, is how many ethnic minority women engage in 'relations of dependence'? Is the concept of 'unfree labour' a general one and which extends to all or most women workers from ethnic backgrounds? In much of the analyses presented above, it is not at all clear whether such relations of dependence are a general or specific condition, or how they may be affected over time particularly if the scale of economic activity increase.

Another problem with analyses by patriarchy theory pointing towards relations of dependence is that such relations are dismissed lightly. After all, the whole point of household unfree labour power is that it cannot be composed of a 'disposable' workforce. This labour power, unlike other labour costs in capitalist relations has a fixed rather than a variable cost. The translation of this to enterprise functions means that whilst it may be true that constituent household members cannot dispose of each other, this need not apply to hired workers. These sorts of problematics are not apparent in approaches which do not make the distinction between family labour and waged workers. Rather, there is the tendency for general assumptions which consist of seeing ethnic minority women workers are generally 'captive' by 'other than' wage relationships. One conclusion which may be drawn from the application of patriarchy theory is that if women's inclusion is conceptualised in general terms as characterised by extra-market relations of dependence, this would suggest that a labour market does not exist or, if it does, it does not exist fully enough to indicate that capitalist social relations predominate. This has important implications, since if women wage workers do not exist to the degree of being incorporated in the labour market, then there is little basis to self-organisation amongst a non-existent or barely-existent class of women wage workers.

The experience of the Cypriot entrepreneurs in the North London garment industry was underpinned by a great fear of 'losing' women machinists during 'slack periods', and complaints over labour 'disloyalty' were frequently expressed by contractors. 'Finding machinists' was cited as the single largest problem confronting employers. This was specified in 34 out of 78 establishments. By size group this was cited as a problem by 13 out of 32 small establishments, (employing between one and 25 workers), 15 out of 30 medium establishments (employing between 25 and 50 workers), but only six out of 16 large factories (employing 50 and more workers) (see Panayiotopoulos, 1996a). This not only suggests that a labour market exists, but also that emergent firms in the medium sized group faced greater problems with labour supply. What the study revealed was one impact of economic differentiation, in that the larger Cypriot employers (contractors and manufacturers) faced with exhausted available supplies of co-ethnic labour, successfully negotiated labour supply problems by making more extensive use of the labour power of women from other ethnic minorities, primarily as homeworkers. The existence of a general labour market for machinists that drew from a wide range of ethnic minority groups, appeared as a strong feature of the North London Cypriot-dominated garment industry. These kinds of indicators suggested that Cypriot entrepreneurs have pushed, quite significantly, the boundaries of exploitation. A substantial number have risen from the ranks of the petty bourgeoisie, the small employer and the contractor. Many are now large employers, some are manufacturers and most of the women workers employed by them come from a variety of ethnic minority backgrounds.

Labour relations in immigrant enterprise

An understanding of labour relations in immigrant enterprise needs, for analytical purposes, to be clear about what are and what are not, wage relationships. For a labour market and wage relationships to exist a necessary presupposition is the existence of competition and commodity production. Karl Marx (1970:167–169) argued that labour power itself as a commodity ('free wage labour') was conditional on two factors: that the exchange of commodities, i.e. money (wages) for labour power 'implies no other relations of dependence' and that the labourer is in no position to sell commodities other than 'that very labour-power, which exists only in his (her) living self'. Analyses of labour markets and labour relations in immigrant enterprises characterised by a reliance on own-labour (the self-employed) and/or family labour, poses problems for the above categorisation. Since component members of the family enterprise do not act as 'free' wage labour (as they are indeed tied by 'relations of dependence'), then how do we conceptualise the incorporation of households in capitalist production? Marx (1975) writing on the position of independent handicrafts producers and the petty bourgeoisie, suggested that whilst many such producers may employ no labourers and therefore do not produce as capitalists they can, however, act as producers of commodities. In this capacity they confront us as sellers of commodities and not as sellers of labour. This relation, Marx asserted, 'has nothing to do with the exchange of capital for labour' (pp. 407–408). One further observation was the possibility that these producers, working with their own means of production, not only reproduce their own labour power, but may also create surplus-value.

The garment, leather, catering, retail and other industries can be seen as examples where households (as Family Units of Production) can engage in the production of goods and services on contract for large multinational companies in a functional relationship with the most concentrated forms of capitalist marketing. Immigrant enterprises relying exclusively on their own labour, (but at the same time producing commodities for some or other capitalist buyer) may be seen as an example of household units of production integrated into capitalist relations (see, Basu and Altinay, 2003). As such, they engage in capitalist relations 'with the world around them' whilst retaining the capacity to part-appropriate their own surplus labour through formal ownership of its own labour and the means of production. If one made a distinction, however, between formal ownership and real control over productive activities, this may suggest that many family units of production (if they continue as such) may be found in the matrix of economic compulsion intrinsically associated with capitalist wage work. In this context, households using their own labour to produce goods and services for markets, could be understood through the concept of 'disguised wage-labour' households (Gerry, 1987).

The peculiarities of the part-appropriation of surplus value by the household, also suggests that households in this position may in part be their own oppressors and own exploiters. If the petty bourgeoisie wishes to wage war against the bourgeoisie over a redivision of the spoils (of its own) surplus labour then the 'pygmies' of capital have to grow bigger. To do this implies the acquisition of more commodities, not least of all the labour power of other hired workers. Whatever the particular trajectory of any small unit of capital may be, what is certain is that the petty bourgeoisie does not 'survive' as an historical curiosity but, on the contrary, whilst it is a precarious strata it is also a resilient strata with strong capacities for self-reproduction.

The emergence of a class of employers from the ranks of immigrant wage workers can be seen as a concrete manifestation of the reproduction of class society. Much of the evidence suggests that the status of ethnic employer is an emergent and submergent phenomenon, characterised by high levels of entry and exit. Evidence from a study of immigrant entrepreneurs in the Parisian garment industry (Morokvasic *et al.*, 1990:167), points to the ambiguity of the contractor's status such that the contractor 'may be literally employer and employee at the same time' and that 'some immigrants regularly shift from one status to another several times a year'. The *Sentier* system is characterised by high rate of firm turnover (failures) (Green, 2002). In a similar way Anthias (1992:132–133) pointed to a high degree of mobility amongst Greek Cypriots in London between the status of small employer, the self-employed, shopkeeper and wage worker (largest group).

The worldview associated with the repositioning of members of an ethnic group from labour migrants to petty employers has important implications for the bargaining process. One implication of mobility between strata is that since 'objective' class positions are themselves frequently inter-exchangeable, so are ideas about class. Analyses which attempted to understand the 'contradictory class location' of the strata between wage workers and small capitalists, (Wright, 1978, 1985; Poulantzas, 1975; Bechhofer and Elliot, 1981) can be seen as useful, in a context where ideas about class are indeed confused, as the development of class society itself may be 'in formation'. Erik Olin Wright argued that in situations where family and waged workers were employed, then the relative ratio between family and waged workers can act as a method of defining their relative (class) position. The significance of the extension of wage labour, is noted by Wright (1978:80) in these terms,

> When a petty-bourgeois producer employs a single helper, there is an immediate change in the social relations of production, for the labour of a worker can now be exploited. Still, the surplus-value appropriated from a single employee is likely to be very small; most importantly, it is likely to be less than the surplus product generated by the petty-bourgeois producer him/herself. This is especially likely since frequently in petty-bourgeois production a considerable amount of labour is contributed by unpaid family members. As additional employees are added, the proportion of the total surplus product that is generated by the petty-bourgeois family declines. At some point it becomes less than half of the total surplus product, and eventually becomes a small fraction of the total surplus. At that point, the petty-bourgeois producer becomes firmly a small capitalist. There is no *a priori* basis for deciding how many employees are necessary to become a small capitalist. This number would vary considerably for different technologies employed in production and for different historical periods.

The extension of wage labour and the size of the enterprise have important implications for workplace relations. One illustration is in how the emergent capitalist employer physically relates to the establishment. The size of the enterprise may determine the physical form in which the proprietor takes part in the enterprise. If the size and capital of the workshop is still very small, the small capitalist frequently works side-by-side with other shopfloor workers. If the capital and size of the establishment grows larger, then the proprietor may give up manual working and specialise in commercial, marketing and other functions associated with expansion. These may detach the entrepreneur from the establishment altogether for prolonged periods and may, therefore, increasingly detach the entrepreneur from the common experience of physical labour.

Ideas about ethnic solidarity held by immigrant workers who have become entrepreneurs are attempts to construct and reconstruct a conscious explanation of the changing world around them. This process should not be seen as Gramsci (1971:333) argued, as 'fixed' or as the cultural property of individuals, classes or ethnic groups. Rather, ideas are a reflection of the relationships between people and with the world around them and, as such, 'as the terms of that relationship changes, so consciousness itself is thrown into turmoil'. This concept when applied to a class of ethnic capitalists who have risen from the ranks of workers may translate (to paraphrase Gramsci), as one where amongst small employers, the migrant 'man in the mass' contains two consciousnesses: vestiges of his/her artisanal or working class origins (or what may be seen as a theoretical consciousness) and, the other, his/her actual practical consciousness as a petty or larger employer. In this sense, the emergent ethnic capitalist may be seen as the bearer of two consciousnesses, or of one contradictory consciousness.

Nowhere is this contradictory consciousness more apparent than in attitudes towards trade unions. One study of contractors in the London garment industry, showed that most of the entrepreneurs had risen from the ranks of wage workers and many were previously members of trade unions. Sixteen (out of 78) specified that they had been members in their home country and two actually held full-time positions in Communist-led trade unions. Some continued membership of English trade unions and 13 specified previous membership in the UK. Three were shop stewards and one was a District Official. When the question was asked, 'Is there a trade union here?' the answer in 77 out of 78 cases was negative, with a typical response consisting of, 'what, for 15 people?'. When the question was asked 'what do *you* think of trade unions?', many entrepreneurs (particularly amongst the 'first'-generation immigrant group) saw them in a positive light. It was illustrative that at one left-wing meeting, seven respondents were present and that the meeting was advertised in three factories with, in two, the poster prominently displayed on the employer's office door (Panayiotopoulos, 1994:334–337).

One assumption made with considerable justification, is that since most immigrant enterprises are small, so their functions will mirror those of small enterprises generally and that this can be equally applied to our understanding of labour relations. Analyses of workplace relations in small firms frequently present a polarity between 'paternal' or 'autocratic' styles of management. Ram (1993; also see, Ram *et al.*, 2002a), in seeking to go beyond this divide pointed towards a more contingent and informal 'negotiated paternalism' in labour relations amongst immigrant enterprises in the West Midlands garment industry. This parallels discussion on ethnic paternalism in New York by Roger Waldinger (see Chapter 3). The conclusions drawn by Ram were that 'the management of workplace relations in the West Midlands does not conform to the prevailing stereotypes of management autocrat' (Ram, 1993:578). Rainnie (1989) drew sharply opposing conclusions from research on the relationship between Marks and Spencer and its many competing, small-scale garment contractors, and identified such firms as 'sites of managerial autocracy' associated with quite harsh conditions. Considerable research and social commentary would support the view that amongst the many competing contractors conditions are indeed harsh and that this has important implications for labour relations (see, Ross, 1997; Bonacich and Appelbaum, 2000; Phizacklea, 1990; Bonacich, 1993b).

Ram (1993:570), argued that negotiated paternalism is informed by high levels of mutual 'trust' between workers and bosses, which makes use of networks based in real or imagined common claims to kinship, religion, caste or ethnicity. The recruitment and management of workers made use of the above classifications. Ram (1993:576) noted that the labour process was organised in the form of section work (assembly-line production) whereby machinists specialised in producing a particular part, or section, of the garment. This specialisation involved five stages: trimmings, pockets, linings, zips and finishing, and necessitated a continuous supply of appropriate work. The supervisory regime, both at the level of the workplace and amongst homeworkers was about the management of women machinists, who form the largest section of the labour force. Typically this is through the piece-rate system. The rate paid inside the factory for each garment produced was subject to individual negotiation: bargaining involved variables such as the time of the year, past rates, availability of external labour, caste and culture. In this supervisory model the workplace is the assumed physical terrain for workplace relations. The above factory assembly-line conditions require a continuous supply of appropriate work. In many small garment workshops, however, section work breaks down, either because work is not available in the right quantities or, more typically, because machinists and other workers are insufficient in number to form an assembly line.

The reliance on homeworking in many situations means that the physical structure of the workplace needs to be more expansively understood. In London and Los Angeles the greatest employment growth was found amongst homeworkers. This has important implications for the bargaining process. Homeworking relies on make-through machining rather than section work: this means that the individual worker undertakes most of the sewing tasks and this calls for high levels of skill, which can be in short supply and which can place machinists in a relatively strong bargaining position. The bargaining process whilst shaped by the structure and seasonal demands of the industry, can also be influenced by the supply and demand for labour, particularly for make-through machinists. In many situations, entrepreneurs experience periodic problems in recruiting female machinists. This, as we noted, is often due to the ageing of first-generation women machinists and the unwillingness of young second-generation ethnic minority women to enter the garment industry, even if they could (since most are not skilled in the needle or sewing trades). During one such period of labour shortages, a study in London found that a general fear of 'losing' women machinists during 'slack periods' and complaints over labour 'disloyalty', were frequently expressed sentiments by CMT contractors. 'Finding machinists' was cited as the single largest problem confronting employers (Panayiotopoulos, 1996a:455). Most of the entrepreneurs were CMT contractors who depended on manufacturers as suppliers of work. The interconnecting problems of the 'CMT syndrome', i.e. 'finding machinists' and 'finding work' at the 'right price', dominated their lives.

> We take low prices from Manufacturers in order to keep going and hang on to staff because otherwise we might lose them' [small CMT unit]. But on the other hand as another put it, 'low prices from Manufacturers means we have to pay low wages leading to loss of staff' [medium CMT unit]. As the proprietor of a large unit put it, 'we don't like the prices but if we get work from somebody else, he [the Manufacturer] would carve us up, especially if it was slack' [large CMT unit]. Finding, hanging-on, or losing machinists was seen in relation to 'busy' and 'slack' periods. As another respondent put it 'In slack periods, the problem is finding work, but when we are busy the problem becomes finding staff' [medium CMT unit]. During 'slack' periods contractors take small dockets; sometimes they were taken 'to try' and at others more regularly. One small place had in its weekly workload blouses, skirts, dresses, trousers and jackets with no docket exceeding 500 garments and most running to a couple of hundred. One result can be that a wide range of garments demands more proficiency from homeworkers, with the possible response to work, that it's 'difficult' or 'doesn't run' (which means pay is low since the worker is on piece-rate). Unless a higher price is paid then this is compensated by homeworkers 'rushing' or showing low diligence, which can add to problems, over quality and standard deviation inherent in make-through machining.
>
> (Panayiotopoulos, 1994:307–313)

The above conditions of labour scarcity encountered in London and elsewhere, are critical in shaping the bargaining process and pushing up piece-rate payments given to machinists. Specific factors were also influential in the precise price given, such as the range of garments produced: whether blouses, skirts, sweatshirts or dresses, with the latter demanding higher payments due to greater effort required. Whilst there was a price benchmark for each garment, it also 'depended on the worker'. The rate was also influenced by the quality and class of the garment and whether it was 'high fashion', 'average' or 'mail order', with the latter two paid significantly less. Payment per garment also depended on 'how easy or difficult it was to make' and this was influenced by the size of the docket. The bigger the order was, the more likely that workers would become more proficient over time, and the rate revised downwards. In reverse (and more common), due to the large number of small dockets produced, workers would complain that the work was 'difficult' and the price had to be adjusted upwards. A complex set of variables formed the basis of negotiation between the individual worker and employer. In the case of homeworkers, isolation added to the individualisation of bargaining. Unlike factory workers, where a collective rate could be set by machinists this becomes more difficult, although not impossible, amongst homeworkers. The high demand for make-through machinists and fashion seasonality with its peaks and troughs in labour demand, however, can create circumstances for effective bargaining by workers. In London, homeworkers made reference to a moral economy in which all were entitled to 'thirds' – 'one third for the machinist, one third for the employer, and one third for finishing' – as structuring payment expectations: many said this had broken down, with homeworkers feeling 'hard done by' and that many of them were 'laying down a line of £30 per day and refusing to work below it' (Panayiotopoulos, 1994:155).

Labour scarcity forced immigrant entrepreneurs to make changes to the ethnic composition of their labour force, and in how it was employed. The result was a greater representation for non-co-ethnic workers, particularly amongst homeworkers who were a growing section of the labour force (Panayiotopoulos, 1996a:442–445). One example is illustrated in the labour force composition of a Cypriot-owned garment factory in Tottenham, North London (see Table 7.4). An account is presented below,

In one workplace in the Tottenham area of north London, the following observations were made. The enterprise is owned by a Greek Cypriot family and various members of the family acted as workers and as managers. The factory produced women's wear (blouses, skirts, dresses) on a CMT basis. Some of the dockets were for less than 500 garments and up to five different styles produced per week was not unusual. The workplace was a medium-sized factory situated on an Industrial Estate employing 40 people, of whom half were employed as homeworkers. Work began at 8.30 am. (later for those with young school children) and finished at 5.30 pm., Monday to Friday and 8.30 am. to 1.00 pm. on Saturdays. Inside the factory and amongst homeworkers directly employed by the firm, the labour force was considerably ethnically interspersed. Greek Cypriot workers and African-Caribbean women machinists were seen more as 'regular', and if laid-off during a 'slack period', had 'first offer' for future work. The employment of young African-Caribbean men was unusual. Many Greek Cypriot factories discriminate (effectively) against second generation West Indian youth. Tottenham, however, is a major West Indian settlement, and this is a factor that influences the local labour market. The elder brother also prided himself on being a 'progressive man' (and was in fact a leading member of the London Branch of the Cypriot Communist Party).

Inside the factory, face-to-face workplace relations were structured by wage relations and patron–client relations. Management showed a high degree of patronage. For example the elder brother part-owned a fish and chips shop that contained live-in accommodation and the top flat was rented to the two African-Caribbean pressers. Lifts were given to some women workers. The aunt and two other workers who lived near one of the brothers were regularly given lifts. If people worked overtime to meet a 'rush' order getting a lift home was an expected favour. Loans were often advanced to workers and sometimes gifts were given. Garments, frequently end of line or slightly damaged, were sometimes given away or bought by workers for small sums. These patron–client relations based on a high degree of informality between labour and management, also had important formal enterprise functions. In this way management estimated that workers would be more likely to show flexibility over their time of work when asked to, particular in meeting 'delivery dates'. Given the small dockets produced, there were many delivery dates and requests to 'work on', which was a source of friction. The giving of lifts was an attempt to regulate in an effective manner the hours worked. The renting of housing to pressers was also an important way of binding workers who have a reputation for disloyalty (moving on) amongst employers in the trade. It is less likely that workers would move on, if this meant the loss of housing.

(Panayiotopoulos, 2001a:109–110)

Future prospects and the colonisation of immigrant enterprise

The United States and Europe have seen an increasing interest by policy makers about the economic arrangements of immigrant and ethnic minority communities. Many see in immigrant enterprise a useful vehicle for the promotion of a range of desirable social objectives ranging from local employment creation to racial equality. Immigrant enterprise in Europe has become a new focus for policy. The realisation that immigrants are here to stay and that their economic activities contribute something to employment and the production of goods and services, is reflected in attempts at what may be seen as a new colonisation of immigrant enterprise. The old colonisation is familiar enough, in the army of immigrant contractors and subcontractors, frequently occupying subordinate positions in flexible systems of exploitation.

What we mean by 'new', are attempts by practitioners to colonise the field of research on immigrant enterprise and move the focus away from concerns at explaining how immigrants cope in hostile labour markets, and towards normative assumptions that solutions to the complex problems facing immigrant communities are best addressed through the medium of small enterprise promotion. This has been a very long mantra from the small business promotion industry (see, Curran and Storey, 2000; Ram and Smallbone, 2001; Smallbone *et al.*, 2002; Rutherford and Blackburn, 2000). Another, and more problematised focus appears in research and policy on the 'integration' of immigrant enterprises and the 'formalisation' of the informal sector (Kloosterman, 2000; Kloosterman and Rath, 2002, 2003; Rath, 2000a). Whilst the integration school and the small business promotion school, have different objectives and different groups of immigrant or ethnic minority entrepreneurs in mind, they can both be equally understood as the proxy beneficiaries of ethnic minority enterprise promotion and research. In part, this is the result of a policy-driven agenda in the European Union to bring immigrant enterprise out of the 'fringes' and to propose practical ideas for policy makers to 'integrate' it. In part it also derives from the small business consultancy services, which are increasingly targeting emergent minority enterprises in their attempts to 'break out' and to enter the 'mainstream'. Both of these approaches can be criticised for showing insufficient appreciation of ethnicity or immigration status as a basis for economic and political mobilisation.

One important political dimension of differentiation is the way it influences promotion. Much of the literature on embeddedness indicates that emergent entrepreneurs, who occupy a strong economic position are more likely to be integrated in the local political-institutional structures of the host society. This means they are better placed to make use for themselves (and others) community resources. It is in part to their leadership of community organisations (whether in Miami, New York or North London) that many benefit from local government support (see Panayiotopoulos, 1992; Panayiotopoulos and Dreef, 2002). A number of the entrepreneurs have shown strong capacities for political brokerage. Frequently it is the most successful of the entrepreneurs who act as representatives of the community and as intermediaries with policy makers. The reasons for this are complex and reflect on the restructuring of the particular industries, the economic power of the entrepreneurs, the nature of local economies and policy makers themselves. One revealing consequence of the repositioning of a significant section of entrepreneurs out of the ranks of contractors, subcontractors and the self-employed and into stronger economic positions in cities such as London, Los Angeles, and New York and elsewhere, is that a significant group have become an important focus for local government support and are now well placed to become beneficiaries of mainstream business support agencies. This book suggests that the differentiation of minority enterprise is an important factor in the re-shaping of institutional relations and influences the selectivity of the promotional effort.

Much of the material reviewed, indicates an increasing diversity presented in the broad polarity between survival-orientated enterprises confined to the 'ethnic niche' and growth-orientated enterprises trying to 'break out' of the confines of the ethnic economy.

Enterprises are also differentiating themselves in an upward direction away from the small enterprise milieu, or in a sideways direction away from traditional sectors such as garments and retailing. It is these groups that business consultancy and local government authorities, have targeted as major beneficiaries of strategic small business promotion. Small enterprise promotion and business consultancy firms have concluded that these emergent ethnic entrepreneurs have the potential to enter the economic mainstream and at the same time offer high yield return for strategic networking by enterprise support agencies. At the same time, many of the support organisations which have grown in response to government funding in the UK and wider European Union, appeared as lacking adequate information on the profile and dynamics of minority entrepreneurs in their localities. Many showed a lack of understanding of the diversity of the minority enterprise sector and the diverse needs of the entrepreneurs and were confused about the objectives of enterprise support (Ram and Deakins, 1998). One conclusion is that diverse enterprises have different needs and types of institutional support. The new emphasis on the needs of emergent entrepreneurs trying to break out of the ethnic niche, however, is what is capturing policy makers' attention about future directions (see, Ram and Jones, 1998).

Policy makers who see in immigrant enterprise a vehicle for social integration (and 'social justice') prevaricate between whether the objectives of the promotional effort are to address ethnic disadvantage or to promote the extension of viable emergent businesses. Whilst there is an increasing recognition of diversity, questions are raised for ethnic minority enterprise support as an agency for equality. Promotional agencies are driven by their need to produce results and to meet and reach competitive and self-financing criteria and are under pressure to adopt more selective criteria in the targeting of beneficiaries of enterprise development support. The targeting for expansion of 'fewer but better' enterprises from the ranks of existing minority enterprises trying to break out of the ethnic niche offers a potentially higher yield and lower risk area. One consequence is to give strength to those approaches that emphasise 'wagering on the strong' i.e. favouring emergent enterprises. This may well conflict with equity objectives which want to address issues to do with gender, racial and other forms of social exclusion and which place more emphasis on start-up amongst groups under-represented in the enterprise spectrum. This, points to future directions and tensions in ethnic minority enterprise policy and support.

Conclusions

The book in following much of the contemporary sociological analyses of immigration and ethnicity suggests that far from being a state reflecting ineradicable differences and highly durable cultural traits, ethnicity and its economic arrangements are an emergent and submergent phenomenon. This becomes doubly apparent in studies of ethnic minority and immigrant participation in particular industries. Material from comparative research indicates that the supply and demand for labour can reconfigure the ethnic composition of the labour force in immigrant enterprises. This has been the experience of the garment industry in New York and East London, both once dominated by the Jewish community and now by other immigrant and ethnic groups. Edna Bonacich, as we noted, applied Leon's (1946) argument about the 'end' of the 'people class' i.e. an occupationally-based ethnicity, which advances and recedes in different historical circumstances, to explain these changes. Waldinger notes (in the New York garment industry) that 'in all the size of the firm made it necessary to recruit beyond the owner's kinship network' (Waldinger, 1986:157). Similarly, evidence from London shows a decreasing role for Cypriot wage workers in Cypriot-owned factories and an expansion in the employment of, in particular, women homeworkers from other ethnic groups (see, Panayiotopoulos and Dreef, 2002). Bonacich (1998) notes that in the Los Angeles garment industry the antagonism between contractor and workers takes on inter-ethnic dimensions between Asian contractors and Hispanic women workers. The above provide the material conditions for the development, as Ivan Light *et al.* (1994) argue, of an immigrant, rather than ethnic enclave.

The book argued that the differentiation of immigrant enterprise has critical implications for how entrepreneurs respond to changes in the market and institutional environment, how they manage their enterprises and in how they relate to the production process. The experience of immigrant participation in the North London garment industry and elsewhere, indicate that differentiation typically represented a move away from the ranks of the many small CMT contractors and towards the ranks of the fewer manufacturers. A much smaller number have become owners of considerable property. This process, as much as the informalisation of production and its negative impact on labour rights, has been a significant experience of Cypriot participation and informed conclusions in early research, about the community as an 'achieving' minority, which more recent ethnic entrants in the garment sector (in New York, Berlin, Paris, Amsterdam) might 'emulate' (see, Waldinger *et al.*, 1985:587).

As we noted, the size and complexity of the enterprise may determine the physical form in which the proprietor takes part in the enterprise. That in small workshops the entrepreneur frequently works side-by-side with other shopfloor workers and in larger workshops the proprietor may give up manual working and specialise in commercial, marketing and other functions, which may detach the entrepreneur from the establishment and from the common experience of physical labour. Material that points to the role of non-co-ethnic labour, such as in Cypriot, Jewish or Korean-owned factories, typically through the employment of women homeworkers from various ethnic groups, raises one major issue. In our application of the problematic – if an employer no longer sweats side-by-side with other workers, of whom an increasing proportion may come from an ethnic group different from that of the employer – then the claim to a common identity based on common ethnic origins and experience which may unite the employer and the worker, is considerably weakened. The above can become amplified in emergent enterprises, which employ larger numbers of workers and within which family workers, constitute a smaller proportion of the labour force.

Ethnicity as an emergent and submergent phenomenon, needs however to be qualified. It is too broad to conclude that the tendency in many immigrant factories to show a considerable ethnic interspersion in labour recruitment results in the undermining of the occupational basis of ethnicity as a collective identity, for all social strata in an ethnic group. This is subject to variation, not least of all in opportunities available for working-class immigrants. The tendency for a significant proportion of workers *not* to be employed by an employer from the same immigrant group, poses questions for embeddedness theories, which see ethnic solidarity as a necessary precondition for ordering workplace relations and in structuring the redistributory functions of immigrant enterprise (Portes, Waldinger, *passim*). This creates problems for a negotiated paternalism, which applies ethnicity (however defined) as the basic unit for classification and analytical purposes. One conclusion is that research on workplace relations in immigrant enterprise needs to show more regard for internal differentiation. The tendency to reduce analyses of immigrant enterprise and ethnic identity to ethnic identity and claims associated with a common origin rather than to common experiences which themselves are subject to change, which may sharply diverge between particular sections of the same group, and which more generally may be subject to a tension between the ideal values of a particular community and the everyday life of its constituent members, however defined, needs to be questioned. The book suggests that stratification analyses pose problems for culturally driven claims to common identities applied in workplace relations, and in doing so invites questions about 'who benefits' from immigrant enterprise.

Future trajectories are for the foolhardy. What is certain is that the future for immigrant enterprise will continue to be influenced by the restructuring of particular sectors, localities, neighbourhoods and cities, substantially under the impact of the storm and stress which is the global economy, and ultimately involving a relationship between 'capital' and immigrant communities. In this process there are winners and losers and much of it is pretty predictable stuff. If you are a machinist your life is going to be tough; so is the life of your children, especially if you work at home. At the same time there is a new-found confidence amongst second-generation youth in the gateway cities of Europe and the United States, which in cases builds on proud traditions. Despite the rampant xenophobia sweeping across Europe and the United States, the book ends on a note of optimism in the message sent during the May 2005 British general election by the people of Bethnal Green in East London, when Respect, a political party which came out of the anti-war movement, shook the political establishment by sending, at its first appearance, George Galloway to Parliament and taking the seat from the pro-war New Labour candidate. In the neighbouring constituencies of East and West Ham and Poplar, Respect came second and it also polled well in Birmingham Sparkbrook, Tottenham and Hackney. In an area of North-east London containing something like one million people, Respect has become the main challenge to New Labour. There is an excitement in the air as activists from the Bangladeshi, Pakistani, Turkish, Kurdish, West Indian and other communities, Muslims and atheists, SWP members and old Communist Party veterans, men and women, unions like the RMT and restaurant owners, assembled in an alliance which first came together to oppose war in Iraq and which points to one possible future direction. This was articulated in one of the messages of congratulations sent to Respect (in this instance by Fausto Bertinotti of Italy's *Rifondazione Communista*), which talked of the victory of a political experiment bringing together an original combination of different political projects and the idea of a multi-cultural society. East London during the late nineteenth century was the birthplace of the Labour Party and the new industrial trade unionism. The same streets of Bethnal Green were turned by Jewish immigrants into a centre of economic, cultural and political life and bedrock of support for the Communist Party, returning one Member of Parliament (Phil Piratin) until 1945. In the same streets, the Blackshirts of Oswald Mosley were turned back in the 1930s. Today, it is Bangladeshi immigrants who have picked up the cudgels against war, racism and xenophobia, defending in the process civil liberties and rights held dear by many of Albion's sons and daughters. The idea of a multi-racial, multi-ethnic mobilisation, which challenges the xenophobes and enters the political mainstream, demanding amongst others, respect for immigrants and refugees. Here is a project worth fighting for.

Bibliography

Alba, R. D. (1999) *Ethnic Identity: The Transformation of White America*, New Haven, CT: Yale University Press.

Aldrich, Howard and Albert Reiss Jnr (1981) 'Continuities in the Study of Ecological Succession: Changes in the Race Composition of Neighbourhoods and their Businesses', *American Journal of Sociology*, Vol. 81, pp. 846–866.

Aldrich, Howard, Trevor Jones and David McEvoy (1984) 'Ethnic Advantage and Minority Business Development', in Robin Ward and Richard Jenkins (eds) *Ethnic Communities in Business*, Cambridge: Cambridge University Press, pp. 189–210.

Allen, Richard A. (1969) *Black Awakening in Capitalist America*, New York: Pathfinder Press.

Anderson, Harriet and John Flatley (1997) *Contrasting London's Incomes: a Social and Spatial Analysis*, London: London Research Centre.

Anson, R. (1997) 'EU Clothing Production may have a Future', Editorial, *Textile Outlook International*, September, pp. 128–144.

Anthias, Floya (1992) *Ethnicity, Class, Gender and Migration: Greek Cypriots in Britain*, Aldershot: Avebury.

—— (1983) 'Sexual Divisions and Ethnic Adaptations: The Case of Greek Cypriot Women', in Annie Phizacklea (ed.) *One Way Ticket. Migration and the Labour Market*, London: Routledge, pp. 59–74.

Anthias, Floya and Gabriella Lazaridis (2000) (eds) *Gender and Migration in Southern Europe: Women on the Move*, Aldershot: Ashgate.

Arbruster, R., K. Geron and E. Bonacich (1995) 'The Assault on California's Latino Immigrants: The Politics of Proposition 187', *International Journal of Urban and Regional Research*, Vol. 19, No. 4, pp. 655–663.

Asad, Talal (1973) *Anthropology and the Colonial Encounter*, London: Ithaca Press.

Asian Week (2001) 'What Now?', 29 June 2001 (available at www.asianweek.com/2001_06).

Atema, James and Prodromos Panayiotopoulos (1995) *Promoting Urban Informal Enterprises: A Case Study of the ActionAid-Kenya Kariobangi Savings and Credit Programme*, Swansea: Papers in International Development No. 15, Centre for Development Studies.

Barnes, P. (1994) 'Profile of Marks and Spencer: A Growing International Presence', *Textile Outlook International*, November, pp. 3–5.

Barret, Giles, Trevor Jones and David McEvoy (2003) 'United Kingdom: Severely

Constrained Entrepreneurialism', in R. Kloosterman and J. Rath (eds) *Immigrant Entrepreneurs: Venturing Abroad in the Age of Globalization*, Oxford: Berg, pp. 101–123.

—— (1996) 'Ethnic Minority Business: Theoretical Discourse in Britain and North America', *Urban Studies*, Vol. 33, Nos. 4–5, pp. 783–809.

Barth, Frederick (1969) 'Introduction', in Frederick Barth (ed.) *Ethnic Groups and Boundaries: The Social Organisation of Culture Difference*, London: George Allen and Unwin, pp. 9–38.

Basch, Linda, Nina Schilier and Cristina Blanc-Szanton (1994) *Nations Unbound: Transnational Projects, Post-colonial Predicaments and De-territorialized Nation-States*, Langhorne, PA: Gordon and Breach.

Basu, Anuradha and Eser Altinay (2003) 'Family and Work in Minority Ethnic Business in the UK', Joseph Rowntree Trust: Findings Number 13 (www.jrf.org.uk).

Bayar, Ali (1996) 'Ethnic Business Among Turkish Immigrants in Europe', *Forum*, Vol. 3, No. 4. December, pp. 1–7.

Bechhofer, Frank and Brian Elliot (1981) *The Petite Bourgeosie: Comparative Studies of the Uneasy Stratum*, London: Macmillan Press.

Becker, H. (1956) 'Middlemen Trading Peoples: Germ Plasm and Social Situations', *Man in Reciprocity*, New York: Praeger, pp. 225–237.

Beja, J. and W. Chunguang (1999) 'Un Village du Zhejiang a Paris, Migration Chinoise', *Hommes et Migration*, No. 1220, pp. 65–82.

Bell, Nicholas (2002) Contribution to the Conference on 'Borders on Migration' organised by the Austrian League for Human Rights, Vienna 29–30 October: European Civic Forum.

Benoit, Bertrand (2005) 'Germany restricts Jewish immigration', *Financial Times*, 6 January.

—— (2004) 'Germany shines the spotlight on its shadow economy', *Financial Times*, 6 February.

—— (2003) 'Germans wake up the call of the muezzin', *Financial Times*, 4 November.

Benton, Gregor and Frank N. Pieke (eds) (1998) *The Chinese in Europe*, Houndmills, Basingstoke: Macmillan Press.

Bermant, Chaim (1975) *London's East End: Point of Arrival*, New York: Macmillan.

Bhachu, Parminder (1988) 'Fast Food, Fettered Work: Chinese Women in the Ethnic Catering Industry', in Sally Westwood and Parminder Bhachu (eds) *Enterprising Women: Ethnicity, Economy and Gender Relations*, London: Routledge, pp. 58–75.

Bickerton, Ian (2004a) 'From tolerance to division? Murder and extremism shake Dutch faith in an open society', *Financial Times*, 17 November.

—— (2004b) 'Attacks on Muslims raise Dutch fears over integration', *Financial Times*, 9 November.

Bird, Sharon R. and Stephen G. Sapp (2004) 'Understanding the Gender Gap in Small Business Success', *Gender & Society*, Vol. 18, No. 1, pp. 5–28.

Blackburn, R. and R. Rutherford (1999) *Enterprise for Culturally Diverse Communities*, London: Kingston University.

Body-Gendrot, Sophie (1996) 'Paris: a "Soft" Global City?', *New Community*, Vol. 22, No. 4, pp. 595–605.

Bohning, W. R. (1972) *The Migration of Workers in the United Kingdom and the European Community*, Oxford: Oxford University Press.

Boisevain, Jeremy (1984) 'Small Entrepreneurs in Contemporary Europe', in Robin Ward and Richard Jenkins (eds) *Ethnic Communities in Business: Strategies for Economic Survival*, Cambridge: Cambridge University Press, pp. 20–38.

—— (1981) *Small Entrepreneurs in Contemporary Europe*, Work and Social Change, No. 4, Maastricht: European Centre for Work and Society.

—— and Hanneke Grotenbreg (1988) 'Culture, Structure and Ethnic Entreprise. The Surinamese of Amsterdam', in M. Cross and H. Entzinger (eds) *Lost Illusions: Caribbean Minorities in Britain and the Netherlands*, London: Routledge, pp. 221–249.

—— J. Blaschke, H. Grotenbreg, J. Isaac, I. Light, M. Sway, R. Waldinger and P. Werbster (1990) 'Ethnic Entrepreneurs and Ethnic Strategies', in R. Waldinger, H. Aldrich and R. Ward (eds) *Ethnic Entrepreneurs*, London: Sage Publications, pp. 131–156.

Bonacich, Edna (1998) 'Organising Immigrant Workers in the Los Angeles Apparel Industry', *Journal of World-Systems Research*, Vol. 4, No. 1 (http://csf.colorado.edu/jwsr/archive/).

—— (1994) 'Asians in the Los Angeles Garment Industry', in Paul Ong, Edna Bonacich and Lucie Cheng (eds) *The New Asian immigration in Los Angeles and Global Restructuring*, Philadelphia: Temple University Press, pp. 137–163.

—— (1993a) 'The Other Side of Ethnic Entrepreneurship: A Dialogue with Waldinger, Aldrich, Ward and Associates', *International Migration Review*, Vol. xxvii, No. 4, pp. 685–692.

—— (1993b) 'Asian and Latino Immigrants in the Los Angeles Garment Industry: An Exploration of the Relationship Between Capitalism and Racial Oppression', in Ivan Light and Parminder Bhachu (eds) *Immigration and Entrepreneurship: Culture, Capital and Ethnic Networks*, New Brunswick: Transaction Publishers, pp. 51–74.

—— (1973) 'A Theory of Middleman Minorities', *American Sociological Review*, Vol. 38, pp. 583–594.

—— (1972) 'A Theory of Ethnic Antagonism: The Split Labour Market', *American Sociological Review*, Vol. 37, pp. 34–51.

—— and Richard Appelbaum (2000) (eds) *Behind the Label: Inequality in the Los Angeles Apparel Industry*, Berkley: University of California.

—— and John Modell (eds) (1980) *The Economic Basis of Ethnic Solidarity: Small Business in the Japanese American Community*, Berkeley: University of California.

—— and John Turner (1980) 'Towards a Composite Theory of Middleman Minorities', *Ethnicity*, Vol. 7, pp. 144–158.

—— I. Light and C. Wong (1976) 'Korean Immigrants: Mall Business in Los Angeles', in E. Gee (ed.) *Counterpoint: Perspectives on Asian Americans*, Los Angeles: Asian American Studies Center, UCLA, pp. 437–449.

Booth, Peter (1998a) National Secretary, Transport and General Workers Union, quoted from, *Observer*, 'Final Cut', 13 September.

Booth, William (1998b) 'One Nation, Indivisible: Is it History?', *Washington Post*, 22 February.

Borjas, George (1999) *Economic Research on the Determinants of Immigration: Lessons for the European Union*. World Bank Technical Paper No. 438: Washington, DC.

—— and Marta Tienda (1993) 'The Employment and Wages of Legalised Immigrants', *International Migration Review*, Vol. xxvii, No. 4, pp. 712–747.

Boulange, Antoine (2004) 'The Hijab, Racism and the State', *International Socialism*, No. 102, Spring, pp. 3–26.

Bourdieu, Pierre and Jean-Claude Passeron (1977) *Reproduction in Education, Society and Culture*, London: Sage Publications.

Boyes, Roger (2004) 'Germans fear Islamic unrest', *The Times*, 17 November.

Buck, Tobias and Daniel Dombey (2004) ' "Islamisation" warning clouds Turk's EU drive', *Financial Times*, 8 September.

Burgess, Kate (2004) 'City leads the west in Islamic Financial products', *Financial Times*, 15 August.

Callinicos, Alex (1993) *Race and Class*, London: Bookmarks.

Campell, Duncan (2000) 'Janitors clean up in strike settlement', *Guardian*, 25 April.

Capps, Gavin and Prodromos Panayiotopoulos (2001) 'South Korea: Free Market Miracle or Mirage?', in G. Gavin and P. Panayiotopoulos (eds) *World Development: An Introduction*, London: Pluto Press, pp. 133–147.

Carter, B., M. Green and R. Halpern (1996) 'Immigration Policy and the Racialization of Migrant Labour: The Construction of National Identities in the USA and Britain', *Ethnic and Racial Studies*, Vol. 19, No. 1, pp. 135–157.

Carvel, John (2004) 'Census shows Muslims' plight', *Guardian*, 12 October.

Castles, Stephen (2004) 'Why migration policies fail', *Ethnic and Racial Studies*, Vol. 27, No. 2, pp. 205–227.

—— (2000) *Ethnicity and Globalisation: From Migrant Worker to Transnational Citizen*, London: Sage Publications.

—— and Godula Kosack (1973) *Immigrant Workers and Class Structure in Western Europe*, Oxford: Oxford University Press.

—— Heather Booth and Tina Wallace (1984) *Here for Good: Western Europes New Ethnic Minorities*, London: Pluto Press.

Chaffin, Joshua (2004) 'Florida's new Hispanics', *Financial Times*, 13 April.

Cheng, Lucie and Philip Q. Yang (1996) 'Asians: The "Model Minority" Deconstructed', in Roger Waldinger and Mehdi Bozorgmehr (eds) *Ethnic Los Angeles*, New York: Russell Sage Foundation, pp. 305–344.

Chin, K. (1999) *Smuggled Chinese: Clandestine Immigration to the United States*. Philadelphia: Temple University Press.

Chin, Ku-Sup, In-Jin Yoon and David Smith (1996) 'Immigrant Small Business and International Economic Linkage: A Case of the Korean Wig Business in London Angeles, 1968–1977', *International Migration Review*, Vol. xxx, No. 2, pp. 485–510.

Clark, William (2003) *Immigrants and the American Dream: Remaking the Middle Class*. New York: The Guildford Press.

Cohen, Abner (1974) 'The Lesson of Ethnicity', in Abner Cohen (ed.) *Urban Ethnicity*, London: Tavistock Publications, pp. ix–xiii.

Cohen, Robin (1997) *Global Diasporas: An Introduction*, London: University College Press.

Cole, Mike and Gareth Dale (1999) (eds) *The European Union and Migrant Labour*, Oxford: Berg Publishers.

Coleman, James (1988) 'Social Capital in the Creation of Human Capital', *American Journal of Sociology*, Vol. 94, pp. S95–120.

Cornwell, Rupert (2003) 'American jail population hits two million', *Independent*, 8 April.

Cowan, Rosie (2004) 'Young Muslims "made scapegoats" in stop and search', *Guardian*, 3 July.

Cummings, Scott (1980) 'The Unique Legacy of Immigrant Economic Development', in Scott Cummings (ed.) *Self-Help in Urban America*, Washington DC: Kennikat Press, pp. 5–32.

Curran, James and David S. Storey (2000) *Small Business Policy: Past Experiences and Future Directions*, London: Kingston Business School (http://business.kingston.ac.uk/research/kbssbs.html).

Das, Subesh K. and Prodromos Panayiotopoulos (1996) 'Flexible Specialisation. New Paradigm for Industrialisation for Developing Countries?', *Economic and Political Weekly*, December, No. 28, pp. 57–61.

Davis, Mike (1992) *City of Quartz: Excavating the Future in Los Angeles*, London: Vintage.

Denton, Nancy and Douglas Massey (1989) 'Racial Identity Among Caribbean Hispanics: The Effect of Double Minority Status On Residential Segregation', *American Sociological Review*, Vol. 54, pp. 790–808.

Desnyder, V., M. Diazperez, A. Acevedo and L. Natera (1996) 'Perceptions of Wives of Documented and Undocumented Mexican immigrants to the United States', *Hispanic Journal of Behavioural Sciences*, Vol. 18, No. 3, pp. 283–296.

Dombey, Daniel (2004) 'Ankara accepts deal after war of nerves', *Finacial Times*, 18 December.

Douglas, Mary and Baron Isherwood (1979) *The World of Goods*, New York: Basic Books.

Drennan, Mathew (1991) 'The Decline and Rise of the New York Economy', in John Mollonkop and Manuel Castells (eds) *Dual City: Restructuring New York City*, New York: Russel Sage Foundation, pp. 25–41.

Eade, John (1989) *The Politics of Community: The Bangladeshi Community in East London*, Aldershot: Ashgate.

Ehrenreich, Barbara and Arlie R. Hochschild (eds) (2003) *Global Women: Nannies, Maids and Sex Workers in the New Economy*, New York: Metropolitan Books.

Ellis, Mark and Richard Wright (1999) 'The Industrial Division of Labour Amongst Immigrants and Internal Migrants to the Los Angeles Economy', *International Migration Review*, Vol. 33, No. 1, pp. 26–54.

Esping-Anderson, Gosta (1990) *The Three Worlds of Welfare Capitalism*, Oxford: Oxford University Press.

Fallers, Lloyd (1967) *Immigrants and Associations*, The Hague: Mouton Press.

Fernandez Kelly, Patricia (1995) 'Social and Cultural Capital in the Urban Ghetto: Implications for the Economic Sociology of Immigration', in Alejandro Portes (ed.) *The Economic Sociology of Immigration: Essays on Networks, Ethnicity and Entrepreneurship*, New York: Russell Sage Foundation, pp. 213–247.

—— and Anna Garcia (1989) 'Informalisation at the Core: Hispanic Women, Homework, and the Advanced Capitalist State', in Alejandro Portes, Manuel Castells and Lauren Benton (eds) *The Informal Economy: Studies in Advanced and Less Developed Countries*, London: John Hopkins Press, pp. 247–264.

Fine, Ben (1999) 'The Developmental State is Dead – Long Live Social Capital?', *Development and Change*, Vol. 30, No. 1, pp. 1–19.

Fishman, William (1976) *East End Radicals 1875–1914*, London: Duckworth.

Flap, Henk, Adem Kumcu and Bert Bulder (2000) 'The Social Capital of Ethnic

Entrepreneurs and their Business Success', in Jan Rath (ed.) *Immigrant Businesses. The Economic, Political and Social Environment*, Houndmills: Macmillan, pp. 142–161.

Foo, Lora (1994) 'The Vulnerable and Exploitable Immigrant Workforce and the Need for Strengthening Worker Protective Legislation', *The Yale Law Journal*, Vol. 103, No. 8, pp. 2213–2237.

Friedman, Jonathan (1990) 'Being in the World: Globalization and Localization', in M. Featherstone (ed.) *Global Culture: Nationalism, Globalisation and Modernity*, London: Sage, pp. 101–125.

Friedman-Kasaba, Kathie (1996) *Memories of Migration. Gender, Ethnicity and Work in the Lives of Jewish and Italian women in New York, 1870–1924*, Albany: State of University Press.

Fukuyama, Francis (1995) *Trust: The Social Virtues and the Creation of Prosperity*, New York: Hamish Hamilton.

Fulton, William (1997) *The Reluctant Metropolis: The Politics of Urban Growth in Los Angeles*, Pt Arena, CA: Solano Press.

Gaffney, Declan (2002) 'Capital of child poverty', *Guardian*, 19 November.

Geddes, Andrew (2003) *The Politics of Migration and Immigration in Europe*, London: Sage Publications.

—— (2000) *Immigration and European Integration: Towards Fortress Europe*, Manchester: Manchester University Press.

Georgakas, Dan and Marvin Surkin (1998) *Detroit: I Do Mind Dying*, London: Redwords.

Gerry, Chris (1987) 'Developing Economies and the Informal Sector in Historical Perspective', *The Annals of the American Academy of Political and Social Science*, No. 493, 101–119.

—— (1985) 'The Working Class and Small Enterprises in the UK Recession', in N. Redclift and A. Mingione (eds) *Beyond Employment: Household, Gender and Subsistence*, Oxford: Basil Blackwell, pp. 288–316.

van Geuns, Roeland (1992) 'An Aspect of Informalisation of Women's Work in a High-Tech Age: Turkish Sweatshops in the Netherlands', in Swasti Mitter (ed.) *Computer-aided Manufacturing and Women's Employment: The Clothing Industry in Four EC Countries*, London: Springer-Verlag Press, pp. 125–137.

Gilbertson, Greta (1995) 'Women's Labor and Enclave Employment: the Case of Dominican and Columbian Women in New York City. *International Migration Review*, Vol. 29, No. 3, pp. 657–670.

Glasgow, Douglas (1980) *The Black Underclass: Poverty, Unemployment and Entrapment of Ghetto Youth*, San Fransisco: Jossey-Bass Publishers.

Glanz, Rudolph (1976) *The Jewish Woman in America: Two Female Immigrant Generations 1820–1929*, 2 vols. New York: Ktav.

Glazer, Nathan (1997) *We Are All Multiculturalists Now*, Cambridge, MA: Harvard University Press.

—— (1983) *Ethnic Dilemas 1964–1982*, Cambridge, MA: Harvard University Press.

—— and Daniel Moynihan (1975) 'Introduction', in Nathan Glazer (ed.) *Ethnicity: Theory and Practice*, Cambridge, MA: Harvard University Press, pp. 1–26.

—— and Daniel Moynihan (1970) *Beyond the Melting Pot: The Negroes, Puerto Ricans, Jews, Italians and Irish of New York City*, Cambridge, MA: M.I.T. Press.

Goffman, Erving (1968) *Asylums*, Harmondsworth: Penguin.

Van Gogh, Theo (2003) *Allah Knows Best*, Amsterdam: XProductie.

Goldenberg, Suzanne (2002) 'Greatest wave of migrants drives US engine', *Guardian*, 3 December.

Gokturk, Deniz (1999) 'Turkish Delight – German Fright: Labour and Migration', Transnational Communities Programme WPTC-99-01, London: ESRC (www.transcomm.ox.ac.uk/working_papers.htm).

Goodwin, Mark (1996) 'Governing the Spaces of Difference: Regulation and Globalisation in London', *Urban Studies*, Vol. 33, No. 8, pp. 1395–1406.

Government of Cyprus (1970) *Industrial Production Survey*, Nicosia: Government Printers.

—— (1962) *Industrial Production Survey*, Nicosia: Government Printers.

—— (1959) *Annual Report, Ministry of Labour*, Nicosia: Government Printers.

Government of the Philippines (1995) *The Overseas Development Programme*, Manila: Department of Labor and Employment.

Government Office for London (2001) *Researching African Caribbean Business in London*, London: ABI Associates (www.abi.co.uk/reports.htm).

—— (2000) *Review of Business Support for Ethnic Minority Owned Businesses in London*, London: ABI Associates (www.abi.co.uk/reports.htm).

Graham, Robert (2003) 'French secularism unwraps far more than headscarves in the classroom', *Financial Times*, 21 December.

Graham, D. and N. Spence (1995) 'Contemporary Deindustrialisation and Tertiatisation in the London economy', Urban Studies, Vol. 32, No. 6, pp. 885–911.

Gramsci, Antonio (1971) *Selection from the Prison Notebooks of Antonio Gramsci*, London: Lawrence and Wishart.

Granovetter, Mark (1995) 'The Economic Sociology of Firms and Entrepreneurs', in Alejandro Portes (ed.) *The Economic Sociology of Immigration: Essays on Networks, Ethnicity and Entrepreneurship*, New York: Russell Sage Foundation, pp. 128–165.

—— (1985) 'Economic Action and Social Structure: The Problem of Embeddedness', *American Journal of Sociology*, Vol. 91, No. 3, pp. 481–510.

Greater London Authority (2002) *Ethnic Minorities in the Labour Market*. Cabinet Office, London: ABI Associates (www.abi.co.uk/reports.htm).

—— (2003) *The Contribution of London's Diverse Ethnic Communities to London's Economy*, London: Report No. 5, Economic and Social Development Committee.

Green, Nancy (2002) 'Paris: A Historical View', in Jan Rath (ed.) *Unravelling the Rag Trade: Immigrant Entrepreneurship in Seven World Cities*, Oxford: Berg Publishers, pp. 29–47.

Greenhouse, Steven (2001) 'As the Rich Do Without Extras, Service Workers Do Without', *New York Times*, 29 November.

Grennier, Guillermo and Alex Stepick (2002) 'Miami: Ethnic Succession and Failed Restructuring', in Jan Rath (ed.) *Unravelling the Rag Trade: Immigrant Entrepreneurship in Seven World Cities*, Oxford: Berg Publishers, pp. 135–150.

Grimes, Christopher (2003) 'Harlem reaps mixed blessing of gentrification', *Financial Times*, 19 November.

Gumble, Andrew (2002) 'A decade on LA South Central still smoulders', *Independent*, 30 April.

Haberfellner, Regina (2003) 'Austria: Still a Highly Regulated Economy', in

Robert Kloosterman and Jan Rath (eds) *Immigrant Entrepreneurs. Venturing Abroad in the Age of Globalisation*, Oxford: Berg, pp. 213–232.

Hamilton, Guy (1978) 'Pariah Capitalism: A Paradox of Power and Dependence', *Ethnic Groups*, Vol. 2, pp. 1–15.

Hamnett, Chris (1996) 'Social Polarisation, Economic Restructuring and Welfare State Regimes', *Urban Studies*, Vol. 33, No. 8, pp. 1407–1430.

Harris, Nigel (2002) *Thinking the Unthinkable. The Immigration Myth Exposed*, London: I.B. Tauris.

—— (1995a) *The New Untouchables: Immigration and the New World Worker*, London: Penguin.

—— (1995b) 'Can the West Survive?', *Competition and Change*, Vol. 1, pp. 111–122.

Hartog, Joop and Aslan Zorlu (1999) *Turkish Confection in Amsterdam: The Rise and Fall of a Perfectly Competitive Labour Market*, Amsterdam: Tinbergen Institute.

Henry, Nick, Cheryl McEwan and Jane Pollard (2001) 'Globalisation from below: Birmingham – post-colonial workshop of the world', *Transnational Communities Programme*, WPTC-2K-08, London: ESRC (http://www.transcomm.ox.ac.uk/working_papers.htm).

Hernandez, Ramona (2002) *The Mobility of Workers Under Advanced Capitalism: Dominican Migration to the United States*, New York: Columbia University Press.

Hilmann, Felicitas (2000) 'Are ethnic economies the revolving doors of the urban labour markets in transition', Paper presented to the Conference on 'The Economic Embeddedness of Immigrant Enterprise', Jerusalem, 18–20 June.

—— (1999) 'A Look at the "Hidden Side": Turkish Women in Berlin's Ethnic Labour Market', *International Journal of Urban and Regional Research*, Vol. 23, No. 2, pp. 267–282.

—— and Hedwig Rudolph (1997) *Redistributing the Cake – Processes of Ethnicisatiion in the Food Sector of Berlin*, WZB-Discussion Paper 97-101, Berlin.

Holzer, Harry J. (1991) 'The Spatial Mismatch Hypothesis: What Has the Evidence Shown?', *Urban Studies*, Vol. 28, No. 1, pp. 105–122.

Hondagneu-Sotelo, Pierrette (2001) *Domestica: Immigrant Workers Cleaning and Caring in the Shadows of Affluence*, Berkeley, CA: University of California Press.

Hood, Marlowe (1998) 'Fuzhou', in Lynn Pan (ed.) *The Encyclopedia of the Chinese Overseas*, Richmond, Surrey: Curzon Press, pp. 33–35, 268.

Hoogvelt, Ankie (1997) 'From Fordist to Flexible Production', in Ankie Hoogvelt (ed.) *Globalisation and the Post-colonial World: the New Political Economy of Development*, London: Macmillan, pp. 92–113.

Horton, John (1995) *The Politics of Diversity*, Philadelphia: Temple University.

Howe, Irving (1976) *The Imigrant Jews of New York*, London: Routledge.

Hughes, Donna M. (2000) 'The "Natasha" Trade – The Transnational Shadow Market of Trafficking in Women', *Journal of International Affairs*, Spring (www.uri.edu/artsci/wms/hughes/).

Hum, Tarry (2001) 'Mapping Global Production in New York City: The Role of Sunset Park, Brooklyn's Immigrant Economy', Paper presented to the Conference on 'Public Policy: the Institutional Environment and Immigrant Business', Liverpool 17–19 June.

Human Rights Watch (2001) 'Hidden in the Home: Abuse of Domestic Workers with Special Visas in the United States', Vol 13, No. 2 (www.hrw.org/reports/usadom/).

Husbands, Chris (1994) 'Crises of National Identity as the "New Moral Panics": Political Agenda Setting about Definitions of Nationhood', *New Community*, No. 20, pp. 191–206.

Institute for Migration and Ethnic Studies (1998) *Immigrant Businesses in Manufacturing: The Case of Turkish Businesses in the Amsterdam Garment Industry*, Amsterdam: University of Amsterdam.

International Organisation for Migration (2003) *Managing Migration – Challenges and Response*, IOM: Blackwell Publishing.

James, C. L. R. (1980) *Toussaint Louverture amd the San Domingo Revolution*, London: Alison and Busby.

Jenkins, Richard (1984) 'Ethnic Minorities in Business: A Research Agenda', in Robin Ward and Richard Jenkins (eds) *Ethnic Communities in Business: Strategies for Economic Survival*, Cambridge: Cambridge University Press, pp. 231–238.

Jiang, Joseph (1968) 'Towards a Theory of Pariah Entrepreneurship', in Gehem Wijeyewardene (ed.) *Leadership and Authority: A Symposium*, Singapore: University of Malaya Press, pp.147–162.

Johnson, Jo (2004) 'Nearly 2m French people live in ghettos, says report', *Financial Times*, 6 July.

Jones, Trevor (1993) *Britain's Ethnic Minorities*, London: Policy Studies Institute.

Jordi, Jean-Jaques (2003) 'The Creation of the Pieds-Noirs: Arrival and Settlement in Marseilles, 1962', in A. Smith (ed.) *Europe's Invisible Migrants*, Amsterdam: Amsterdam University Press, pp. 61–74.

Josephides, Sasha (1988) 'Honour, Family, and Work: Greek Cypriot Women Before and After Migration', in Sally Westwood and Parminder Bhachu (eds) *Enterprising Women: Ethnicity, Economy and Gender Relations*, London: Routledge, pp. 34–57.

—— (1987) 'Associations amongst the Greek Cypriot Population in Britain', in John Rex, Daniele Joly and Wilpert Czarina (eds) *Immigrant Associations in Europe*, Aldershot: Gower, pp. 42–62.

Kabeer, Naila (2000) *The Power to Choose: Bangladeshi Women and Labour Market Decisions in London and Dhaka*, London: Verso.

Kashem, Noushad (2001) 'More Bangladeshis Are Owning Taxis Today', *Weekly Thikana*, 17 August (translated for the *Gotham Gazette*).

Kerner Commission (1968) *Report of the National Advisory Commission on Civil Disorders*, New York: E. P. Dutton.

Kershen, J. Anne (ed.) (1990) *London: the Promised Land? The Migrant Experience in a Capital City*, Aldershot: Avebury.

Kindleberger, Charles (1967) *Europe's Post-War Growth. The Role of Labour Supply*, New York: Harvard University Press.

King, Desmond (2000) *Making Americans. Immigration, Race and the Origins of the Diverse Democracy*, Cambridge MA: Harvard University Press.

Kloosterman, Robert (2000) 'Immigrant Entrepreneurship and the Institutional Context: A Theoretical Exploration', in Jan Rath (ed.) *Immigrant Businesses. The Economic, Political and Social Environment*, Houndmills: Macmillan, pp. 90–106.

—— (1996) 'Mixed Experiences: Post Industrial Transition and Ethnic Minorities on the Amsterdam Labour market', *New Community*, Vol. 22, No. 4, pp. 637–653.

—— and Jan Rath (eds) (2003) *Immigrant Entrepreneurs: Venturing Abroad in the Age of Globalisation*, Oxford: Berg.

—— and Jan Rath (2003) 'The Netherlands: A Dutch Treat', in Robert Klooster-man and Jan Rath (eds) *Immigrant Entrepreneurs. Venturing Abroad in the Age of Globalisation*, Oxford: Berg, pp. 123–146.

—— and Jan Rath (2002) 'Working on the Fringes. Immigrant Businesses, Economic Integration and Informal Practices', in *Marginalisering eller Integration*, Stockholm: NUTEK, pp. 177–188.

—— and Jan Rath (2001) 'Immigrant Entrepreneurs in advanced economies: mixed embeddedness further explored', *Journal of Ethnic and Migration Studies*, Vol. 27, No. 2, pp. 189–202.

—— Joanne van der Leun and Jan Rath (1999) 'Mixed Embeddedness: (In)formal Economic Activities and Immigrant Businesses in the Netherlands', *International Journal of Urban and Regional Research*, Vol. 23, No. 2, pp. 252–266.

Kuper, Adam (1973) *Anthropologists and Anthropology: The British School 1922–1972*, London: Penguin.

Kwong, Peter (1998) *Forbidden Workers: Illegal Chinese Immigrants and American Labor*, New York: New Press.

—— (1997) 'Manufacturing Ethnicity', *Critique of Anthropology*, Vol. 17, No. 4, pp. 365–387.

Ladbury, Sarah (1984) 'Choice, Change or no Alternative: Turkish Cypriots in Business in London', in Robin Ward and Richard Jenkins (eds) *Ethnic Communities in Business: Strategies for Economic Survival*, Cambridge: Cambridge University Press, pp. 105–125.

—— (1979) Turkish Cypriots in London: Economy, Society, Culture and Change. Unpublished Ph.D. thesis, London: School of Oriental and African Studies.

Lai, L. Mark (1998) 'The United States', in Lynn Pan (ed.) *The Encyclopedia of the Chinese Overseas*, Richmond, Surrey: Curzon Press, pp. 261–273.

Lankevich, George (1998) *American Metropolis A History of New York City*, New York: New York University Press.

Lam, Jabez (2000) 'They are treating us like criminals', *Socialist Worker*, 1 July 2000.

Lapper, Richard (2004) 'Workers throw a lifeline. Migrant earnings are now a leading source of foreign exchange', *Financial Times*, 29 March.

Lawrence, Felicity (2005) 'The precarious existence of the thousands in Britain's underclass', *Guardian*, 10 January.

Lee, Dong (1992) 'Commodification of Ethnicity. The Sociospatial Reproduction of Immigrant Entrepreneurs', *Urban Affairs Quarterly*, Vol. 28, No. 2, pp. 258–275.

Leon, Abram (1946) *The Jewish Question. A Marxist Interpretation*, Mexico City: Ediciones Pioneres (www.marxsist.de/religion/leon/index.htm).

Levi-Strauss, Claude (1967), *The Scope of Anthropology*, Inaugural Lecture, Chair of Social Anthropology, College de France, 5 January 1960. London: Jonathan Cape.

Lewis, W. Arthur (1954) 'Economic Development with Unlimited Supplies of Labour', *Manchester School*, Vol. 22 (May), pp. 139–191.

Light, Ivan (2000a) 'Globalisation and Migration Networks', in Jan Rath (ed.) *Immigrant Businesses. The Economic, Political and Social Environment*, Hound-mills: Macmillan, pp. 162–181.

—— (2000b) 'Immigrants in Real Estate Development and Promotion in Los Angeles, 1970–2000', Paper presented to the Conference on 'The Economic Embeddedness of Immigrant Enterprise', Jerusalem, 18–20 June.

—— (1982) 'Immigrant and Ethnic Minority Enterprise in North America', Paper presented at the 10th World Congress of the International Sociological Association, Mexico City, August, pp. 1–33.

—— (1972) *Ethnic Enterprise in America: Business and Welfare among Chinese, Japanese and Blacks*, Berkeley, CA: University of California Press.

Light, Ivan and Parminder Bhachu (1993) *Immigrations and Entrepreneurship: Culture, Capital and Ethnic Networks*, New Brunswick: Transaction Publishers.

—— and Edna Bonacich (1988) *Immigrant Entrepreneurs: Koreans in Los Angeles 1965–1982*, Berkeley: University of California Press.

—— and Steven J. Gold (2000) *Ethnic Economies*, San Diego: California Academic Press.

—— and Stavros Karageorgis (1994) 'The Ethnic Economy', in Neil Smelser and Richard Swedbergh (eds) *The Handbook of Economic Sociology*, New York: Princeton University Press, pp. 647–671.

—— and Victoria D. Ojeda (2002) 'Los Angeles: Wearing out Their Welcome', in Jan Rath (ed.) *Unravelling the Rag Trade: Immigrant Enterpreneurship in Seven World Cities*, Oxford: Berg Publishers, pp. 135–150.

—— and Elizabeth Roach (1996) 'Self-Employment: Mobility Ladder or Economic Lifeboat?', in Roger Waldinger and Mehdi Bozorgmehr (eds) *Ethnic Los Angeles*, New York: Russell Sage Foundation, pp. 193–214.

—— and Carolyn Rosenstein (1995) 'Expanding the Interaction Theory of Entrepreneurship', in Alejandro Portes, (ed.) *The Economic Sociology of Immigration: Essays on Networks, Ethnicity and Entrepreneurship*, New York: Russell Sage Foundation, pp. 166–212.

—— Richard Bernard and Rebecca Kim (1999) 'Immigrant Incorporation in the Garment Industry of Los Angeles', *International Labour Review*, Vol. xxxiii, No. 1, pp. 5–25.

—— Georges Sabach, Mehdi Bozorgmehr and Claudia Der-Martirosian (1994) 'Beyond the Ethnic Enclave Economy', *Social Problems*, Vol. 41, No. 1, pp. 65–80.

Lloyd, John (2002) 'No to immigration: how rightwing populism entered the mainstream', *Financial Times*, 28 November.

Locher-Scholten, Elsbeth (2003) 'From Urn to Monument: Dutch Memories of World War Two in the Pacific', in Andrea Smith (ed.) *Europe's Invisible Migrants*, Amsterdam: Amsterdam University Press, pp. 105–128.

London Skills Forecasting Unit (2001) *Ethnic Capital Shaping London's Local Economies*, London: European Community Social Fund (www.abi.co.uk/reports.htm).

—— (1999) *Strength Through Diversity: Ethnic Minorities in London's Economy*, London: European Social Fund (www.Londoncentrallsc.gov.uk/).

Luu, M. (1997) 'French-speaking refugees and the foundation of the London silk industry in the sixteenth century', *Proceedings of Huguenot Society*, Vol. 26, No. 564–576.

McCracken, Grant (1988) *Culture and Consumption: New Approaches to the Symbolic Character of Consumer Goods and Activities*, Blomingtonn, IN: Indiana University Press.

MacGaffey, Janet and Bazenguissa-Ganga, Remy (2000) *Congo-Paris. Transnational Traders on the Margins of the Law*, Oxford: James Currey.

Magatti, Mauro and Fabio Quassoli (2003) 'Italy: Between Legal Barriers and Informal Arrangements', in Robert Kloosterman and Jan Rath (eds) *Immigrant Entrepreneurs. Venturing Abroad in the Age of Globalisation*, Oxford: Berg, pp. 147–172.

—— (2000) 'The Italian case: Socio-economic characteristics of immigrant businesses in Italy', Paper presented to the Conference on 'The Economic Embeddedness of Immigrant Enterprise', Jerusalem, 18–20 June.

Mahler, Sarah (1995) *The Dysfunctions of Transnationalism*, Russel Sage Foundation, Working Paper No. 73.

Manco, Ural (2004) *Turks in Western Europe*, Centrum vor Islam in Europe: University of Ghent.

Marable, Manning (1993) 'Beyond Racial Identity Politics', *Race and Class*, Vol. 35, No. 1, pp. 113–130.

Martin, P. L. (1994) 'Good Intentions Gone Awry – IRCA and United States Agriculture', *Annals of the American Academy of Political and Social Science*, Vol. 534, pp. 44–57.

Marx, Karl (1975) *Theories of Surplus Value, Part 1*, London: Lawrence and Wishart.

—— (1970) *Capital*, Vol. 1, London: Lawrence and Wishart.

Mavrou, Vasilis (1994) *Patronage, Ethnicity, and the Secondary Economy*, unpublished Ph.D. thesis, London: City University.

Meng, Shui, N. (1998) 'Laos', in Lynn Pan (ed.) *The Encyclopedia of the Chinese Overseas*, Richmond, Surrey: Curzon Press, pp. 169–171.

Min, Pyong Gap (1996) *Caught in the Middle. Korean Communities in New York and Los Angeles*, Berkeley, LA: University of California Press.

—— and Mehdi Bozorgmehr (2000) 'Immigrant Entrepreneurship and Business Patterns: A Comparison of Koreans and Iranians in Los Angeles', *International Migration Review*, Vol. 34, No. 3, pp. 707–738.

Mitter, Swasti (1986) 'Industrial Restructuring and Manufacturing Homework: Immigrant Women in the UK Clothing Industry', *Capital and Class*, No. 27, pp. 37–80.

Model, Suzanne (1992) 'The Ethnic Economy: Cubans and Chinese Considered', *Sociological Quarterly*, Vol. 3, pp. 63–82.

—— and David Lapido (1996) 'Context and Opportunity: Minorities in London and New York', *Social Forces*, Vol. 75, No. 2, pp. 485–510.

Mohann, Giles (2002) 'Diaspora and development', in Jenny Robinson (ed.) *Development and Displacement*, Open University: Oxford University Press, pp. 77–140.

Molyva, Demetra (2005) 'Seven Cypriots in new top 1,000 of Britains's rich', *Cyprus Weekly*, 8 April.

Morokvasic, Mirjana, Roger Waldinger and Annie Phizacklea (1990) 'Business on the Ragged Edge: Immigrant and Minority Business in the Garment Industries of Paris, London and New York', in R. Waldinger, H. Aldrich, R. Ward and J. Blaschke (eds) *Ethnic Entrepreneurs: Immigrant Business in Industrial Societies*, London: Sage Publications, pp. 157–176.

Moules, Jonathan (2005) 'With no expense spared, Asian weddings prove costly affairs', *Financial Times*, 15 January.

Mung, Emmanuel Ma and Thomas Lacroix (2003) 'France: The Narrow Path', in Robert Kloosterman and Jan Rath (eds) *Immigrant Entrepreneurs. Venturing Abroad in the Age of Globalisation*, Oxford: Berg, pp. 173–194.

—— (2000) 'Context and "Economic Arrangements" of Immigrant Enterprises', Paper presented to the Conference on 'The Economic Embeddedness of Immigrant Enterprise', Jerusalem, 18–20 June.

National Migration Forum (2002) 'Immigrants in the Crosshairs: The Quiet Backlash Against America's Immigrants and Refugees', *Backrounder*, 16 December, Washington, DC.

National Statistics Online (2004a) available at: www.statistics.gov.uk/census2001/profiles/commentaries/ethnicity.

—— (2004b) available at: www.statistics.gov.uk/census2001/profiles/commentaries/london.

Neale, Jonathan (2004) *What's Wrong With America? How the Rich and Powerful Have Changed America and Now Want to Change the World*, London: Vision Paperbacks.

Nearchou, Vickie (1960) 'The Assimilation of the Cypriot Community in London', Unpublished M.A. thesis, University of Nottingham.

Norman, Peter (1998) 'German jobs crisis hits Turks harder', *Financial Times*, 13 February.

Nutter, Steve (1997) 'The Structure and Growth of the Los Angeles Garment Industry', in Andrew Ross (ed.) *No Sweat: Fashion, Free Trade and the Rights of Garment Workers*, New York: Verso, pp. 113–122.

Oakley, Robin (1972) *Cypriot Migration and Settlement in Britain*, unpublished D. Phil. thesis, Oxford University.

OECD (2003) *Development Co-operation Report*, Paris: Organisation for Economic Co-operation and Development.

—— (1998) *Immigrants, Immigration and Cities: Exploring the Links*, Paris: Organisation for Economic Co-operation and Development.

Ong, Paul, Edna Bonacich and Lucie Cheng (1994) 'The Political Economy of Capitalist Restructuring and the New Asian Migration', in P. Ong, E. Bonacich and L. Cheng (eds) *The New Asian Immigration in Los Angeles and Global Restructuring*, Philadelphia: Temple University Press, pp. 3–38.

Owen, David (1997) 'Labour Force Participation Rates, Self-employment and Unemployment', in Valerie Karn (ed.) *Ethnicity in the 1991 Census*, London: HMSO, pp. 29–66.

Pai, Hsiao-Hung (2004) 'Inside the grim world of the gangmasters', *Guardian*, Special Report, 27 March.

Panayiotopoulos, Prodromos (2005) 'A study in the globalisation of care for the elderly: Filipina domestic workers in Cyprus', *Capital and Class*, May, No. 116, pp. 99–133.

—— (2004) Amsterdam, personal observation, 11–25 July.

—— (2004) Sentier, personal observation, 3 January.

—— (2003/2004) Champs-Elysees/Sevran Beaudottes, personal observation, 31 December/1 January.

—— (2003) Barcelona and Madrid, personal observation, 12–25 April.

—— (2002) 'Anthropology Consultancy in the UK and Community Development

246   *Bibliography*

in the Third World: a Difficult Dialogue', *Development in Practice*, Vol. 12, No. 1, pp. 45–59.

—— (2001a) 'Globalisation and Immigrant Enterprise', in Prodromos Panayiotopoulos and Gavin Capps (eds) *World Development*, London: Pluto Press, pp. 98–113.

—— (2001b) 'The Global Textile Industry: An Engendered Protectionism', in Prodromos Panayiotopoulos and Gavin Capps (eds) *World Development*, London: Pluto Press, pp. 192–207.

—— (2001c) 'The Emergent Post-Colonial State in Cyprus', from *Praktika tou Diethnous Kyprologikou Synethriou* (Proceedings of the Third International Congress on Cypriot Studies, held in Nicosia 16–20 April 1996, Vol. 3), Nicosia: Imprinta, pp. 583–608.

—— (2000a) Venice, personal obervation, 12–25 May.

—— (2000b) 'The Labour Regime Under Conditions of Globalisation in the Cypriot Garment Industy', *Journal of Southern Europe and the Balkans*, Vol. 2, No. 1, pp. 75–88.

—— (1999) 'The Emergent Post-Colonial State in Cyprus', *Commonwealth & Comparative Politics*, Vol. 37, No. 1, 31–55.

—— (1997) 'Small enterprise Development: "making it work" and "making sense"', *Brainstorm Magazine*, Deutsche Gesellschaft fur Technische Zusammenarbeit, January No. 1, pp. 3–11 (www.gtz.de/cefe).

—— (1996a) 'Challenging Orthodoxies: Cypriot Entrepreneurs in the London Garment Industry', *Journal of Ethnic and Migration Studies*, Vol. 22, No. 3, pp. 437–460.

—— (1996b) 'The State and Enterprise in the Cypriot Clothing Industry Under Conditions of Globalisation', *Cyprus Journal of Economics*, Vol. 9, No. 1, pp. 5–29.

—— (1994) 'Cypriot Entrepreneurs in the Clothing Industry. North London and Cyprus: A Comparative Analysis', Ph.D. thesis, Centre For Development Studies, University of Wales, Swansea, U.K.

—— (1992) 'Local Government Economic Initiatives. Planning, Choice and Politics: The London Experience', Papers in International Development, No. 7. Swansea: Centre for Development Studies.

—— (1990) 'Cypriot Entrepreneurs in the North London Clothing Industry: A Colonial Legacy', in the Proceedings of the *First International Symposium on Cypriot Migration: A Historical and Sociological Perspective*, Nicosia: Social Science Research Centre, pp. 285–331.

—— (1984) *Labour migration: Alentejo and the Greater Lisbon Region* (unpublished undergraduate thesis), Centre for Development Studies: Swansea.

Panayiotopoulos, Prodromos and Gavin Capps (2001) 'Globalisation in the Millennium', in Prodromos Panayiotopoulos and Gavin Capps (eds) *World Development*, London: Pluto Press, pp. 53–63.

—— and Marja Dreef (2002) 'London: Economic Differentiation and Policymaking', in Jan Rath (ed.) *Unravelling the Rag Trade: Immigrant Enterpreneurship in Seven World Cities*, Oxford: Berg Publishers, pp. 49–73.

Pang, Ching Li, (2003) 'Belgium: From Proletarians to Proteans', in Robert Kloosterman and Jan Rath (eds) *Immigrant Entrepreneurs. Venturing Abroad in the Age of Globalisation*, Oxford: Berg, pp. 195–212.

—— (2000) 'The Economic Embeddedness of Immigrant Businesses: The Case of

Belgium', Paper presented to the Conference on 'The Economic Embeddedness of Immigrant Enterprise', Jerusalem, 18–20 June.

Parkes, Christopher (2002a) 'Anti-terror legislation programme in US runs into controversy', *Financial Times*, 20 December.

—— (2002b) 'Little change in Los Angeles tinder-box', *Financial Times*, 30 April.

—— (1999) 'Californians urged to raise a cheer for Asian immigrants', *Financial Times*, 3 July.

—— (1998) 'Something stirring in the melting pot', *Financial Times*, 7 June.

Parsons, Talcott (1952) *The Social System*, London: Tavistock.

—— and Neilson Smelser (1957) *Economy and Society: A study in the Integration of Economic and Social Theory*, London: Routledge.

Pavlova, Natasha (New York City's Mayor's Office) (2001) 'Immigrants and the Economic Revitalisation of New York City', Paper presented to the Conference on 'Public Policy: the Institutional Environment and Immigrant Business', Liverpool 17–19 June.

Pecoud, Antoine (2001) 'Weltoffenheit schafft Jobs: Turkish Entrepreneurship and Multiculturalism in Berlin', *Transnational Communities Programme*, WPTC-01-09, London: ESRC (www.transcomm.ox.ac.uk/working_papers.htm).

Penninx, Rinus, Jeannette Schoorl and Carlo van Praag (1993) *The Impact of International Migration on Receiving Countries: The Case of the Netherlands*, Amsterdam: Swets and Zeitlinger.

Pennsylvania Crime Commission (1991) *Organised Crime in Philadelphia – A Decade of Change Report*, Conshohocken, PA: Pennsylvania Crime Commission.

Perlmann, J. and R. Waldinger (1997) 'Second Generation Decline? Children of Immigrants, Past and Present a Reconsideration', *International Migration Review*, Vol. 31, No. 4, pp. 893–922.

Petras, Elizabeth M. (1992) 'The Shirt on Your Back: Immigrant Workers and the Reorganisation of the Garment Industry', *Social Justice*, Vol. 19, No. 1, pp. 76–114.

Phizacklea, Annie (1990) *Unpacking the Fashion Industry*, London: Routledge.

—— (1988) 'Entrepreneurship, Ethnicity, and Gender', in Sally Westwood and Parmindar Bhachu (eds) *Enterprising Women: Ethnicity, Economy and Gender Relations*, London: Routledge, pp. 20–34.

Pieke, Frank N. (2002) *Recent Trends in Chinese Migration to Europe: Fujianese Migration in Perspective*, Geneva: International Organisation for Migration.

—— (1999) 'The Netherlands', in Lynn Pan (ed.) *The Encyclopedia of the Chinese Overseas*, Richmond, Surrey: Curzon Press, pp. 322–327.

—— (1998) 'Introduction', in G. Benton and F. Pieke (eds) *The Chinese in Europe*, Houndmills, Basingstoke: Macmillan Press, pp. 1–17.

—— and Gregor Benton (1998) 'The Chinese in the Netherlands', in G. Benton and F. Pieke (eds) *The Chinese in Europe*, Houndmills, Basingstoke: Macmillan Press, pp. 125–167.

Portes, Alejandro (1997) 'Globalisation from Below: The Rise of Transnational Communities', ESRC Transnational Communities Project, Working Paper WPTC-98-01 (www.transcomm.ox.ac.uk/workingpapers_htm).

—— (1996) 'Globalisation from Below: The Rise of Transnational Communities', in W. Smith and W. Korczenwicz (eds) *Latin America in the World Economy*, Westport: Greenwood Press, pp. 151–168.

—— (1995a) 'Economic Sociology and the Sociology of Immigration: A Conceptual Overview', in Alejandro Portes (ed.) *The Economic Sociology of Immigration: Essays on Networks, Ethnicity and Entrepreneurship*, New York: Russell Sage Foundation, pp. 1–41.

—— (1995b) 'Children of Immigrants: Segmented Assimilation and Its Determinants', in Alejandro Portes (ed.) *The Economic Sociology of Immigration: Essays on Networks, Ethnicity and Entrepreneurship*, New York: Russell Sage Foundation, pp. 248–280.

—— (1994) 'The Informal Economy and its Paradoxes', in Neil Smelser and Richard Swedbergh (eds) *The Handbook of Economic Sociology*, New York: Princeton University Press, pp. 426–449.

—— (1984) 'The Rise of Ethnicity: Perceptions Among Cuban Exiles in Miami', *American Sociological Review*, Vol. 49, pp. 383–412.

—— (1981) 'Modes of Structural Incorporation and Present Theories of Immigration', in M. Kritz, C. Keely and S. Tomasi (eds) *Global Trends in Migration*, New York: CMS Press, pp. 279–297.

—— and Robert Bach (1985) *Latin Journey: Cuban and Mexican Immigrants in the United States*, Berkeley: University of California Press.

—— and Leif Jensen (1989) 'The Enclave and the Entrants: Patterns of Ethnic Enterprise in Miami Before and After Mariel', *American Sociological Review*, Vol. 54, pp. 929–949.

—— and Leif Jensen (1987) 'What's an Ethnic Enclave? The Case for Conceptual Clarity', *American Sociological Review*, Vol. 52, pp. 768–771.

—— and Patricia Landolt (1996) The Downside of Social Capital', *The American Prospect*, No. 26. May–June (www.prospect.org/authors/portes-a.html).

—— and D. MacLeod (1996) 'What Shall I Call Myself? Hispanic Identity Formation in the Second Generation', *Ethnic and Racial Studies*, Vol. 19, No. 3, pp. 523–547.

—— and Min Zhou (1996) 'Self-employment and the Earnings of Immigrants', *American Sociological Review*, Vol. 61, No. 2, pp. 219–230.

—— and Min Zhou (1993) 'The New Second-Generation: Segmented Assimilation and its Variants among Post-1965 Immigrant Youth', *Annals of the American Academy of Politics and Social Science*, No. 530, pp. 74–96.

—— and Ruben G. Rumbaut (2001) *Legacies: The Story of the Immigrant Second Generation*, Berkeley: University of California Press.

—— and Sensenbrenner, Julia (1993) 'Embeddedness and Immigration: Notes on the Social Determinants of Economic Action', *American Journal of Sociology*, Vol. 98, No. 6, pp. 1320–1350.

—— and Alex Stepick (1993) *City on the Edge. The Transformation of Miami*, Berkeley: University of California Press.

—— and Alex Stepick (1985) 'Unwelcome Immigrants: The Labour Market Experiences of 1980 (Mariel) Cuban and Haitian Refugees in South Florida', *American Sociological Review*, Vol. 50, pp. 493–514.

—— Manuel Castells and Lauren Benton (eds) (1989) *The Informal Economy: Studies in Advanced and Less Developed Countries*, London: Johns Hopkins Press.

—— William Haller and Luis Guarnizo (2001) 'Transnational Entrepreneurs: The Emergence and Determinants of an Alternative form of Immigrant Economic Adaptation', *Transnational Communities Programme*, WPTC-01-05. London: ESRC (www.transcomm.ox.ac.uk/working_papers.htm).

Poulantzas, Nicos (1975) *Classes in Contemporary Capitalism*, London: New Left Books.

Poutziouris, Panikkos (1999) 'The development of ethnic family business ventures: lessons for the "breaking-out" strategies of Anglo-Cypriots', Paper delivered to 'The Conference on Cypriot Society in the Millennium', held at the University of Greenwich, 4–5 December.

—— (1998) 'The Growth and Control Dilemma in the Family Business: The Taramasolada Kings. Business Development Centre: Manchester Business School, UK.

Proper, Carl (1997) 'New York: Defending the Union Contract', in Andrew Ross (ed.) *No Sweat: Fashion, Free Trade and the Rights of Garment Workers*, New York: Verso, pp. 113–122.

Putnam, Robert (1993) *Making Democracy Work: Civic Traditions in Modern Italy*, Princeton, NJ: Princeton University Press.

—— (1993) 'The Prosperous Community: Social Capital and Public Life', *The American Prospect*, No. 3 (www.prospect.org/authors/putnam-r.html).

Quassoli, Fabio (1999) 'Migrants in the Italian Underground Economy', *International Journal of Urban and Regional Research*, Vol. 23, No. 2, pp. 212–231.

Raes, Stephen (2000a) *Migrating Enterprise and Migrant Entrepreneurship: How Fashion and Migration Have Changed the Spatial Organisation of Clothing Supply in the Netherlands*, Amsterdam: Het Spinhuis Publishers.

—— (2000b) 'Regionalisation in a Globalising World: The Emergence of Clothing Sweatshops in the European Union', in J. Rath (ed.) *Immigrant Businesses. The Economic, Political and Social Environment*, Houndmills: Macmillan, pp. 20–37.

—— Jan Rath, Marja Dreef, Adem Kumcu, Flavia Reil and Aslan Zorlu (2002) 'Amsterdam: Stitched Up', in Jan Rath (ed.) *Unravelling the Rag Trade: Immigrant Entrepreneurship in Seven World Cities*, Oxford: Berg Publishers, pp. 89–111.

Rainnie, Al (1989) *Industrial Relations in Small Firms: Small isn't Beautiful*, London: Routledge.

Ram, Monder (2002) *Access to Finance and Business Support by Ethnic Minority Firms in the UK*, London: British Bankers Association.

—— (1993) 'Workplace Relations in Ethnic Minority Firms – Asians in the West Midlands Clothing Industry', *New Community*, Vol. 19, No. 4, pp. 567–580.

—— and David Deakins (1998) 'Enterprise Support and Ethnic Minority Firms', *Journal of Ethnic and Minority Studies*, Vol. 24, No. 1, pp. 143–158.

—— and Trevor Jones (1998) *Ethnic Minorities in Business*, Milton Keynes: Small Business Research Trust, Open University Business School.

—— and David Smallbone (2001) *Ethnic Minority Enterprise: Policy in Practice*, London: Small Business Service (www.abi.co.uk/reports.htm).

—— Bob Jerrard and Joy Husband (2002) 'West Midlands: Still Managing to Survive', in Jan Rath (ed.) *Unravelling the Rag Trade: Immigrant Entrepreneurship in Seven World Cities*, Oxford: Berg Publishers, pp. 73–87.

—— Tahir Abbas, Balihar Sanghera, Gerald Barlow and Tevor Jones (2001) '"Apprentice Entrepreneurs"? Ethnic Minority Workers in the Independent Restaurant Sector', *Work, Employment and Society*, Vol. 15, No. 2, pp. 353–372.

Rath, Jan (2002a) (ed.) *Unravelling the Rag Trade: Immigrant Entrepreneurship in Seven World Cities*, Oxford: Berg Publishers (www.users.fgm.uva.nl/jrath/download.htm).

—— (2002b) 'Needle Games: A Discussion of Mixed Embeddedness', in Jan Rath (ed.) *Unravelling the Rag Trade: Immigrant Entrepreneurship in Seven World Cities*, Oxford: Berg Publishers, pp. 1–27.

—— (2002c) 'Sewing up Seven Cities', in Jan Rath (ed.) *Unravelling the Rag Trade: Immigrant Entrepreneurship in Seven World Cities*, Oxford: Berg Publishers, pp. 169–191.

—— (2001) 'A Game of Ethnic Musical Chairs? Immigrant Businesses and the Formation and Succession of Niches in the Amsterdam economy', in S. Body-Gendrot and M. Martiniello (eds) *Minorities in European Cities. The Dynamics of Social Integration and Social Exclusion at the Neighbourhood Level*, Basingstoke: Macmillan Press, pp. 26–43.

—— (2000a) (ed.) *Immigrant Businesses. The Economic, Political and Social Environment*, Houndmills: Macmillan.

—— (2000b) 'Introduction', in Jan Rath (ed.) *Immigrant Businesses. The Economic, Political and Social Environment*, Houndmills: Macmillan, pp. 1–19.

—— and Robert Kloosterman (2000) 'Outsiders' Business: A Critical Review of Research on Immigrant Entrepreneurship in the Netherlands', *International Migration Review*, Vol. xxxiv, No. 3, pp. 657–681.

Rekers, Ans and Ronald van Kempen (2000) 'Location Matters: Entrepreneurs and the Spatial Context', in J. Rath (ed.) *Unravelling the Rag Trade: Immigrant Entrepreneurship in Seven World Cities*, Oxford: Berg Publishers, pp. 54–69.

Rex, John and Sasha Josephides (1987) 'Asian and Greek Cypriot Associations and Identity', in John Rex, Daniele Joly and Czarina Wilpert (eds) *Immigrant Associations in Europe*, Aldershot: Gower, pp. 11–41.

—— and Robert Moore (1967) *Race, Community and Conflict: A Study of Sparkbrook*, London: Oxford University Press.

Rhea, J. T. (1997) *Race, Pride and the American Identity*, Cambridge MA: Harvard University Press.

Rinder, Irwin (1959) 'Strangers in the Land: Social Relations in the Status Gap', *Social Problems*, Vol. 10, No. 6, pp. 340–354.

Roberts, Richard (2002) Head of SME Research, Barclays Bank, quoted from, *Financial Times*, 'Fair play and ethnic businesses', 26 September.

Robinson, Jenny (ed.) (2002) *Development and Displacement*, Open University: Oxford University Press.

—— (2002) 'Introduction', in Jenny Robinson (ed.) *Development and Displacement*, Open University: Oxford University Press, pp. 1–18.

Rosenbaum, Emily (1996) 'The Influence of Race on Hispanic Housing Choices: New York City, 1978–1987', *Urban Affairs Review*, Vol. 32, No. 2, pp. 217–243.

Ross, Andrew (1997) (ed.) *No Sweat: Fashion, Free Trade and the Rights of Garment Workers*, New York: Verso.

Rutherford, R. and Blackburn, R. (2000) 'The diversity of ethnic minority small firms: issues for business support providers', Paper presented at the 23rd National Small Firms Conference, Aberdeen, November.

Sabagh, Georges and Mehdi Bozorgmehr (1996) 'Population Change: Immigration and Ethnic Transformation', in R. Waldinger and Mehdi Bozorgmehr (eds) *Ethnic Los Angeles*, New York: Russell Sage Foundation, pp. 79–107.

Salt, John (2000) 'Trafficking and Human Smuggling: A European Perspective', *International Migration Quarterly Review. Special Issue: Perspectives on Trafficking of Migrants*, Vol. 38, Part 3, pp. 31–56.

—— and J. Stein (1997) 'Migration as Business: the Case of Trafficking', *International Migration Quarterly Review*, Vol. 35, No. 4, pp. 467–492.

Samuelson, A. (1948) 'International trade and the equalisation of factor prices', *Economic Journal*, No. 59, pp. 181–197.

Sanders, Jimy and Victor Nee (1996) 'Immigrant Self-Employment and the Value of Human Capital', *American Sociological Review*, Vol. 61, pp. 231–249.

—— (1992) 'Problems in Resolving the Enclave Economy Debate', *American Sociological Review*, Vol. 57, pp. 415–418.

—— (1987a) 'Limits of Ethnic Solidarity in the Enclave Economy', *American Sociological Review*, Vol. 52, pp. 745–773.

—— (1987b) 'On Testing the Enclave-Economy Hypothesis', *American Sociological Review*, Vol. 52, pp. 771–773.

Sassen, Saskia (2004) 'The migration fallacy', *Financial Times*, 27 December.

—— (1998) *Globalisation and its Discontents: Essays on the New Mobility of People and Money*, New York: New Press.

—— (1996) 'New Employment Regimes in the Cities: The Impact of Immigrant Workers', *New Community*, Vol. 22, No. 4, pp. 579–594.

—— (1995) 'Immigration and Local Labor Markets', in Alejandro Portes (ed.) *The Economic Sociology of Immigration: Essays on Networks, Ethnicity and Entrepreneurship*, New York: Russell Sage Foundation, pp. 87–127.

—— (1994) 'The Informal Economy. Between New Developments and Old Regulations,' *Yale Law Journal*, Vol. 103, No. 8, pp. 2289–2304.

—— (1991) *The Global City: New York, London, Tokyo*, Princeton, NJ: Princeton University Press.

—— (1988) 'New York's Informal Economy', ISSR Working Papers, Volume 4, No. 9.

Saxenian, Analee (1999) *Silicon Valley's New Imigrant Entrepreneurs*, Santa Barbara, CA: Public Policy Institute of California (www.ppic.org).

Schermenhom, R. A. (1970) *Comparative Ethnic Relations*, New York: Random House.

Schlesinger, A. M. Jnr (1992) *The Disuniting of America*, New York: W. W. Norton.

Schmiechen, James (1984) *Sweated Industries and Sweated Labor. The London Clothing Trades, 1860–1914*, London: Croom Helm.

Schonwalder, Karen (2004) 'Why Germany's Guestworkers were Largely Europeans: The Selective Principles of Post-war Labour Recruitment Policy', *Ethnic and Racial Studies*, Vol. 27, No. 2, pp. 248–265.

Scott, Allen J. (1996) 'The Manufacturing Economy: Ethnic and Gender Divisions of Labor', in Roger Waldinger and Mehdi Bozorgmehr (eds) *Ethnic Los Angeles*, New York: Russell Sage Foundation, pp. 215–246.

Scott, James C. (1985) *Weapons of the Weak: Everyday Forms of Peasant Resistance*, New Haven, CT: Yale University Press.

Seller, Maxine (1986) 'The Uprising of the Twenty Thousand: Sex, Class and Ethnicity in the Shirtwaist Strike of 1909', in D. Hoerder (ed.) *Struggle a Hard Battle: Essays on Working-Class Immigrants*, DeKalb, IL: Northern Illinois University Press.

Shaikh, Asima (1995) 'Industrial Restructuring, Informalisation and Casual Labour in the "East End" Clothing Industry', Working Paper No. 69, Development Planning Unit, University College London.

Simon, Gildas (1990) *Immigrant Entrepreneurs in France: A European Overview*, Institute of Social Science Research, Working Paper Series 9: University of Poitiers (translated by Jeffrey Arsham).

Simonian, Haig (2004) 'Swiss reject calls to ease rules on citizenship', *Financial Times*, 28 September.

Skeldon, Robert (2000) *Myths and Realities of Chinese Irregular Migration*, Geneva: International Organisation for Migration.

Smallbone, David, Monder Ram, David Deakins and Robert Baldock (2002) 'Assessing Finance and Business Support by Ethnic Minority Businesses in the UK', London: British Banker's Association (www.abi.co.uk/reports.htm).

Smith, Andrea (2003) (ed.) *Europes's Invisible Migrants*, Amsterdam: Amsterdam University Press.

Smith, Michael (1998) 'EU moves against black economy', *Financial Times*, 8 April.

Smith, Sharon (1994) 'Mistaken Identity', *International Socialism Journal*, No. 62, pp. 3–51.

Sorensen, E. and F. D. Bean (1994) 'Immigration Reform and Control Act and the Wages of Mexican Origin Workers – Evidence from Current Population Surveys', *Social Science Quarterly*, Vol. 75, No. 1, pp. 1–17.

Spielberg, Elinor (1997) 'The Myth of Nimble Fingers', in Andrew Ross (ed.) *No Sweat: Fashion, Free Trade and the Rights of Garment Workers*, New York: Verso, pp. 113–122.

Staring, Richard (2000) 'International Migration, Undocumented Immigrants and Immigrant Entrepreneurship', in Jan Rath (ed.) *Immigrant Businesses. The Economic, Political and Social Environment*, Houndmills: Macmillan, pp. 162–181.

Steadman, Gareth Jones (1976) *Outcast London: A Study in the Relationship between Classes in Victorian Society*, London: Peregrine.

Stepick, Alex (1989) 'Miami's Two Informal Sectors', in Alejandro Portes, Manuel Castells and Lauren Benton (eds) *The Informal Economy: Studies in Advanced and Less Developed Countries*, London: Johns Hopkins Press, pp. 111–134.

—— Guillermo Grennier, Max Castro and Marvin Dunn (2003) *This Land is Our Land: Immigrants and Power in Miami*, Berkeley, CA: University of California Press.

Steward, Margaret and Leslie Hunter (1964) *The Needle is Threaded. The History of an Industry*, London: Heinemann.

Storkey, Marian (1993) *Identifying the Cypriot Community from the 1991 Census*, London: London Research Centre.

—— and Rob Lewis (1997) 'London: A True Metropolis', in Peter Ratcliffe (ed.) *Ethnicity in the 1991 Census*, London: HMSO, pp. 210–225.

Stryker, S. (1959) 'Social Structure and Prejudice', *Social Problems*, Spring No. 6, pp. 340–354.

Tana, Li (1998) 'Vietnam', in Lynn Pan (ed.) *The Encyclopedia of the Chinese Overseas*, Richmond, Surrey: Curzon Press, pp. 228–233.

Tichenor, Daniel (2002) *Dividing Lines: The Politics of Immigration Controls in America*, Princeton and Oxford: Princeton University Press.

Tienda, Marta and Rebeca Raijman (2000) 'Immigrants' Pathways to Business Ownership: A Comparative Ethnic Perspective', *International Migration Review*, Vol. xxxiv, No. 3, pp. 682–706.

Tollenaere, Herman de (2004) 'Theo van Gogh: Hero, Anti-Semite, Misogynist or Islamophobe?', *What Next?*, No. 29, pp. 1–3 (www.whatnextjournal.co.uk).

Tomba, L. (1999) 'Exporting the "Wenzhou Model" to Beijing and Florence: Suggestions for a Comparative Perspective on Labour and Economic Organisation in Two Migrant Communities', in F. N. Pieke and H. Malleo (eds) *Internal and International Migration, Chinese Pespectives*, Richmond: Curzon, pp. 280–293.

—— (1996) 'Exporting the "Whenzhou Model" to Beijing and Florence: Ideas for a Comparative Perspective on Labour and Economic Organisation in Two Migrant Communities', Paper presented at the 'European Chinese Migrants' Workshop', Oxford, 3–5 July.

Trimikliniotis, Nicos (1999) 'Racism and New Migration to Cyprus: The Racialisation of Migrant Workers', in Floya Anthias and Gabriela Lazaridis (eds) *Into the Margins*, Aldershot: Ashgate, pp. 139–178.

Turkish Research Centre (2000) 'Turks in the European Union', April, Essen: Institut An Der Uinversitat GH Essen.

Turner, David (2005) 'Poor prospects and low wages at the bottom of the ladder', *Financial Times*, 20 January.

Turton, David (2002) 'Forced displacement and the nation-state', in Jenny Robinson (ed.) *Development and Displacement*, Open University: Oxford University Press, pp. 19–76.

UK Department of Employment (1976) *Immigrants in the Labour Market*, Unit of Manpower Studies Project Report, London: HMSO.

Uzzi, Brian (1996) 'The Sources and Consequences of Embeddedness for the Economic Performance of Organisations: the Network Effect', *American Sociological Review*, Vol. 61 pp. 674–698.

Waldinger, Roger (2001a) 'Conclusion. Immigration and the Remaking of Urban America', in R. Waldinger (ed.) *Strangers at the Gates: New immigrants in Urban America*, Berkeley: University of California Press, pp. 308–330 (www.sscnet.ucla.edu/soc/faculty/Waldinger).

—— (2001b) 'Up from Poverty? "Race", Immigration and the Fate of Low-Skilled Workers', in R. Waldinger (ed.) *Strangers at the Gates: New immigrants in Urban America*, Berkeley: University of California Press, pp. 80–116.

—— (2000) 'The Economic Theory of Ethnic Conflict: A Critique and Reformulation', in Jan Rath (ed.) *Immigrant Businesses. The Economic, Political and Social Environment*, Houndmills: Macmillan, pp. 124–141.

—— (1996a) 'Ethnicity and Opportunity in the Plural City', in Roger Waldinger and Mehdi Bozorgmehr (eds) *Ethnic Los Angeles*, New York: Russell Sage Foundation, pp. 445–470.

—— (1996b) *Still the Promised City? African-Americans and New Immigrants in Post-industrial New York*, Cambridge MA: Harvard University Press.

—— (1996c) 'From Ellis Island to LAX: Immigrant Prospects in the American City', *International Migration Review*, Vol. xxx, No. 4, pp. 1078–1086.

—— (1995) 'The "Other Side" of Embeddedness: A Case-study of the Interplay of Economy and Ethnicity', *Ethnic and Racial Studies*, Vol. 18, No. 3, pp. 555–580.

—— (1986) *Through the Eye of the Needle: Immigrants and Enterprise in New York's Garment Trades*, New York: New York University Press.

—— (1985) 'Immigration and Industrial Change in the New York City Apparel Industry', in Maria Tienda and George Borjas (eds) *Hispanic Workers in the United States*, Orlando: Academic Press, pp. 323–349.

—— (1984) 'Immigrant Enterprise in the New York Garment Industry', *Social Forces*, Vol. 32, No. 1, pp. 60–71.

254   *Bibliography*

—— and Mehdi Bozorgmehr (1996) (eds) *Ethnic Los Angeles*, New York: Russell Sage Foundation.

—— and Mehdi Bozorgmehr (1996) 'The Making of a Metropolitan Metropolis', in Roger Waldinger and Mehdi Bozorgmehr (eds) *Ethnic Los Angeles*, New York: Russell Sage Foundation, pp. 3–38.

—— and L. Feliciano (2004) 'Will the second generation experience "downward assimilation"? Segmented Assimilation Reassessed', *Ethnic and Racial Studies*, Vol. 27, No. 3, pp. 376–402.

—— and Michael Lapp (1993) 'Back to the Sweatshop or Ahead to the Informal Sector', *International Journal of Urban and Regional Research*, Vol. 17, No. 1, pp. 6–29.

—— and Jennifer Lee (2001) 'New Immigrants in Urban America', in R. Waldinger (ed.) *Strangers at the Gates: New Immigrants in Urban America*, Berkeley: University of California Press, pp. 30–79.

—— Robin Ward and Howard Aldrich (1985) 'Trend Report, Ethnic Businesses and Occupational Mobility in Advanced Societies', *Sociology*, Vol. 19, No. 4, pp. 586–597.

—— Howard Aldrich, Robin Ward and Jochen Blaschke (eds) (1990) *Ethnic Entrepreneurs: Immigrant Business in Industrial Societies*, London: Sage Publications.

Wallman, Sandra (1974) 'Status and the Innovator' in John Davis (ed.) *Essays in Honour of Lucy Maier*, London: Athlone Press, pp. 230–251.

Wassener, Bettina (2002) 'New laws spur on foreign voters', *Financial Times*, 13 September.

Watson, Robert, Kevin Keasy and Mae Baker (2000) 'Small Firm Financial Contracting and Immigrant Entrepreneurship', in Jan Rath (ed.) *Immigrant Businesses. The Economic, Political and Social Environment*, Houndmills: Macmillan, pp. 70–89.

Watts, Julie (2002) *Immmigration Policy and the Challenge of Globlisation: Unions and Employers in an Unlikely Alliance*, Ithaca: Cornell University Press.

Weber, Max (1968) *Economy and Society: An Outline of Interpretative Sociology*, Berkeley, CA: University of California Press.

—— (1958) 'The Protestant Sects and the Spirit of Capitalism', in H. Hans Gerth and C. W. Mills (eds) *From Max Weber*, New York: Oxford University Press, pp. 302–322.

Westwood, Sally and Parmindar Bhachu (eds) (1988) *Enterprising Women: Ethnicity, Economy and Gender Relations*, London: Routledge.

—— (1988) 'Introduction', in S. Westwood and P. Bhachu (eds) *Enterprising Women: Ethnicity, Economy and Gender Relations*, London: Routledge, pp. 1–20.

Willems, Wim (2003) 'No Sheltering Sky: Migrant Identities of Dutch Nationals from Indonesia', in Andrea Smith (ed.) *Europe's Invisible Migrants*, Amsterdam: Amsterdam University Press, pp. 33–59.

Wilpert, Czarina (2003) 'Germany: From Workers to Entrepreneurs', in Robert Kloosterman and Jan Rath (eds) *Immigrant Entrepreneurs. Venturing Abroad in the Age of Globalisation*, Oxford: Berg, pp. 233–260.

—— (1993) 'Ideological and Institutional Foundations of Racism in the Federal Republic of Germany', in John Wrench and John Solomos (eds) *Racism and Migration in Western Europe*, Oxford: Berg.

Wilson, Kenneth and Alejandro Portes (1980) 'Immigrant Enclaves: An Analysis of the Labour Market Experiences of Cubans in Miami', *American Journal of Sociology*, Vol. 86, pp. 295–319.

Wilson, William (1987) *The Truly Disadvantaged: The Inner Cities, the Underclass, and Public Policy*, Chicago: University of Chicago Press.

Wirth, Lewis (1938) 'Urbanism as a Way of Life', *American Sociological Review*, Vol. 44: pp. 1–24.

Wong, Aliza (1999) 'Italy', in Lynn Pan (ed.) *The Encyclopedia of the Chinese Overseas*, Richmond, Surrey: Curzon Press, pp. 319–321.

World Bank (1995) 'Workers in an Integrating World', Annual World Development Report. Washington, DC: Oxford University Press.

Wright, Erik Olin (1985) *Classes*, London: Verso.

—— (1978) *Class, Crisis and the State*, London: New Left Books.

Yeager, Jolly (2002) 'Chasing the Latino dollar', *Financial Times*, 23 August.

—— (2000) 'The Hispanic vote', *Financial Times*, 4 September.

Young, Gary (2003) '30% of black men in US will go to jail', *Guardian*, 19 August.

Yu-Sion, Live (1999) 'France', in Lynn Pan (ed.) *The Encyclopedia of the Chinese Overseas*, Richmond, Surrey: Curzon Press, pp. 311–317.

—— (1998) 'The Chinese Community in France: Immigration, Economic Activity, Cultural Organisation and Representations', in Gregor Benton and Frank N. Pieke (eds) *The Chinese in Europe*, Houndmills, Basingstoke: Macmillan Press, pp. 96–124.

Yun, Gao (2004) *Chinese Migrants and Forced Labour in Europe*, Working Paper No. 32, Geneva: International Labour Office.

Zhou, Min (1992) *Chinatown: The Socioeconomic Potential of an Urban Enclave*, Philadelphia: Temple University Press.

—— and John Logan (1989) 'Returns on Human Capital in Ethnic Enclaves: New York and Chinatown', *American Sociological Review*, Vol. 54, pp. 809–820.

Zhou, Yu (2002) 'New York: Caught under the Fashion Runway', in Jan Rath (ed.) *Unravelling the Rag Trade: Immigrant Entrepreneurship in Seven World Cities*, Oxford: Berg Publishers, pp. 113–133.

Index

African 38; continent 168; diaspora 14, 37; exclusion from West Germany 110; immigration to France 197; immigration to UK 143; shopkeepers in France 197; street-sellers in Italy 134; *see also* Congolese; Maghreb

African Americans 3, 36–7, 71, 72, 97, 253; entrepreneurs 19; entrepreneurs and under-representation 33, 115; *Kerner Commission* 241; Mexicans 'taking jobs' of 93, 108–9, 111, 20; migration and urban ghetto 35–6; migration to northern cities 37, 94; riots 34; as section of US working class 97–8; socio-economic indicators 93, 95; Watts 1965 35; working class and job losses 99, 111; working class in auto and steel 109; *see also* Black; Los Angeles; race

African-Caribbean entrepreneurs in UK 145, 239; banks and start-up capital 19; *see also* West Indian

ageing 19, 23, 204; and elderly care 125; of entrepreneurs 61; European working population 118; immigrant women 155; UK population 119; *see also* youth

agency 9–10, 16, 21–2, 184, 204; in entrepreneurship 21, 139; and immigration 12; *see also* structure

Aldrich, H. and A. Reiss 42

Algeria 185, 195; immigrants and Berber traders 196; immigrants to France 189; *see also* France

Americanisation 51; and Americanization 72, 86; as mainline assimilation 24; in South Central 97; Tammany Hall as a path 52; *see also* assimilation; New York

Amsterdam 164–82; and Chinatown 178; Chinese–Indonesian restaurants 164, 169, 175–8; in crisis 180; as early gateway city 164; Italian artisans 169; Moroccan *halal* butchers and bakers 167–70; recent entrants 169;

Surinamese 165–6; Surinamese in personal services 170; Turkish 166–7; Turkish and crisis 174; Turkish as butchers and restaurant owners 170; Turkish as contractors in garment industry 171–5, 180; Turkish in confectionaries 169; Turkish in employment 169; Turkish number of firms 173, *177*, 178; Turkish raids 165, 181–2; *see also* informal sector; Netherlands

Anomie, concept used by Wirth 32; and adaptation by social capital theories 33

Anthias, F. 218, 222

Arab 5; Americans 6, 130; bakers 132

Armenians 14, 105, 195

Asia 55

Asia and immigrant exclusion: West Germany 118; South-East Asia 56, 68, 105, 194, 199; UK 143

Asia and immigrants 10, 93, 106, 113, 162; to Europe 14, 133; to France 187; labourers 44; New Asian migration 93, 109, 206; New Asian Migration to California 101, 206; role of Chinatowns 139; South Asia to UK 115, 145; South Asia to US 99

Asian Americans 3, 36; as 'achieving minority' 100, 113; criticism of 113–14; Asian Pacific Americans 100

Asian entrepreneurs 101, 106, 113, 161–2, 196; as contractors in garments 151, 230; *see also* Chinese; Korean; Silicon Valley

assimilation 24, 26, 36–9, 95; crisis of in Europe 34, 48, 206; crisis of in US 34, 41, 96; downward 91, 254; enclave as alternative path 86; mainline 50–2; segmented 248; straight-line 69; *see also* ethnicity; modernisation

asylum seekers 116; ban in Switzerland 121; denied right to work 1; detention

LaVergne, TN USA
06 October 2009

160002LV00002B/20/P